KING ARTHUR CONSPIRACY

Proudly produced and published by

Cymroglyphics Ltd

April 2022

1st edition - 2005

with the kind permissassistance of
Alan Wilson & Baram Blackett

ISBN - 978-1-9162875-6-3

Copyright Cymroglyphics Ltd

All rights reserved. No part of this publication may be reprinted, reproduced, stored or transmitted in any form or by any means electronic, mechanical, photocopying, recording or otherwise, without the prior written permission of Cymroglyphics Ltd.

Inquiries concerning the reproduction or use of any of the elements should be sent by post to Cymroglyphics Ltd or by email to

info@cymroglyphics.com

10 Lansdale Drive, Tonteg, Pontypridd, Glamorgan

Wales CF38 1PG

KING ARTHUR
CONSPIRACY

Volume 1
From Babylon to Britain

Wilson & Blackett

The Historical Cataclysm

Nineteen Eighty-Four

History is a lie, which is generally agreed to. Voltaire.

"History is continuously rewritten. This day-to-day falsification of the past, carried out by the Ministry of Truth, is as necessary to the stability of the regime as the work of repression and espionage carried out by the Ministry of Love. Past events have no objective existence, but survive only in written records and in human memories. The past is whatever the records and memories agree upon. And since the party is in control of all records, it is equally in control of the minds of its members, it follows that the past is whatever the Party chooses to make it. To make sure that all records agree with the orthodoxy of the moment is merely a mechanical act. **But it is also necessary to remember that events happened in the desired manner. And if it is necessary to rearrange one's memories or to tamper with written records, then it is necessary to forget that one has done so.**

George Orwell.

Acknowledgements

Reproducing *King Arthur Conspiracy* was a bigger challenge than was first expected. Sad to say, many of the original text files and images had degraded over the intervening seventeen years since the initial publication in 2005. The first edition had also been produced in an unusual shape and size which created its own production problems and would need resizing to sit well with the other books in the Wilson and Blackett range being republished by Cymroglyphics Ltd.

So a decision was made to bite on the bullet and to create entirely new print files with the original as a base. This required a huge amount of typing and checking against the original and would not have been possible without the volunteers from the *BritainsHiddenHistory* group that stepped forward to help with this huge task. For which sincere thanks go to Adrian and Andrea Maratty, Patricia Gilcash, Mark Austin, Margaret Taylor-Hill, Janet McArthur, Bob Morgan, Michael Tomboline, Chris Wood, James Clark, David Hooper, Darren Cole, David Moseley, Monika Escobar, Stephen Pole, Peter Smith, Angela Zhang and Sally Alden.

Peter Smith and Michael Tomboline then stepped in to help with reproducing the graphics and pages of transcriptions. Michael has also created digital fonts for Coelbren and Cymroglyphics which will be available soon and will create some exciting opportunities to bring these almost-lost writing systems into the twenty-first century.

Special mention must also be given to Marchell Abrahams for the countless hours of dedicated proof-reading that were required to bring the work to the professional standard that a book of this magnitude warrants.

If errors have crept through, they will undoubtedly be owing to any last-minute changes and additions made by me rather than any mistakes by the conscientious volunteers who have been diligent and painstaking in their efforts throughout.

And last, but by my no means least, our ongoing thanks to Alan Wilson and Baram Blackett for their decades of commitment and brilliance in revealing our hidden history before it was lost for ever – as very nearly happened. The whole project has been done with joyous hearts and with so much more of their work still to be published the next project is never far away!

Diolch pawb (thank you all)

Heddwch (peace)

K Ross Broadstock, April 2022

Contents

Acknowledgements vii
Contents viii
Introduction xi

Chapters

1 Grave Creek West Virginia   1
2 The British Cold War   39
3 The Coming of Albyne   69
4 The Discovery of a Mystery   97
5 The Stones in Britain   129
6 The Etruscan Challenge   164
7 The Longer Etruscan Inscriptions   195
8 In Search of Brutus   231
9 The Arthurian Dynasty   266
10 The Myth of a Celtic and Roman Britain   293
11 Back to Britain   322

Bibliography   340
Index   341

Contents

Pictures and photographs

Grave Greek tablet 7
Elucidator   10
Braxton county stone   13
Blackett, Baram   13
Dungi tomb - plan and relief   77
Dungi tomb photo 78
Gorddyfwn Stone, Briarmail   108
Ancient Bards of Britain   109
Migrations map   111
Coelbren print 1794   124
Newton Stone   131
St Vigean Stone   133
St Paul's stone   138
Arthur II stone + W&B   144
Arthur I stone   144
Bridekirk script   152
Book of St Teilo   155
Stones-Theodosius & Theoderic 160
Tomb of Orcus scene   166
Etruscan wall painting   171
Etruscan Fallen Warrior   173
Etruscan mirror   174
Bronze mirror   174
Etruscan stones   182
Mesocco, Davesco, Stabio stones 182
Romanche deer horns   186
Romanche deer horns   186
Tuscany coffin   187
Pyrgi tablets 200
Agnone/Oscan tablet   208
Lemnos stone   237
Eski-Sher Temple   243
Gordion Inscription   250

Translation illustrations

5-1 St Vigeans Stone   135
5-2 Newton Stone   135
5-3 Coelbren alphabet   148
5-4 Bridekirk stone   154
Stitula and wine jug   177
Sarteano statue   178
Vulci drinking vessel   178
Mesocco stone   182
Stabio stone 183
Davesco stone   183
Vipanana sacophagus   189
Gordium - phrygian   251
Vel Arna Sarcophagus   188, 190
Agnone/Oscan tablet   209-18
Lemnos stone   238-9
Eski-Sher Temple   244-5

Bronze Statue of Brutus

INTRODUCTION

Our British Christian values are being undermined and our nation's cultural heritage is tottering on the verge of obliteration. History has many faces and all but one are false. In the case of recording a war, the history written by the winner is routinely very different from the history written by the losers. In some cases, as with Julius Caesar's disastrous defeats in Britain in 55 and 54 BC, the loser resorts to portraying a catastrophic defeat as a victory in order to survive politically in his distant homeland.

The most common form of Historical deception is practised for political ends for History is one of the most powerful, if not the most powerful, of all political weapons. The ever-present danger is that the history of a nation will be re-written and re-styled to meet the requirements of the dominant group, and this means that the real history, as it actually happened, will be remodelled and changed to meet whatever are the requirements of the dominant Political and Religious groups.

In 1956 Alan Wilson slowly began to realize that the history of the area of South East Wales that was being presented to the people bore virtually no relationship to the evidence that lay around in abundance. The older generations of his own extended family and their acquaintances had been taught and had knowledge of a totally different version of the past. In a casual way, when time and opportunity permitted, Alan Wilson began to try to probe into the fogs and mists that appeared to shroud a tangled and obscured situation. He began to gather information and to test it against the visible physical remains of the past, and to investigate the bland politically and religiously correct versions that were being marketed.

The collection of data went on casually until, in 1976, Alan Wilson met Baram Blackett who wanted to know who the great Prince Urien Rheged who had ruled the ancient North of Britain in the late sixth century AD, and how did it come about that his daughter Elwiri had married a Glamorgan King named Morgan.

It was this coming together of two minds that sparked a full-scale project to delve into the muddled morass of clearly perverted records that was masquerading as ancient British History. It was immediately apparent that the whole history of Britain had been treated as if it were a shapeless lump of plasticine that could be bent and pressed into any shape that was required by the political and religious correctness of the dominant social and national group in Britain. The ancient records and the multitudes of surviving physical evidence bore no relationship whatsoever to the propaganda versions of the past that were being used to "educate" the current and future generations of the British Nation.

In 1976 Alan Wilson and Baram Blackett set up their Research Project that was designed to resurrect correct and accurate Ancient British History. They see the history of Britain as the inalienable right and the property of the British Nation. The heritage and culture of the Nation is enshrined in the national history, and it must be free of religious and political tampering and the grotesque inventions and manipulations of these self interest groups. In short, they believed that just for once the records that are advertised should be honest.

There is much quoted evidence that the Romans knew of the existence of lands far to the north and the west of the Atlantic. To this may be added the cryptic line in an ancient Khumric- "Welsh" poem, which mentions such lands under the reference "according to the ancients." In modern times more notice has been taken of the late sixth-century voyage of St Brendan, who sailed to America because he had heard of the previous voyages of the Teyrn, or the Monarch, and notice has been taken of the twelfth century voyage of Leif Ericsson, and the 1397 voyage of the Earl Henry Sinclair of the Orkneys.

In these volumes, the voyage in AD 562 by the Prince Madoc Morfran, in AD 573 by the Admiral Gwenon, and in AD 574 by Arthur II and Madoc, both sons of King Meurig, and their brother-in-law Amwn are examined and traced. In 1625 the Lord, George Abbott, the Archbishop of Canterbury, wrote a *History of the World* and in that history he stated that 'King Arthur knew of America and that a Welsh Prince had discovered it.'

This means unequivocally that Madoc sailed to America in the sixth century AD as "King Arthur" is either, king Arthur I son of Magnus Maximus and Ceindrech the daughter of Rheiden, who was of around AD 346 to AD 400: or King Arthur II son of King Meurig and Queen Onbrawst the daughter of Gwrgan Mawr (Aurelian the Great), who was of circa AD 503 to 579. It seems obvious that Arthur II was intended by the Archbishop of Canterbury, and the fact that Arthur II had a well recorded brother named as Madoc Morfran (the Cormorant) supports this. Arthur I, son of Magnus Maximus had two full brothers and three half-brothers, none of whom was named Madoc

What was not known for some time to Alan Wilson and Baram Blackett was that Gerhard Kremer, the famous sixteenth century cartographer, known as Mercator, was corresponding with John Dee, the court Mathematician and Necromancer for Queen Elizabeth I. In this correspondence between Dee and Mercator, a letter was sent by Mercator that referred directly to the story of King Arthur's voyages into the far Northern Oceans in the Sixth century. This information came from Bob MacCann of Yowie Bay, Australia. In this letter Mercator cited sources showing that some four thousand descendants of survivors of members of a supposedly lost expedition led by King Arthur still survived in America, and the proof was that eight of these descendants had arrived at the court of the King of Norway in AD 1354, some 138 years before Columbus sailed.

This letter written by Mercator exists and it has been translated and was

Introduction

published in E.G.R.Taylor (1956) "A letter dated 1577 from Mercator to John Dee, 'Imago Mundi,' Vol 13, pp 56-68."

The original letter is in the British Library-MSS Cottonian Vitelius.C. vii, f264 ct seq. The extraordinary maps drawn by Mercator as early as 1538 showed amazing details of the coast-lines of the North and South American continents, which were at that time still "undiscovered" and equally remarkable detail of "undiscovered" Antartica. This production and publication of accurate Maps of as then undiscovered continents by Mercator and other early Cartographers, was the subject of a thorough research project conducted by Professor Charles H. Hapgood, published in his *The Maps of the Ancient Sea Kings*. The ancient maps of Antarctica actually showed the correct land geography before the land was covered by ice. Professor Hapgood and his colleagues came to no firm conclusion on the origins of the sources of information for these maps, and examined all manner of possible sources with the quite normal total exclusion of the ancient British.

The early maps of Mercator and his correspondence with Welsh John Dee supports the massive array of evidence in the form of Manuscripts and Inscribed Stones, which details the voyages of AD 562, 573, and 574, made from Britain to America.

The problem facing researchers is one where it is difficult to trace and assemble the widely scattered evidence, and that evidence is forbidden and censored by academia. One lesson, that the researchers of this volume were constantly compelled to re-learn is that not all the evidence is concealed and not known. Nor is it necessary to travel to far-away places to seek out hidden knowledge, as what is sought is often freely available. At least one ancient sixth century British-Khumric manuscript records an epic poem, which contains the phrase concerning the existence of the Americas, which states concerning this knowledge, "according to the ancients." This clearly implies a historical tradition that more ancient people knew of the Americas.

If we look a little further, we see that the Christian Bible contains only a selection of the early Christian writings, and a very large number of texts were excluded from the Bible compilation of texts at Lyons that was used to form the present Standard Version. Many of these excluded texts are published as Apocrypha, and others as merely stray Christian texts, whilst others are ignored. One early Christian document is *The First Epistle of St Clement to the Corinthians*, and the author Clement is none other than Clement, the second Bishop of Rome after Linus the son of King Caradoc I. In modern times this First Epistle of St Clement was published by Gramercy Books of New York, under the title of *The Lost Books of the Bible*.

The preamble of the text of this Epistle states that-

'Clement was a disciple of St Peter and afterwards Bishop of Rome',

(not mentioning Linus the first Bishop), and proceeds to state-

'Clemens Alexandrinus calls him as Apostle, Jerome, around 350, says he was an apostolical man, and Ruffinus that he was almost an Apostle. Eusebius, writing around AD 325, calls this the wonderful Epistle of St Clement, and says that it was publicly read in the assemblies of the primitive church. It is included in one of the ancient collections of the Canon Scripture.'

Then comes the bombshell-

'Its genuiness has been much questioned, particularly by Photius, patriarch of Constantinople, in the Ninth Century, who objects that Clemens speaks of worlds beyond the ocean.'

Around AD 850 the Patriarch Photius attacked the *First Epistle of Clement* on the grounds that Clement wrote of the existence of other worlds beyond the ocean, which means west beyond the Atlantic. The mentions of the Epistle by Eusebilts, some five-hundred years earlier around AD 325, and those made by Jerome, and Ruffinus, and Clemens, confirm the document's antiquity, and that Photius was simply a dyed-in-the-wool fundamentalist churchman is fairly clear. The existence of other worlds would upset the dogmas that the entire human race has descended from the children of Noah after their near annihilation by the Biblical Flood.

In Chapter Nine, Verse 12, Clement wrote-

'The ocean unpassable to mankind, and the worlds that are beyond it, are governed by the same commands of their master (=god).'

There is no doubting the import of these words which clearly state that there are other worlds beyond the Atlantic Ocean to the west of Europe. The British-Khumry knew of those opposing Clement's statement. Clement of course was no peasant Christian, nor were the majority of early Christians drawn from what we might call the 'lower classes.' As shown elsewhere, the martyr and Bishop of Rome named Clement was almost certainly Titus Flavius Clemens, the son of Sabinus, who was a brother of the Emperor Vespasian. As a member of the leading family of Rome, Clement would have been very well educated, and there is no doubt amongst scholars that this Clement was well educated.

The preamble to this First Epistle of St Clement to the Corinthians shows how in later ages Archbishop Wake attempted to reason out Clement's thinking on the comparison of the rising and reincarnation of the legendary Phoenix of Egypt, to the resurrection of Jesus the Nazarene. This comparison would also have offended Photius, as the five-hundred years cycle of the reincarnation of the Phoenix was a mythical legend that was not believed in, and then the reincarnation of Jesus the

Introduction

Nazarene could also be regarded in the same light.

The translation used by Gramercy Books was that done by Archbishop Wake, and was taken from the ancient Greek copy of the Epistle, which is found at the end of the Alexandrine Manuscript of the Septuagint and New Testament, which Cyril the Patriarch of Alexandria presented to King Charles I, and which is now in the British Museum. The main point is that Clement in the first century AD knew of the existence of "other worlds" out across the Atlantic Ocean. That Clement would have had direct contact with the early British Christians in Rome after AD 51 is a certainty. The detail tracing of Clement's various writings by other ancient scholars is well known and well authenticated.

Hundreds, if not thousands of those who had access to this Epistle down the ages would have known of the "Otherworld", which was far out to the west across the Atlantic. This is the real "Otherworld" which is described in a plethora of authentic ancient sixth century British texts. It was not a place of the corporate British national imagination, but simply the two continents that the Spanish and Portuguese of a thousand years later were to call "The New World."

Grant Berkley 20 April 2004

THE KING ARTHUR CONSPIRACY

Chapter One

Grave Creek West Virginia

It was in the fall of 1989, and mild, lemon sun-rays filtered low through the pale iron-grey sky, carpeting the autumn landscape with a medley of melted browns and casting long gentle shadows. With winter coming on and the daylight hours shortening, Jim Michael sat in his office in his home in La-Grange, Kentucky, pondering on a message he had received from Dana Olsen in Indiana. James B. Michael was President of the Ancient Kentucke Historical and Epigraphical Association. A former U.S. Army helicopter pilot, and now a recently retired marketing man with a major proprietary pharmaceutical company, Jim was finally able to throw himself into his long-time prime interest of the ancient history of the American Mid-West. The message from Dana Olsen had started a train of thought and Jim Michael decided there and then to pursue it and see where it went.

Dana Olsen had written a book in 1987 intending to prove that the ancient Prince Madoc of Wales had been present in his native Clark County in Indiana around AD 1170. Don Weber up in Illinois had bought a copy and had sent it to Baram Blackett and Alan Wilson, who were then in Cardiff, in Wales. Don knew something of their research into ancient British History, and of the four books that they had already published through books sold by Mark Slater in Annapolis in Maryland. The trail of contacts led back through Sun City and Orange County and New York in that strange way that information trickles about.

Alan Wilson and Baram Blackett had read Dana Olsen's book and found it as strange as most other modern attempts at Khumric-'Welsh' history. Ely was said to be untraceable, yet the river Ely still runs through Cardiff, and some thirty-thousand people still live in the Ely district. William Fleming was said to be unknown, and also untraceable, yet the prominent Fleming family lived at Flemingston just eight miles west of Cardiff from around AD 1100, and anciently had held office as Sheriffs of Cardiff. Walter Map was misplaced, yet Walter Map was son of Blondel de Mapes who had married Nefydd the daughter of the Lord Gweirydd of Llancarfan just nine miles west of Cardiff. Walter Map had criticised Fleming's poetry on Prince Madoc, and the two were close neighbours. There was a plethora of errors.

In common with most other Madoc searchers, Dana Olsen was struggling with a lack of basic information. This was no surprise to Baram Blackett and Alan Wilson, who had been struggling in the same web of censorship, conspiracy and misdirection for many years. They knew about Madoc, 'The Cormorant', and had decided not to get involved in what would almost certainly be another mud-slinging stalemate engineered by imperious academics.

They did however pass on basic information about William Fleming and his family, about Ely, and Walter Map, and many other details. So it transpired that Dana Olsen passed the information on to Jim Michael. Jim sat silent in awe of what might now become reality. A powerful sense of realisation came to him and with mixed emotions he foresaw that there would be powerful contradictions within his own preconceived theoretical framework. Yet it was as if there was a psychological link or connection already being forged.

Around two hundred years ago when the West was being opened up to settlement, Kentucky was the centre of Prince Madoc interest. Stories abounded of encounters with Welsh-speaking, native Americans - misnamed 'Indians' - and physical relics lay scattered all through Kentucky and the neighbouring States. Large hill-forts of typical Khumric 'Welsh' style lay strategically placed. Ditched circles similar to ancient Khumric cors lay around, and there were grave mounds by the hundred. Most decisive for Jim Michael however were the many ancient rock-cut inscriptions throughout the Mid-West and the many similarly inscribed artefacts. He reasoned that given the huge weight of traditional evidence on Madoc, there was just a chance that these inscriptions, which were found along the Ohio Valley and elsewhere might be in Khumric.

Jim Michael had become enchanted with the Madoc legend, and now there was a prospect of perhaps achieving something positive. He wrote a letter to Wilson and Blackett and suggested that they collaborate with these fresh mysteries.

In 1838 a strange and momentous discovery was made in the United States of America. Investigators digging into a vast grave mound at Grave Creek in West Virginia came upon a small, stone tablet deep down inside the sixty-feet-high mound. This tiny, stone tablet was of monumental importance because it had three lines of clear alphabetic inscriptions cut into its smooth face, and below these inscriptions was an unmistakeable Christian cross. The people excavating the huge Grave Creek mound were, unfortunately, by modern standards woefully amateur in their methods and they made a totally inadequate record of this large-scale enterprise. Their records were all too brief, devoid of detail, and with little attention to measurement, yet there are extant accounts of a general nature.

In defence of the researchers and excavators at Grave Creek it should be noted that their methods were far better controlled and recorded than the looting and grave robbing which passed for excavation in contemporary Etruria, in Egypt, or ancient Assyria and Chaldea, or elsewhere. Mounds are not unusual in the American Mid-West, and estimates of the number still surviving along the Ohio valleys after several centuries of being built over, flattened, and robbed, vary between eight thousand and twelve thousand.

No native American people of North America had been identified as possessing an alphabet and using any form of written language and so the discovery of this tablet inscribed with a very clear written alphabet was a sensation. Some of the Native American nations used pictographs and some kept their national historical records in picture and sign form on wooden sticks, but none knew or used an alphabet.

The scale of the problem can be gauged from the fact of the sheer bulk of this, the largest, of the Grave Creek mounds. Even when probably eroded by time it stood sixty feet high, and measured some two-hundred-and-fifty feet in diameter at its base. The mound was surrounded by a ditch or moat, which is variously estimated at perhaps originally some four feet deep and up to thirty feet wide. The mound does in fact bear an uncanny resemblance to some of the major tomb mounds in Britain, and is virtually a replica of Twyn Tudor Tumulus of Tudor on Mynydd Islwyn in Gwent.

To the surprise of the 1838 excavation team at Grave Creek the mound turned out to be two mounds. An earlier mound some thirty-feet-high had been used as a base and a second mound had been erected on top of it, raising the level of the finished structure to sixty feet. Box-like burial chambers made of heavy logs were discovered inside both the upper and the lower mounds. The upper burial chamber contained two skeletons, one of which was surrounded by six-hundred-and-fifty shell beads. The lower chamber or vault contained ten haunting skeletons.

Fortunately, all this was recorded by Abelard Tomlinson, one of the excavation team, who kept notes of the excavations, detailing the construction of the timber-built log chamber tomb vaults and other data. It was not until Abelard Tomlinson published the detail of the excavation in 1840 that the news of the inscribed stone tablet, which had been discovered on 16th June 1838, reached and shook the public at large. The tablet was a small limestone disc of oval shape, just one and a half inches in diameter (60 mm) and three-quarters of an inch thick (30 mm).

Abelard Tomlinson and his colleagues may have had very good reasons for being careful in the manner in which they announced the discovery of this tablet at Grave Creek. Most Europeans may find it difficult to understand why such a momentous find should have been made known simply as part of the general account of the excavation. Those were, however, extremely delicate times for anyone to discover an inscribed stone tablet in an ancient grave. Joseph Smith had announced his finding of inscribed gold tablets on a hill named Cumorah in 1823 and this had led him to found the Mormon Church. The uproar that this founding of a new style, Christian-related church in America had caused was huge. Without getting into too much detail, the Mormons were attacked and persecuted and they fought back, and finally they set out and founded their own State based on Salt Lake City in Utah.

Feelings were running high and Senators urged United States Presidents to make war on these unorthodox Christians who practised polygamy and believed that Joseph Smith was a latter-day prophet. Folk whose ancestors had fled persecution in Europe were indignantly demanding that those who differed from themselves in belief should now be persecuted. Difficult times. Almost universally people all across America leapt to predictable hasty conclusions and linked the discovery of the Grave Creek Tablet to the Joseph Smith account of his dream and visitation by an angel which led him to find the inscribed golden tablets upon which the Mormon religion was founded.

None of the excavators at Grave Creek were Mormons, but the Grave Creek Tablet was in many places perceived as a major threat to Christian orthodox beliefs. This additional fuel on an already dangerous political fire now involved the Government. At the time a number of nations had major interests in the North American continent, much of which was still in the hands of the Native Americans, which meant that it was available for seizure. Britain held Canada, and did not recognize the United States' claims to Oregon until 1846, Spain was still antagonistic over the annexation of Texas, and still held New Mexico and California, and Russia owned Alaska.

The furore over this tiny piece of stone, now known as the Grave Creek Tablet, brought a well-known scholar onto the scene. Henry Rowe Schoolcraft now became a central figure in the strange story of the inscribed tablet found at Grave Creek. Schoolcraft was as well qualified as anyone to deal with the problem of discovering the nature and origin of the alphabet on the tablet, which might then lead to the language in which it was inscribed and thus bring about the possibility of a decipherment. His efforts however appear to have resulted in a series of lamentable failures.

Born in New York State, Schoolcraft had studied Mineralogy at college and, sometime after 1812, he went west through Pittsburgh, and engaged on a mineralogical survey of the territories beyond the Alleghenies. He returned with cases loaded with samples, which revealed the natural wealth of the Mississippi Valley, and as a natural consequence his work had brought him into contact with the Native American peoples of the area. Henry Schoolcraft had developed an interest in the indigenous native people of North America.

Henry Schoolcraft, the college-trained Mineralogist, was about to enter into the

Chapter 1 - Grave Creek, West Virginia

realms of History, Archaeology, and Language Studies. He was apparently self-conscious and unsure of himself through a lack of formal training. Perhaps he failed to realize that as an organized study Archaeology - then known as Antiquarianism - hardly existed, and History - apart from 'classical' Roman and Greek literature - was traditionally parochial and confined to national boundaries and political interests. The Grave Creek Mound was however obviously ancient, and it lay in what had been Native American territory, and so it was deemed that knowledge of Native Americans was suitable.

In 1820-1821 Schoolcraft had been a member of Government expeditions into Native American territories to obtain geological mineralogical reports. In 1822 he was appointed as Agent for Indian affairs at Sault Ste Marie, which was then a frontier outpost of the American Northwest. He married a half-Ojibwa girl and learned the Ojibwa language and compiled a book on Ojibwa grammar. He collected Ojibwa poetry, folklore, myths and legends, and after seventeen years he published *Algic Researches*, establishing himself as an anthropologist. Then in 1836 he became acting Superintendent of Indian Affairs for the State of Michigan.

From this point onwards Schoolcraft began accumulating various public appointments and he engaged in the foundation of scholastic societies. Inevitably he built up a circle of correspondence with antiquarians (early archaeologists), and ethnologists in other countries. With Albert Galletin he founded the American Ethnology Society in 1842. Then in 1842 he travelled to London where he read a paper before the British Association for the Advancement of Science. So Henry Schoolcraft advanced along the routine academic path of publications, society memberships, and presenting and reading papers.

Armed with the necessary paper-trail of qualifications and a circle of international scholastic contacts Henry Schoolcraft appeared to be a good choice for the task of unravelling the secret of the intriguingly inscribed Grave Creek Tablet. He was not a historian, nor was he a linguist, he was a mineralogist and a government official; but he had the necessary contacts and some knowledge of disciplined enquiry techniques.

Nonetheless Henry Schoolcraft examined the tablet from Grave Creek, and based on observation, on advice from others, and on comparison with known alphabets, his first stated opinion was that the twenty-five characters on the stone represented twenty-two letter characters and one hieroglyph. Presumably he saw what appears to be a cross as a hieroglyph or he was not prepared to call it a cross because of the possible Mormon connection. It would seem to be logical that the other two characters on the stone were either also letters or perhaps numerals.

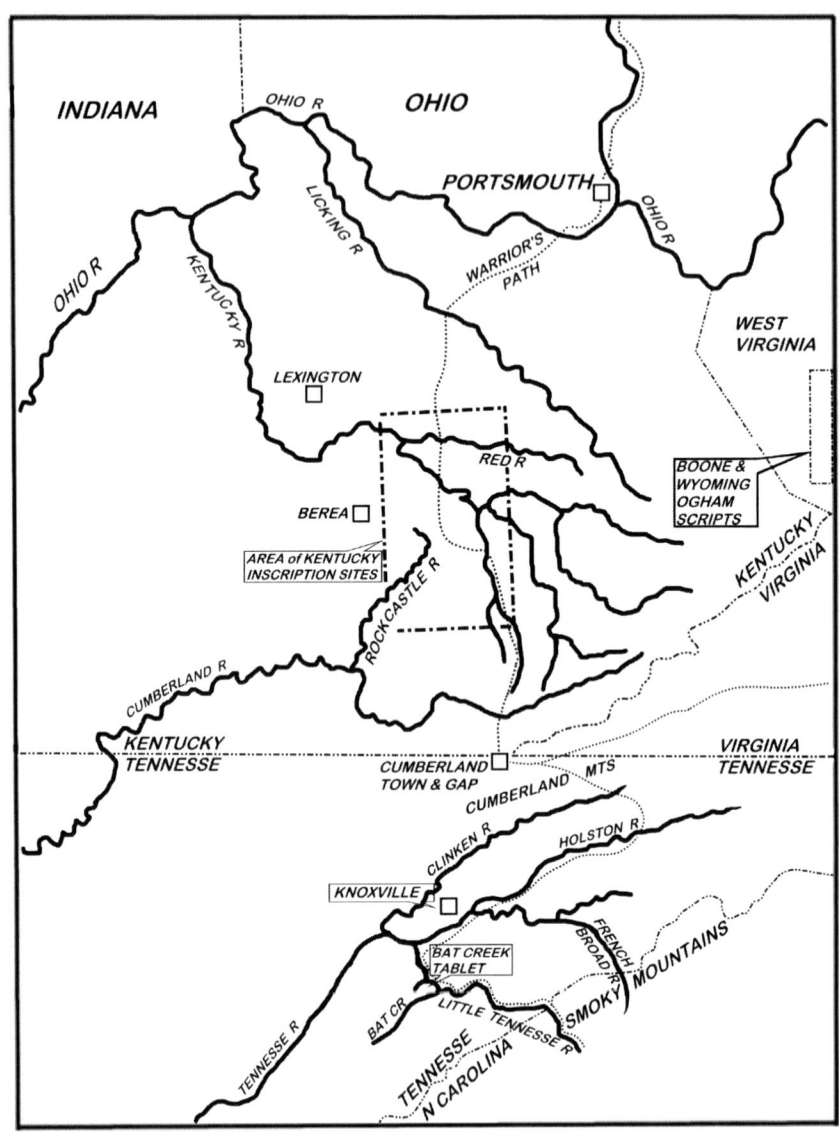

Bat Creek Map
Kindly produced and provided by Peter Smith

Chapter 1 - Grave Creek, West Virginia

Grave Creek Tablet

Schoolcraft may not have been a historian or a philologist, but he was prepared to make a positive beginning. He actually stated that he thought that fourteen of the ancient letters were from the ancient 'Celtic' alphabet. This statement is in itself confusing, but it appears to have meant that they were letters from the ancient British Coelbren Alphabet preserved by the Khumry-'Welsh'. There is no such preserved language or alphabet as 'Celtic', certainly not in Britain; and the 'Welsh' are correctly the Khumry and are not 'Celtic'. Neither are the Irish 'Celts', but instead correctly Gaels, and their recorded migration trail starts from the upper Tigris, down to Egypt, along the coast of North Africa to the Gibraltar Straits after passing through the Egyptian Delta, and then sailing from Spain to Ireland.

It seems however that Schoolcraft was at first identifying the Grave Creek Tablet as being possibly inscribed in the British Coelbren or Khumric Alphabet. Yet even this is uncertain, for there are three ancient runic or stroke alphabets to be found in Britain, plus one other set of straight stroke symbols. The most important is the very ancient British Coelbren Alphabet which was used by the Khumry-'Welsh', who trace

7

their origins in Britain back three-thousand-six-hundred-years to two great fleet migrations *circa* 1567 BC and 504 BC. Another alphabet is in a similar runic style and is currently identified as 'Anglo-Saxon', and this is found on a few relics in Eastern and Northern Britain, and in Dark Age texts. A third alphabet is the runic form found extensively inscribed in the Isle of Man, and this can be confidently dated as from the ninth and tenth centuries AD.

There is also the fourth straight style known as Ogham - believed by some to stem from Ogimos or Orpheus. It is very doubtful that Ogham is a true alphabet as it appears to be the foundation of very early musical scores. It probably represents musical chants when found on inscribed stones. The Latin or Khumric text is the verse or chant and the Ogham is the musical score.

Anyone comparing the Grave Creek Tablet with the ancient British Coelbren Alphabet will be able to see the obvious similarities between the two. It is in fact an unavoidable identification.

Schoolcraft's identification of the Grave Creek Tablet being inscribed in what he called 'Celtic' would appear to indicate that he meant the ancient British Coelbren Alphabet. This is significant, as in the era from 1760-1870, the legend that a Khumric Prince named Madoc had sailed to America in antiquity was known to everyone in the Mid-West of America and elsewhere. No less than twenty-five reliable accounts are recorded of encounters between responsible migrating investigative explorers moving westwards in the growing U.S.A., with Native Americans who spoke and understood the Khumric language. Many of these encounters had taken place before the Grave Creek Tablet was discovered. These are not stories brought back by illiterate trappers or traders, but instead they are reports from educated men, army officers, some of high rank, ministers of religion, and professional men involved in surveying, geology, mineralogy, and so on.

At the same time that these encounters were being reported, there were no fewer than five reports of travellers actually being shown ancient books, which were wrapped in leather and carefully preserved by the Native Americans. These books were written in a strange script and alphabet, and were said to be Bibles. A scramble had ensued to get hold of these Bibles, with the French Governor of Canada sending emissaries who were said to have obtained two of these books around 1750, and several decades later President Thomas Jefferson sent representatives to try to get hold of another book.

Henry Schoolcraft may well have been associating the Grave Creek Tablet and its strange alphabet with these accounts of the Khumric language and these Bibles which were preserved and scattered through the Mid-West of the U.S.A. He would have been equally aware of the expedition of John Evans, sent from Wales in 1792 to try to make

Chapter 1 - Grave Creek, West Virginia

contact with Khumric-speaking 'Indians'. Evans was in St Louis in 1793 and went up river to seek out the Mandan tribe, who were regarded as likely candidates of his search, in the spring of 1795. It was John Evans's map, extending fifteen-hundred miles north of St Louis, which President Jefferson sent to Captain Meriwether Lewis and Captain William Clark on 13th January 1804 when they were about to set out north on their voyage of exploration, up the Missouri river. If the Prince Madoc had reached the Mid-West, then there should be no surprise if Bibles did exist in the middle of America, as the Khumry had been Christians since AD 37 – 'the last year of Tiberius'.

In the context of Bibles and Christian contacts many researchers have noted the strong and strange resemblance between many Native American tribal rituals with recorded Hebrew and Christian practices. The late Dr Joseph Mahan of Columbus, Georgia, who with his wife endeavoured to assist Jim Michael, Alan Wilson, and Baram Blackett, was a leading exponent of this research in his books.

Armed with the widespread knowledge of and interest in the Prince Madoc traditional histories, and the widespread reportage of the Khumric Language and even Bibles in the Mid-West, an enquiry into the possibility of the Grave Creek Tablet being written in the very ancient British Coelbren Alphabet and in the Khumric tongue, would seem to have been an obvious course. This did not take place, and the question has to be: 'Why did this not happen?' It would have been a simple, quick, inexpensive, and definitive exercise. The Khumric language was still spoken by some 95% of the native Khumric-'Welsh' population around 1842, and the alphabet was well known and well published. In fact, John Williams at Oxford published it widely in a book printed in 1846. Given these circumstances the Grave Creek Tablet could have been deciphered and read in minutes rather than hours. This did not happen despite Henry Schoolcraft seeing immediately that the letters are not just very similar, but are in fact identical.

What the politics of this might have been is another matter. The young nation of the United States of America may have had a government that might have tactfully wished not to recognize an ancient British colonisation of the Mid-West proven. 1842 was not so long after the era when the three rival European imperial powers of Spain, pushing up from the deep South, France, pushing up from the South and down from the Canadian North, and Britain, pushing over from Canada and the North East Coast, had all warred over American Empires. The War of Independence of 1776 to 1783 was still a fresh memory, and the war of 1812 to 1814 with the English burning Washington and the White House would not have helped matters. This is speculation on what appears to be inexplicable.

Illustration.
The Ancient British Coelbren Alphabet.
There are some variant Signs occurring in the Alphabet.

Vowels

Consonants

The Bardic Alphabet contained 16 radicals and 24 derivatives, formed from the radicals by the addition of a bud or shoot to the original symbol

The Elucidator was a frame composed of a number of sticks, some 3 sided, others squared, on the flat surface of which were carved the Bardic aphorisms. The 3 sided ones contained a complete triad; the 4 sided ones a stanza (See Ezekiel xxxvii 16.)

Basic Coelbren Alphabet

Chapter 1 - Grave Creek, West Virginia

More likely Henry Schoolcraft was self-conscious about his lack of formal training in the study of history and languages. He may have felt insecure without the confirmation of his opinion from persons regarded as 'experts' in these fields. What is certain is that he failed to even try to make contact with a few Welsh scholars who would certainly know the ancient language and alphabet. Schoolcraft visited London in England in 1840, and he may, like most Americans, have failed to appreciate the massive gulf between Khumric-'Welsh' culture, history, heritage, and language, and English politics. If he made his contacts in London, Oxford, and Cambridge, then he would have found few friends or supporters of the Khumry and Wales in that heated political era. In fact, the centuries old political campaign to eradicate entirely the Khumric language, culture, and history, was gaining momentum and about to reach an all-time peak.

The Genie is out of the Bottle

Why Henry Schoolcraft failed to trust all his frontiersman instincts, which surely must have directed him to go straight for the Old British Alphabet to seek a possible reading of the Grave Creek Tablet, we will never know. It is not impossible that he enjoyed or even revelled in the heady atmosphere of equal contact with scholars at much revered old-world universities. A quick simple and easy solution to the problem might well have cut very short what turned out to be many years of basking in the cosy intellectual warmth of academic society.

Either way, for inexplicable reasons, he did not bother to contact scholars in South Wales, who would know the old British Coelbren Alphabet and the Khumric Language. As Alan Wilson put it to Jim Michael, 'at that time any two educated Welsh people in a crowd of three could have told him how to read it'.

So perhaps doubting the advice given to him and failing to trust his own judgement that at least fourteen of the Grave Creek Tablet characters were of the Old British = Khumric, Henry Schoolcraft began to write letters. Logically the first letters should have gone to Western Britain, to Wales, or to the well-known Welsh Societies in London. But no, Schoolcraft first wrote to Professor Jomard of Paris, France, and then he wrote to a Professor Page in Copenhagen, Denmark.

This extraordinary choice of correspondence set in motion a train of events, which were to confuse and distort the study of ancient North America for a hundred and fifty years. Perhaps Schoolcraft had ideas of eliminating other possibilities, leaving British as the unchallenged candidate. Certainly Professor Page confirmed that the Grave Creek script was not Runic Norse thus eliminating the Danes, Swedes, and Norwegians, and Vikings in general. If this was the plan then it came to grief, however.

From Paris Professor Jomard sent a long laborious analysis that presented the astounding view that the letters were ancient Lybian writing deriving from North Africa. In 1842 France controlled almost all colonial North Africa, and after many centuries of hostility, including Wolfe's victory in Canada, by Nelson's and Wellington's joint defeat of Napoleon, and the British seizure of India from the French, no self-respecting Frenchman would have ever acknowledged a British claim of ancient presence in North America.

With Professor Jomard's amazing statement the genie was out of the bottle, and nothing would get it back in. Schoolcraft continued in his new bureaucratic career and sent out more letters, and the correspondence grew and flourished. Opinions multiplied like bacteria, and the script from Grave Creek was seen as Greek, Etruscan, ancient Gallic, Erse (Irish), Phoenician, Norse Runes, Hebrew, and a dozen other languages or alphabets, and again the Old British Khumric Coelbren alphabet. In a frenzy of jingoist nationalism everyone, except the London regime, wanted their nation to own the proud claim of the pre-Columbus discovery of America. These opinions meant that every European and Mediterranean country was put forward as a claimant.

Actually, it was all more than ridiculous as there were an estimated eighty million native Americans living in North America and it was their ancestors who were obviously the discoverers of America.

The Scandinavians came up with the voyage of Leif Ericsson around AD 1120, but the Scots record of the Sinclair voyages around 1398 were not pressed. The Irish put forward the voyage of St Brendan - probably around 580 AD. However, given the tangle and twists of the religious and political history of that era now emerging, there is no guarantee that Brendan was Irish. The British put forward the untraceable voyages of Madoc son of Owen Gwynedd around AD 1170. Only one nation possessed a massive core of recorded history detailing large-scale transatlantic fleet voyages in antiquity to America and this was firmly ignored.

Schoolcraft must have been very naïve politically if he thought for one second that any preconceived mindset would support the veracity of ancient British Khumric history in any way whatsoever in his era. He must have been even more naïve/f if he thought that a French Professor would know anything whatsoever of ancient British History, or even of the existence of the Khumric Language and ancient Coelbren alphabet. As stated, that a Frenchman in 1842 would agree to recognize such evidence, even if he knew of it, is inconceivable given the fierce rivalries of these European nations in all things.

Chapter 1 - Grave Creek, West Virginia

Braxton County Stone

Baram Blackett, Cardiff office 1993

Schoolcraft consequently failed to realise that several of the various opinions and claims made actually supported the original view that the Grave Creek Script was Old British. Some views supported Etruscan origins, without evidence of such voyages, yet both the British and the Etruscans claim a common origin in Asia Minor. The Asia Minor alphabet loosely termed Pelasgian is again near-identical with British Coelbren and Etruscan, and this fact was published in 1793, in 1846, and again in 1906. That these alphabets should be the same given the common origin of both the British and the Etruscans in western Asia Minor is logical. In the same way the idea that the alphabet from Grave Creek had similarities with the ancient Iberian script from Spain is understandable, as Brutus, the British founding King, is recorded as picking up three groups of kinsmen from Iberia who had gone ahead of the main force on its way to invade Britain in circa 504 BC.

The record of the trail of these ancient migrations matches geographically with the known locations of the spread of the Coelbren Alphabet. Henry Schoolcraft would not have known of this as he would not have been told of the ancient Khumric-British histories.

The result of his widespread correspondence was the birth of a disaster. Theories grew and multiplied. Ancient Egyptians were proposed as voyaging to America - and over a hundred years later Thor Heyerdahl almost proved this a possibility - and then the ancient Carthaginians, the Phoenicians, and the Romans were put forward as discoverers and even as regular trans-Atlantic visitors to America. Iberian 'Celts' were proposed as settlers, Irish monks - ignoring the detail in the Life of Brendan - were advanced as the first discoverers, and Lydian sailors were introduced. Greeks were written in as discoverers of America and so were ancient Sumerians. In fact, any and every ancient nation was a candidate for the discovery and colonization of America, with one notable exception - no one put forward the ancient British even though Julius Caesar wrote in 55 BC of their massive ocean-going ships and of their alphabet.

The astounding discovery at Grave Creek in 1838 is matched by the extraordinary fact that the mass of detailed evidence preserved in Khumric Historical record was in the public domain having been published in modern book form in 1800, 1804, and 1806. Even more extraordinary this published evidence was resolutely ignored. It was available, it still is available, it can be read, and it is very clearly stated. It was and is politically incorrect and unpopular, but it is nonetheless extant, published, and preserved. This perhaps is the real mystery.

The fiasco, which grew out of the muddled attempt to discover the language and origin of the Grave Creek Tablet, was to have lasting effect. Faced with a vast array of theories involving unrecorded, and in most cases, highly improbable voyages from all over the ancient world, the modern archaeologists have simply put up the shutters and closed the shop. In America they have almost universally adopted the equally unproven, untenable and unprovable theory that no ancient migrations came from East across the Atlantic to North America. Two opposing groups have emerged, one of which represents the camp of the Pre-Columbians who generally aver that numerous migrations came and went in the ancient world of America, while the Pro-Columbians occupy the other camp and hold that no migrations of any kind from anywhere arrived in America before Christopher Columbus in 1492. This second view then maintains that as a result of total isolation all burial mounds, artefacts, forts, alphabets, and everything else found is a direct result of indigenous ancient American progress.

This second isolation position is as unseemly as it is absurd. *Bona fide* scholars and researchers should be prepared to examine any and all credible evidence. It is both extraordinary and unsound to propose that ancient Sumerians, Egyptians, Cretans, Greeks, Phoenicians, Romans, Etruscans, Hebrews, and Carthaginians all made such huge voyages spanning both the Mediterranean and the Atlantic Oceans, and that they all discovered America, and then they all completely forgot to record these facts. It is equally extraordinary that anyone can take up a position holding that no one arrived from the West before Columbus in 1492, particularly as Christopher Columbus had at least one map to guide him.

It is inescapable that the voyage by Brendan claimed by the Irish was and is recorded. It is equally inescapable that the voyages of Leif Ericsson around AD 1120, and the voyages of Henry Sinclair Earl of Orkney of around 1397, are equally well recorded. In fact, modern scholars can show physical evidence in support of both Leif Ericsson's and Henry Sinclair's voyages. To ignore all the evidence that indicates or proves a pre-Columbian arrival in America from the East is an untenable position for any reputable scholar or researcher to adopt.

The current situation owes more to emotive and political thinking and reactions than it does to sanity. This is precisely why Wilson and Blackett had put all thoughts of Madoc Morfran away on the back burner before being persuaded to co-operate with Jim Michael and his colleagues in 1989. Matters are reminiscent of, and almost as farcial as, the crazy war between the tiny people of Lilliput and Brobdignag in Swift's *Gulliver's Travels*, where one faction demanded that boiled eggs should be opened at the small end, whilst the others insisted that boiled eggs be cut open at the thicker end.

It seems to have been forgotten that some Native American Nations preserved their histories, and that their records contained accounts of the arrival in antiquity of a powerful race of White Men from the East. Details of the wars with these ancient White Men, locations, battlefield sites, and so on, exist.

The reactionary "Columbus Only" theory is probably the result of the opinions of the Director of Native American Studies, one Cyrus Thomas, and his contemporary disciple and successor John Wesley Powell. Cyrus Thomas did in fact perform truly prodigious feats in excavating and examining the ancient mound grave monuments of North America. Maybe he excavated too much and paid too little attention to detail and to the wider world. He wrote a book of seven hundred pages and he certainly attempted the beginning of the necessary archaeological research. How well he fared given that there were no historical yardsticks or inscriptions related to such histories to guide his dates, and Radio Carbon 14 dating had not been discovered, is open to question. What appeared to emerge was that of the eight to ten thousand mound graves in the Ohio River Valley, and the many thousands elsewhere, several levels of cultural attainment were evident from the nature of the artefacts found. A great diversity of origin was clearly apparent, and in the South funeral mounds were still being erected until around 1600 to 1750.

Despite the huge diversity found, Cyrus Thomas was determinedly opposed to even the thought that there was ever any origin other than that of the indigenous Native American populations. When Cyrus Thomas retired, his successor, John Wesley Powell, continued to maintain this uncompromising political view.

The successive directors of Native American Studies were not unchallenged. A number of more open-minded investigators were of the opinion that independent Native American cultural advancement had occasionally been enhanced by some form of immigration from abroad. E.G. Squier worked away trying to relate artefacts found in American grave mounds to artefacts from antiquity abroad. Dr Samuel Morton took the path of comparing skulls from American grave mounds with crania from other continents and from different areas of America. These nineteenth-century researchers were handicapped by the lack of the necessary tools to work effectively. There were no scientific aids like Radio Carbon 14 dating techniques, no analytical tree ring dating - dendrochronology - and obviously nothing like modern D.N.A. comparative analysis.

Squier and his contemporaries took little or no notice of the growing number of inscriptions found on stones in caves, under rock cliff overhangs, on cliff faces, and on artefacts. This reluctance to get involved with inscriptions, which would form the most important part of any archaeological work anywhere else, may have resulted from the fiasco which was born of Henry Schoolcraft's open house enquiry into the Grave Creek Tablet. A form of lunacy appeared to grip would-be decipherers of the inscription. In 1875 Levi Bing declared the letters to be Canaanite and gave a trumped-up reading to the Congress of Americanists at Nancy in France. Jules Opert translated the inscription as Sumerian, and others declared that the writing was that of Israelite Hebrews fleeing from Roman persecution, which was a favourite theme.

Chapter 1 - Grave Creek, West Virginia

No one ever attempted to read the sixth-century British-Khumric records, and no one ever attempted to use the ancient British-Khumric alphabet and its ciphers to read the inscriptions as Khumric. Yet the entire Mid-West was alive with the stories of the legendary Khumric Prince Madoc.

When President Thomas Jefferson sent an aide to recover an ancient Bible in a strange script, which was kept by a Native American lady in her cabin, the cabin somehow got burned down and the book burned with it. Perhaps we need to remember that when a later President ordered the removal of the Cherokee Nation from their homelands in what is remembered as 'The Trail of Tears', he was advised that his action was illegal and also unconstitutional. He simply replied: "Who will take the matter to court?" One year later the Law was amended in order retrospectively to legalize this illegality, which had resulted in untold hardship and the death of the majority of the Cherokee. Perhaps they did not want that ancient Bible, possibly written in the British Coelbren script, to survive.

So, the Grave Creek Tablet along with many other similar inscriptions remained unread. Archaeological opinions hardened and declined into the realm of the absurd. Only artefacts and items discovered by those designated as 'archaeologists' could be accepted as genuine - as if archaeologists were alone trustworthy, and all items found by the vast 99.99% of the population are therefore ignored as suspect. As the overwhelming majority of honest Americans moving about their vast country are not labelled as 'archaeologists', and they make the vast majority of discoveries, the situation is as ludicrous as it is in Britain.

The majority of archaeologists spend most of their time as university employees teaching their students what they were themselves taught. The assumption that all other citizens are uninformed, untrustworthy fakers is unjust. The notion that only some two thousand persons - the employed archaeologists - in a population of some two hundred and sixty million are intelligent and trustworthy is nonsense. In fact, it is simply a form of protectionism that is designed to render everyone else inactive and to 'keep them off the grass.

The result is predictably stagnation and stalemate, exactly as it is in Britain where centuries'-old political deceptions render almost all progress in historical and related archaeological fields impossible. There have been fakers in the U.S.A., and these are almost invariably religiously motivated persons desperately trying to fabricate proof and 'evidence' on the theme of the Lost Ten Tribes of Israel sailing off five-and-a-half thousand miles to ancient America, or otherwise Judean groups fleeing from Roman oppression. The danger that is inherent in these fabrications is that genuine ancient inscriptions will be also set aside and dismissed. Rather like the little shepherd boy who cried "Wolf!" when there was no wolf, until the day came when there was a wolf and no one took any notice.

Now at this time of writing, in 2004, it was a hundred and sixty-six years since the Grave Creek Tablet was found, and a hundred and sixty-four years since Henry Schoolcraft began to try to find its source and meaning. There are now a growing number of obviously genuine inscriptions in this same Alphabetical Script and all can be read. It is a time of opportunity. It is also a time of danger to the 'professionals', as these long-ignored inscriptions may yield information which undermines and destroys years of academic theorising and speculation. Reputations will be at stake.

As Jim Michael pointed out to Alan Wilson and Baram Blackett, the tragedy is ongoing as no protection is offered to the majority of ancient carvings and inscriptions. Several generations have badly mutilated many of them by using them for rifle target practice. Other relics are often illegally collected by private persons, who are prepared to cut away slices of rock that carry ancient carvings, and sometimes these are the very people who are employed to protect them.

The American Initiative

After a hundred and fifty years of growing confusion concerning the increasing number of anciently inscribed rocks, stones, animal horns and claws, and man-made artefacts found in the U.S.A., a positive course of action was set in motion. I.S.S.A.C. (The Institute of Scientific Study of American Cultures) was set up to endeavour impartially to assess the validity of signs of early foreign influences. The Ancient Kentucke Historical and Epigraphical Association was founded with Jim Michael as its President, and the majority of the inscriptions are found in the Mid-West of the U.S.A., and it is in his region that the strategically placed mound banked hill-fortresses of British type are found. There are religious sites of the flattened bell-mound style, and the entire Ohio Valley is peppered with grave mounds. Wales is peppered with grave mounds and most of the large mounds are named for Kings and Princes, and some for Queens and Princesses.

Study of ancient American culture had made Jim Michael very well aware of the well documented encounters between white explorers and settlers of good repute, and Native Americans who spoke the Khumric-'Welsh' language. Frequently there were Native people who had hair, eyes, and general physical characteristics exhibiting at least a possible white ancestry. He also knew of numerous reports of European and Eastern Mediterranean ancient artefacts and coins found in the Mid-West, and had made study of the reports of ancient Bibles preserved by Native Americans in the 1760-1840 era. He was also intrigued by the early discovery of a huge rock cliff carved into the shape of a typical Welsh Dragon - still the national symbol of Wales - and many other mysteries.

Jim Michael had extensive medical contacts as a direct result of his job, and he leant heavily towards the forms of scientific evidence that medical expertise might

Chapter 1 - Grave Creek, West Virginia

produce. Native Americans have three Inca bones in their skulls, and Caucasian Europeans and others do not. The bicuspid teeth of the Native American are different from the bicuspid teeth of the Caucasian race, and traces of diseases which were not present in ancient America but which are anciently found in Europe, are found in the Caucasian-type skeletons unearthed in America.

At least one very large mound cemetery existed which bore a resemblance to the well-recorded ancient burial ground guarded by monks, which was the graveyard of 'the multitudes of the illustrious of the British'. The great Snake Mounds of North America matched the great Snake Mounds of Britain and Ireland, some of which still exist. The best recorded Snake Mound still existing is near Oban in Scotland. The record of the Welsh St Patrick tells how he lit fires in the 'egg' circles in the mouths of the great earth-banked snakes, and so defiled these sites and frustrated the Irish Druid priests. Patrick did not drive out live snakes from Ireland, and there are plenty of grass snakes still there. In our modern times a Snake Mound and Egg were rebuilt on a hill East above Pontypridd in Wales, and predictably it has been attacked by Christian groups.

Jim Michael had other powerful weapons in his armoury. One was the Historical record of the Delaware Tribal Confederation. The recorded Histories of the Delaware Nation are known as the *Wallum Ollam of the Lenni Lenape* and they have a known reputable and reliable provenance and pedigree. The story of the acquisition of these records is that a Dr Ward first obtained them from the Delaware in Indiana in 1820. With his people stricken with imported European diseases against which they had no natural immunity, a Delaware Chief who feared that his entire Nation would pass away and be forgotten, decided to give the record of the Delaware to Dr Ward. In this way he hoped that the record would live on even if the people did not.

The Wallum Ollam record that was incised in pictographs on sticks, finally came into the hands of Constantine Rafinesque, a scholar of some distinction who taught Botany and Natural History at Transylvania University at Lexington, Kentucky. Rafinesque made careful copies of all the sticks and subsequently a number of researchers working with Delaware people have produced translations of these histories.

Curiously, 'Wallum Ollam' looks very much like the Khumric 'Gwalad Oll-am', which means 'the order/arrangement of everyone'. Then 'Lenni Lenape' is suspiciously like 'llenu', meaning 'veiled'', and 'llen' meaning 'knowledge', with 'af' meaning 'a going on', or 'a progress', and 'E' is simply 'it' or 'he'. 'Llenu Llen-af-e', meaning 'the veiled knowledge the going on of it', looks and sounds remarkably like Lenni Lenape.

The outstanding feature of these Histories of the Delaware is that they record how in antiquity a great race of White Men migrated into the Mid-West of the U.S.A. and occupied lands which are firmly identified by Native American leaders as the Kentucky area, and some surrounding lands. Bitter wars were fought between these ancient White Men and the ancestors of the Native Americans, and there are still remembered battlefields and associated areas which yield up the skulls that have no 'Inca bones'. It has also passed unnoticed that for millennia the Khumry also wrote on sticks, using knives and small axes to cut the straight strokes of the Coelbren Alphabet into the sticks. Coelbren is held to mean 'a record or letter stick'.

Whether this writing on sticks has any common relevance or not, the whole mass of available evidence seemed to Jim Michael and his colleagues to warrant an enquiry into Khumric-'Welsh' records. They decided to approach the only people interested in and capable of researching Khumric records, and contacted Alan Wilson and Baram Blackett in Cardiff. Jim Michael sent a letter and enclosed a photograph of one of the many American inscriptions, and asked: "Do you know what writing this is?" and so Wilson and Blackett turned the photograph upside down and wrote back and said: "It is the ancient Khumric Coelbren Alphabet, and the inscription is written in 'Welsh', no problem".

At the time, in late 1989, Wilson and Blackett were disinclined to get involved with the U.S.A. inscriptions. They had seen a photograph of the Bourne Stone in 1984 and had translated it. Alan Wilson's mother had brought their attention to the publication of the Yarmouth Bay, Nova Scotia stone in *Y Drych*, a Welsh language paper, in 1948, but attempts at making contact in North America had brought no worthwhile responses. Past experience deterred them from getting involved in stirring up another hornets' nest of frightened university employees. They preferred to let the vast herds of the sacred cows of unfounded academic theories graze in peace. There was also the matter of time periods, as it was their firm policy not to investigate later than the end of the reign of King Iestyn ap Gwrgan (Justin son of Aurelian) in AD 1091. A line had to be drawn somewhere and King Iestyn (Justin) offered a convenient date.

Wilson and Blackett had quite naturally associated the existence of Coelbren carved inscriptions in North America with the voyages of the Prince Madoc to the Americas. Some hundred and fifty volumes on library shelves proclaimed Madoc as sailing to America around AD 1170, which meant that this was another subject to be avoided. The historian Caradoc of Llancarfan was universally alleged to have written on Prince Madoc's voyages, yet if Madoc sailed in 1170, this was impossible was Caradoc died in 1156. Then there was the problem of Walter Map son of Blondel de Mapes who married Nefydd the daughter of the Lord Gweirydd (George) of Llancarfan just nine miles west of Cardiff. Walter Map wrote satirically on the quality of the poetry written by his near neighbour William Fleming. If Walter Map wrote well before 1156, and William Fleming wrote even earlier, then the problem is that there would need to have been two Walter Maps, father and son. From this and other

Chapter 1 - Grave Creek, West Virginia

evidence the universally accepted dating of Madoc's voyages was ludicrous.

Madoc had in fact been historically 'time-warped', being transferred from the mid to late sixth century AD to late in the twelfth century, a mere six hundred years out of time. Madoc had also been transferred from the Royal Dynasty in South East Wales and placed into the relatively minor royal branch of the Princes of the North West. Wrong time, wrong family, and wrong geography.

The villain of the piece appears to be one Richard Hakluyt, who wrote around 1582 in the reign of Elizabeth I Tudor. The Tudors descended from Gwynedd Princes in North West Wales, and Richard Hakluyt had more prudence than to identify Madoc with the older senior royal house in South East Wales.

Once this fake scenario had been set in motion, every other writer predictably followed this absurd false trail. No one did any basic research into the earliest sources, or if they did then they kept very quiet about it. Finally, in modern times, the absence of any positive evidence on voyages of this Prince Madoc of North West Wales around AD 1170 led to a general conclusion that the matter was spurious. No one dares to offend the ruling London Establishment by investigating the sixth-century voyages of Madoc Morfran – "Madoc the Cormorant"; well-recorded expeditions in multiple records, all of impeccable South East Wales' sources, recording voyages of between AD 562 to 574.

When Jim Michael from Kentucky was trying to persuade Wilson and Blackett to get involved, they were re-reading the book by Dana Olsen of Indiana sent to them by Don Weber in Illinois. The extent of the muddle in America and clear ignorance of the mass of information which was available, leading to the total hash of well-meant attempts to try to make some progress, finally persuaded them tentatively to become collaborators.

The catalogue of chaos was endless. Ely in West Cardiff, home of some twenty-thousand people, was said to be untraceable. William Fleming whose family lived at nearby Flemingston and in a manor house in Ely, was said to be unknown despite that fact that his family served as Sheriffs of Cardiff, as Jurors, and as soldiers of some repute, and were well-recorded local nobility. Walter Map son of Blonde) de Map of Llancarfan, seven miles from Ely, was now a Breton from Hereford. Abercerrig is clearly the harbour at Porth Ceri in South Wales, was being vainly sought in the North West. Three ship owners, all prominent men who are easily traceable in the South East around AD 1100, were equally being sought as elusive phantoms in the North West, and so on. It was the nature of the total disaster of the Madoc fiasco that finally moved Wilson and Blackett to try to do something to clear up the mess.

So, by persistent persuasion Jim Michael managed to get co-operation from an extremely reluctant Cardiff group. There were unexpected difficulties until it dawned upon Wilson and Blackett that the Kentucke Association had no idea at all that the Khumric 'Welsh' language is as different from English as German is from Japanese. They at first thought it was some 'ye olde Englyshe' dialect, and there was a near disastrous collision which would have ended all contact. Then Alan Wilson, in conversation with a colleague, realized what might be happening and went to the Post Office and got bi-lingual Welsh and English Information manuals, and bi-lingual Driving Licence application forms and electricity bills, and so on, and sent them to Kentucky. Once the complete difference in the languages was understood the difficulties evaporated.

Wilson and Blackett were for years heavily involved in tracing the ancient British Khumric ancestral histories back in time along the ancient migration trails, which were set out in the neglected histories. This meant that they were going back in time some four thousand years, and going eastwards with remarkable success. The people in Kentucky wanted them to go forward in time and to go westwards. This meant a complete change of plans, and at first Alan Wilson and Baram Blackett flatly refused to do this. The British came to Britain by sea in two great fleet migrations. The first came from Syria c.1600 BC, and the second from Trojan-Phrygia around 504 BC. The Etruscans left the same Trojan-Phrygia area of Western Asia Minor in c. 650 BC, and the Etruscan, the British, and Phrygian alphabets of antiquity are virtually identical. This was the line being followed by Wilson and Blackett, and unexpected developments were taking them back confidently to 2000 BC.

Most academic and general book-writing research is nothing more than simply reading all the books previously written by other university employees. Very rarely does anyone go right back to the earliest and most original sources and start from scratch. Anyone doing this runs the great risk of discovering that the consensus opinion and theories are probably incorrect. Then there is the great risk of saying something quite different from the speculations and guesswork of the other writers in the herd. Getting out of step and breaking ranks is a guaranteed way of ruining a promising university career. Telling the truth about the Madoc voyages would certainly get anyone straight to the top of the unpopularity lists in Britain. This lack of comprehension is typical of a pre-conceived mindset within an inaccurate framework.

It dawned upon Wilson and Blackett that in this new situation they could work to transfer their research activities away from Britain and play on a different pitch, with a different referee, a different rule book, and a new ball. All the barriers to progress and overt censorship in Britain would not mean a thing in the United States. If the problem in the U.S.A. centred around the decipherment and translation of a number of clear Coelbren Alphabet inscriptions in America, written in the Khumric Language, and by simply matching up the very clear accounts of the voyages of c. 562, 572, and

574, with the Native American records and traditional memories of the White Nation which had occupied Kentucky and other areas some fourteen hundred years ago, then the solution to their problems might be at hand.

They had been aware of American inscriptions for years, and even the academics had reluctantly recognized the Yarmouth Bay stone in 1948-1949. An abandoned search for useful American contacts might yet be revived with an organized group in Kentucky ready and willing to help. Forty-three pages of a proposed book on the British voyages to America had been finished and typeset in 1984, and a further eight chapters prepared, but the inability to fit the British evidence with the American unknown had caused a cancellation of this project. Half a story was not good enough.

For better or worse the massive decipherment exercises which had been the major preoccupation for over six years, following the information in the Khumric Triads which pointed East through Asia Minor to Armenia, then to Palestine, and on down to Egypt, was reluctantly put under wraps. Reluctantly, because the British-Khumric Histories had consistently proved to be truthful and accurate, and the detail which was emerging from this line of approach was extraordinary. By mid-1990 Wilson and Blackett had re-orientated their activities and they were prepared to work very seriously with Jim Michael. The mystery of the White Nation, which had lived in Kentucky in ancient times, and the large number of inscriptions in the Mid-West was targeted as a major project.

The Arthurian research Involvement

The International Arthurian Research Foundation was established in 1976, based upon and using work done on a casual basis since 1956. Explained simply, the investigations centred around the Histories of the British Kings generally preserved in South East Wales. This is perhaps the most detailed and accurate collection of ancient records in Western Europe. These detailed British Histories are routinely avoided by all university employees, and the rare mentions made of them are invariably to denigrate these records.

History in Britain has long been a political football to be kicked about in any direction as required. Successive régimes have finally arrived at the stage where the British History is regarded as a piece of plasticine to be moulded, bent, and twisted into any shape desired. The Church of Rome and its branch in England were opposed to British History, which exhibited the arrival of Christianity in Britain in AD 35 or 37 from where it spread East to Rome and through Gaul. Rome was not the centre or the fountain of Western Christianity. The secular politics of England demanded the obliteration of all early British History simply because the separate histories of Khumry- 'Wales', of Ireland, and of later Scotland, were powerful divisive influences which worked to oppose the desired centralized London-controlled unified single

State.

The detail is well known but rarely publicized. For seemingly endless centuries the never-ending stream of attacks were made by the English establishment upon the Khumry, and it was long ago that the policies of obliterating differences were established. The Christianity practised in Wales had to be eliminated. The Khumric legal system had to be destroyed. The Khumric language had to be destroyed, and with it the heritage of history and culture. The same policies applied to Ireland after the Norman invasion and conquest by Richard Strongbow, and they also applied to equally to Scotland. This is not said to reopen old wounds and sores, but simply because we live today with the consequences of those actions of cultural genocide.

Suffice it to say that as early as Richard II of England prohibitions were attempted against writing in Khumric, and during the reign of Henry IV the use of, and even the making or importation of all writing materials, was forbidden in Wales. This failed because the Khumry were still able to revert to their ancestral Straight Stroke Coelbren Alphabet and simply cut messages on sticks, which of course the English could neither recognize nor read. Khumric men were prohibited from holding any office - bailiff, reeve, juror, sheriff - that is, anything and everything. All Court cases were heard in entirely English, which none of the Khumry could understand, with predictable outcomes of verdicts. In this way a mentality developed which held non-English persons and speakers to be ignorant and inferior. Their language and culture were thought to be inferior, and subsequently also their histories.

Whilst printing was practised in England from AD 1474 when William Caxton set up his printing press in London, it was illegal to print in Wales until 1694. In a thousand different ways the process of eradication was carried out. Sadly, this naïve policy prevented the entire British Nation from enjoying the fruits of their true cultural heritage.

The result is still one of imbalance. It is absolutely forbidden for one single word of the most ancient British language to be spoken in the British (?) Parliament. This has some comic results. In 1996 Mr P. Flynn, the Member of Parliament for Newport in Gwent, in South-East Wales, rose and made a few comments and began reading from a book. The Speaker of the House of Commons - a former theatre chorus girl - rose to the bait and shouting and bawling in her best fishwife manner she proclaimed that as Mr Flynn well knew - not one single word of that language is to be spoken in this House'. Amid laughter Mr Paul Flynn patiently explained what almost everyone else knew, that the book he was reading from was Chaucer, written in fourteenth-century Old English. In the previous year, 1995, an Israeli Prime Minister was assassinated, and Members of Parliament queued up to eulogize this politician. Curious, because in his younger days his man was a terrorist. He was a member of the Stern gang, which kidnapped British soldiers and after holding them prisoner for a while, then murdered them in cold blood. When a Jewish Member got up to speak, he proceeded to make a long unintelligible series of statements and quotations in the Jewish language, and the Speaker of the House of Commons sat silent and did nothing.

Without labouring the point, the train has reached the end of the tracks, for it is perfectly all right to speak in a non-British foreign tongue at some length, but it is not permissible to use one single word of the ancient, four thousand-year-old British Language. This typifies the endless series of double standards which are routinely applied to all ancient Khumric history and heritage in what is dubiously termed 'the United Kingdom'.

It is laughable that in the 1914-1918 World War the British military recruited large numbers of educated Welshmen, schoolteachers and clerks. All British military messages were first translated into the despised and hated Khumric language and then encoded. At the other end of the line the messages were decoded into Khumric and then translated into English. The Germans never got anywhere near deciphering one single British message. Yet London governments had beavered away for centuries to determinedly trying to obliterate this same Language. Alan Wilson remembers how the headmaster at his school was said to have been a spy in the 1914-1918 War, when actually he was encoding and decoding military messages. This is another example of stupidity revealed.

The United States military used the Navajo Native American language to encode and decode their secret messages during World War II, and again there is the paradox of eighteenth- and nineteenth-century persecution and cultural demolition of a smaller nation and then the vital recourse to that despised culture.

Extraordinary as it may seem, the Khumry had been playing the same game of coded messages for long centuries with the English. Secret messages, which are of the most extraordinary significance, proliferate through their ancient records.

The Tudor monarchy can be used to give a hint of the politics involved. Henry Tudor, a Welsh claimant to the English throne, landed in South-West Wales in 1495 with a tiny handful of followers and sat in an Inn nervously waiting to see what would happen. Military contingents arrived from Gwent and Glamorgan in South-East Wales and Henry Tudor was uncertain whether they would arrest him or aid him. Conveniently it is forgotten that it was a centuries'-old custom for the Khumry to hire out in large local regiments as mercenaries in Europe, particularly to Italian city states. At Crécy in AD 1346, and at the famous 'English' victory of the Black Prince at Poitiers in AD 1356 where his small army of five thousand defeated some fifty thousand French was actually won by two thousand three hundred Khumric archers with a thousand Irish infantry standing firm with them. The same thing happened at Agincourt in 1415 where Henry V with a similar tiny force, raised by Gruffydd Gam, was able to defeat another French mass of around sixty thousand. So in 1485 the men coming to join Henry Tudor were almost all Khumric professional mercenaries and not levies.

It is forgotten that the nobility and barons of England in the reign of King John refused to fight for the King outside Britain. John, who owned huge tracts of Gaul, was in difficulty facing a military coalition led by the French King. His English subjects would not fight for him in France. The situation is revealed in Shakespeare's play *Henry V*, in which Henry cries out that the Englishmen home safely in bed will rue the day that they were not with him in the forthcoming battle at Agincourt on St Crispin's day. Edward I defeated the Scots with Irish infantry and hordes of Welsh archers.

The problem Henry Tudor had was that the local great lord in West Wales, one Rhys, had been bullied into signing an agreement on oath to Richard III that he would only allow Henry Tudor to pass through his land 'over his body'. So, being confronted with a growing army of experienced soldiers all eager to be granted rich lands in England, Rhys and Henry Tudor came up with a typical Khumric solution. The oath simply specified the Henry could only pass by over Rhys's 'body', and not 'dead body'. So Rhys rode his horse into a river and sat under a bridge and Henry rode over the bridge thus fulfilling Rhys's obligation of oath to the English King. He joined Henry and the war was as good as won: ten thousand men were left at the Welsh border and Henry Tudor went forward with five and a half thousand picked soldiers, and defeated and killed Richard III at Cuddington, just over a mile from Bosworth. The Welsh had now conquered England and that was about to destroy them.

The Tudor heirs did the Khumry no good at all. In 1536 Henry VIII got Parliament to literally annex all Wales, and in 1546 English settlers in the five counties of the Welsh Marches petitioned their Parliament that Gloucester, Hereford, Worcester, Shropshire, and Cheshire, should be annexed out of Welsh territory and made part of England. It is odd that English Parliaments proclaim Hitler's annexation of Poland illegal, and strange that they were furious when German settlers in Czechoslovakia successfully petitioned Hitler to seize the Sudeten lands.

In 1604 the last Tudor, Elizabeth I, died and the English throne passed by virtue of the marriage of Henry Tudor's sister Margaret to the Scottish and Stuart King James VI, known as James I of England. The Stuart pedigree, originally Stewart or Steward from their position, traced back to King Gruffydd ap Llewellyn of Gwynedd, so the Tudor history from the mountains of far North-West Wales.

North-West Wales had to be preserved and it also had to be inflated to conceal the senior line of ancient Khumric Kings in the South-East. The same situation applied when in 1714 German George I of Hanover became King of England by virtue of a marriage with the Stuarts of Scotland. The policy of obliterating most Khumric-

British history and inflating the Tudor heritage to try to fill the void was continued. This situation solidified and worsened. To paraphrase George Orwell:

> '... when you have rewritten and reinvented history it is then necessary to forget that you have done so.'

Henry VII Tudor started the rot by appointing himself as the head of a commission of Heraldry and listing every ancestor he had. The book of his parents, grandparents, eight – sixteen – thirty-two – sixty-four – a hundred and twenty-eight - etc, etc, etc. ancestors, is still available. Henry Tudor re-orientated all Khumric history around his Gwynedd-North West Wales ancestors, and everything else had to go. Even so a small statuette of St Arthmael-Iron-Bear-Arthur II, dressed in full armour, is in his mortuary chapel in Westminster.

The result is chaos and the jingoistic racism of superiority preached by the Professor Bishop Stubbs of Oxford University and Edwin Guest at Cambridge some hundred and fifty years ago, saw the false notion of ancient Irish and Khumric barbarity fully established. Strange that when King Alfred - curiously modernly termed 'the Great - ruled southern England in 871-899 he found that not one single person in his English Kingdom could read or write. So he sent to Wales for the monk Asser - Geraint y Ffardd Glas - and he sent to Ireland for John Erigerna, whose great manuscript still lies untranslated in Dublin, and he sent for John Scottius, to set up learning in his illiterate land.

At the end of the day the squabbles, stupidities, and jealousies, of our various ancestors have left us all with a fine old mess on our hands in Britain. By throwing out all ancient British History, Bishops Stubbs, Edwin Guest, and their adherents had effectively thrown out Brutus and the Khumric-Trojan origins, and along with this, inevitably, the great Lloegres or English record of the earlier Geauntes Albyne. Out as well went all the ancient Kings and this included 'King Arthur' in the well-known identities of Arthur I son of Mascen or Magnus Maximus, and his direct descendant Arthur II son of King Meurig. It also was necessary to vilify the great British Queen Empress, Helen of the Cross, and her son the British Emperor Constantine the Great. The simplistic racist propaganda tumbled everything, the Hanoverian monarchy was German, the Angles and Saxons were German tribes, and therefore Anglo-Saxonism had to be exalted. Julius Caesar was claimed to have won when he lost. Roman defeats in later centuries were translated into ghostly victories, and everything originally British had to be denigrated.

Today it is common for politicians to speak of Anglo-American agreements and Anglo-Irish agreements, instead of British-American or British-Irish agreements. Who are these Anglos? They are not Khumric-Welsh, nor Scots, nor Northern Irish, nor Cornish, nor Manx, nor Midland Mercians, nor Worcester Hwiccae, nor Southern and South West Ealde Cyrcenas-Old Syrians, or Gewissae, nor North-West Cumbrian Khumry. This demonstrates the Establishment mind.

The fact that Britain had some ten million war-like inhabitants who were difficult to be easily explained away as effeminate clods who were defeated by three boat loads of Saxons, was simply avoided. The fact that almost the entire country was devastated by impacts of comet débris *c.* AD 562 was simply ignored and left out of the newly invented histories. The new histories claimed reduced, primitive and barbaric British populations in place of the highly developed, advanced, and scholastic culture, which was reported in antiquity by Greek, Roman, and British writers.

One of the leading fabricators of the new History was one Edwin Guest, who although he did not offer himself as a candidate for the position of Master at Caius College, in Oxford, was nonetheless nominated and elected by his friends. His technique was a little more insidious than that of Stubbs, and in making what he claimed were researches into the origins of the British, he began by simply discarding the Albyne and Brutus-Trojan Histories and ignoring at least 95 % of the Native Khumric Histories completely. The parallel would be to ignore all Greek records and traditions and then to attempt a history of the Greeks, or alternatively to ignore all Hebrew, Israel, Judean, records, or to ignore all Roman records, and start from that point on the Histories of the Jews or of Rome.

Incredibly, Edwin Guest was prepared to recognize the legendary histories of the Irish and Scots as preserved in the Welsh histories by the Welsh monk Nennius. Anything and everything British-Khumric was determinedly ignored, with the exception of vague, mystical, or misunderstood snippets. For example, Guest prognosticated on the Khumric Triad reference to Defrobani and the Gwlad yr Haf as Khumric places of origin. Defrobani was accepted as Ceylon - properly Sri-Lanka - as Tropobane, yet 'Def-Rho-Ba-Ni' means 'A place given to us for our own', and Gwlad yr Haf does not mean the 'Summer Land' = 'Somerset', but it means 'Land of Plenty'. These are statements redolent of the Promised Land and a Land Flowing with Milk and Honey. It bothered no one that Ceylon-Sri Lanka is not geographically on any migration route to Britain.

The Guest technique was basically simple. First discard all native British Histories and records, and then second, trace every nation of Europe, including the British, back to the names of the Hebrew patriarchs descended from Noah in Biblical record. This was done by scouring the ancient Greek and Roman writings for names of people and places, and by then comparing them and 'deciphering' them. The result was a pompous proclamation of the inhabitants of Britain being the descendants of the Biblical Gog and Magog. No reason was given for discarding Khumric and British records. This buffoon was actually held in high repute throughout Europe. By showering a bemused audience with myriads of ancient place names and tribal or city identities, all quoted from a vast array of revered Greek and Latin writers, a vast illusory mirage of credibility was set up to support the newly invented British Histories.

Guest held that the name Britain derived from Greek etymology and meant 'the painted men' through Britanni. It seemed not to matter to him that Brutus was the founding King and that Arab historians as late as AD 1100 were still referring to Britain as Brutusland. When he died his political supporters, including Bishop Stubbs, gathered to publish the *Origines Celticae* which he had planned as the bogus History of Britain in total disregard of the fact that the were no Celts in Britain, none of the British or Irish are Celtic, and there are no Celts in Britain. One of those eulogising Guest in the Preface of this work signs himself as 'E.V. The Preceptory, Lincoln', and referring to a work of Edwin Guest he states:

> 'It was one which afforded Dr Guest the opportunity of exhibiting his marvellous genius, as 'the discoverer', almost 'the creator' of the early history of Britain.'

Anyone who begins by totally setting aside and ignoring the entire corpus of national history without investigating it, and then labours to invent and create a new history based on speculation and surmise is hardly a genius. Bishop W. Stubbs, writing on 17th April 1882, proclaims the work as one "which bears so characteristic an impress of his genius, his faith, and his devout labour". Here we have it, everything had to conform to Biblical record and the myths of descendants of Noah and Abraham. British History did not conform, and neither did it suit the political requirements of the Regime. In 1793 the identical nature of the British Coelbren Alphabet with ancient Etruscan and "Pelasgian" Phrygian of Asia Minor was published. In 1846 John Williams at Oxford had published these Alphabets and similarities, and by the time Stubbs was writing this, German scholars were investigating the British-Khumric Alphabet.

It may or may not be genius to see that if the National History points to a specific ancient route, and that the same alphabet is found all along that route, then the same national language was probably used along that route. It is a short step then to consider that the same alphabet is written in the same language found in the inscriptions in Britain, in Italy, in Switzerland, in the Aegean, and in Asia Minor, and further East. Guest was just another 'Classical' scholar playing word games. This however was the era of the Treachery of the Blue Books of 1846, and the London Parliament was hell-bent on obliterating the Khumric Language and Alphabet. Guest's task was to give this cultural genocide the aura of bogus respectability. If there was no ancient culture then there was no moral guilt in destroying it.

Logically, if everything had to go to promote the new fake history manufactured by Bishop Stubbs as Professor of History at Oxford, then the ancient Coelbren Alphabet also had to be rejected. All the British Emperors of Rome had to be re-identified.

This new fabricated history might have succeeded totally were it not for the great grey rock-like ghost of 'King Arthur'. Nothing could get rid of the Arthurian sagas, records, histories, traditions and romances. That 'King Arthur', a composite figure of two warrior kings, was always known amongst the Khumry. Printing was banned in Wales until AD 1694, but by 1734 the Rev Williams had published a book identifying both Arthurs, and Wilson and Blackett came across this as confirmation after they had made the same identifications. In fact, several hundred Khumric authors had correctly exhibited Arthur II in manuscript and book form over the centuries.

The Historical Triads tell of Arthur killing Rhitta Gawr, a powerful Irish prince in a battle near Snowdon. The romance tales identify Rhitta Gawr as 'King Ryons', and the histories name him as Reueth, killed *c.* AD 367. The 'King Arthur' of the Brut (History of) Tyssilio and of Gruffydd ap Arthur (Geoffrey of Monmouth) relate how Arthur invaded Gaul, besieged Paris, and defeated the Roman Emperor and his barbarian generals at Soissons = Sassy. Then they tell how Arthur killed the Roman King = Emperor. These are the exploits of Arthur I, eldest son of Magnus Maximus the grandson of the British Constantine the Great, who as Magnus' chief general did invade Gaul in AD 383, and capture Paris, the stronghold of the Lady St. Genevieve. This Arthur -copiously recorded in ancient manuscript genealogies - then defeated the massed armies of the Roman Emperor Gratian at Soissons, and chased him South to Lugdunum = Lyons, where he killed him.

The campaigns of this Arthur I through Switzerland and on down through Italy, over to Greece, and up into the Balkans are well known and recorded. He fought two major battles against Theodosius of Constantinople in Illyria = Yugoslavia, where he was greatly outnumbered and finally defeated. Arthur I, known to Latins as Andragathius, made his way back to Britain in 388. This is the Arthur who just as the Histories tell was succeeded by his cousin Constantine Coronog = the Crowned, who invaded Gaul in AD 406 and set up as yet another British Emperor. Constantine Coronog was powerful enough to seize Gaul and Spain and to defeat the Germanic confederation of the Vandals, Sueves, and Alans.

Removing both Arthurs from all British history is no mean feat of brainwashing and propaganda, given the remarkable quantities of impeccably authentic historical data which is preserved about both these kings. Bishop Stubbs and his conspirator colleagues nearly succeeded, but as Abraham Lincoln observed: "You can fool all the people some of the time, and you can fool some of the people all of the time, but you cannot fool all the people all the time". In fact, Stubbs came perilously close to proving Lincoln wrong.

The second Arthur was of course Arthur II son of King Meurig son of King Tewdrig, and so on back to Brutus. He was a sixth-generation direct descendant in the male line of Arthur I, who was born *c.* AD 503 and was killed in 579. This Arthur II fought the Jutes, Angles, Saxons and others. He also had trouble over his heirs, and fought the Civil War battles with his nephew Modred ap Liew ap Cynfarch Oer of Llongborth, at Llongborth in Cardigan Bay, and at Camlann in the Camlann Valley below Camlann mountain just ten miles south of Dollgelly. Fatefully it was in his time that the Comet débris struck Britain in 562, decimating the entire population and rendering much of Britain an uninhabitable great wasteland for between seven to eleven years. Evidence lies around in mountainous quantity. Winston Churchill recognized the dangers of fabricated history when he inserted into his history volumes the reference to King Arthur being from South Wales, indicating Arthur II.

There are clear, precise accounts giving directions to the grave of Arthur I in the great ancient graveyard of the "illustrious of the British" in Warwickshire. There is a glut of detail preserved of the death and burial of Arthur II, and two three-line verses in the Songs of the Graves pin-point the exact spot and grave mound in Glamorgan. The grave of his father Meurig = Maurice is known, that of Tewdrig = Theoderic his grandfather is known, and was excavated twice, in 1609 and in 1881. Graves and memorials of his ancestors, his brothers, cousins, kinsmen, and descendants, are identifiable in profusion. Another alleged 'mystery', the grave of Gwrtheyrn = Monarch of Men, *alias* Vortigern = High Ruler, in fact a King Trahaearn, was excavated in AD 1776. The real 'mystery' of Arthur is how on Earth did Stubbs, and Guest, and the London Régime get away with this for a hundred and fifty years. Integrity is crucial in historical research, and this vital integrity is not apparent here.

Possibly in keeping with the proverb 'Fools rush in where angels fear to tread', Wilson and Blackett had set about detailing and restoring these correct and precisely recorded ancient British Histories. In doing this they were discovering the harsh reality of the other proverb, 'Let him who wishes to write the truth declare war upon the world'. The reaction was as bad as their worst nightmares. This was politically forbidden history, which could be set aside, ridiculed, and abused, in the cause of political correctness, but heaven help anyone who simply sought to trace and exhibit its plain truths and extreme accuracy.

The significance of all this is that an integral part of the ancient British History is the language and the alphabet. The History was politically undesirable and was destined and condemned to extinction, but 'King Arthur' would not go, and so he was made a comic unreal figure of myth and legend. The language was legislated against and forcibly eliminated through seizure of the education system. This left only the awkward ancient Coelbren Alphabet lying mute on pre-Christian coins, on ancient stones of the Kings who now officially no longer existed, on fonts, and carved on wood and written in manuscripts. This seemingly insoluble problem was solved by simply declaring that the ancient British Coelbren Alphabet to be a forgery of around AD 1800, and by ignoring all the ancient inscriptions in all their forms, and of course turning a blind eye to the writings of Julius Caesar, Strabo, Ammianus Marcellinus, and others.

The audacity and barefaced insolence of the London Establishment are breath-taking beyond all comprehension. In the only state on Earth without a written constitution to protect the people from extremist politicians, anything can be done by Government. If the alphabet was declared false then everything written in it became also false. As a logical consequence all inscribed stones could be ignored or re-dated by several hundred years. Worse still, with the Trojan inheritance being declared false meant that the key to the decipherment of related ancient Etruscan, Rhaetian, and Phrygian texts was thrown away. These ancient languages and links were to remain indecipherable, for how could texts written in 650 BC be read using an alphabet allegedly forged in AD 1800?

The knock-on effect was that the clear Coelbren inscriptions in North America could not be read either. Nor could any of the historical records in Britain, which explain how these writings exist in America, be used to solve these mysteries, for the British histories were now prohibited. Absurd phrases such as "it all began in 1066" proliferated in a country whose recorded history stretched back three thousand six hundred years to around 1600 BC. The scholars of the Western World were denied access to the tool and the key to unlock the barred and bolted rusted doors of the misted shrouded ancient past. The Madoc Legend only survived because it was removed from South East Wales and the very undesirable ancient British royal family, and transferred into the Tudor heartland of Gwynedd and re-dated by six hundred years.

Explaining all this to Americans was no easy task, but they understood corruption and President Nixon, and the "who shot Kennedy?" farrago. Ferreting out the academic weasels who have deliberately fabricated falsehoods since around 1840 to the present day was a time-consuming but remarkably rewarding exercise. Demonstrating their bent methods and inanities is remarkably simple once they have been identified. Add what can only be described as wholesale wilful mistranslation of ancient texts to the time-honoured courtroom tactic of the Prosecution declaring dangerous evidence to be inadmissible in the case, and the truth emerges. The skull-duggery constitutes a project in itself, and would take a volume to detail. The extent of the fabrications published is staggering in its dishonesty, and the Establishment clearly understood the academic mind. No one would bother to look at the original of a translated and published text, and if rarely someone did then prudence to protect a career and reputation would ensure silence.

Chapter 1 - Grave Creek, West Virginia

Jim Michael and the Ancient Kentucke Historical Association had been going in the same ever-decreasing circles and heading towards vanishing point, and in the same way as Henry Schoolcraft. They were not surprised when in 1992, just two weeks before Alan Wilson arrived on a five-week tour to speak in the U.S.A., an article appeared in a widely distributed and leading American epigraphical magazine ridiculing Wilson and Blackett and alleging the Coelbren alphabet to be a forgery. The authors and editors of this piece did not even have a clue what Coelbren actually looked like, and had no idea what Wilson and Blackett were saying. The attempt to smear Wilson and Blackett as insane amateurs and incompetents failed because Wilson and Blackett had predicted that this would probably happen, and the source was quickly traced to a government-funded agency in Cardiff.

Fortunately, Jim Michael and his colleagues were also already aware that the ancient alphabet was written in the *Manuscript Bodleian No. 572* in Oxford *c.* 1520, and Jim Michael had seen the inscribed stone dug up in St Paul's church yard in 1852. They knew of the then Prince of Wales' bard writing in 1784 concerning the ancient alphabet, and they knew of references to the alphabet made in poetry of pre-1367, in *c.* 1425, and 1450 and 1475, and also of a long five-hundred-and-twenty-page Manuscript recorded in 1773. The fact that the alphabet existed carved on stones of between AD 200 to *c.* AD 1140 in Britain had been made known to them, and the attempt to torpedo the investigation in the U.S.A. and Alan Wilson's visit fell flat.

With a different personality than Jim Michael in contact it is highly likely that the 'hands across the water' co-operation, which was being set up between Kentucky and Cardiff, would have collapsed. The enquiry would have been aborted, and Wilson and Blackett would never have known why. Instead, Jim Michael went steaming in to the authors of the offensive article, and he knew that they had already published and had supported publications in several contentious books which would be largely discredited once the British Coelbren Alphabet was exhibited and put to use in deciphering the U.S.A. inscriptions.

Just how many thousands of allegedly learned books will need to be re-written or simply pulped once the accurate history of the British-Khumric nation is re-admitted into the forums and courts of the nations of Planet Earth is not Wilson and Blackett's problem. The problem is a political problem. It requires the same type of changed open attitude amongst the academic historical and archaeological fraternity that is clearly common in scientific scholarly circles.

The story of vanishing collections of ancient manuscripts, of libraries burned down by arson, of legislation passed to destroy the language and the alphabet, and many other barbaric misdeeds can be told elsewhere. Perhaps it should be remembered that since Columbus set foot in the Caribbean West Indies the industrialised imperial powers of Europe have demolished the records, the culture, and the heritage, of nations in Asia, in Africa, in South America, through the Pacific, and in Australia. Non-Christian and non-European cultures were wrong and inferior, and non-Christian religion was wrong and inferior, and anything which was different was inferior and could be destroyed. Even people in South America and Africa were held to be inferior beings and could therefore be enslaved. In past centuries the only morality was that of power.

Civilization levels were measured by architecture and by industrial achievement alone, and this is still thought to be so by many academics. The ancient people who built the biggest buildings and temples were the 'highest civilizations'. Which of course presents a problem with two-thirds of the population of Athens being slaves, and the Roman slave empire building massive amphitheatres solely for the purpose of public exhibitions of mass murder and cruelty in a thousand forms. Being civilized means how we conduct ourselves, and how decently we behave towards others, how honest and honourable our institutions are. The country which can build the fastest war-planes and the most devastating weapons is not necessarily the most civilized.

A group of African native elders sitting in conference in the shade under a tree are far more likely to conduct their affairs in a truly civilized manner than the modem style vote- and publicity-conscious career politicians of London, Washington, Brussels, or elsewhere. This is what this project is all about: the tracing of British civilization.

Edwin Guest and the Wonderland of Gog and Magog

Whilst Henry Schoolcraft was setting about the task of identifying the origin of the Grave Creek Tablet, over in England a religiously inspired fanatic was organizing the destruction of the ancient culture that had produced it. Few people today have heard of Edwin Guest, who was a major figure in the assassination of ancient British history. He was a product of his times, born in AD 1800 into a land-owning family of country gentry in Worcestershire, his father having amassed a fortune in the Napoleonic Wars, and Edmund Guest, the Bishop of Salisbury who died in 1578, was an ancestor.

The schools and university system in which he was educated was then still firmly under religious control. Growing Protestantism in Britain and Europe and perhaps the advent of Mormon belief in America was causing alarm and a backlash amongst the upper classes of England, and Edwin Guest was destined to become involved. He took his degree at Caius College, Cambridge, and became a Fellow in 1824. He then spent a year travelling in Europe, mostly in Germany, before returning to London. He became a lawyer - the pupil of Lord Campbell - and finally a Barrister. Working on the Oxford circuit was gradually set aside for literary pursuits, and he ceased work in the courts.

Chapter 1 - Grave Creek, West Virginia

He began by publishing *English Rhythms* in 1838, just when the Grave Creek mound was being excavated, and to do this he had to study the few surviving ancient English manuscripts containing poetry. This led him into the field of Philology and he formed the Philology Society. From ancient Philology it was but a short step to dabbling in ancient history. Most of the leading members of Guest's Philology Society were major orthodox convinced Christian clergymen. The Bishop of St David's was the first President, a Mr Stanley of University College, Oxford, who later became Dean of Westminster, set out to interest Oxford notables in joining Guest's Cambridge contacts, and the ultra-religious Dr Arnold of Rugby gave Guest 'valuable assistance'.

The study of Philology was totally in the hands of a group of orthodox clergymen and faithful believers. This has to be seen against the background of current events at that time. On 27th December 1831, Charles Darwin had sailed in the surveying sloop H.M.S. *Beagle* on a momentous five years' voyage, and in 1839 he published his *On the Origin of Species*. The screams of outrage from the orthodox Christian community still echo around, for Darwin had totally demolished the Christian theory of World History. The world was not created by the god Yahweh, at 9 a.m. on a Thursday morning around 4130 BC. Nor did the god create all the plants and animals exactly as they are today. Evolution and development and changes, which spanned many millions of years, were now demonstrated.

The Christian dogmas, which had exhibited the Creation, had also established Hebrew ancient history as the sole ancient history. Greek and Roman history had to be allowed as classical, but all others were relentlessly ignored as pagan and heathen. At this very time explorers were discovering ancient Sumerian, Chaldean, Assyrian, Egyptian, and other city sites, and the sublime nature of many of the religious hymns and the sagacity of their laws was becoming apparent. This was no time to discover an ancient tablet of unknown antiquity and inscribed in an unknown alphabet in America. Copernicus, Bruno, Gallileo, and others had brought the theology of the Earth being the flat centre of the universe crashing down. Otto von Guerick had publicly demonstrated the vacuum and its properties, Robert Meyer had discovered the 'Law of the Conservation of Energy', sending the academic world almost crazy and resulting in the magnificent Meyer being incarcerated in a lunatic asylum by frightened and jealous academics. Dozens of other discoveries too numerous to mention were shaking the old religious edifice to pieces.

So the men in black fought back and they did it through Philology. They took the Bible record of the descendants of Seth the third son of Adam and Eve, and the descendants of Noah and set to work. The Biblical idea was that all the people on Earth were direct descendants of Noah and his sons and grandsons and so on. These descendants of Noah were to have constantly divided and each to form a new tribe or nation, and this of course did not include Africans, Asians, Chinese, and ancient Americans, and so on. This was no obstacle and Edwin Guest set about his great work.

We find clues in the words of the Master of his College:

> 'his sound judgement and deep Christian feeling were invaluable; he could always be relied upon, he never wavered in his convictions.'

Guest's first move was to abandon almost all of ancient British history completely, and here he did something very strange. He took the historical records of the Welsh monk Nennius from Bangor in North Wales and threw out all Khumric British records. Then from amongst these same unwelcome records he proceeded to publish the brief account of the main Irish history of migration, and he also published the brief Scottish record in the same source. It is an understatement to say that Guest was extremely selective, but as will be shown these records do not pose the same political threat as do the British.

Guest laboured mightily scouring the allegedly ancient Greek and Roman records for the names of races, nations, peoples, tribes, cities, and subjecting them to his analysis and 'criticism'. He construed meanings of names, he sought comparisons of sound and spellings, and he sought snippets of migration notations, and so he claimed to track the movements of ancient peoples across Asia and Europe. For the hapless British he came up with the astonishing conclusion that they were the descendants of the Biblical Gog and Magog, and they were also 'Celts'. There was no need of recorded British History for the determined Edwin Guest.

So the British were disinherited. Edwin Guest - although he did not apply for the job - was elected as Master of Caius College, Cambridge, 'by his friends', in 1852, giving his ravings the aura of respectability. He picked up the usual set of academic memberships to disguise his incompetence - Fellow of the Royal Society in 1839; Member of Society of Antiquaries in 1852; D.L.C. et eundum at Oxford in 1853, and so on. As one of those writing eulogies on his death in 1880 put it-

> 'It was one which afforded Dr Guest the opportunity of exhibiting his marvellous genius as 'the discoverer', almost 'the creator' of the early History of Britain," and adding that this was "the province he had made so peculiarly his own.'

It was his own - he fabricated it.

So, British History was flushed away down the drain by Edwin Guest and Biblical theology, and Gog and Magog were installed instead. The wrecking went on after his death as Bishop E. Stubbs, Professor of History at Oxford, along with other die-hard religionists gathered to publish *Origines Celticae* which Guest had threatened to publish before he died. It is a source of total wonder to Alan Wilson and Baram Blackett that almost without exception British historians and archaeologists are still blindly following the path laid down by this pseudo-academic without questioning.

Chapter 1 - Grave Creek, West Virginia

To study the history of any nation the first recourse is to its national records. This is the only way to proceed, and in common with all other nations on Planet Earth, the British record must be adjudged innocent until proven guilty, and not condemned as being guilty without trial. *No other national history is alleged to be a total forgery.* Henry Schoolcraft had no chance of success in this religious war where the innocent victim was all British ancient record, heritage, culture, and history.

It was Bishop Stubbs of Oxford, the eager disciple of Guest, who proclaimed that absolutely nothing whatsoever in the heritage of the new Anglo-Saxon England was owed to any way to any ancient British sources. All pre-Anglo-Saxon sources were played down and Anglo-Saxon achievement was played up. British records were banished to the newly created 'Celtic fringe' and discredited, and these records were irrelevant to the English anyway. Stubbs effectively completed the demolition of the British past as designed by Edwin Guest.

The ancient colleges of Wales were destroyed long centuries before, and the only persons able to refute the Bible-based absurdities of Guest, Stubbs, and company, were individual scholars who lacked the institutional credibility of Oxford and Cambridge. These scholars could easily be disposed of by simply labelling them as forgers and cranks, without of course needing to prove these allegations.

It seems not to have been understood that a group of African tribal elders sitting in conference under a Banyan tree are just as civilized as Senators in Washington and Members of Parliament in London as Nelson Mandela is living proof. The only difference is the buildings. Given the conduct of many modern politicians it may well be that sitting under a Banyan tree is to be preferred. So it was that the Romans were exalted as a mirror-image in nineteenth-century Anglo-Saxon England. British victories over the Romans were to be either disregarded or turned into defeats. All British cultural achievement was denied and denigrated.

In amongst this bedlam of religious fanaticism prepared to destroy anything and everything in the name of religion, which was badly frightened by Charles Darwin's publication, and confused by growing scientific discovery, worried by threats posed to the comfortable social order, deeply disturbed by ongoing Protestant breakaways and Unitarianism, poor Henry Schoolcraft had no chance of establishing whether or not the Grave Creek Tablet was written in Old British, for now the highly literate ancient British had been decreed to have been illiterate by men of religion at Oxford and Cambridge.

Roman piracy and pillaging of other nations was justified as civilizing. Invading other nations, stealing their goods, herds, and lands, was justified. Slaughtering their men-folk in battle and enslaving their women, children, and old people, was 'bringing civilization'. Exploitation by Rome of other nations' natural resources was 'expanding civilization'. The destruction of other nations' religions and holy shrines was simply spreading the Roman civilization. In the nineteenth century every nation in Western Europe was busily doing the exact same thing in Africa, Asia, all across the Pacific, and in South America. Western Europe was developed industrially and could build the biggest buildings, the biggest ships, and the biggest and the most destructive weapons, and therefore they were the most 'civilized'. Today we are learning differently.

Chapter Two

The British Cold War

The vast majority of people everywhere are oblivious of the relentless cold war that has been waged for many centuries in what is optimistically styled the United Kingdom. This cold war is the one-sided battle which has raged over the preservation of all ancient British heritage, culture, and history. This is the unholy mess into which Henry Schoolcraft would have stepped if he had enquired too deeply into the Old British lettering on the Grave Creek Tablet.

How to write about this cold war and how to exhibit its disastrous consequences has been the major concern for Alan Wilson and Baram Blackett as it involves secular and religious politics from which the authors would prefer to refrain. This however is not possible, and describing the events that brought about the current situation is wholly unavoidable before concentrating on the abundance of evidence available. What has been paraded as ancient British history is in fact a confection of squalid and unreliable decadence. Only by employing incisive analysis and microscopic examination of the data available in an unbiased and dispassionate climate unaffected by controversial nationalist and religious emotions does a clear historical scenario emerge.

It is as if there is a great ruined castle hidden deep in a forest, and its massive iron bound doors are firmly locked. Very little can be seen of the castle's treasures and secrets until the key of knowledge is found, and then by entering and opening the shutters and pulling back the curtains, and lighting up the darkened rooms, we can see everything. No longer do we blunder about fumbling with uncollated abstracts. With the clear light of day, we can see things. We can proceed to collect, collate, assess, and disseminate the new information. These are the recognized four basic tenets of any military intelligence work, and they allow for accurate assessments.

Until around AD 1700 the ancient traditional histories of Britain were firmly believed and published. The first was the tradition that the Geuantes - Gutian - Albyne had sailed with a fleet from Syria around 1600 BC, to seize the great Tin Island of Britain. This is evidenced from the sudden emergence of a remarkable metal-working culture in Southern England and Wales which archaeologists have called the Wessex culture. The second migration was that of Brutus who sailed from Trojan Western Asia Minor in circa 504 BC and again another new advanced metal-working culture erupted as if out of nowhere in Britain. The archaeologists prove what the 'historians' deny. Overland migrations - probably of tribal groups - are also mentioned in the records, but the two main organised large-scale military migrations which were fixed firmly in the British mind were those of Albyne and Brutus.

These British histories were arbitrarily abandoned in England during the eighteenth and nineteenth centuries. The Albyne migration was thought to involve Giants: a simple misreading of 'Geauntes', and without evidence. The Brutus tradition was ridiculed as it involved the survivors of the wreck of the Trojan War, and academic opinion was that the city of Troy never actually existed, and was instead a fairy-tale place which had existed only in the imagination of Melesigenes – 'Homer'. The fact that the groups known as the Ealde Cyrcenas - Old Syrians are listed in early Mediaeval Manuscripts, and the name Surrey is traceable in foreign ancient texts as well as still existing, seems not to have been noticed. As for Brutus, the great grandson of Aeneas, the evidence is overwhelming as is the evidence for the Trojan War of c. 650 BC once British records are understood.

If the history of a nation is arbitrarily abandoned then something else has to take its place to fill the void. The something else was the invention of 'British barbarism'. The massed array of evidence exhibiting that the British were a technically advanced, literate, cultured, and well-ordered nation was simply thrown aside. British victories over the Romans were translated as defeats, and barbaric piratical attacks by the Romans on yet another civilized group of nations were disguised as bringing Roman order to barbarians.

The founding of Christianity in Britain in AD 35-37, well before Rome knew of it, and the arrival of Christianity in Rome with the family of the British King Caradoc I in AD 51, are admitted by the Church of Rome - but not very loudly or too frequently. Clearly this was less than welcome to the Roman Church. As is well recorded the débris from a comet struck Britain and parts of Ireland in AD 562, and the entire country, the vast population, the cities, and towns, the villa palaces, and castles were laid entirely waste. In 1986 Dr Victor Clube of Oxford University Astrophysics Laboratory estimated the blast as equivalent to a scatter of a hundred Hiroshima atomic bombs. This allowed the mass infiltration of Britain by tribes from Heligoland, the Netherlands, and Germany. The catastrophic disaster also provided the opportunity for the Bishop of Rome to send a mission to the Jutes, Angles, and Saxons, in Britain.

Chapter 2 - The British Cold War

The destruction of Arthurian Britain by the comet débris passed on into folklore as well as historical record. Centuries later the Romance writers on the sagas of King Arthur related the strange great blast which wrecked the Greal Castle and devastated the Arthurian Kingdom. They wrote of the Great Wastelands that held death for all who dared to enter, and amazingly none of this was believed to be factual and true. By denying the destruction of Britain by débris - comet or asteroid - from outer space in AD 562 it was easily possibly to pour scorn on the records that a great powerful and highly civilized British state had ever existed. Read the records, and there is the story of the destruction of Britain by impact from the heavens. Ignore the record, and the history of ancient Britain can be jeered at as false, for how could such a vast state disappear?

Theology also held that a god had created the whole Earth and its many life forms in six days. Even the heavens and the light of the sun were simultaneously created. The Earth, the solar system and galaxy, even the universe, were a stable safe creation of the god. Isaac Newton had postulated the serene, secure, celestial mechanics of the solar system, which he thought worked like a great harmonious and unstoppable mechanical clock. Whilst Newton's mentor Edmund Halley was studying the ancient records from bygone civilisations it seems never to have occurred to either of them that a comet or an asteroid might collide with planet Earth. The researches of Copernicus, Gallileo, Giodarni Bruno, and others were still anathema to the Church of Rome, and the Church of England was simply an errant sheep from the Roman fold.

No one could take up a Professorial Chair in an English University unless he could show that he was an orthodox Christian of the State Church. Education and religion were inextricably entwined and so also was the teaching of history. History is a hugely powerful political weapon, and as George Orwell put it: "Who controls the past controls the present, and whoever controls the present controls the future."

In 1485 the Welsh Henry Tewdwr - anglicized as Tudor - defeated King Richard III of England at Cuddington near Bosworth and became King of England. The Tudor Dynasty ended in 1604 with the death of Elizabeth I, and by virtue of the marriage between Margaret, the sister of Henry VIII Tudor, and the Scottish King James III, the crown ultimately passed to James VI of Scots and I of England. As a dynasty the Stuarts were a disaster, and by 1688 a second revolution had seen James II deposed, defeated by William of Orange, and driven into exile. This 'Glorious Revolution' of 1688 saw the future government of Britain pass into the hands of a junta, who needed puppet monarchs to front their rule. Queen Anne, who left no heirs, was succeeded by Queen Mary and William of Orange, who again left no heirs, and finally by virtue of a marriage between a Stuart Princess (on her mother's side) and an Elector of Hanover, whose family were also suitably Protestant, a German family sat on the throne.

George I became King in 1714 and a Scottish rebellion took place in 1715. A second revolt in 1745 under 'Bonnie Prince Charlie' shook the hoped-for tranquillity of the régime, and the savagery of the reprisals taken against the Scots demonstrates the fear of the régime. The new monarchy was not generally popular and the heavy-handedness of the London government caused the revolt of the twelve American colonies and the War of Independence in 1776. Some fifty percent of the British population supported the cause of their American emigrant kinsmen and friends. The shattering blow of the loss of the American colonies was followed by the French revolution in 1792, with the public execution of the King, the Queen, and most of the aristocracy, causing great alarm in London. Wolf Tone had formed his United Irishmen organisation in 1790 causing further alarm in London, and in Britain the Chartist movement was worrying by its sheer strength of numbers. In 1838 three groups of Welshmen numbering five thousand marched into Newport in Gwent and an armed confrontation involving cannon saw twenty killed by English soldiers.

A very sizeable proportion of the ordinary British population originally supported the French struggle for freedom. Leading British philosophers supported these revolutions, and the printing-press set up by William Caxton in London in 1474 was at last doing its work. The Englishman Thomas Payne was tried and condemned in his absence for his support of the Americans and the French, and the more scholarly Richard Williams of Glamorgan was made a citizen of the United States by Congress. Then with the rise to power of Napoleon and his military successes, which allowed him to depose most of the royal houses of Europe, the unpopular British monarchy, and the aristocracy, whose future depended upon maintaining the monarchy, was in a very worried state.

Unity and unification in Britain were the new targets. The ancient immigrating Angles and Saxons were promoted to create a new identity of Anglo-Saxonism. Everyone in England would become Anglo-Saxon, disregarding the obvious fact that the vast majority were neither Angle nor Saxon descended. The ancient British Khumry of Lancashire, Cumberland, and Westmorland were not Anglo-Saxon, nor were the mixed Mercian, Ealde Cyrcenas (Old Syrians) and British Khumry of the Midlands. Nor were the Cornish, and Gewissae (Wessex people) of the South; whilst the Yorkshire and Derbyshire people were predominantly of Danish origin. Even the Hwiccae of Worcester and the mixed Gewissae, Khumric, and Mercian populations of Welsh borders - Welsh until 1546 - Herefordshire, Gloucestershire, Shropshire, and Cheshire, were emphatically not Anglo-Saxon.

In place of the comet disaster, which overwhelmed the powerful ten million-strong British in AD 562, there was to be a newly minted Anglo-Saxon Conquest. Just how three boat-loads of Saxons, hired as coastguards by the usurper Gwrtheyrn (Vortigern) in the civil war raging in AD 426, could defeat the militarily aggressive

Chapter 2 - The British Cold War

British who had invaded Gaul and seized all Western Europe under Magnus Maximus and his eldest son Arthur I in 383 with an army of sixty-two thousand, and repeated the act under a cousin Constantine Coronog – 'the Crowned' - in 406, is not explained. Instead, a new, minimal population in ancient Britain was proposed. This nation instead of constantly defeating the Romans was now said to have been weak and cowardly and defeated by the Roman. History stood on its head.

The re-writing was endless. The wholesale destruction of cities, towns, and villas, described in the records and evident in ruins, was explained away by newly created 'British barbarism'. Primitive people, who were totally uncultured and allowed the ruins left by departing Romans to decay utterly. These people could therefore never be the descendants of the high metal-working civilization of ancient Chaldean Syria. Nor could they be of Trojan descent, even if Troy had existed outside the imagination of Homer. Troy was declared a myth and all ancient British history was therefore also totally mythical and untrue.

The construction of the new, politically correct history of Britain was to be founded on the new Roman Conquest of Britain, contrary to the records, and upon the amazing new Anglo-Saxon Conquest of England. The new history was developed by strict adherence to the Biblical record of the descendants of Noah and the tribes and nations, which they founded. The British histories did not conform to the religious requirements of this paper exercise and so they were automatically discarded. Religious conformity was enforced in the few universities existing and so British history became the Roman Conquest, followed by the Anglo-Saxon Conquest, the partial Danish Conquest, and the Norman Conquest; every conqueror was an English ancestor and contradictory record was flung out as treacherous and forged.

The ages old policy of eradicating different languages in Ireland, Scotland, and Wales, and thus eroding the culture, was accelerated. The first Superman comic-book heroes were created by novelists - Ivanhoe could defeat limitless numbers of huge well-armed enemies even when he was badly wounded - and various others like Quentin Durward appeared. The practice of historical studies in the universities rapidly became a purely political concern. Ancient British histories written before 1688 bear little or no resemblance to the later nineteenth-century politically correct histories.

The obliteration of British history may have been desirable for the Church of Rome but the accomplishment of this obliteration was brought about by politics in England.

In summary - the present bogus political history requires that the people believe that for at least a thousand years several hundreds of Welsh scholars, bards, poets, and historians - including a king who wrote a history - living in the North East on the Dee, over to Gwynedd and Anglesey in the North West, and spread two hundred miles South to Dyfed, and two hundred miles East to the Wye and Severn, ALL conspired to write a gigantic interlocking forgery, complete with ancient tombs, grave mounds, stone memorials, coffins and skeletons, along with ancient battlefields and the vast grave mounds of their dead, ruined castles, forts, manors and churches, and much more.

The Defence of the National Legacy

Baram Blackett had developed the habit of occasionally browsing the antiquarian book shops, and amongst his purchases was a copy of Percy Enderbie's history of Britain entitled *Cambria Triumphans, or Brittain in its Perfect Lustre*, published in 1661, just one year after the democracy of Oliver Williams - alias Cromwell - ended and the monarchy was restored in the person of Charles II. This book boldly and confidently states the origins of the British from Brutus, and right up front it illustrates a genealogy of Charles II as a descendant of Howell Dda ap Cadell of Dyfed, from a Llewellyn of Powys, and from Gruffydd ap Llewellyn ap Seisyllt of Gwynedd. It avoids Morganwg in the South East.

Throughout this long History, numbers of genealogies of the dukes and earls and other great lords of Britain are displayed and in almost every case there is an original claim of descent from an ancient Khumric king or prince. The royal family of the paramount British kings located in Essyllwg - later Morganwg - in South-East Wales, who were the direct descendants of Brutus, is generally avoided. This is probably because the Stuart - Steward - descent is from Walter the Steward, the son of Nest the daughter of King Gruffydd ap Llewellyn of Gwynedd and Fleance son of Banquo. The Essyllwg descent (or 'Silures', as misnamed by the Romans) included the Imperial descents and both Arthurs as well as the Holy Family descents.

This unmistakably points to a firm belief in the simple fact that the Khumry were in Britain for a thousand years before the Angles and Saxons, and that the right of British kingship resides with the descent from the first king, who was Brutus. There is no mention of supposed descents from the minor Northern lines such as Aidan ap Gafran ap Aidan Fradog (the Traitor) or Kenneth Mac Alpin, or any others. The throne is claimed through Cambrian = Welsh descent and so from Brutus.

Another of Baram's purchases was the 1794 book of Edward Jones the Bard to the then Hanoverian Prince of Wales, George Augustus Frederick. The book, entitled *The Musical and Poetical Relicks of the Welsh Bards, etc.*, is in fact an openly determined defensive publication which constantly rebuts and refutes false allegations from English sources. From 1661 to 1794 there was a complete sea

Chapter 2 - The British Cold War

change in the matter of British history. By 1794 everything Khumric was despised and derided and was obviously being condemned without evidence or trial.

That the struggle for British history was being waged at this time is evidenced by the republication of Enderbie's *Cambria Triumphans* in 1810. The defence of heritage is plainly evident on Page 1 in Edward Jones' book, where he cites numerous instances of destruction.,

The Welsh nobles who were captives in the Tower of London (formerly called the White Tower, and part of it known by that name) obtained permission that the contents of their libraries should be sent to them from Wales, to amuse them in their solitude and confinement. This was a frequent practice so that in the process of time the Tower became the principal repository of Welsh literature. Unfortunately for our history and poetry, all the manuscripts thus collected there were burnt by the villainy of one Scolan (Scholasticus, a monk) of whom nothing more is known. Gutto'r Glyn, an eminent Bard, who flourished in the fourteenth century, has in one of his poems the following passage –

> 'The books of the Cymru and their remains,
> went to the White Tower where they were hid;
> cursed was Ysgolans act,
> in throwing them in heaps into the fire.'

The interesting feature of Edward Jones' book is that it opens up with clearly defensive statements and brings to attention the fact that there are plenty of pre-Roman and pre-Christian ancient inscribed coins known in Britain. So, literacy is proven.

He then proceeds to quote Julius Caesar from his *De Bello Gallico - The Gallic Wars*, where Caesar in 54 BC describes the British alphabet. Caesar remarked upon the clear similarities of the British and Greek alphabets. Caesar also described British cities, roads, and universities, where students from all over Western Europe, and particularly Gaul, flocked to study. It is immediately evident that this book was being written in 1794 as a defence against the propaganda that the Khumry were illiterate primitive barbarians.

Edward Jones went on to quote the report of Strabo around 50 BC on his encounter with the British where he is fulsome in his admiration for British learning and culture.

> 'He' [a Briton] 'came to Athens not clad in skins like a Scythian, but with a bow in his hand, a quiver hanging on his shoulders, a plad wrapped about his body, a

gilded belt encircling his loins, and trowsers reaching from the waiste down to the soles of his feet. He was easy in his address; agreeable in his conversation; active in the dispatch, and secret in the management of great affairs; quick in judging of present occurrences; and ready to take his party in any sudden emergency; provident withal in guarding against futurity; diligent in the quest of wisdom; fond of friendship; trusting very little to fortune, yet having the entire confidence of others, and trusted for everything with his prudence. <u>He spake Greek with a fluency, that you would have thought he had been bred up in the Lyceum, and had conversed all his life with the academy of Athens.'</u>

Some barbarian. The Lyceum was the great University at Athens, which lasted for nine hundred years. It is perhaps worth noting that the Imperial family of Rome intermarried with these alleged 'primitive barbarians', and a number of British native princes were Roman Emperors. Certainly, the Greek travelling geographer and historian Strabo would not agree with the present distorted view of the ancient British.

Edward Jones also cited the Roman historian Ammianus Marcellinus who also described the British alphabet and was clear that the Greeks had obtained their similar alphabet from the British. This is wholly possible, as the second ancestral British migration arrived in Western Asia Minor around 650 BC and very substantial numbers of these culturally advanced people remained there until around 504 BC. So, for a hundred and fifty years they lived right alongside the originally illiterate Greeks.

These records would of course be very 'politically incorrect' in England where the false idea that there was no ancient Lloegrean (English) history was firmly established as a mindset. By basing their historical education system on a series of blurred unproven theories of ancient Conquests, the modern English saw their history as beginning with the arrival of the two Jute leaders Hengist and Horsa in c. AD 450. They solved their problem of now having no ancient history of their own by importing the foreign Greek and Roman 'classical' histories. As these foreign histories were adjudged to be pagan and heathen they solved the problem of now having no theological ancient record by importing the Hebrew, Israel, and Judean, records as history. In short, for generations they dressed themselves in borrowed garments.

Whereas normal nations have always named their warships after figures from their own native culture, using the names of rulers, great men of achievement, and native place names, the bizarre English practice was usually to give British warships the names of ancient alien Greek or Roman mythical figures. Warships named

Chapter 2 - The British Cold War

Bellepheron or *Hermes* and *Ajax* and *Achilles* and so on, ploughed the oceans and no one ever thought how absurd these choices of foreign alien names for British warships were.

All the ancient pre-Norman universities in Wales had long ago been destroyed in the centuries of ceaseless attacks. There was no native institution left surviving to defend the British cause. With the German House of Saxe-Coburg-Gotha married to the Guelphs, and on the English throne and uneasy as well as unpopular, the ancient History of Britain posed a powerful threat to the regime. The mass of the English who are in fact mainly Ealde Cyrcenas - Old Syrians, - Vandal Mercians, Old British, Cornish, Herules, Bretons, Normans, and others, were aggressively persuaded that they were 'Anglo-Saxons' and Conquerors. A mendacious campaign, which has control of the university and school system, can re-educate the mass of the people in a few years.

Henry Schoolcraft could never have succeeded in this environment. With the open attacks being made on British history the records of Madoc's voyages to America were being thrown out and discarded. As records of Madoc's voyages were rejected, there was also automatically a rejection of the plethora of records of King Arthur, son of Magnus Maximus - known as Andragathius to Latins - and his conquest of Western Europe in AD 383 - 388, and an equal rejection of his sixth-generation direct male descendant Arthur II son of Meurig. The Arthurian histories were already muddled by the lying monks of Glastonbury, who were serving the political purposes of Henry II of England in AD 1189. Now the ridiculous Arthurian Mystery was created.

Along with the confusion of wholesale rejection of factual records the ancient British Coelbren alphabet was also rejected, and in fact it became a specific target for obliteration. So, the prize and objective of Professor Schoolcraft's search, an ancient language and its alphabet, which had been carefully and faithfully preserved for three thousand six hundred years in Britain, and was a marvellous archaeological and historical treasure and relic, was under organised official attack. The British alphabet is clearly traceable all along the ancient historical migration routes, in Iberia - Spain, in Etruscan Italy, in Rhaetia - Switzerland, in the Aegean, in Trojan Phrygia in Asia Minor, and further back into ancient Assyria and Palestine, with pointers towards Egypt, and yet this marvellous relic was targeted for destruction.

Sadly, this savage assault upon British cultural heritage preserved in a small ancient nation can be documented in great detail and with unmistakable clarity. The political ideologies of that era demanded that there should be absolute conformity in every way. Ancient Gaelic was to be eradicated in Ireland and Scotland, and this almost succeeded. The Scots were forbidden from wearing the kilt or tartans, and bagpipes were banned, which is precisely why they wear and play these items so determinedly today. The Khumry posed the larger threat with their dogged adherence to their language and history, and because of the very uncomfortable facts that those histories preserved.

Even today when everyone with one ounce of intelligence knows that great numbers of ancient stones and manuscripts clearly exhibit the Coelbren alphabet between AD 200 and 948, and even earlier, the general university line remains the falsehood that this alphabet was forged around 1800. This disregards the Bodleian Library MSS no 572, and well-known poetic references to the alphabet in pre-1367, in 1425, in 1450, in 1475, and so on. It also disregards the great discovery in 1945 by Mr Mohammed Ali of an entire Gnostic Christian library at Nag Hammadi in Egypt. This collection in fourteen leather satchels in a five-foot-high clay jar was buried around AD 400 and rediscovered in 1945, and in it and the Mannasses Manuscript contains a description of the alphabet allegedly forged by Edward Williams around 1800. This almost comical ostrich-like posture then renders all the many valuable inscriptions in Britain, Spain, Switzerland, Italy, the Aegean, Turkey, and Assyria, and elsewhere, including Palestine and Egypt, indecipherable.

This was the state of on-going cultural and historical genocide, which was well under way when Henry Schoolcraft began his search for the language and alphabet of the American inscriptions. This has to be understood in order to re-discover the people who wrote the American inscriptions scattered through the Mid-West and along the East Coast. In order to get to the truth, it is necessary to speak the truth, and to expose the sophistry.

Were Julius Caesar, Strabo, and Ammianus Marcellinus, and others all liars? Are the pre-Christian British coins dating back to *c.* 200 BC all counterfeit forgeries? Are all the stones found in England, Scotland, and Wales, all fakes, although the majority were known and recorded many centuries before 1800? Are the clear records of British everyday cultural achievement all mistakes? These people did everything the Romans and Greeks did, and often did it better. They did not construct vast buildings of an extremely complicated design such as the Romans did with their Colosseum and amphitheatres, all dedicated to mass murder and animal slaughter. They mined ores, mainly tin and iron and some gold, and they smelted and cast metals. They were masters of the complex engineering of war-chariots, and they made large, strong ocean-going ships, which Julius Caesar found impressive.

These were people who minted coins, made pottery, built houses of Britain's plentiful timber, spun wool and wove cloth, and farmed their innumerable herds. But above all they were educated, they were literate, and they were organised as a State, which provided for universities and colleges to which not only their own young people went to study, and which drew thousands from all across Western Europe. Members of the Imperial Roman and senatorial families were happy to intermarry with them, and several British kings ruled as emperors.

The allegation of British barbarism is a humbug. Roman history is perfectly clear that they encouraged the wealthy British royalty and nobility to build palaces, and villas, and public buildings, in the Roman style, and to live themselves in these buildings. Much the same as the oil rich Arab kings, princes, and sheikhs, of our times who employ European and other architects and builders to assist in them in the development of their countries.

Prince Madoc, son of King Meurig ap Tewdrig, and brother of Arthur II, could not be admitted to have discovered America in AD 562, even accidentally, because the entire history enshrining this event had to be obliterated. Subsequent proving voyages checking star readings and the fleet of seven hundred ships then sailing also had to be prohibited. Troy was declared a fiction and so the Trojans were fictional people, and it followed that therefore, British claims of Trojan descents were therefore absurd fictions. The Queen-Empress Helen of the Cross became a daughter of a Yugoslavian Innkeeper, thus making the British Emperor Constantine the Great non-British and illegitimate; and therefore his eldest son Flavius Caesar Crispus and his grandson Magnus Clemens Maximus were illegitimate and not British. The Holy Cross was not therefore brought to Britain; and the now barbarous uncouth illiterate British could not have been the cradle of Western Christianity.

Alas for Henry Schoolcraft and the Khumry, it was not until 1873 that Heinrich Schliemann sailed from the U.S.A. to Turkey and proceeded to re-discover Troy. One might think that this momentous discovery might have led to a re-assessment of British history, but by 1873 too many academic careers had been built on Bible Philology and alleged British barbarism. Even in 1891, eighteen years after the discovery of Troy by Heinrich Schliemann, Oxford-educated academics were publishing that all British history was a sham because Troy was a fiction.

In 1794 Edward Williams wrote that the ancient British, the Etruscan, and the Pelasgian alphabets were near-identical. He was clearly pointing to the idea that these alphabets littered the ancient British migration route, although he did not actually state this. Then in 1846 John Williams, of Oxford, published a book exhibiting the ancient alphabets of Britain and also stating clearly the near Identicality of the ancient British, Etruscan, and Pelasgian alphabets. This was ignored, and then six years later, in 1852, a stone inscribed in the ancient British alphabet was found buried twenty-six feet down in St Paul's churchyard in London. The stone exhibits the Dragon Comet of AD 562 and a supporting inscription in the alleged non-existent Coelbren alphabet. A furore erupted with the already brainwashed followers of Edwin Guest and Bishop Stuhbs viciously attacking any suggestion that it was an ancient British inscription as they alleged that the British had been illiterate. What people will do in the name of religion.

The situation was bizarre as Austin Layard had discovered the great archives of the Assyrian Emperors at the ruins of Nineveh in 1846 and sent them to London. These stones named the Ten Tribes deported from Israel as 'the Khumry', and this is still the name of the British Khumry who are misnamed as 'Welsh' by the English. 'Wallische' is 'strangers' in old High German, and the immigrant Angles and Saxons actually called the British 'strangers' in their own land. As we will see, the Khumry of the Assyrians between 720 - 687 BC were the Kimmeroi and Kimmerians of the Greeks in Asia Minor from 690 - 650 BC when they reached Trojan lands at the Dardanelles.

The situation created by Edwin Guest, Bishop Stubbs, and other supporters of Biblical omnipotence had already gone past Disneyland proportions. Now at the very same time that they were busily demolishing ancient British historical record evidence was surfacing from Khumric records, from the depths of St Paul's churchyard, and out of the débris of long-buried ancient palaces in Nineveh, which could prove that history correct. Like sharks in feeding frenzy academics at British universities vied with each other to claim to 'disprove' this or that ancient Khumric manuscript. This still goes on as none of them think that they are British.

The seven-hundred-year-old onslaught on the Khumric culture and language was gaining momentum in Henry Schoolcraft's era and would include Acts of Parliament outlawing the speaking of even one single word of Khumric-'Welsh' in the schools in Wales, where it was the national tongue, and enforcing the use of English.

The battle for the survival of the marvellous key to ancient world history had entered a crucial phase. Americans, blocked off from the obliterated true source of the alphabet and language of the American inscriptions, were left with a plethora of untruths, half-truths, and misdirections. The inscriptions in the U.S.A. looked something like Hebrew, and so they should if the Khumry were the descendants of the lost Ten Tribes. There was a resemblance to Etruscan in these American inscriptions, and so there should be, for the main group of the Kimmeroi passing through Asia Minor from 687 - 650 BC were the Y-treres = 'travelling homes' people.

Half the nation sailed for Italy to found Etruria (see Herodotus), and is not Y-Treres perhaps Etruscan or Tuscan? The U.S.A. inscription looked something like ancient Iberian, and so they should for three tribal groups went ahead of the main fleets of Brutus to Spain, and they combined when he got there.

Chapter 2 - The British Cold War

The British mysteries were created in the nineteenth century at Oxford and Cambridge. The learned Edward Lluyd, Keeper of the Ashmolean Library and Museum around 1700, clearly identified Arthur I son of Magnus as the eponymous folk hero 'Guy of Warwick', which correctly placed him in the Midlands. This is explained in detail in the forthcoming volume *King Arthur I of Warwickshire*. In 1734 a Revd. Williams published that there were two King Arthurs: correct. Well over a hundred books written in English and Khumric between 1760 and 1920 specify that Arthur II was the son of Meurig ap Tewdrig. It is as if there exists a cultural Iron Curtain between England and Wales.

The Riddles in the Histories

When in 1976 Baram Blackett found a notation in a book that interested him, he had no idea where it would lead him. The statement was that a great lord named Urien Rheged had ruled in the north of what is now England around AD 590 before the Angles invaded that area, and he had fought them. What was intriguing however was that this Lord Urien had a daughter named Elwiri and she had married an ancient Glamorgan king named Morgan. He wondered why he had never heard of any of this. Schools, books, radio, and television all poured out information on Romans and on Normans and bits on the Angles and Saxons, but virtually nothing about the British.

A few attempts to get at books that might reveal something were frustrated as there was someone else always using them. In that strange quirk of human nature common to almost everyone, whilst he was only mildly interested at first, the fact that he was being prevented from simple enquiry increased his determination to make it. Finally, feeling a little irritated, he was directed by a librarian to the man sitting at a table near the window, and who was obstructing his search. And so he came to meet with Alan Wilson.

This was his introduction to that strange invisible kingdom whose giant remains are scattered everywhere all across Britain, and are daily passed by millions who never ever see any of it. In talking with Alan Wilson, it seemed obvious to Baram that if this man was just half way right, then there could be all manner of opportunities and possibilities in this fortuitous yet apparently correct situation. There was a coffee bar across the square in front of the library and they went there to talk, and so began a crusade of miraculous happenings.

King Morgan Mwynfawr was real and he did marry Elwiri, daughter of Urien Rheged. Morgan was the successor of a King Arthur son of King Meurig, who was in turn son of a King Tewdrig, and so on and on who were South Wales kings. Meurig was only Maurice pronounced 'My-rig', and Tewdrig was Theoderic. Urien was the

'Sir Uriens' of the Arthurian Romances, and he had brothers named Liew or 'Sir Leoline', and Arawn who was 'Sir Agravaine', and in fact all the knightly characters of the Arthurian Sagas were easily traceable. A Prince Llywarch Hen (the Aged), whose epic poetry still exists, had been translated into Sir Lamorack', and Liew alias 'Sir Leoline' had married Gwyar, a sister of King Arthur son of Meurig, and they had two sons named Modred and Gwalchmai, or 'the Hawk of May' or 'Sir Walwayne'.

Publishing opportunities were recognised and he knew that King Arthur was a major topic and said to be a total mystery, on whom there was almost no information. Alan was familiar with this situation and he believed that British history warranted more fortitudinous research. At that time Alan had masses of various notes and copies of information and he had been pursuing the topic as a hobby since 1956, in a casual manner rather than with any organised intent. He described it as a gigantic British haystack, which had been deliberately scattered to the winds, and the pretence was that there never was a haystack.

A small part of what has emerged over the years from this meeting is the subject of this book. What is clear to Alan and Baram is that no one has ever studied British ancient history in the modern era. As correctly discerned by them in 1976, the use of industrial investigative and organizational techniques, with which Alan Wilson was an expert, could bring about a restoration to eliminate the hiatus within the long scattered British historical haystack. Everything down to the smallest detail has to be checked and verified.

Sadly, the average university employee working in a history department is usually more concerned with protecting the institutional *status quo*. Any authentic synthesis that lies outside the preconceived framework will inevitably be perceived as both dubious and unreliable. The erroneous beliefs in the currently preferred theories have resulted in an unhealthy climate of silence and even chicanery, emanating from irreverent and philistinic individuals who possess neither the knowledge of the subject nor the foresight to recognize the value of discoveries. Their only concern has been the protection of reputations, both individual and corporate, and of their considerable financial vested interests. The total mishandling of the situation, particularly in South Wales, is the main cause of the difficulties and the depredations of our cultural heritage.

Nothing should be assumed. The first assumption is that the Romans conquered all Britain: wrong. It is assumed that the Romans totally dominated Britain for either four hundred and fifty or four hundred years: incorrect. It is assumed that early Christianity spread from Rome out westwards across Europe to Britain: bunkum. It is assumed that there was political collapse in a serf-like servile British population after AD 411 and that there was then a subsequent Anglo-Saxon conquest of Britain:

wrong. It is assumed that the ancient British were barbarian 'Celts: a nonsense. It is assumed that the ancient British were of a low culture and illiterate: untrue. It is assumed that they were few in number and primitive: wrong. In short, all the most basic and fundamental points upon which any standard approach is made towards ancient British historical study is based upon are provably false assumptions.

To reiterate what has been aforesaid, there are two histories in Britain. One is the phony version dreamed up and invented in the nineteenth century, and which has been marketed like a modern soap powder. The other is the real history of Britain, shrouded in a myopic fog of misdirections, unfounded assumptions, and indolence. The one can be shown to be mendacious, and it is therefore 'politically and religiously correct'. The other can be verified and proven over and over again and yet has been discarded.

There is an old story of a Briton holidaying on the far West Coast of Ireland and asking an Irishman for directions so that he could return to Dublin and get back to London. The Irishman thought for a while and said: "If I was going to Dublin and on to London, then I wouldn't start from here". Alan Wilson firmly believes that the average university employee would not last a week in industry: "He would start Monday and get fired on Tuesday." If anything is to be attempted then it is unavoidable that a start be made at the beginning, and that absolutely nothing is taken for granted.

Alan's and Baram's experience of working with American colleagues taught them much about this problem of an assumed base from which to work. Amateur approaches are everywhere. To begin with the simplest form of enquiry: 'what is a name?' This may sound crazy, but it is fundamental. The British universally use Latin forms of ancient British designations, and this strange preference for alien terms and sources characterises the whole approach, and can only be described as asinine. If we take the 'names' of Beli Mawr and his son 'Caswallon' who completely defeated and humiliated Julius Caesar in 55 and 54 BC, we find that neither is a name. 'Beli' is 'tumult' and 'Mawr' is 'great', and the appellation is titular; one who ruled in a time of 'great tumults'. The same applies to Caswallon, which means 'a viceroy', in fact 'ruler of a separated part of the state', the paramount king's son. By mangling 'Caswallon' into a ludicrous Latin 'Cassivelaunius' the information that he was a Viceroy is lost.

The same thing applies to 'Cynfelyn' – 'Yellow hair', who is twisted into 'Cunobelinus', which is of course meaningless. This practice of referring to named kings and princes of Britain in a titular manner permeates the entire history. In AD 434 a lord titled as Cuneda succeeded to the military command in wars against the Irish, and this much quoted 'Cuneda' is again not a name. He restored order with his victories, and 'Cun' means a 'lord', and 'Edau' means 'restoration', so he was the Lord of Restoration. The question is then: who were Beli Mawr, Caswallon, and Cuneda, and Gwrtheyrn 'monarch of men' (known to the English as Vortigern), and the Uthyrpendragons and dozens of others? Where are they in the genealogies and how are they related to each other, and what were the politics, and what does this tell us of the history?

The academic preference for using useless alien Latin corruptions of titles serves only to obscure the histories of Britain. This then brings us to the matter of genealogies and it is no exaggeration to state that the Khumry were viewed as being genealogy-mad. The saying 'as long as a Welshman's pedigree' was a commonplace joke and here we have a culture clash. The Khumry did not use surnames, and the English did. So in England people were mostly known by their hereditary family trades or by their place of domicile. This results in Jack Tailor (Taylor), and Jim Cartwright, and Joe Butcher, and so on, and with others like John Bradford, and Harry Preston. In stark contrast, a Khumro could only identify himself precisely by a recitation of his name, his father's name, his grandfather's, and so on; so Griffith ap Rhodri ap Ifor, was seen to be different from Griffith ap Rhodri ap Iestyn, and this worked. This system established his place and status in the society in which he lived.

The matter of national obsessions with genealogy had a purpose. It was not unusual for an eighteenth-century cobbler to exhibit a list of ancestors of thirty-three names going back to the kings of Powys. In the doubling of ancestors with each generation it effectively meant that everyone was descended from everyone and in this lay the national strength of family, clan, tribe, and nation. In the passage of five hundred years everyone had five hundred thousand ancestors, and somewhere amongst them was always the 'indispensable ancestor', the nobleman who led the way back into the noble and royal families. In a nation of great antiquity tracing itself back two-and-a-half thousand years in Britain and some fifteen hundred years before that elsewhere, everyone was bound to everyone else. There was also the law of Gavelkind, which existed in Wales, whereby an inheritance was split equally between all the heirs as far as was possible. This meant that estates devolved down to small units and the marriage of first and second cousins was common to prevent land from going out of a family. It also resulted in any heiress having a host of suitor;, and a major bargaining weapon in these marriage stakes was a prominent genealogy going back to the kings and princes.

The matter of genealogy and its importance in society is not peculiar to the Khumry, as is evident by the importance of genealogy in the scant records of the Saxons and Angles, and in Norse records, to say nothing of the still-evident and preserved tribal and ancestral identifications of the Hebrew peoples. Royal genealogy is the backbone of all ancient histories. Of course, one of the major reasons for the rejection of Khumric genealogy by the majority English was the constant theme of tracing back ancestors to Brutus and Aeneas and Anchises of Troy, and also tracing back through Israeli and Judean pedigrees to Noah and Adam. The idea that the Khumry were of Trojan origin was dismissed totally as outright nonsense, and the idea of an ancient Israel descent was regarded as impossible. Yet this is precisely what the national histories stated, and all down the long centuries the royal, noble, and countless other genealogies were firmly based upon this.

It is safe to say that the average would-be researcher into British history in general and into Arthurian matters in particular has not the slightest idea of the massive array of preserved genealogies all based upon these constant themes. The genealogies were the very bricks, the mortar, the cement, which held the fabric of the nation together. Is it not self-evident that everyone likes to 'belong' somewhere? People from Australia, New Zealand, America, all like to trace ancestors and places of origin, to claim identity as with a Scottish clan by their names; old soldiers identify with their regiments, sailors with their ships, and airmen with their squadrons; and many people now associate themselves with football and baseball clubs.

There were other outcomes of the law of Gavelkind. Primogeniture in England, with everything going to the eldest son, resulted in there being larger estates in England but down the long centuries it meant that more men were peasants, serfs, vassals, villeins, and churls, and tied to the land in servile lives. These people were non-combatants in times of war and were generally safe from harm in the conflicts. The Khumric- 'Welsh' could call upon a far greater proportion of men ready and able and motivated to fight. Notable victories in France were actually won by Khumric- 'Welsh' archers and Irish infantry mercenaries. At Poitiers in 1356 where the Black Prince's tiny professional army of five thousand defeated sixty thousand French, three thousand Welsh archers shot the French knights to pieces with their longbows. These men from Glamorgan were known as the Black Army and Edward the Black Prince granted them common grazing lands. Even today an annual meeting is held in an ancient pub in the town of Llantrisant - Holy Estate of the Three Saints, and anyone who can prove descent from a man of Poitiers in 1356 can claim grazing rights. This requires correct genealogy.

At Crécy, another famous victory, the Welsh archers were decisive. Sir Howell Griffith brought the largest contingent to the battle: two knights, eight hundred men-at-arms, and four thousand archers. At Agincourt in 1415, it was Dafydd Gam of Abergavenny who raised Henry V's army in Britain from the Welsh Marches, and again two thousand Welsh archers, guarded by one thousand Irish infantrymen, shot the armoured French knights to shreds. A culture clash occurred when the Irish and Welsh then slit the throats of the richly decorated French wounded, to get their valuable rings, chains, necklaces, and bracelets. This was against the rules as noblemen were supposed to be captured alive for the King to extract ransoms fur their release. To the Irish and Welsh, it was better to kill them and prevent them coming back to fight again, and the loot was theirs.

The tomb of Dafydd Gam (David the Lame) exists, and he is famous for his report to Henry V who sent his General to assess the strength of the French army at Agincourt: "enough to kill, enough to capture, and enough to run away." Hardly Shakespeare. He and two other Welsh knights died saving Henry V's life at a critical moment of the fighting. The genealogy aspect emerges from a tombstone of a descendant of Dafydd Gam - one Edward Games who died in 1617, and all his seven ancestors back to Dafydd Gam are listed, and then Dafydd Gam is listed back to Iestyn ap Gwrgan, the Glamorgan king who was deposed in AD 1091. As Iestyn is a direct descendant of Arthur II ap Meurig ap Tewdrig, it is obvious why Khumric genealogies might worry the English establishment. See Harleian MSS 6821. Numbers of such tombstones exist.

To disregard the vital importance of native genealogy in Britain is to guarantee failure before beginning. If the first Angles and Saxons were brought to Britain in AD 389 and began arriving in numbers in Britain around AD 500, then there is no point in seeking ancient British origins or record amongst them. Equally there is no point in searching amongst the Scots who moved over from Ireland after AD 562. The only place to find records is amongst the Khumry, part of whom arrived in Britain around 1600 BC, and the remainder around 500 BC.

1-   Genealogy is an essential part of British and Khumric history and must be considered as an aid to its understanding.

2-   Genealogy was an essential part of Khumric law and land-tenure.

3-   The massive array of Khumric genealogical manuscripts form an essential part of Khumric literature.

4-   Genealogy played an important part in the formation of and development of the Khumric character. It was essential to racial consciousness.

5-   The tradition of genealogy is unbroken from the earliest times and is a surviving characteristic, and it grew down the ages like snowballs rolling down a hill.

The genealogy is in fact the key to Britain's past. To quote Francis Junes:

'That Welsh genealogy cannot be dismissed as useless lumber, and it cannot be ignored by historians or literatures who propose to present an adequate and true

Chapter 2 - The British Cold War

picture of our national life. Neither can it be studied as a subject on its own: as part of our heritage it cannot separate itself from the conditions that produced it.'

The Royal British Genealogies are in fact the key to the histories. They are the firm skeleton which all the other information fleshes out. As if the situation were not desperate enough there is the added incompetence of those regarded as 'translators' and indeed experts, who look at the Dynastic King Lists and ancient poetry and who are quite unable to differentiate between a name, or a noun, or adjective, or pronoun, or even a verb or adverb, let alone to discriminate between a name and a title.

The situation that Alan Wilson was even then learning about was stunning to Baram Blackett in 1976. What if the British history of a migration from Syria some three thousand six hundred years ago was true, and no one bothered to investigate this?

What if the story of a migration to Britain from the Trojan area around two thousand five hundred years ago was true and no one investigated it?

What if these neglected histories enshrined two King Arthurs, and no one bothered to look?

What if Christianity arrived in Britain in AD 35- 37 and then spread to Rome and Gaul from Britain and that this was true?

What if a mass of other historical tradition was true and for various reasons it was ignored?

This is where the investigation into British History begins: at the beginning. Nowhere in any British records is there any mention whatsoever of the British nation or any part of it being 'Celtic'. Therefore the glib modern archaeological label of 'Celts' and 'Celtic' is totally contrary to the national record. To label the Khumry as 'Celtic' is to defy and to ignore a vast accumulation of historical record and to state that which is neither evident nor proven. It is in fact a colossal misdirection, which subverts all British ancient history. This perhaps is the major weed to be uprooted.

Lemprière's *A Classical Dictionary* has this to say: 'Celtae, a name given to the nation that inhabited the country between the Ocean and the Palus Maeotis, according to some authors mentioned in Plutarch in Mario. This name, though anciently applied to the inhabitants of Gaul, as well as Germany and Spain, was particularly given to a part of the Gauls, whose country, called Gallia Celtica, was situate between the rivers Sequanna and Garumna, modernly called La Seine and La Garonne. The Celtae seemed to receive their name from Celtus a son of Hercules or of Polyphemus. The promontory which bore the name Celticum is now called Cape

Finnisterre, see *Caesars De Bello Gallico I*, c. I. etc, -*Pomponius Mela*, 3. c. 2. Herodotus, 4. c. 49.

Finally in 1995 Professor John Collis of Sheffield broke ranks and stated that there were no Celts in Britain and there never ever had been any, when speaking at an Archaeological Conference in Cardiff. In 1998 Professor Collis published his thoughts. In 1999, the British Museum Press published a volume by Professor Simon James, an archaeologist, who again stated that there were no Celts in Britain, and that Celticism as such was a nonsense. For two decades Alan Wilson and Baram Blackett had been called idiots and much worse for saying exactly the same, and with masses more evidence to offer.

The overall conspectus which has confined British history from defervescence to stagnation is one where a large expansionist country has incorrectly perceived a relatively small nation as inferior and even as culturally primitive. Rather than assess all the elements, the policy, which is still prevalent, has been to promulgate a centralised hypothesis and thus to curtail the extant historical evidence and religious beliefs from the primordial. This calculated sophism and misdirection have resulted in total anachronistic confusion.

In a moment of supreme optimism in 1976 Baram Blackett stated: "We have the field to ourselves; no one else can come close." It all seemed so simple. Read the histories and see where they take you. The problem is that there are scores of 'No Entry' signs, countless 'Keep off the Grass' and 'No Trespassing' notices, and an army of anxious, desperate saboteurs lying in wait. If British ancient history was shown to be correct then the institutional reputations of British universities may not shine so brightly, nor will the bubble reputations of the denizens of these institutions, which bask in the descriptive political glow of the term 'centres of excellence.'

The plain truth is that no one else in modern times has ever conducted a proper, fair and unbiased enquiry into ancient British history. Just what Henry Schoolcraft from America was told if he made enquiries about the ancient British Coelbren alphabet is not known. The few British universities at that time can be shown to have contravened albeit, and were often devoid of candour.

Incredible as it must appear in the comedy of errors, German scholars - Mommsen, Bunsen, and Scheebohm - all began taking interest in the ancient British history as preserved in South East Wales, as the English scholars triumphantly completed its total demolition. In 1946 an Englishwoman named E.O. Gordon wrote a small volume entitled *Prehistoric London*, attempting to probe into what had been cast away. Even Gordon got it wrong as she was dealing with history and not prehistoric times. On page 76 she quotes from Bunsen's *Christianity and Mankind* vol.

iv. p.158:

> 'The Kymric Language prevailed in different dialects over the whole of Europe and a large part of Asia. It is the substructure of all the Keltic tongues and the Archaic element in the Greek, the Latin, the Sanskrit, and the hieroglyphic Egyptian. It is the key to the affinity between the languages of the East and the West. All other languages can be traced to an alien source—this alone cannot. It is certain it was brought by the Kymry into Britain, as it was spoken by their forefathers in Armenia, B. C. 1700, and that its purity and integrity have been guarded by them in all ages with jealous care. It is the witness, alike above suspicion and corruption, to the extreme antiquity of their nationality and civilization.'

Bunsen and E.O. Gordon had guessed at the truth, and Alan Wilson and Baram Blackett, armed with modern industrial techniques of investigative control, and better equipped to do the job than university employees, set out to put the matter to the test.

Mary Thomas and the Old Book

Around 1860, the titled lady of a great manor house in Powys in North East Wales, was afflicted with the dreaded disease of smallpox. This was a contagious, feared and dreaded disease, and the unfortunate victims mostly died or were badly facially scarred for life. Immunisation was still unknown and there were no curative medicines.

Within days, twenty-two of the twenty-three servants had left, and only the cook - Mary Thomas - remained in the great echoing empty mansion to take care of the desperately sick lady of the house. Mary Thomas nursed her employer through her illness in the silent, still mansion, and the lady actually recovered. As a reward for her devotion this very rich woman gave Mary Thomas an ancient book.

At that time the ironworks of South East Wales - old Morganwg - were prospering, and a great new steel industry was about to develop. The major industrial expansion was in the vast anthracite coalfields, with all their attendant engineering works and foundries, and the ports and railway systems to export the 'black diamonds', as coal was jokingly called. Industrial development meant some, in fact many, people grew rich, and they and the hotels and restaurants needed cooks. Mary Thomas came south to Cardiff, bringing her old book with her.

In Cardiff, Mary Thomas met Robert Roberts, from Anglesey in North West Wales, who had also made the long walk south for work. Robert Roberts worked with a team of men employed in actually digging out - sinking - the vertical mine shafts for the ever-increasing number of new coal pits, and he then moved to Cardiff and found work on the docks. They were married at St John's Church in central Cardiff in 1876, and had a son, John, and daughters, Elizabeth, Mary Ann, and Margaret.

In due time Mary Ann, whose parents were from Gwynedd and Powys, met William Owen Williams, who was born in Dinas Cross in Dyfed in West Wales, and they were married. William Owen in common with most of his family had been a seaman, and he was now looking to settle down in the newly prosperous South East. In time Mary Thomas, now Roberts, died, and her husband Robert moved to live with his daughter and her husband William Owen, bringing the old book with him. Finally, he died in 1930 and the old book passed to Mary Ann.

Families go on, and William Owen and Mary Ann had children in Elizabeth, Mary, and Breeze. The name Breeze was a family name from Dinas Cross and the story is that there were two named Breeze, one the father of William Owen a Master Mariner. His father before him had been a captain of a sailing vessel and sometime around 1840 with his wife on board ship with him - not so unusual as might be thought - the ship was becalmed for days with no winds.

A son was born to the captain's wife and within the hour the winds sprang up. So the child was named Breeze.

However, in the mid-1930s it occurred to Mary Ann and William Owen that the old book given to Mary Thomas might be valuable. Most family opinion was that the lady in Powys had not treated Mary Thomas very kindly by giving her a useless book and a substantial cash present would have been more fitting. The book was useless as it was handwritten in a strange script that no one could read. There was then a chance that it might have been a valuable gift. So they resolved to find out.

William Owen's brother John lived about seventy yards away down the street, and he was an avid reader and collector of books, with rooms full of books. He could find no parallel with this strange writing in the many enquiries he made, and neither could the host of much-travelled former sailors known to William Owen. These men had literally sailed the world and had been to places that were only names to others: Yokohama, Singapore, San Francisco, Suez, Hong Kong, Amsterdam, Genoa, and a thousand other ports. But no one knew this writing.

Until recently the Cardiff Central Library had been one of the best city libraries in Britain, as it was developed at a time when the National Library for Wales was being

Chapter 2 - The British Cold War

proposed to be located in Cardiff. The Welsh National Library had however been deliberately located in Aberystwyth, a village-town of some five thousand souls, 'up in the sticks' in Mid- to North Wales, as far away from the majority of the population and as inaccessible as possible. It was as if the British = English National Library had been located in Exeter or Carlisle where 95 % of the population could not get at it. So, William Owen and Mary Ann went to the Cardiff Library and no one there claimed to recognise the alphabet of the book, but they gained the impression that there was something that they were not being told.

As the book was from Powys in North East Wales it was baffling that the script was apparently unrecognisable. Next, they visited the National Museum of Wales and again they were told that the alphabet of the book was unknown. Again, they thought that the persons whom they spoke with were somewhat uncomfortable. This left the Cardiff University College and so they went there as well. Whom they saw they never recorded, but they definitely got what generally called a very swift 'brush off'. The old book went back on the shelf.

By this time their eldest daughter Elizabeth had met and married Luke Wilson, whose father had been recruited from the Durham area in the North East around 1905 as one of a nucleus of experienced steel workers to lead the manning of the new steel-works being constructed alongside Cardiff Docks. The marriage caused a huge family rift on both sides as Elizabeth was a Baptist and Luke's family were Catholics. Elizabeth, like her uncle John, was also an avid reader and book person, and she had also attempted to discover the writing in the old book. No one was talking to either Elizabeth or Luke, however, as result of the unacceptable marriage, and then one day in a fit of frustration the house-proud, always cleaning and dusting Mary Ann threw the apparently useless book into the trash bin. It was destroyed. Why she did not give the book to her brother-in-law John, or to Elizabeth her daughter, both of who were enthusiastic book readers and collectors, will never be known.

It was not until the 1960s that Alan Wilson, the second son of Elizabeth and Luke and the grandson of William Owen and Mary Ann, showed his mother and grandmother what the ancient Welsh Coelbren alphabet looked like that they both recognised it as the script in Mary Thomas's old book.

It doesn't take a genius to recognize that there is a great deal wrong with the lop-sided version of Khumric 'Welsh' history, which is peddled around the schools and colleges. Anything and everything that allegedly happened took place in Gwynedd in North West Wales, with peripheral events occurring in Powys in the North East and Dyfed in the South West. Nothing whatsoever occurred in the major zone of the South East. This is a stark contrast with the Romans, who recorded that their most determined and inveterate powerful enemies ever were these 'invisible' people from the South East of Wales. As an example of the cover-up, there are on the upper floor of Cardiff City Hall, in South East Wales, a set of twelve imaginative statues which purportedly represent twelve great ancestral figures of Wales. All are from North West and South West Wales.

Few people will have heard of Griffith John Williams, and the pity is that anyone ever did. This man from North Wales was a dedicated disciple of the incredible scholastic fraudster J. Gwenogfran Evans, who lectured at Bangor University College in Gwynedd. It is almost impossible to conceive of the idiocy of J. Gwenogfran Evans in our times. The politics of the times change, however, and from a nation whose colleges had been destroyed long centuries ago, the pennies donated by slate quarry workers, farm labourers, and miners were gathered to found two tiny colleges: the first in 1872 in Aberystwyth and the second in Bangor in North Wales. The only way to get recruits to teach was to hire people educated in the English universities, and so they came in already educated into massive misconceptions.

Equally it suited the defensive mentality of these small rural populations to follow the fake Tudor line on history, that the North Wales Tudor ancestry was all there ever was and it was superior. It gave the poorer hill-billy and country yokel villagers of the North West a fake inflated balloon-like past and a sense of ancestral superiority over the prosperous densely populated South East. J. Gwenogfran Evans clearly believed the Tudor moonshine history, and he declared as an article of faith that there was no older Khumric history or record before AD 1100; appropriately the time of the collision with the Normans.

J. Gwenogfran Evans' methods were unusual to say the least. He constantly referred to his intuition. As a prime example he took the ancient sixth-century epic poem *Y Goddodin*, which concerns the South East Wales massacre at Caer Caradoc around AD 456, and said it was a fourth copy of poems written about a battle on the Menai Strait in 1098. He explained the total difference in poetic style of the sixth to the late eleventh - early twelfth century by stating that an unknown family had owned the manuscript and were displeased with the poem because it showed their ancestors in a poor light. This unnamed unknown family then had a series of unknown unnamed bards who, to please their employers, had mutilated the poem down the centuries.

This is hugely important to British history. These fabrications enabled J. Gwenogfran Evans to mangle the ancient text. He alleged that the names of the notables of the battle of 1098 were missing because they had been removed. The strict twelfth-century poetic style of Cynhanged was nowhere because the unknown bards had mutilated the poem. He then claimed to know exactly which words had been deleted and what they were, and also which words had been added. He knew

Chapter 2 - The British Cold War

which words had been altered, so he could change any word to any other. He claimed to know which phrases and lines were added or omitted or moved about, all this through his very remarkable intuition. In this great epic historical poem of some six thousand, three hundred words he admits to over three thousand, four-hundred alteration; and adds that this is an incomplete list. It would be easily possible to change Mrs Beaton's Cookery Book into a section of the Holy Bible by using J. Gwenogfran Evans' intuitive' methods.

He actually took the sixth-century masterpiece, *Preiddiau Annwn*, very definitely *The Migration to the Otherworld*, re-entitled it *King Richard's Voyage to Acre and Joppa*, and proceeded to insert the name of Saladin into the text where it nowhere appears. English readers of this incredible mush would have no idea of the extent of the disgraceful fabrications that produced it. J. Gwenogfran Evans was following the Oxford and Cambridge line, and was butchering the entire Khumric History to force it to conform with the desired political model. Sir Ifor Williams wrote: "It is impossible to believe anything he' [J.G. Evans] says." Yet this total idiot was held "to have laid the foundations of modern Welsh scholarship." It is a bizarre experience to read some of the jiggery-pokery of his followers as they transform three-letter words into brand new seven-, eight-, even ten-letter words which bear no relationship to the originals, and *vice versa*. Anything can be added, altered, or deleted.

So it was that in 1932 that Griffith John Williams, the poetry expert from the blacksmith's shop in Cellan near Aberystwyth, arrived in Cardiff and was shocked to find a totally different history from the rubbish preached in the North at Aberystwyth and Bangor. Never having heard anything of the real history of Wales this moron immediately came to the conclusion that it all was wrong, and the only way to explain this was that it was a forgery. If there was a forgery then there had to be a forger, and Griffith. J. Williams selected the remarkable scholar Edward Williams, (1748 - 1827), known as Iolo Morganwg as his innocent victim.

Edward Williams was one of many scholars copying ancient Welsh manuscripts and participating in their publication around 1800. Everything known about him and his life resounds of integrity, but now the young and foolish Griffith J. Williams from the North boldly alleged that Iolo Morganwg was a total forger - without a shred of evidence to back up this falsehood. Now in the way of all things, all ancient Khumric history and record of South East Wales was therefore forged or at least suspect. Not only history but also the ancient Coelbren alphabet of Britain was forged by Edward Williams; and pre-Christian coins in the museums were therefore forgeries. Julius Caesar, Strabo, Ammianus Marcellinus and others were all mistaken and wrong; the ancient manuscripts containing the alphabet were forged by some means of time-travel by Iolo Morganwg; and Khumric scholarly references to it by poets of 1367, 1425, c. 1450, c. 1475, and later were wrong. Even very ancient stones with Coelbren lettering were now discredited and the lettering was henceforth to be 'Irish'.

This was the highly charged atmosphere into which William Owen and his wife Mary Ann Williams stepped when they innocently enquired into the origin and nature of the alphabet of Mary Thomas' old book. Very few people knew enough about the subject to challenge the absurdities of Griffith John Williams; no one had ever dreamed of their history being forged before this rash fool, blessed with the cloak of ignorance, launched his assaults on 90% of the Khumric population. Anything which did not match with the Tudor and later political and religious fabrications of British universities was proclaimed as forged.

It took years for Alan Wilson to find time to delve through the forest of fears created by Griffith John Williams, and by the story of his own family he knew without doubt that Griffith John Williams was a fraud and that there was no forgery.

The Bigger the Lie the Better

The strange thing about history is that no one ever seems to learn anything from it. If we refer to the dictums of a modern master-strategist of propaganda in Dr Joseph Goebbels, the propaganda minister in Adolf Hitler's Third Reich, he said: "The bigger the lie the more likely it is to be believed". Goebbels also came up with: "If you tell people something often enough and long enough, then they will believe it." Wilson and Blackett do not admire Goebbels or Hitler, but they are very interested in how they succeeded in marketing their abhorrent views so effectively.

There is a direct parallel in Britain in the assassination of ancient British history in our modern times. How did Griffith John Williams get away with it? How did this poetry fanatic succeed in demolishing all the most valuable history and particularly South East Wales records? One answer is BBC Radio in London: the monopoly of the British Broadcasting Corporation. The London Government realised the propaganda power and value of radio from the moment George S. Kemp of Cardiff sent the first messages from shore to the Mumbles Lifeboat, and shortly after sent his epoch-making radio signal from Lavernock Point in Glamorgan, three-and-a-half miles to Echni Island (Flat Holm) in Cardiff Bay, on 18th May 1897. G. S. Kemp and James Kemp later constructed the radio antennae complex to send a transatlantic message from Cornwall to Canada. Radio in Britain became state-controlled, and the BBC was set up.

The fiction is that the BBC is independent, but the Government appoints and fires

Chapter 2 - The British Cold War

the governors and directors who run it. Well, Griffith John Williams was an ambitious man and he cultivated patrons and sought openings, and soon he was jumping on the train from Cardiff once a week to pour out his destructive bile across the airwaves from the BBC's London headquarters. In those pre-television and mass-media days the BBC state monopoly had the aura and reputation of respectability and infallibility. If it came from the BBC it was true. No one else was allowed to parade the airways to contradict the ravings of Griffith J. Williams, for he was saying precisely what the public school-educated, Oxford- and Cambridge- indoctrinated mob running the BBC wanted to hear. Dr Edwin Guest was right, and Bishop Stubbs was right, and they were vindicated.

In Wales, the Archdruid Brinley Thomas, a native of Maesteg in the South East, erupted, and wrote a book exposing and denouncing Griffith J. Williams. Being the Archdruid he wrote his book in Welsh and whereas everyone could hear what Griffith was spouting for free, very few people could read the Archdruid's book even if they could afford it. Letters flew around and back and forth, and letters held in collections in the Welsh National Library in North Wales remain unpublished.

At the time, in the 1930s and 40s, the Cardiff University College was, like the other Welsh Colleges, a tiny incestuous affair. With some five hundred and ten students on three-year courses, or a hundred and seventy a year, and twenty-three departments of around seven or eight per class per year, all were too tightly knit. Lack of cash meant that the staff were not top grade, and in fact Aberystwyth in its early years often had difficulty in paying them. Not enough people were studying the history, and Cardiff and Swansea Colleges, founded in 1892, were younger and less confident, and the lunacy of J. Gwenogfran Evans prevailed.

What about Edward Williams - Iolo Morganwg - now posthumously the great alleged forger? Well, he began life as a stonemason and soon became a building contractor, and was often employed repairing the ancient tottering churches in his native South Wales. He developed an interest in the national history, and began to persuade the clergymen and the gentry whose manors and mansions he repaired to allow him to copy their old crumbling manuscripts. He developed contacts with educated men and literati and he became a leading figure in the Khumric literary circles of his day.

Iolo was a founding member of Unitarian Churches, believing in one God and nothing else - no trinities - and this would not endear him to those in authority. He backed the campaign to elect the first non-noble-gentleman to Parliament from Glamorgan, and he probably favoured and supported the American War of Independence. He founded a small library and he owned a bookshop, and he owned shares in a ship. He was one of the group that organised the funding of John Evans' epic journey to America to map the upper Missouri river in 1792-95 in the search for 'Welsh Indians' descended from Prince Madoc and his followers.

In addition, Iolo re-founded Eisteddfods in Wales, and he founded the annual Welsh National Eisteddfod. He was also, with Dr Owen Jones and Dr William Owen Pughe, responsible for the publication of the massive *Myvyrian Archaiology of Wales* in 1800, republished in 1804 and 1806. This vast tome contained several hundred ancient epic Khumric poems, a number of the Khumric Histories, the Triads (Historical, Religious, and Philosophical), the Khumric Laws, and ancient Music, and so on. He was also responsible for the public excavation and discovery of important ancient inscribed stones.

Now Griffith J. Williams was very reluctant to attack the Oxford University-educated Dr Owen Jones and Dr William 0. Pughe in his witch-hunt, and so he selected Iolo or Edward Williams, who had not been to an English University. He alleged that some one third of the *Myvyrian Archaiology* was forged, and that one third was the section for which Iolo was responsible. Recent research shows that Dr Pughe and Dr Jones were in fact responsible for this section and not Iolo. He then alleged that Iolo was a secret drug-addict, something that none of his contemporaries had noticed. Two television programmes in the early 1990s made by H.T.V. entitled *Not Bad For A Junkie*, and *Some Junkie*, called upon modern knowledge of drugs, their effects on character and health, visible effects, and so on, and of course the fact that Iolo died aged seventy-nine, finally exploded this lie. Iolo did have a chronic chest problem, and he did take laudanum for it, which does contain some cocaine. Alan Wilson's grandmother had a similar problem and took considerable quantities of Dr Collis Browne's Cough Mixture containing Laudanum for many years and died aged eighty-seven, perfectly sane.

Griffith John Williams stated, and actually wrote to the effect that-

'Whilst all the members of his household, his family and servants, and all his neighbours, were fast asleep Iolo sat up until three in the morning forging documents by lamp light.'

Now amazing as it might appear, no one asked how it was that, if none of Iolo's family, his servants, or neighbours, knew that he was busy forging in the dead of night in 1800, then how did Griffith John Williams from a hundred and fifty miles away in North Wales know this a hundred and fifty years later?

For years, every enquiry into South East Wales history made by Alan Wilson was met with the childish chant of 'Iolo Morganwg was a forger'. People who had never

Chapter 2 - The British Cold War

ever read a single word of the histories, and who actually did not even know the name of the ridiculous publicity-hunter Griffith John Williams, repeated this parrot-like refrain. No one even questioned the matter. Not until a few years after Wilson and Blackett published their fourth book in 1986 did a young lady set out to begin research for a book on Iolo the Forger, presumably to rebut Wilson and Blackett. She gave up because she constantly found that manuscripts allegedly forged by Iolo Morganwg around 1800 exist in earlier copies made by others around 1500 to 1700, or earlier.

Other researchers who were better trained and equipped to make tracks through the archive jungles were persuaded to ignore the abuse and bile being flung at Wilson and Blackett in exactly the same personal manner as the vicious attacks on Iolo, and they also began to find much earlier copies of manuscripts alleged to be forged by Iolo Morganwg around 1800. A search by Brian Davies for the alleged forged Triads led to his finding groups of these Triads in varying numbers scattered through older texts. He found over a hundred and eighty of two hundred and eight allegedly forged Triads in earlier manuscripts, and he also found whole earlier allegedly forged manuscripts which were clearly a century or two before Iolo's time.

Strange as it is, other researchers earlier than Iolo, and some who were contemporary with him, published the same records which he is said to have forged. As everything has been thrown out in a rush to demonstrate political correctness and to conform with the braying asinine dictates of Griffith John Williams it seems that these publications are now also retrospectively forgeries by association. The entire subject has now become taboo and contaminated.

Actually, the resurrection of ancient British history can be done very comfortably without using the records honestly and honourably collected by Edward Williams *alias* Iolo. This man walked from village to village from manor to manor, come rain, hail, or shine, in all winds and weather, from one end of Wales to the other. He kept the most meticulous records ever, noting down the roads and bridges and their condition, the inns and houses he stayed in, the menus and quality of food, whom he met, what he saw, etc., etc., etc. He was detailed in who had and owned what manuscript, and he posted these records of his journeys twice weekly to his sponsors. The National Library of Wales in the north is reluctant to admit that it has no less than twenty-three thousand pages of Iolo's journals in its vaults. They allegedly hold ancient manuscripts written in ancient British Coelbren. They know Iolo was no forger.

On one journey through North Wales collecting and copying manuscripts Iolo arrived in Aberystwyth with a considerable bundle. His sponsors were not rich and they put up what cash they could, and so, short of funds, Iolo placed the package of manuscript copies on the stage-coach, paid the postage fee, and set off to walk the hundred and forty miles back to Cardiff. He arrived home and waited months and nothing arrived by stagecoach. So, he set off again and walked back north to Aberystwyth where he found that the depot manager of the stagecoach company had removed his large package after he left, and had taken it to a local literary gentleman who had promptly hidden it. These crooks, surprised by Iolo's reappearance, and his visit to the local magistrate, handed over the manuscript bundle to Iolo who carried it back the hundred and forty miles to South Wales.

If it is any consolation to the sad shades of Iolo then Wilson and Blackett can give an assurance that nothing has changed. In the early 1980s Alan Wilson wrote five times to the National Library of Wales in Aberystwyth for information, and enclosed paper and stamped addressed envelopes in his last three letters, and never got any reply.

In 1986, John Dudley Davies, then manager of the Welsh Book Council Warehouse, again sadly in the remote Aberystwyth area, told Alan Wilson and Baram Blackett that he could have easily sold three or four times more of their books if it were not for the opposition corning out of Aberystwyth University and the Library. As they had bitter experience of several hostile actions from these quarters this was no surprise to them.

The matter is now simply one of institutional and individual academic reputation. It is also now one of absurd regional pride and stubbornness. It has nothing whatsoever to do with the accuracy and truthfulness of the records. It is all about who gets what share of public funds and grants. It is all about the Old Pals acts with too small an incestuous and inbred group. If J. Gwenogfran Evans and Griffith John Williams were a pair of academic imbeciles, and probably also crooks, then it is time to admit it. The time to clean house is long overdue.

Alan Wilson and Baram Blackett work on the basis that the ancient texts are inviolate. Not one word can be added or deleted or changed. Nor can any name be added or changed or deleted. Nor can anyone, with the exception of J. G. Evans and G. J. Williams and their followers, be accused of forgery. Britain has a great and very ancient history and we should all cherish and protect it.

Chapter Three

The Coming of Albyne

All nations have their traditions and take pride in their historical origin and exhibit marmoreal permanence with relics, be they castles, grave mounds, temples, antique statues, or ancient stone circles. In Western Europe for many centuries almost all these traditional histories were submerged and reduced to the level of legends and myths, and even mocked as fairy tales. This was necessary so that the religious importation of the Hebrew myths and legends beginning in phases with Adam and Eve, then Noah and his ark, then Abraham and his family, and so on, could replace all other histories of origin.

Religion, with its blackmail threats of eternal damnation and millions of years of horrendous torture of souls after death to those who refused to submit, and loss of office and status and property, and even torture or death to the living, was the most powerful force in mediaeval Europe. Part of the price exacted by the men in black was the elevation of Biblical Hebrew history to be virtually the only ancient history.

The first History of Britain is that of the Voyage of Albyne. This was published in modern times by the Early English Text Society in 1906. This Society struggled to make available to the public at large the ancient manuscripts of England. In 1906 they hired Friedrich W.D. Brie, of Marburg, to produce a composite version of the Bruts of England sometimes called The Chronicles of England. No fewer than a hundred and sixty-nine manuscripts of this Brut (History) survive, and they cover the continuous period from Albyne, whom Khumric scholars place around 1567BC, to AD1479. Friedrich Brie used the MSS Rawlinson B.171. Bodleian, the MSS Douce 323 Bodleian, and the MSS Trinity College Dublin 490.

The records of the Early English Text Society show that they were constantly short of funds for publishing and had more editors and manuscripts available than they had funds to permit them to work and publish.

'An urgent appeal is hereby made to Members to increase the list of subscribers to the E.E. Text Society. It is nothing less than a scandal that the Hellenic Society should have 1000 members and the E.E.Text Society should have only 300.'

The problem of the records was not therefore entirely confined to Khumric sources, and the misdirection of the education system towards the irrelevant foreign ancient mythical histories of distant Greece and Rome was having its destructive effect.

Not many people were interested in the fact that a fleet led by Albyne had sailed from ancient Syria to Britain some three thousand six hundred years ago. The 'history', when it was occasionally discussed, was automatically labelled as myth and legend, and no one asked why. Asking questions was however the business of Blackett and Wilson, and in 1982 they decided to give the Bruts of England a long overdue fair trial, beginning with the story of Albyne. The voyage of Albyne was to the British what the migration of Abraham from Ur of the Chaldeans was to the Hebrews and we would do well to remember this. The *Brut or Chronicle of England* in MS Douce 323.

Bodleian opens with Line 1; - How King Dioclisian wedded his 33 Daughters to 33 Kings whom they afterwards murdered; and how these Widows came to England, & had children by the Giants of the land. This Prologue is a later summary of the original tale.

The story begins on Line 2: -

'In the noble lande of Surrye ther was a noble kyng and myghty, & a man of grete renoun, that me called [himself] Dyoclician ...'

So, the tale opens in ancient Surrye or Syria. In Line 12 we are told; -

'Hyt befell thus, that this Dioclician spousede a gentyl damysele that was wondyr fair that was hys Eemys doughter, Labana...'

So, Diocletian the great King of Syria married the daughter of his enemy Labana.

The account in the Bruts proceeds to tell how King Diocletian *'who ruled all the lands about him'*, numbering thirty-three other subject territories, married thirty-three of his daughters to these subject Amyralles (Emirs), Princes, and Dukes. These daughters believed that they far outranked their lesser husbands and

The Brut

OR

The Chronicles of England.

EDITED FROM

MS. RAWL. B 171, BODLEIAN LIBRARY, &c.

BY

FRIEDRICH W. D. BRIE, Ph.D.

WITH INTRODUCTION, NOTES, AND GLOSSARY.

PART I.

LONDON:
PUBLISHED FOR THE EARLY ENGLISH TEXT SOCIETY
By KEGAN PAUL, TRENCH, TRÜBNER & CO., LIMITED,
DRYDEN HOUSE, 43, GERRARD STREET, SOHO, W.
1906.

(Title page of the *The Brut*)

The Brut, a Chronicle of England.

[MS. Douce 323, Bodleian Library.]

[THE PROLOG.]¹

[How King Dioclisian wedded his 33 Daughters to 33 Kings whom they afterwards murderd; and how these Widows came to England, & had children by the Giants of the land.]

IN³ the noble lande of Surrye⁴ ther was a noble kyng and myghty, & a man of grete renoun, þat me called Dyoclician, þat wel and worthily hym gouernede, & rewlede thurgh his noble chiualrye, so þat he conquered alle þe landes abowte hym, so that almoste all þe kynges of þe world to hym were entendaunt. ¶ Hyt befell thus, þat this Dioclician spousede a gentyl damysele þat was wondyr fayr, þat was hys Eemys doughter, Labana; & sche loued hym as reson wolde, so þat he gate vpon here xxxiij doughtres, of þe which þe eldest me called Albyne. And þese⁵ Damysels, whan þey comyn in-to⁶ Age, bycomen⁷ so fayre þat it was wondyr. ¶ Wherfore this Dioclician anon lete make A sompnyng, & comaundid by his lettres þat Alle þe kyngys þat heldyn of hym schulde come at A certayn day, as in his lettres was⁸ conteyned, to make A ryal feste. At which day, þedir þey comyn, & brought with hem Amyralles, Pryncez & Dukes, & noble Chiualrye. Þe feste was ryally Arayd; & þere þey lyved in ioy and merthe y-now, that it was wonder to wete.

¶ And hit befelle þus, þat þis Dioclician þoughte maryen his Doughtres among all þo knyghtys⁹ þat tho were at that solempnite;

---

¹ The text to the end of Chapter V is taken from MS. Douce 323, as it is wanting (except just the latter part of Chapter V, which is too blurred and indistinct to be copied) in MS. Rawlinson B 171. The collation following is of MS. Trin. Coll. Dublin 490 (D). ² leaf 1.
³ D has this heading: Her may a man hure How Engelande was ferst callede Albyon and through whome it hade the name.
⁴ Syrrie ⁵ þis ⁶ vnto ⁷ bicome ⁸ were ⁹ kynges

BRUT. B

Opening page of *The Brut*

troubles began in these marriages. The sub-kings made complaints to King Diocletian, and at a conciliatory conference, which he called, the thirty-three daughters each murdered their respective despised husbands. As a result, Diocletian banished his daughters, who were led by Albyne, and they sailed for Britain in a fleet with their followers. Albyne brought her god Apollyon with her.

Now these are major pieces of information. The first thing of note is the name Surrye or Syria, because this name is still extant in Britain in the County of Surrey. This is a name which has long puzzled philologists, and one academic in recent times wrote a paper hypothesizing that as Surrey lies to the south of the river Thames then there was possible an ancient long forgotten Norrey on the north banks of the Thames. The name Surrey that still exists in England is more likely to stem from the Albyne migration.

If anything is to come out of this investigation then the false doctrine that scepticism is wisdom needs to be abandoned. A sceptic is a man who simply does not know how to, why to, or where to, go about doing anything. Concerning the Bruts of England and how to regard them. Freidrich Brie wisely wrote –

> 'The value of those parts of the story which are incapable of external authentication depends upon the generally faithful character of the text where they have been proved.'

In short, where it is possible to check the veracity of the Bruts they are generally shown to be correct and true. It then follows that where it may not be possible to check the Bruts, it is reasonable to assume that these parts may also be considered true. Settled in the confines of their study with its peacock blue walls and white ceiling against the red-brown rosewood Victorian furniture Blackett and Wilson set out to plan the methods of checking out what was universally perceived as being uncheckable.

Next, Blackett and Wilson turned to the obvious information held in The Odyssey, written around 650BC, by Melisigenes, *alias* Homer. In this account of the voyages of Odysseus following the Trojan War, the hero has been away from home for ten long years and is presumed dead by most folk. Suitors have gathered, pressing the faithful Penelope, the presumed widow of Odysseus, to re-marry and to choose one of their number. They clearly want the rich estates of Odysseus. When Odysseus returns home unrecognized, he is assisted in his plan to kill these gluttonous suitors by his farm bailiff, Eumaeus. In conversation, Odysseus asks Eumaeus of his origins, and he is told; -

'You were asking about my early days. Let me give you the tale. There is an island called Syrie - you may have heard the name - out beyond Ortygie, where the sun turns in his course.' Homer, *The Odyssey*, Book 15, v. 403.

The phrase 'where the sun turns in his course' implies 'away in the far west from Greece, out beyond the Pillars of Hercules' - the Gibraltar Straits. Ortygia is thought to have been the birthplace of the goddess Diana and of the god Apollo, and the Bruts record the god of Albyne of Britain as Apollyon. Ortygia is the name of a small island in Sicily in the bay of Syracuse, where the fountain of Arethusa rose, and once, one of the four quarters of that ancient city, as in Virgil's *Aeneid* 3, l. 694, and Homer's *The Odyssey*. So, beyond Ortygia is far to the west beyond Italy.

Virgil, writing *The Aeneid* around 50BC, names a Rutulian prince named Ortygius who was killed by Caeneus. This again indicates Ortygia as Italy and so beyond Ortygia from Greece again means far west of Italy. Vergil-The Aenead, 9. v. 573. The island described by Eumaeus is large, very fertile, very green, and had a temperate climate free from diseases. The heat of summer was always the time and season of diseases in the hotter countries of Eastern Mediterranean, and so once again the more welcome and cooler climate indicates Britain.

The *Bruts of England* also name a powerful Laban as the major enemy of the Great King Diocletian, and in the era around 1600-1550BC there is the obvious Biblical Laban. In Genesis between 24:49 and 46:25 there is the story of the Hebrew Prince, Isaac, son of Abraham, sending his second son Jacob, north to Haran to get one of his first cousins for a wife. Laban is very clearly identified as son of the Aramean woman named Bethuel, and sister of Rachel who was Isaac's wife, and Laban's father Nahor was Abraham's brother. Whether this is Laban the enemy of the Diocletian of the ancient Bruts of England is yet to be seen.

It might be well to get the geography of the tale correct. Haran (Carrhae) is on the upper reaches of the Balih (Nahr Balikh) River, a major tributary of the Euphrates, in what was northern Suri (now Syria) at 36° 56' North and 39° 04' East, and further North is ancient Ur (later named Callirrhoe and then Edessa) at 37° 15' North and 38° 54' East. This northern Ur is traditionally and almost certainly the Ur from which Abraham migrated going South. At this point we need to recognize that there were two ancient cities named Ur, and the southern Ur lies six hundred miles south on the lower Euphrates, some two hundred miles south of Babylon, at around 30° 34' north and 48° 59' East.

From 1922 to 1934 the very able archaeologist Leonard Woolley conducted large scale excavations at the southern Ur on behalf of the Trustees of the British Museum and the Museum of the University of Pennsylvania. The primary objective of these excavations was scholarly interest in these Eastern civilizations and perhaps a Biblical interest in the name of Ur being associated with Abraham. Demonstrating remarkable skills and abilities Woolley excavated the ancient city of Ur in a prodigious twelve-year exercise which uncovered the ruins of whole cities, ziggurats, temples, palaces, libraries, market-places, shops, and houses, and also the royal necropolis of the huge tombs of the kings and queens of the southern Babylonian Ur.

These were remarkable excavations by any standards, and brought astonishing discoveries, but in the way of things, Woolley's marvellous discoveries were completely overshadowed by the sensational find of the insignificant boy-Pharaoh Tutankhamun by Howard Carter in Egypt.

Digging out the royal graves of the emperors and queens of Ur involved excavating enormous grave-pits and carefully entering the lower floors of vast funerary palaces. Huge grave-pits were filled with the remains of dozens of servants, courtiers, and soldiers, who had accompanied their royal masters into eternity. Soldiers with their weapons, ladies with their jewellery, funeral ox-carts and sledges and the great beasts which pulled them, and all manner of utensils, artefacts, musical instruments, and personal belongings. Belief in an after-life was undoubted.

Huge difficulties were encountered in recovering and preserving these relics. The burials were often below the level of the local subterranean water tables. Rainfall in the area, which by contrast was almost non-existent in Egypt, had over the millennia completely rotted away both wood and fabrics. Only dark stains and faint outlines in the soil marked where harps and wooden statues had lain. The gold and jewels and traces of silver, which had covered these items, remained crushed and twisted. Yet the technical skill and patience was such that quite astonishing reconstructions were made.

The massive fortress-like mausoleum tombs of the emperors of Ur were located and dug out. These were the great emperors of the ancient world, but in the strange and perverse ways of fate, the historical vicissitudes of the times, and the coinciding discoveries in 1922 in Egypt diminished their importance in the public mind. The hoard of well-preserved furniture, vases, personal possessions, chariots, beds, religious and funerary items, which accompanied the boy-king of Egypt into eternity in his intact burial chambers, mesmerised the world's media. Given the comparatively easy accessibility of Egypt and the mass evidence of a complete undisturbed burial of an ancient god-king, this is perhaps understandable.

At Ur, Leonard Woolley and his team were uncovering massive mausoleum tombs built like great fortresses. Massive outer walls protected inner complexes of courtyards, warehouses, offices, and living quarters, built two storeys above ground. Here the officials and workers responsible for the estates which provided for the upkeep of the King's mausoleum, lived and worked. Here also dwelt the priests who carried out the necessary daily rites of the worship of the dead god-king. Below ground were two more storeys of corridors, storerooms, and ritual and funerary apartments.

These were the religious votive areas, the treasure-chambers containing the riches required by the king in eternity, and the burial chamber of the king himself.

The sanctuaries and administrative offices which had packed the above-ground areas inside these massive slab-walled fortress structures, still held records and accounts on baked clay tablets. Descending stairways of mud-brick, still in good condition, led down to the lower levels of these multi-storey fortress monastery temples. Buildings intended to perpetuate the memory of, and continue the religious services dedicated to, the Emperors of Ur were still in remarkably good condition.

Here lay the great Emperors of the Third Dynasty, the rulers who had calmly styled themselves as 'King of the World' and 'King of the Four Quarters of the World', and the greatest of these was Dungi. The largest of the great tombs in the royal necropolis at the southern Ur was that of the Great King Dungi, the most powerful ruler of the illustrious Third Dynasty of Ur. His tomb was originally a four-storey fortress or palace-like building, with two floors below ground, and Woolley excavated it thoroughly.

There may well be objections over the dating of King Dungi of Ur, but further work, which will be published, will resolve any difficulties. The nineteenth-century chronological structures based on the Egyptian model are known to be unsound and these problems can be resolved. Another problem is that modern scholars, many of who have a somewhat quixotic approach, have endeavoured to find some tiny niche to call their own, and have mangled Dungi into Shulgi.

Dungi the great King of Ur has much in common with Diocletian of the English Bruts, for he claimed to rule the Four Corners of the Earth, namely Akkad-Babylonia in the South East, Elam in the North East, Amurru (Syria, Palestine,

Chapter 3 - The Coming of Albyne

Lebanon, and Phillistia) in the South West, and Gutium in the North West. Harran of Laban and the northern Ur of Abraham lay on the borders of Gutium. Dungi also claimed to rule over thirty-three subject provinces just as Diocletian of the Bruts did.

Dungi also made some of his daughters rulers over subject provinces, and this is yet another strange echo from the past. That Dungi was the ruler over Suri - ancient Syria - is evident, and Diocletian of the Bruts also ruled Sirrye, or Surrye, as it is variously spelled. Then when Albyne arrived in Britain, she and her sisters are said to have married with Geauntes, who are not Fairy Tale Giants but instead perhaps the people of Coele Syria, and Syria proper, known as Gutians from Gutium.

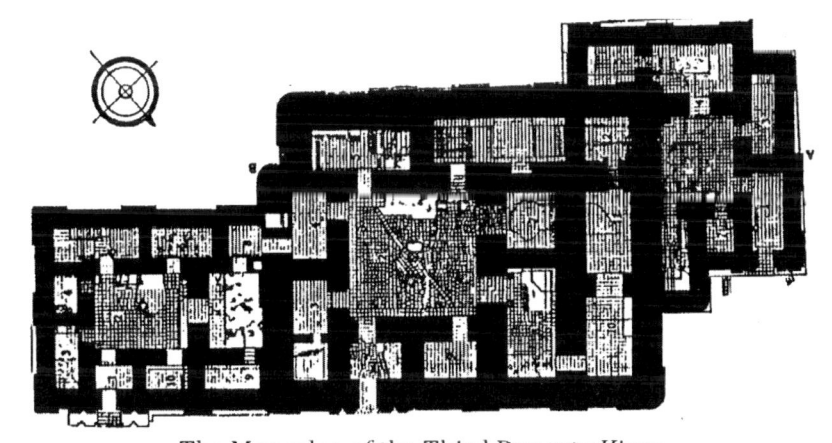

The Mausolea of the Third Dynasty Kings

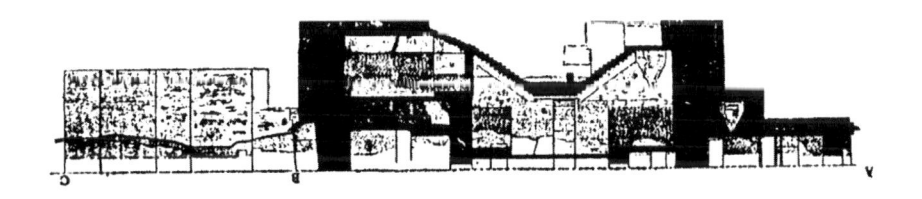

Plan and relief of the mausolea of Dungi-Diocletian

Under Dungi-Diocletian's Mausoleum

Chapter 3 - The Coming of Albyne

The Hittites

For many centuries the name of a people known as the Hittites was just that, simply a name and nothing else. Brief passing references in the Christian Bible were all that was known of them, and they were either thought irredeemably lost or otherwise they were considered to be irrelevant and amorphous. Even their 're-discovery' in modern times exhibits a chapter of accidents.

In Biblical references the Hittites are referred to in contexts which indicate that they were a powerful nation with strong military capabilities, and yet they had somehow vanished without a trace. They figure in the story of Abraham buying land for the burial of his wife Sarah in Genesis 23.

> 'And Sarah was a hundred and seven and twenty years old; these were the years of the life of Sarah. And Sarah died in Kirjathoarba; the same is Hebron in the land of Caanan, and Abraham came to mourn for Sarah and to weep for her.
>
> 'And Abraham stood up before his dead, and spoke unto the sons of Heth saying –
>
> 'I am a stranger and a sojourner with you; give me a possession of a burying place with you, that I may bury my dead out of sight.'

So, Abraham bought a cave and a field for the price of four hundred silver shekels from Ephron the son of Zohar. It is generally accepted that these sons of Heth were Hittites and that they owned at least part of ancient Canaan.

In 2 Kings 7:6 there is another mention -

> 'For the Lord has made the host of the Syrians to hear a noise of chariots, and a noise of horses, even the noise of a great host, and they said unto one another, Lo, the king of Israel has hired against us the kings of the Hittites, and the kings of the Egyptians to come against us.'

This again indicates a powerful Hittite nation. King David made himself infamous by arranging the death of one of his most able and loyal military commanders, Uriah the Hittite, so that he could marry his widow Bathsheba. Solomon married Hittite wives, as in 1 Kings 11:1, and he traded horses imported from Egypt to the Kings of the Hittites and the Kings of the Arameans, as in 2 Chronicles 1:17

The Hittites are referred to in lists of the Nations in Genesis 15:19-21, and similarly in Joshua 3:10. Esau son of Isaac married Hittite wives as stated in Genesis 26:34 and 36:1-3, and the city of Jerusalem is said to be the bastard offspring of an Amorite and a Hittite in Ezekiel 26:3. In the geography of Palestine in Numbers 13:29 it is related that: 'Amalek dwells in the land of the South, and the Hittite, and the Jebusite, and the Amorite, dwell in the mountains ...' *and so on.*

In Joshua 1:2-4 it appears that the Hittites held all the land between Lebanon and the Euphrates, and how much further north or west into Asia Minor is not stated.

Every indication is that the Hittites were a powerful ancient nation located in areas north of Syria stretching over to the Euphrates in the east and westwards into Asia Minor.

Johann Ludwig Borchardt was born in Lausanne on 24 November 1784, into a family of gentleman scholars. He studied Natural Science and Arabic in the universities of Leipzig, Göttingen, and London, and was later employed by the British Africa Society. In 1809 he sailed to Malta and dressed himself in oriental clothing, before going to Syria where he lived as a merchant in Aleppo and then Damascus. He spent his life travelling the Arab nations, soaking up their culture, history, geography, and perfecting his use of their language. He became a Moslem and was buried as Sheikh Ibrahim and as Hadji, in Cairo in 1817.

Johann Borchardt's amazing travels are well known, and whilst in the bazaar of Hama on the Orantes in Syria, the Biblical Hamath (later Epiphaneia), he noticed a stone built into the wall of a house. The stone was covered with strange signs and figures, which had the appearance of a form of hieroglyphs, which were quite different from those of Egypt. Borchardt's book titled *Travels in Syria and the Holy Land* was not published until 1822, five years after he died, and on page 146, he made reference to the strange stone at Hama in Syria.

No one took any notice of this reference to a strange stone in Hama, until sixty years later, the American Consul-General, Augustus Johnson, was in the bazaar with a friend, Dr Jessup, and they saw the stone in the corner of a house. They enquired about the stone and were told that there were three other similar stones nearby. An attempt by these 'infidels' to copy the stone led to something of a riot, and Johnson and Jessup were forced to withdraw in some haste. Next year, 1873, Drake and Palmer, of the American Palestinian Exploration Society, were equally unsuccessful, but the notable English traveller, explorer, and writer, Captain Richard Burton, managed to make some rough sketches. With the local people

Chapter 3 - The Coming of Albyne

now being whipped up into religious fanaticism and threatening to destroy these stones, Shubi Pasha, the new Governor of Syria, who was appointed in 1872, came to Hama to see for himself. He took with him the British Consul at Damascus, a Mr. Kirby Green, and William Wright, an Irish missionary living in Damascus.

The main concern and interest of European and American exploration was Biblical, and this Christian orientation of research was inevitably to arouse suspicion amongst local Moslem communities.

Shuhi Pasha took soldiers with him to Hama and they were needed. Five inscribed stones were found in Hama and as workmen removed them from the walls of the houses they were built into, armed sentries stood guard. Amid a near riot the stones were taken away and sent to Constantinople (now Instanbul, the capital of the Turkish Empire. Plaster casts of the inscriptions were made by William Wright and sent to the British Museum in London, making these inscriptions available to scholars.

William Wright guessed at a Biblical solution to the strange writing, that these strange inscriptions were in the language and script of the 'sons of Heth.' An American, Hayes Ward, made a comparison with seals found in the excavations at Nineveh in 1849 by Austin Layard. No one mentioned Hittites. Then in 1876 George Smith, the remarkable English researcher and explorer, had with W.H. Skene, the British Consul at Aleppo, identified the site of the great Hittite fortress city of Carchemish, which had anciently dominated northern Syria, on a bend in the Euphrates. A British Museum expedition soon began unearthing more stones with Hama-type inscriptions and sculptures.

These sculptures electrified Henry Archibald Sayce (Sayce is from Seisyllt which in English would be Cecil, a scholar with family descent from the ancient Welsh nobility. He lar sculptures on rock faces near Boghaz-had seen a whole series of simikeui in Asia Minor just seventy-five miles east of Ankara, and others at Marash in north Syria, and more at Karabel on the Asia Minor coast. He guessed that these inscriptions must be Hittite, and so the Hittites were re-discovered, just a few decades after the History of Albyne was abandoned in Britain. Suffice it to say that Henry A. Sayce made the first inroads into the decipherment of Hittite cuneiform.

The past century has seen a reconstruction of the geography of the Hittite Empire in antiquity; and Harran, the city of Laban, the father-in-law of Jacob, lies inside the borders of its eastern territories.

From the reconstruction of Hittite and Chaldean History, the lists of the Great Kings have emerged, and the first King was named Labarnas. This King Labarnas can be roughly dated to around 1600BC and his successor was Labarnas II- Hattusilis.

Therefore, there were Kings named Labarnas clearly available as the Laban, the enemy of King Diocletian of Syria in the English Bruts, who ruled all the thirty-three states of the Four Quarters, along the Euphrates and the Tigris. All the subsequent Hittite Great Kings are now known to have adopted the throne name of Labarna just in the same way as the Emperors of Rome used the name Caesar in titular fashion.

Labarnas II- Hattusilis expanded the empire south and east down into Syria and seized the prosperous Kingdom of Yamhad with its capital at Aleppo, called Halap by the Hittites. This Hittite invasion of one of their northern provinces obviously would have brought the rulers of Ur into conflict with Labarnas II-Hattusilis I, and the Bruts of England state that King Diocletian of Sirrye had an enemy named Laban.

Significantly the adopted son of Labarnas II was Labarnas-Mursilis I, and this Great King of the Hittites records how he attacked and conquered almost the whole of Syria and then marched south down along the river Euphrates and attacked the Babylonian Amorite kingdom, which collapsed under his assault. This record precisely matches the events of the Third Dynasty of Ur following the death of Dungi (modernly misnamed as Shulgi). His successor Bursin, ruled for only eight years, and then Shusin, who again lasted only eight years, was compelled to build a line of fortifications along the western frontiers to try to hold off invaders. Then early in the reign of Ibbisin, the last of the line, a major invasion launched from the West swept clear across all Sumer and Akkad, devastating the whole land. This matches perfectly with the records of the Hittite King Labarnas-Mursilis I.

This attack led to the collapse of the Dynasty of Dungi and the Empire of Ur slowly disintegrated. There appears to have been little thought to the political conditions which allowed Semite Princes, whose wealth lay in raising cattle, sheep, and goats, rather than horticulture, to migrate south from Harran. It may well be that the invasion of Labarnas-Mursilis I forced them to migrate south away from Harran.

To Blackett and Wilson, it would appear logical that Terah, Abraham, and Lot, were able to move south from over-crowded mountain grazing lands around

Harran because the Labarnas-Mursilis I had shattered the Empire of the Third Dynasty of Ur. There was no longer any power able to stop them. Equally Abraham may have bought the field and cave at Machpelah for burial of his family from Hittites who had seized these lands in Palestine. Significantly the Hittites who sold him the land said in response to his request-

'Harken to us, sir. We look upon you as a mighty leader.' (Genesis 23:5) and they had so little regard for the land and money that they offered to give it to him for nothing.

The prevalent idea that Abraham and his descendants were poor simple harmless folk, wandering about with their flocks and herds, does not stand up to examination. Most important however, is the fact that there was a credible King Diocletian of Sirrye in the Emperor Dungi who ruled ancient Suri-Syria, and he had a terrible enemy for Laban of the English Bruts in the Hittite King named as Labarnas. Dungi like Diocletian, ruled over thirty-three subject provinces, and as Leonard Woolley discovered he appointed some of his daughters to rule over provinces.

Wilson and Blackett ask the questions- "How did our British ancestors of a thousand years ago know of Dungi or Diocletian of Syria, and of his enemy Laban or Labarnas. How did they know that Dungi or Diocletian ruled over thirty-three other nations? How did they know that Dungi or Diocletian made his daughters rulers of provinces? As the Hittites were not rediscovered until 1876 none of this makes sense, unless our ancient British ancestors did the obvious easy simple thing that all other nations did, and they simply recorded and remembered their history."

What Blackett and Wilson regard as significant, is that contrary to the current mind set of there being ancient Khumric 'Welsh' manuscripts which differ from, or are in conflict with, ancient English manuscripts, the ancient texts corroborate with each other. The story of Albyne appears in Khumric texts as well as in the English. The story of Brutus and the migration from Trojan lands follows immediately after the story of Albyne in the Bruts of England, and it is peppered through the Khumric manuscripts in total corroboration.

The Ealde Cyrcenas in Britain

One major question, which needed to be addressed in the carefully planned programme of investigation into The Coming of Albyne, was: "Is there solid evidence surviving in Britain?" This appeared to be so obvious as a line of enquiry that both Alan Wilson and Baram Blackett were perplexed that there appeared to be little or no effort made in this direction previously.

They were later to find that in 1908 Sir Norman Lockyear and others at Cambridge University had made some attempts to identify possible links between ancient Syria and Britain.

Mr. Ray Hudson, of Pontypool, and Terry DeLacy, of Cardiff, a well-known television producer and director, drew this to their attention, and even obtained a loan of a book written on this research. This investigation was discontinued at the outbreak of World War I in 1914, and never recommenced. The investigation made no real progress and appears to have been archaeologically orientated and mainly directed towards ancient Syrian artefacts. It was however encouraging to know that the matter of Albyne had been taken seriously at a major scholastic institution.

The first and most crucial move in the investigation of a Nation's history is however to read the histories available. This is so obvious that it should not need to be stated. Surprising as it may appear however this had not been done, and it is apparently a typical dereliction amongst archaeologists.

The first thing that Wilson and Blackett did was to examine the name of the people, and the ancient inhabitants of England were known as Lloegrwys, and the country was Lloegres. This would imply that these people were Moon worshippers, from the words *lloer'* meaning the Moon, and *'lloergan'* for moonlight, and *'lloerog'* which is *'like the moon'*. It is a fact that the people of ancient southern Babylonian, Ur, were Moon worshippers. The great temple and ziggurat of the Moon god Nannar, dominated the ancient city of Ur, and Nannar, son of Bel-Enlil, and his wife Nin-gal, the Moon goddess, were the patron deities of the city. Small beginnings, but still a beginning.

Next, they looked at the Language of the Lloegrwys, and again nothing is quite as it appears. The Welsh Histories state under the date AD 826, '*The Language which prevailed in Lloegres was the language of the Icinglas.*' In the context in which this appears it means that out of Old British Khumric, Latin, German, Angle, and Saxon, and Danish, the language which remained native to Lloegres was the language of the Iceni tribal nation. The Iceni are perhaps best remembered through their Queen Boudicca who rose against the barbarian Roman invaders in the time of Nero, and slaughtered many thousands of them, and her statue stands outside the palace of Westminster.

Chapter 3 - The Coming of Albyne

At first sight this might appear questionable given the mindset implanted in the British education system by nineteenth-century demagogues. A parallel can be drawn with the fact that in AD 383, the British armies seized Brittany and Lydaw (Normandy) in the North West of France and colonized these areas with British settlers. Alan Wilson can remember how before the 1939-45 War, the Breton trawlers would arrive once a year in the South Wales ports loaded with the annual onion crops, and Breton men would drape masses of strings of onions over bicycles and go door to door through the city and the towns and villages selling them. They were known as 'Johnny Onions'.

These Bretons were able to speak with Alan's grandfather and his Welsh speaking friends once a few initial difficulties were overcome; even after sixteen hundred years they could get by.

If the records preserved from pre-Norman England are, as alleged, Anglo-Saxon, then why is it that no Englishman could ever simply get talking with a German? It appears that the language is not a form of German, and therefore it may not be Anglo-Saxon. Next Alan and Baram noticed that many scholars had remarked that the early writers of these alleged Anglo-Saxon texts all had British names, with Caedmon being the best known. The idea that a form of German replaced the native language of Lloegres is an assumption made without analysis, and the politics of the nineteenth century within the limits of its own misconceptions tended to favour unctuous self-worth and academic stagnation in place of the truth. The early writers were native British and there is no evidence that the migrating Angles and Saxons brought an alphabet with them. More was found of this later, and an example is that there are no extant Continental copies of the Beowulf saga.

This brought light to another curiosity. In the mid-1970s, three writers, named respectively Michael Baigent, Richard Leigh, and Henry Lincoln, wrote a book speculating on the possible settlement of a Jewish Christian community in Southern France in the first century AD. Later they continued their individual researches and publications and one wrote of a Frenchman who researched the origins of the English Language and came up with the answer that English derived from ancient Chaldean. And of course, the Frenchman either could not or would not state why this was so. This line of research is interesting as it points to the Albyne migration from ancient Chaldea. It may not be a popular line of enquiry to follow in a British University, but it remains fairly obvious that the English language never seems to have been Germanic.

The Khumric British histories are provably accurate and they may well be right about the ancient Language of Lloegres. Wilson and Blackett were able to find significant references in these Histories, and the most widely published is that in the historical records attributed to William of Malmesbury (1090-1143), and was published by E. K. Chambers, in 1922 under - From interpolations (12th-13th cent) in *De Antiquitate Glastoniensis Ecclesiae* (1129-39) edited by T. Hearne, and included in his history, *Adam of Domerham* (1727).

> 'quod mala mali illius Ealdcyrcenas eppel, i veteris ecclesiae poma, vocantur; sus quoque Ealdecyrce suge idciro nominabatur,'

Now Ealde-Cyrccnas means simply the 'Old Syrians', and here we have writers of over eight hundred years ago informing us of these Old Syrians in Britain. The entire text actually places these Old Syrians right into the middle of England. What we know as the County of Surrey may well be old Sirrye or old Syria, and no one has been looking.

The next logical item on the list for Blackett and Wilson was the pre-Christian era coins of Britain, which are inscribed. The lettering on these coins does appear to be in a form of the British Coelbren Alphabet, which would generally relate to Western Britain and to the Khumric people of the Brutus migration around 504 BC. It seems that scholars have been beguiled into thinking that old English texts are Anglo-Saxon, and no attempt has been made to interpret these coins as inscribed in the same language five hundred years before the arrival of these Saxons and Angles, albeit much of the evidence is diaphanous.

Alan Wilson sees a certain humour in all this, for in their efforts to promote Anglo-Saxonism in the nineteenth century, Edwin Guest and Bishop Stubbs were also demolishing the ancient history of Lloegres, England. The idea, which they created, was that the Welsh, the Irish, and even the Scots, were earlier barbarian peoples who were conquered by the much later English in the persons of the Angles and Saxons. Yet the histories place the Lloegreans (Icinglas - earliest English people) as the first in Britain by at least a thousand years. If Albyne arrived around 1600 BC and Brutus around 504 BC, this is so. Yet the highly advanced civilization of the Eadle Cyrcenas from Syria has proved them to be the most enduring of people.

This then brings matters to what archaeologists have designated as the 'Wessex' Culture which would imply 'West Saxons', in spite of the fact that the 'Wessex' Culture was an amazing metal-working civilization which suddenly erupted out of nowhere all across the southern half of Britain around 1600 BC, some two thousand years before any Saxon arrival in Britain. Every aspect of this extraordinary new culture points to an inward immigration from an existing high-level civilization, which is precisely what the British histories record in the Albyne Story.

The reason for a major fleet sailing to Britain from Chaldea-Syria around 1600 BC is obviously related to Britain being the Tin Island. This was the dawn of the Bronze Age with the much harder bronze weapons being far superior to the earlier softer copper weapons and tools. Tin was the essential ingredient required to smelt soft copper into hard bronze, and tin was in scarce supply.

A plan by the major imperial power in the ancient world to seize control of the Tin Island would seem to be a very logical step. There would appear to be no other explanation for the sudden bursting forth of the remarkable 'Wessex' Culture across southern Britain.

Extraordinary pieces of fine gold work have sometimes been found in the excavation of large 'Wessex' Culture grave mounds, which were obviously raised for important leaders. Only George Bain of Edinburgh realised what might have happened and he began a thorough investigation of the patterns of designs of ancient ornamentation. Ancient jewellery sometimes discovered in Britain yields evidence of common designs. The ancient stone crosses, churches, and memorial stones are mostly embellished with recognisably standard designs, as are coffins. This can also be seen in ancient manuscripts where the scribes and monks frequently took the first letter on a page - at the left-hand top - and embellished that letter with a quite extraordinary embroidery of animals and foliage.

George Bain made comparisons in Britain and Ireland and he also extended the scope of his research to include the ancient patterns used in embellishing the ancient temples, the palaces, the jewellery, pottery, and other artefacts of the ancient civilizations of Asia Minor, Chaldea, Assyria, and Greece. Here he found direct correlations between standard design patterns in Britain and Ireland and the ancient nations of the Eastern Mediterranean and Western Asia. This is research work which could be taken further, and which might now be easier with the access to information available through the modern marvel of the Internet. Bain showed that there are clearly ancient connections between Britain and Ireland and these other civilizations from which the British and the Irish trace their ancestry.

The frequent use of squared-off wave patterns, of entwined swastikas, of wind symbols, of endless entwined rope designs, which symbolize eternity, and chequerboard maze designs, and other legendary motifs are all obvious in every linked culture.

There are also a limited number of other ancient artefacts that are inscribed with the early alphabet found in England. One is the famous Franks Casket with its carved scenes and short texts, which does not appear to read as currently suggested. Also similarly inscribed is the great stone cross at Ruthwell in Dumfriesshire. Then there is, as will be shown later, the otherwise inexplicable discovery of three 'Anglo-Saxon' inscriptions in the Mid-West of the U.S.A. Even the most complex paradox can become clearly illuminated when the parallax view is apparent from a different standpoint.

In the case of the Franks Casket it has been claimed that the scenes are a mixture of Biblical and Teutonic legends. Yet one panel scene is clearly that of Agamemnon and Menelaus attacking Troy, and so it is part of the British experience as the British under Brutus are descended from Troy. Another left-hand scene is claimed to be the lame Smith Volund-Wayland holding the head of one of King Nidhad's sons in his tongs, but this could equally be a representation of the beheading of John the Baptist. This is more than likely as the opposite right-hand scene shows the Magi presenting gifts to the child Jesus in his mother's arms.

Other panels show the siege and overthrow of Jerusalem by Titus, which is again relevant to Britain with the well-attested flight of Judean migrants to Britain in the Apostolic era - see *The Holy Kingdom*. A further panel depicts the exposed twins Romulus and Remus, the founders of Rome, being suckled by wolves. This again has strong British connections with the British descent from Brutus, the grandson of Aeneas. And it was Aeneas who first built the villages of Romulus into a recognisable city, around 600 BC, as modern archaeology is demonstrating.

In short, the Franks Casket shows scenes on all its panels which relate to the British experience. The destruction of Troy, the founders of Rome, the beheading of John the Baptist and the adoration of the Magi, the destruction of Jerusalem by Titus, all relate. All around these carved scenes the panels carry writing and it is the origin of the writing that is important, and the language in which it is written.

We can perhaps rely on the fact that Old British Manuscripts of around AD 1100-1150 and then later, do in fact contain quite clear mentions of British people in the South of England and in the Midlands who are called the Ealde Cyrcenas, and '*the Ealde Cyrcenas*' means very definitely 'the Old Syrians'. As these people were still identifiable in the early twelfth century AD, this should be regarded as major evidence.

Chapter 3 - The Coming of Albyne

Cynfelyn and the Lexden Mound

The policy adopted by Blackett and Wilson throughout their investigations was to 'keep it simple'. Things happened in history; these events were remembered and recorded; and so all that is necessary is to follow the traces, no matter how faint and obscure they may be. In the excavation of the great mausoleum complex of Dungi of Ur, Leonard Woolley had first to find a hidden access entry in a cunningly sealed wall. He then dug his way down two converging flights of steps, to a landing, and then down a further flight of steps into the depths of the tomb.

One room near the burial chambers in these lower levels contained votive equipment, which appeared to have been used in religious ceremonies. As religion is normally the most permanent feature of any civilization the votive items found in the tomb of the Great King Dungi at Ur of around 1600 BC interested Alan Wilson and Baram Blackett. The votive equipment consisted of a metal table, models of reclining rams and hulls, glass balls, and various cups and jars.

Some fifteen hundred and fifty years later the British Viceroy recorded as Caswallon, son of Beli Mawr, had totally humiliated and defeated Julius Caesar in 55 and 54 BC and it has already been explained that this means that 'the Viceroy', son of 'him of Great Tumults', wiped the military floor with Julius Caesar. This means that King Dingad, son of Annyn Grych, or Aeneas the Rugged, gave Julius Caesar a military education.

The successor of the Caswallon, was popularly known as Cynfelyn, which title means 'yellow hair', and Greidiol, successor to Dingad is the most likely candidate to be Cynfelyn. Greidiol was also embroiled in the same wars as Dingad and matters have not been helped by the English predilection of referring to Cynfelyn as Cunobelinus in a foreign, Latin form. Historical tradition holds that after the wars between Julius Caesar and Pompey, and the subsequent chaos of further civil warfare after the assassination of Julius Caesar had ceased, Cynfelyn visited Rome to meet Augustus-Octavian, and his arrival caused something of a sensation in Rome. This is important because, then as now, Heads of State visiting each other exchange costly gifts.

Greidiol means to scorch or to burn, and as King Dingad employed a scorched-earth policy of drawing Julius Caesar on and on into middle Britain and totally depriving him of food for his army, and forcing him to surrender. The younger Prince Greidiol - the Scorcher - probably had this task. The picture is one of Aeneas the Rugged, probably aged about seventy, like some early day Winston Churchill figure, managing the war politically, with Dingad as the Commanding

General in the field, and Greidiol a younger commander at that time.

The scale of the British victory can be gauged from the fact that this same Julius Caesar had defeated an army of Gauls that exceeded three hundred thousand. Yet Aeneas and Dingad allowed him to land his army, to move inland, and upstream, and to cross the Thames with ease at a shallow ford, and then simply drove off all the animal stock, and scorched the earth ahead of him, leaving his army starving.

Dingad actually sent almost all of his army home for winter, and was able to harass Caesar's army of around forty thousand with only four thousand chariots. Aeneas and Dingad then sent one British army to block the ford of the Thames, and another under 'Carvilius', to attack Caesar's base and fleet. In this way the Roman commander was cut off without supplies and learned what Napoleon knew: 'An army marches on its stomach'.

Dingad then had the supreme satisfaction of surrounding Caesar's army with his troops and 'escorting' the Romans back to their ships. The Romans themselves record how they scrambled aboard in great haste and loaded three times as many men as normal onto each surviving ship. Contemporary Roman poets lampooned Julius Caesar for this disastrous campaign and complete humiliation. This is a stark contrast to the ease with which Pompey and later Vespasian and Titus overcame Judea. The political Roman account reads like a victory for Caesar, yet the stated terms, that 'Mandubratius' or Afarwy Fradog, the Traitor, be left unharmed, are false; for Afarwy never again set foot in Britain. Both sides claimed victory, the Caswallon because he won, and Caesar because the admission of defeat would spell political ruination for him at the hands of Crassus and Pompey.

Caswallon-Dingad then celebrated his victory with a feast at London, a pre-Roman city, where some hundred thousand farm animals, forty thousand wild animals (deer and boar), and innumerable poultry were eaten. Amazing as it may seem to sane men the British universities now preach a Roman victory and a British pre-Anglo-Saxon defeat.

Cynfelyn is interesting as his grave mound remained known and in 1922-24, at the same time that Leonard Woolley was digging down into the bowels of the great mausoleum of Dungi, the Emperor of Ur, this mound was excavated. As it was not foreign or alien this excavation of the Lexden Mound excited very little interest in Britain. As has been previously stated the 1922 Tutankhamun discovery of a total historical non-entity was overshadowing everything, and even Woolley was running a poor second in the media attention stakes. However, a votive area was discovered in the Lexden Mound, and this contained a metal table, models of

Chapter 3 - The Coming of Albyne

reclining rams and bulls, and glass balls, along with vessels and containers.

No one noticed that the votive equipment of King Dungi at Ur, and that of the British King Cynfelyn - Greidiol at the Lexden Mound were identical. It is not impossible that some people did notice, but thought it wiser to protect their academic careers and financial security by discreet silence.

The votive equipment found in King Cynfelyn's Lexden Tomb is kept on exhibition in Colchester Museum, and Wilson and Blackett propose that this points towards an identical religion and an origin of the Lloegrean British in the ancient high civilization of Syria. The mound itself is somewhat neglected and currently the local people appear to be unaware of its significance.

One of the other major items found in the Lexden Mound was a magnificent cameo medal of a lion bearing the effigy of the Emperor Augustus Caesar, whom Cynfelyn visited in Rome. This would have been Augustus's personal political gift to this British King, and it represents a major piece of evidence in the reconstruction of British History.

This reinstatement of native British History to displace the imported Greek-Roman secular, and the Hebrew religious histories, then has a fantastic development, for all the well-preserved records of the ancient British past are no longer 'inadmissible in court'. This means that there is available a considerable body of written records, which can be substantially supported and which again point unequivocally towards an ancient Syrian-Chaldean origin.

What has happened in the lunatic labyrinth of academia subsequent to the massacre of all ancient British History is even more incomprehensible, assuming that to be possible. Archaeology is said to begin where history ends. This dictum raises huge problems in Britain as tracing back history no longer ends in either 504BC or in 1600BC, but now is ordered to end around AD 426 with the arrival of Angles and Saxons. Armed with the advantage of ignorance the archaeologists have been charging around, quite oblivious of the fact that there is sound British history, and trampling it beyond recognition.

A volume written by Mr. T. D. Kendrick, an archaeologist at the British Museum, sums up matters appropriately. First, the archaeologists by 1925 were asserting that there were two ancient major invasions of Britain. First, there was a major invasion by an advanced culture of metal working people 'around 2000 BC', and sound chronology is not the archaeologists' forte. This archaeologically demonstrated early invasion would fit exactly with the British historical Albyne records of the arrival from Syria. This, however, is ignored and instead it is postulated, without evidence, that these people were Iberian. Then, amazingly, they are postulated as having their origin in North-West Africa, in the Sahara Desert. It seems that traces of the migration of the Garamantes from Lybia down to Nigeria, well proven in our late twentieth century, are being mistaken for those of British ancestors. Other views were of an arrival from the 'south west', which would of course be the mid-Atlantic.

Next, the archaeological community again correctly propose that there was a second major migration into Britain 'around 600 BC'. This approximation quite obviously corresponds with the arrival of Brutus and his British around 504 BC, again as both the Lloegrean English and Khumric Welsh records testify. This time the newcomers are labelled as 'Keltic'. Bizarre as it is, both the inward ancestral migrations detailed in our histories are confidently archaeologically proven, and then both are deliberately wrongly identified, given false origins, and misnamed.

There is much chatter about the La Tène iron-working culture, yet a trade route can run east to west and also west to east. By a stroke of good fortune, Alan Wilson and Baram Blackett were able to discover the major British iron-working site at a trial excavation in 1990. The surface appearance led them to think that they had a major ancient graveyard, but in 1995 a trial dig with expert help from the experienced Dewi Bowen (Clydach Vale) and Graham Oxlade (Tonyrefail), with Brian Davis, of Pontypridd, revealed a major ancient iron-working smelting site which had been used for countless centuries. Wilson and Blackett, with Richard Wyre, actually discovered the 'Place of the Mausoleum' later, at a different site.

Letters to CADW (Welsh Heritage), the National Museum of Wales, and the Tourist Board, referring to this iron-working site and the probable mausoleum, and offering some co-operation, predictably went unanswered. The archaeologists, having proved British ancient history to be correct, have then denied the fact that they have done so.

So finally, we arrive at the major issue, which has bedevilled everything from 597 AD onwards, the vexed question of British Druidism. Contrary to anxious Christian hopes and assertions British Druidism never really died out, and it was never lost, nor was it forgotten. It was in fact comprehensively recorded and re-recorded down the centuries and we still have it today. As a religious philosophy and a way of life it transcends the harsher and more primitive Christian religion. It is a far more profound and developed system of thought and philosophy, and some researchers believe it a more suitable way of life and religion for the British mind.

Chapter 3 - The Coming of Albyne

The preservation of Druidic thought and practice allows for a comparison to be made between this highly advanced British culture and the cultures of the people of the ancient Lloegrean and Khumric homelands. Many hundreds of ancient village and local customs and festivals can be traced back to Druidic survivals.

Historical evidence for its survival is extraordinary in its amount, and the commencement of publishing the ancient Khumric-Welsh records in AD 1800 undoubtedly contributed to the alarm amongst Edwin Guest and Bishop Stubbs and their adherents. Various facts, amongst a huge number, are the records of the initiation of a major Welsh Prince into the Druidic rites in AD 1156, the Scottish Church Commissioners forcing the ploughing of previously never tilled sacred Druidic land as late as 1678, and the seizure of the image of Darfell Gardam from the Diocese of St Asaph in Wales in AD 1538, where over six hundred offerings, including cattle, had been made. The image and the 'friar' were taken to Smithfield in London and burned. An annual sacrifice of a lame calf was made at St Buena's until these times. This of course to say nothing of the Druids of Pontypridd, reformed and practising in the early twentieth century.

Bulls were sacrificed in the parish of Gairloch in Ross-shire as late as 1649-78, according to the records of the Presbytery of Dingwall. In Cornwall there are still annual horse-ceremonies as at Padstow with the death of the Old Horse on the Eve, and rebirth of the new on May Day, and certainly in Maesteg in Glamorgan a group were still parading the Marie Lluyd decorated Horse skull in the late 1980s. There are many hundreds of these survivals including the well-known Ride of Lady Godiva in Coventry, which is a thinly disguised Ashtar ceremony. Best known of all is the winter fire-ceremony celebrated by all the British for three thousand, six hundred years. It was held on the 1st of November, but after the failure of Guy Fawkes to blow up the King, the Lords, and Parliament in AD 1604, the cunning politicians seized the chance to legitimise the rites, which they could not eliminate, and proclaimed that the fires were lit to celebrate the survival of the professional politicians on the 5th November; a likely story.

In North Wales young men leapt through the Winter bonfire flames 'to escape the black short tailed sow'. In Cornwall the Mid-summer bonfires were lit on June the 23rd starting from Carn Brea, and the young people leapt across the embers to drive off evil and bring good luck. This was disguised by simply transforming it into a pretend 'celebration' of the Eve of St John. Something more on this can be said later, but suffice it to say that most people only know what the enemies of Druidism have said about it. Druidism in fact bears no resemblance whatsoever to the popular notions of meaningless annual sun worship at Stonehenge, well-intended as this may be.

The British adopted some early apostolic Christian ideas in either AD 35 or 'the last year of Tiberius', AD 37. They believed in only one God and no trinity, and at that time so did all Christians, for the idea of the trinity came out of Egypt with Anasthasius the bishop of Alexandria and his followers, and was adopted at the Council of Nicea in AD 324.

Egypt had always had a trinity of Osiris, Isis, and Horus the son, who was also his father, Osiris. British Bishops attended this Council where Jesus the Nazarene was elected God by a narrow majority in the democratic process. They did not attend later Church Councils. Jesus the Nazarene was acceptable because of his willingness to be sacrificed, and so in Druid thought he had become 'eneidfaddau', and early Christianity in Britain was grafted onto the Druid system in a manner suitable to the British mind.

The early Welsh priesthood was then simply a continuation of the Druids. The three levels of Druids were first the Derwydd, the governor or reader, the elder experienced priest; second, the Bard, the recorder of the philosophy, the history, the religious rites, the births, deaths, and marriages, and the singer and propagator of all these things; and third the Ofydd, the novices and disciples of the Bards. So whilst the higher order became increasingly the specialised priesthood, the Bards continued their function of recording and propagating, and training the Ofydds, who would be the next generation of Bards. In the days of book writing, each Bard wrote 'his book', and in turn his Ofydd, when he became a Bard, wrote his own book, which mainly was a reiteration of his master's book with his own continuations.

This process of reproduction rolled on and on down the centuries, and so today we have the copies of copies of copies, many quite old, which preserve for us our own British ancestral philosophy and religion. This had begun to be published piecemeal in 1784 and perhaps earlier, and a comprehensive volume, *Barddas*, was published in 1858, containing the collected works of a number of notable Bards. As these ancient sages knew, life began in the oceans in the most primitive forms and gradually developed in ascending fashion down the millennia, before evolving into advanced mammals and finally man. In this they anticipated Darwin by several millennia. They held that neither time nor space were absolutes, and this thinking, that parallels the theory of relativity, has been remarked by other interested researchers. Abaris, who first taught the Greeks, was a Druidic instructor. That this advanced complex and indeed modern religion would have alarmed Christian fundamentalists in all eras is unquestionable. Druidism also supported and encouraged the advancement of knowledge and science, which they believed would enhance the development of the soul.

An immediate comparison made by Baram Blackett and Alan Wilson was that between the *Epic of Gilgamesh*, and the *King of Uruk*, which survives in five epic poems from ancient Sumerian literature. Two poems, *Gilgamesh and the Land of the Living*, and *The Death of Gilgamesh* have been noted to 'use language much like a lament for Ur-Nammu', the father of Dungi, 'Diocletian' of Ur who is of great interest.

Versions of these poetic epics were found written on clay tablets in the library of Ashurbanipal at Nineveh, and these match elementary themes in the Mediaeval Arthurian Romance Tales. These themes in these ancient Tablets appear to be those of *Y Seint Greal*.

Next there are *The Seven Tablets of Creation*, thought to be of Babylon, and found in the library of the Emperor Ashurbanipal of Assyria (died *c.* 626 BC) at Nineveh, now Kouyonjik. These stories again have distinct parallel themes with the British creation stories as preserved in the Four Branches of the Mabinogi ('Mabinogi' means 'Origins' or 'Genesis', whereas the incorrect 'Mabinogion' means 'Children's Tales'). By labelling the Mabinogi Tales as Mabinogion, or 'Children's Tales', the stories could be protected from the destructive paranoia of Christians. *The Seven Tablets of Creation*, recording the Babylonian creation epic, are now safe in the British Museum and have been published. Several other Mabinogi Tales, which are obviously Solar Stories, also appear to mirror the themes of T*he Seven Tablets of Creation* and other recovered Sumerian epics.

Anyone who has read *Y Seint Greal,* of 1106, will recall that after every two or three pages the narrative is interrupted and a sententious paragraph is inserted that incongruously attempts to explain the text into Christian dogma. This would be to avoid inevitable destruction by the servants of Rome.

In the same way much of the 'mystical' ancient poetry of Britain forms a record of initiation ceremonies into the ancient sacred secrets of the Druids, as has been detailed by several researchers and authors. At the end of the day, we still have the ancient and preserved lore of our ancestors. It perhaps needs to again be made clear that if the same levels of hostile criticism were made against them, then it would be necessary to throw out and reject the *Rig Veda*, the *Popul Vuh*, the *Avestia,* the *Cabala*, all Greek and Roman records, all the Hebrew records and holy scriptures, and much more.

The Philosophical Triads, the Moral Triads, the Religious Triads, and the Historical Triads are all available to us to draw ancient parallels. The Laws of the King Dyfnwal Moelmud (Donald the Bald), of around 420BC, are available, as are the Laws of *c.* AD 920, compiled by the Prince Blegwyryd, to compare tenets of jurisprudence. Reliable accounts of Bardic philosophy and lore are available in plenty.

The most important of many discoveries in Britain was the finding of three ancient ships in the mud of the Humber in 1937.

These were instantly labelled as 'Viking' ships and placed in a museum. Over fifty years passed and finally someone had the idea to Radio Carbon 14 test these ships' timbers. The result was a date of around 1600 BC, with a plus or minus possibility of a few centuries either way. This unmistakeably places these vessels into the era of the Albyne invasion from ancient Chaldean Syria. This posed no problems for the academics and a young lady wrote a book, in which she somewhat absurdly claimed that the ships were of Egyptian provenance. Nothing changes

Chapter Four

The Discovery of a Mystery

Ask any British person about ancient history or ancient archaeological discoveries, and with very few exceptions they will automatically refer to foreign faraway places. In fact, almost anywhere and everywhere will be the subject before Britain. The British have been so educated as to cause them unthinkingly to look for excellence outside the boundaries of their own island. They impute the source of their own palladia to foreign unconnected origins.

The romance of distance has played havoc with our sense of native integrity and identity. Possibly the distant East appears more glamorous than the gentler British environment. Perhaps the conventional academic bias has inclined the nation to assume that it is the East which is the mother of all mysteries. That only the civilizations of ancient Egypt, Akkad and Sumer, Chaldean Babylonia, or the more distant India and China, were the cradles, and world originators, of the most profound religious and moral philosophy. Yet it is in Britain where the great storehouse of ancient record and knowledge is.

A damp, wet, windy street in a tired worn-out area of a Welsh city, on a cold grey February day, is not the popular conception of the start point of an Odyssey-like adventure into the dim and distant past. A second-hand antiquarian bookshop on the rounded corner of a block of dilapidated buildings, scheduled for demolition, has nothing of the aura and overtones of stately scholastic pomp associated with a great library or museum. This, however, is how the story began.

With the rain clattering down hard on the windows outside, Alan Wilson and Baram Blackett had spent an hour checking through the Welsh and Historical antiquarian sections of the quite extensive bookshelves. February of 1982 marked the seventh year of a project that had begun as an investigation into the detailed and well-recorded (but little publicised) ancient histories of South East Wales. Much had been published in the eighteenth and nineteenth centuries, and old books of these periods frequently contained entire reproductions of venerable manuscripts, with numbers of references leading to other valuable sources. The Hayes Bookshop was an excellent place to find the odd volume which held the one or two vital little bits of information which went towards filling in yet another part of the spreading jigsaw-puzzle of the past.

A faded folder of simple brown wrapping-paper, lodged between books, seemed to be strangely out of place amongst the rows of heavy embossed leather-bound volumes. The rows of expensive embossed patterned leather spines, most with gilt set and gleaming, and with impressed titles were the more expensive items in the shop. The practice of our great-great-grandparents of publishing 'important subjects' in expensive, well-presented volumes of a handsome and decorative nature sometimes made obtaining information expensive. So just why was a thin packet made of brown paper there between bulky imposing books?

A hundred years ago ancient manuscripts were published complete in the original Welsh or Latin, often along with English translations. Today the tendency is to publish books 'about Manuscripts', giving opinions, ideas, and theories, with a few selected quotations about the original texts.

A curious Baram Blackett prised out the thin paper packet from between two large bulky books, and carefully opened it up. There were ten sheets of paper inside the worn old paper folder. These were loose, but in good condition. As with the majority of old books these sheets of paper had clearly been little disturbed or read. Both Alan and Baram always carried small sharp penknives as it was frequently necessary to cut apart the still joined pages of books which were over a hundred years old, where the folding, cutting, and binding process originally employed had failed to do so. Books of a hundred or two hundred years old, which no one had ever opened or read, littered the libraries and antiquarian bookstores.

The contents of the folder detailed a paper which had been presented and read to a meeting of antiquarians in London in 1769.

'An account of some remains of Roman and other Antiquities in the county of Brecknock, in South Wales, by John Strange Esquire.'

'In a letter to the President, Council, and Fellows, of the Society of Antiquarians." Read April 13 and 29, 1769.'

Blackett and Wilson were tempted to replace the folder after a few moments. The essay began with the usual scholastic obsession with the Romans, which dulls the brain and clouds the vision, and which of course distorts all British records.

There was however something else towards the end of these papers, set down clearly as a form of afterthought, or to try to make up for the obvious

Chapter 4 - The Discovery of a Mystery

disappointment at finding little or nothing Roman. The diatribe on the sad scarcity of Roman walls, Roman coins, Roman camps, Roman roads, and even Roman bricks, lamented this dearth of things Roman. The frustration of John Strange seeking evidence of his adopted Roman ancestors is very clear. On the last page of his account, he stated-

> 'Having nothing further to observe relative to the Romans in Brecknockshire, give me leave by way of a supplement to add some account of yet another remain I met with in Llandevailog church yard.'

With John Strange disappointed with the scanty Roman evidences of this alien empire in Britain, and which only held brief sway for intermittent periods in this region of the powerful people of Essyllwg - the 'Silures', the British who have occupied the land for some three thousand six hundred years appear to be about to get an unexpected mention. The Invisible Kingdom might be exposed to public notice for one brief moment. Needless to say, John Strange totally fluffed it.

Strange proceeded to describe an extraordinary memorial stone. He also included a quite accurate drawing of the stone, and it was this that persuaded Wilson and Blackett to buy these ten sheets of paper. Wales being colonial Wales, there was no guarantee that the ancient stone was still where John Strange saw it in 1769. In fact, there was no guarantee that it still existed. The wholesale tearing down of ancient Welsh churches in the vast rebuilding programmes of the nineteenth century had resulted in the disappearance and destruction of many ancient inscribed stones of huge cultural and historical value. Some were mutilated, others were cut up to be used as doorsteps, as window sills, or simply as building blocks, and some - very well recorded - simply disappeared.

When a new English vicar was appointed to St Illtyd's at Llan-Illtyd-fawr, or Llantwit Major, in the mid-nineteenth century, he worked mightily to persuade the church council to break up and destroy the marvellous collection of sixth- and seventh-century royal memorial stones. These include the stone of King Ithael, which names his father King Arthmael-Iron Bear, or Arthur II, and St Illtyd, Arthur II's first cousin, and the stones of King Hywel and King Rhys. This planned destruction was only prevented by huge local outcry, all of which is well recorded. Christianity adopted in AD 35-37 had to give way to Austin (Augustine) arriving in Anglo-Saxondom in AD 579, some five hundred and sixty years later.

The stone drawn by John Strange was unknown to Wilson and Blackett at the time they bought his papers describing it. The stone of St Cattwg had been broken up with sledge hammers around 1850, the stone of Constantine son of Magnus

Maximus had disappeared, the famous Gwenora stone of Gwenhwyfar, the wife of Arthur II ap King Meurig ap King Tewdrig, had vanished from Llan-iltern, and so on. Llan-ail-teyrn is 'the holy estate of the alternative monarch', or The Viceroy.

After the usual polite haggling and feigned indifference, four notes changed hands, and the papers of John Strange changed owners. An eyewitness account of a memorial stone, and its precise location over two hundred years ago, might be very valuable information. In this case, it was to be of particular interest.

'There is a flat monumental stone four inches thick, seven feet long, and ten inches wide in the middle, being contracted nearly an inch towards the top and the bottom, where likewise it appears to have been broken. This stone was, I presume, originally sepulchral, but at present serves to cover a low wall contiguous to the outside South wall of the church.'

The drawing accompanying this statement shows the figure, which is clearly that of a king carrying a sword and sceptre.

John Strange realized that the effigy was probably that of a king:

'Upon the upper part is carved in low relief, a rude unpolished figure, representing perhaps, some King, or military chief, arrayed with a tunic, holding a sceptre, sword or some other instrument in each hand.

'Over his head is a cross; and under his feet is an inscription; the characters of which are remarkably plain, exclusive of their being a little disfigured by a fracture in the stone. What is the meaning of this inscription is not easy to determine, as the last letter appears reversed, and some of the others are different from any I can find in British characters.'

As a rare English visitor to 'darkest Wales, John Strange had stumbled upon what was to him a mystery. A large stone bearing the effigy of a King, an inscription to him in an unknown alphabet, and a large representation of a floral cross. His confusion is clear, for although he did not know the alphabet, he was prepared to state that the last letter is reversed. Then, with what Alan Wilson sees as truly incredible illogic, John Strange proceeded to guess that this was the stone of a Christian King in Wales that was that of a Danish-Viking!

Automatically, the inscribed stone of a King in Ireland or Scotland would be thought to be that of an Irish, or Pict, or Scots King. Equally, a royal stone in Assyria is usually Assyrian, and the same applies to Egypt, China, Japan, and anywhere else.

Chapter 4 - The Discovery of a Mystery

Vikings were not Christians, and the presence of a large floral cross on the stone should have told these London 'antiquarians' something. A few sporadic Viking raids are recorded in Wales, but these were limited, and the unpleasant experience of their whole army being trapped on Echni Island (now misnamed Flat Holm) in Cardiff Bay appears to have taught them something. So, a Viking Christian King in the most powerful of the ancient British Kingdoms is an exercise in total absurdity.

The fact that South East Wales-Morganwg was the heartland of the ancient British Coelbren alphabet, and there was an inscription on the stone was apparently also lost on John Strange. In fact, after making his Danish-Viking guess Strange then proceeded to totally disprove it himself.

> 'The whole (except a small fragment broken on one side) is in exceedingly good preservation, although it was probably the workmanship of the fifth or sixth century.'

This now requires a complete and monumental re-writing of all British early history to accommodate a Danish-Viking Christian King in the most powerful Kingdom in Britain in the 500BC to AD700 era.

This is detailed to illustrate the massive gulf existing between Khumric-Wales and England, and the near absolute ignorance in England of ancient British History held in the Khumric manuscript sources that were not available to the English in 1769. Yet the English were busily re-writing the history of Britain at that same time, armed with the major advantage of knowing only some 5-10 % of the evidence. Anything found in Wales was henceforth routinely and alternatively labelled as Roman, Irish, Greek, Egyptian, Viking, or anything, just as long as it is not Welsh.

An illustration of this is the records of the sub-king Gwynlliw of the Newport, Gwent, area. He had fast raiding-vessels, warships which were kept in the Ebbw and Usk estuaries below his fortress. When the Newport docks were being constructed in 1878 a large ancient ship was found intact fifteen feet down in the mud in the former course of the river Ebbw, and it clearly was an ancient warship. Logic might demand that this was one of Gwynlliw's ships, but politics demanded that it be immediately labelled as 'Viking'.

It was 1982, and the extent of the British-Khumric historical catastrophe had not yet been fully appreciated by Alan Wilson and Baram Blackett. So, outside the Hayes bookshop in the now drizzling misty rain, with the early evening traffic of homeward-bound shoppers and workers beginning to fill the roads with squelching blurred cars and yellowed headlights, they made their way back to their car. They had been awakened to a remarkable situation, for Alan still had the memory of the story of Mary Thomas and her mysterious hook, and they knew clear that there were records of the ancient British Coelbren alphabet. They also knew that they had seen the same script on ancient stones in Scotland, England, and Wales. Alan Wilson was also certain that he had seen the same alphabet on Etruscan artefacts in Italy.

All enquiries concerning the Khumric Coelbren alphabet had been routinely met with the childish bleat of 'Iolo Morganwg was a forger'. The indifference and the complete uninterest exhibited towards ancient native British memorials by academics was very well known. John Strange says it in his first paragraph:

> 'It seems that at present generally received amongst the learned that the Principality of Wales supplies very few remains of Roman antiquities. Some of the inscriptions collected by Camden have scarcely been admitted as genuine by succeeding antiquaries.'

Not surprising if these were native British inscriptions. The salient point is that only Roman remains were being sought, and as the Romans did not get a foothold in Wales until AD74 and were driven out by King Baram-Bonassus in AD80-84, as their own records attest, and returned by treaty with Hadrian in AD121, we can see why they left few remains. In fact, Roman interference in Wales thereafter was limited to very brief interludes as can be shown in detail. If it is taken into account that John Strange refers to the Welsh Kingdom as 'the Principality', and confuses Wales with Gwynedd, then the scale of the problem becomes evident.

The questions buzzing around in the minds of Wilson and Blackett as they drove homewards in the evening gloom of February 1982 were many. Why had no one else investigated this strange stone and its inscription? Just how many other such inscribed stones were there? Why not examine the manuscripts which exhibited the alphabet, and make comparisons? Logic however plays no part in unravelling the past in Wales, or for that matter in several other parts of Britain.

The logical approach to this stone was to examine the inscription and to see if it could be deciphered. If it could, this would then prove that the much-abused British Coelbren alphabet was genuine as stated by Julius Caesar, Ammianus Marcellinus, and others. As the inscription represented a king then he should be named. This name could then be sought in the royal genealogies - the Morganwg King Lists. The name of the church needed to be checked as well, as this might give meaningful information.

Chapter 4 - The Discovery of a Mystery

There are over four hundred Dark Age inscribed stones in Wales. Most are in Latin, often ungrammatical, but not all; and some are mixed Latin and British. The supreme importance of these stones is that whilst it is possible to write on paper, vellum, or parchment, it is also possible to write on wood by painting or cutting, as ancient Egyptian coffins show. It is also possible to write in mud tablets and to bake the tablet, and equally it is possible to paint records on stone, or to carve records in stone. Without records in stone, or baked mud, very little would be known of the ancient civilizations of Assyria, Babylonia, Egypt, and others.

In spite of this British academics exhibit a strange muddled thinking on the very rare occasions that they attempt to research British history. Over-confident statements are made that there are no contemporary ancient British records. Yet the contemporary inscribed stones are written records. What is more, these contemporary stone records match with the traditional written historical records and even the imperishable folklore.

Even as they made their journey towards home Alan and Baram realized that if they entered this door which had opened up before them, and delved into this matter, then they would face tremendous opposition from the massed *status quo* ranks of academia. So, stopping and starting in the thickening traffic, and in the gathering gloom, with the streetlights blurred in the rain and people hurrying home in the wet dark of a February night, a journey began. A journey back through the dim mists of long-lost times and far away across thousands of miles.

The Proposition and the Problem

Wilson and Blackett had in their previous researches begun to accept that the much derided and abused British historical records were very accurate and correct. When faced with an ancient alphabet, it seemed logical to propose that the alphabet related to the original language of the British people. Whilst the original Hebrew was lost, the Jewish people still speak the same language and use the same script as did their ancestors some two thousand years ago, despite the disadvantage of being dispersed into many strange countries. The British, in stark contrast, have stayed put, defending their western homeland since their two migrations of three thousand six hundred and two thousand five hundred years ago. Consequently, their language has enjoyed much greater advantages of stability and preservation.

If the British used the ancient tongues spoken by their ancestors in distant lands of origin, before they crossed the seas to arrive in Britain, then those languages should be traceable back into the ancient British fatherlands. The

British and other histories nominate those ancient fatherlands, and therefore the search can be easily directed into the correct areas.

Wilson and Blackett visited the Llandefaelog church in Breconshire on a quiet sunny day and found that the seven-foot stone was safely secured with heavy spikes to the interior wall in the dark of the church tower. The missing piece reported by John Strange in 1769 had been found and replaced and the stone now stood upright and intact. Llandefaelog appears to mean 'the Holy Estate of the Shepherd', and this is unusual as most ancient Welsh churches are named for saints and founders. The location is a quiet one and a few vehicles passed almost unheard along the road outside as Alan and Baram examined the stone. There was no doubt that John Strange had drawn a very good likeness in 1769. The fact that he produced a public record of it, accurately drawn in 1769, meant that there was unquestionable evidence of an ancient British stone inscribed in Coelbren long before Edward Williams was alleged to have forged the British Coelbren alphabet in *c.* 1800. The Llandefaelog stone itself reeks of huge antiquity.

The braying accusations of Griffith John Williams that everything was forged by Iolo collapsed immediately, and were to be silenced forever from that moment onwards. The deliberate sabotage and demolition of all the Glamorgan-Gwent histories which had in fact reached a new climax with astonishing depths of venom in the 1980s was itself the fraud, and this one stone proves it.

There is something very special about actually examining an ancient stone, a certain magic in touching it, and feeling it, and seeing it from all angles. There is a world of difference from looking at a photograph. It was difficult to photograph the stone in the gloom of the tower, and finally Alan and Baram made a copy of the inscription and sat down in the rear pew of the silent, still church to attempt a decipherment.

They took each letter singly and matched it with the Coelbren letter from the Coelbren alphabet preserved by Llewellyn Sion around 1560 and copied by Edward Williams, 'Iolo', around two hundred and fifty years later. Letter by letter they matched the letters of the stone inscription with the manuscript Coelbren, and then one at a time they wrote beneath each Coelbren letter the modern alphabetic equivalent as indicated in the ciphers, and the message unfolded before their eyes. The result was breath-taking, for a coherent statement emerged.

NGH - O - R - T - HW - TH - HW -NH   DE - E - O - LL.
GORTHWFWN   DEOLL.

Chapter 4 - The Discovery of a Mystery

There was almost a sense of disbelief and a scramble to check as the word 'deol' which means 'exile', and 'deolwr' for 'exiled (person)', is close to 'rheol', meaning 'to rule', and 'rheolwr' for 'ruler'. But the inscription clearly stated 'Gorddwfwn the Exile', not 'Gorddwfwn the Ruler'.

The much abused *Genealogy of King Iestyn ap Gwrgan* does in fact name a British ancestral king of around AD 200 as Gorddyfwyn. The entry reads:

46- 'Gorddyfwn ab Gorwg a fu frenin gwallcofus iawn ag am hynny a drowyd allan or frenhiniaeth, ai frawd a gafodd ei le a elwid Rhun.'

46- 'Gorddyfwn the son of Gorwg was a turbulently mad king; for which reason he was deposed, and his brother Rhun placed in his stead.'

It would appear that there was a King Gorddyfwn around two hundred years after Christianity arrived in Britain in AD 35-37, which would account for the floral cross carved large upon the stone. The sword and sceptre are the ancient symbols of royalty. This one stone indicates very clearly that the historical records are accurate and can be trusted, and that the ancient alphabet is genuine. The unfounded theory that the Romans held some form of complete domination over Britain, which is many times disproved in British and Roman records, also goes up in smoke. Other conclusive evidence that the British kings continued right through the alleged unhistorical 'Roman' period is also further supported.

These Khumric kings are listed in a number of manuscript sources including the Harleian MSS 4010 and 4181, and were published in several histories before Iolo copied the records.

As the kings went on right through the alleged 'Roman' period, then the national integrity and language survived, and if the language survived then so also the alphabet and culture survived. The fact that the ciphers preserved by Llewellyn Sion worked accurately to decipher this Gorddwfyn Stone was a mentally staggering experience for Alan and Baram. It clearly meant that there was a certainty that other ancient, similarly inscribed stones could also be deciphered and translated. They now had an immensely powerful tool in their hands, and no one else was aware of it. In 1982, they had not in fact realised the full extent of the hostility towards, and the abandonment of, almost all British history, and in particular the South East Wales histories.

There was one problem with the Llandefaelog Stone. In their usual 'check everything' routine, Baram and Alan checked the names of King Gorddwfyn and his father Gorwg. A problem, which had perplexed them for some time, was that there appeared to be too many kings crowding the period from around AD 170-200. Further to this, neither Gorddwfyn nor Gorwg appeared to be normal names, and this was something that they were to encounter time and again in their researches. Gorwg does in fact appears to be the modern 'gorwr', meaning 'great-grandson', whilst 'gorddwfyn' means 'the upper reaches of a river', or succinctly 'a flowing stream'. This would render Gorddwfyn the Exile ap Gorwg as 'the great-grandson of the flowing stream in exile'.

Alan Wilson had seen similar Etruscan writings in Italy, and was convinced that the alphabet could be traced back along an ancestral trail, and so he and Baram began to formulate and construct a project plan to deal with this extraordinary situation. No support would be forthcoming in Britain, as it was obvious that far too many fragile institutional reputations would be at risk. So the plan had to be simple and effective.

1- There is a well-known tradition that the Khumry were the Ten Tribes of Israel who were transported from their ancient Palestine homelands by the Assyrian Emperor Tiglathpileser III around 740-720 BC. This would account for some scholarly opinions of similarities between the Khumric-Welsh Language and ancient Hebrew.

2- This proposition, if followed, would require tracing a movement of these people from Palestine, to Armenia or Upper Assyria, and then westwards across to western Asia Minor between roughly 740 to 650 BC.

3- Herodotus records that a nation split in two in ancient Phrygia, in Asia Minor, around 650 BC. Half sailed for Italy and almost certainly founded the Etruscan or Tuscan league of twelve cities. Subsequently other leagues of twelve cities were founded; and always twelve. Phrygia was an area of variously described size in antiquity, sometimes huge, presumably through conquest, and other times shrunken small. It was possible that the British Coelbren alphabet might be found in Italian Etruria and in Western Turkey.

4- The ancient British records stated firmly that the second great migration came in a fleet sailing from Western Asia Minor, and that these people were the remnant half of the nation left behind when Aeneas led the other half to Italy around 650 BC, to build the village settlements of Romulus into a city. It was possible that Italian Museums might also have evidence of the British alphabet. As Pliny recorded that the Etruscans set up colonies in Rhaetia, Switzerland might be another location of the alphabet.

Chapter 4 - The Discovery of a Mystery

5-   The key lay in the fact that Virgil and Horace, in Rome *c.* 50 BC, both placed the Trojan War around 650 BC. This date of 650 BC was vigorously supported by the Jewish historian Flavius Josephus, who was writing around AD 80, and who was derisive of the Greek claims of ancient dates. Significantly none of the contemporaries of Virgil, Horace, or Flavius Josephus argued against the 650 BC dating, and most of the great libraries of the ancient world were still then available.

6-   Next, the histories of the kingdom of the Franks also supports a Trojan War of around 650 BC, with the surviving king lists recording a descent from Antenor of Troy. These genealogies only provide a number of names sufficient to stretch back to around 650 BC. This Frankish list of kings then matches the British list, which we know as *The Genealogy of Iestyn ap Gwrgan*, and is preserved in several other ancient manuscript sources. These trace descent from Aeneas, son of Anchises of Troy, and again list only a sufficient number of kings which might provide a dating of around 650 BC for the Trojan War. The Frank records list two marriages between Frankish kings and British princesses, and these serve to link and match the dynastic chronologies.

7-   The histories record Brutus gathering the people from Western Asia Minor in the Trojan areas, and assembling them on an island named Legotia. So, both the mainland and the Aegean islands might hold evidence, in the form of inscriptions.

8-   The fleets of Brutus are recorded as stopping in Iberia, where three advance groups of related peoples had gone ahead of the main body of the people. Therefore, Spain might also contain relics of the ancient Coelbren alphabet.

9-   With the arrival of the people in Britain under Brutus at some time around 500 BC there was the possibility of the ancient British alphabet being found in Lloegres (now England), in Wales, and in Scotland.

King Arthur Conspiracy - Wilson & Blackett

Gorddyfwn or The Cross of Briamail (Llandefaelog)

Chapter 4 - The Discovery of a Mystery

Extract from *THE ANCIENT BARDS OF BRITAIN (sometimes called druids)* By D. Delta Evans ("Dewi Hiraddug") - 1906

British Coelbren Inscriptions

Illustration 4-1: Gorddwfwn the Exile stone - Llandefaelog dating around AD 200

Ceolbren	¥ ◊ ┌ ↕ ◊ ⊤⊓ ◊ ┌┐	▷L◊ 4·ᛉ
Intent	NG O R T HW TH HW NH	DE E O LL
Khumric	GORTH (H) WF (H) WM	DEOLL
English	Gorddwfwn the	Exile

Gorthwfwn-Gorddwfwn the Exile is listed in Glamorgan King Lists as being of around AD 200. This inscribed stone was identified as being ancient when it was sketched by John Strange of London in 1769. It is immediately clear that the scandalous accusation made by Griffith John Williams that the the Coelbren alphabet did not exist before 1800 and that it was a forgery perpetrated by Edward Williams – Iolo Morganwg was a total and appalling lie, no matter how welcome this allegation was to the London Establishment.

Illustration 4-2: Stone of Gwlffert at Llangorse Church dating around AD 900

Coelbren / Latin	HIC IACIT GL3LЬRD		FILIVS	VꞶIVIRK
Intent	HIC IACIT G RD		FILIUS	IVI
Khumric / Latin	HIC IACIT GWIDDERTD		FILIUS	ENIWIOSL
English	here is cast down Gwlffert		son of	Enwystyl

Illustration 4-3: Inscription on the Llandefaelog Font

Coelbren / Latin	ЧIV6IΛ1		9IV6IΛ↑
Intent	S I W DD I A T	or	S I U DD I A T
Khumric / Latin	Sywydd		Syweddyd
English	Star Knowledge		an Astrologer

Illustration 4-4: The inscription on a Brecon Font.

Coelbren / Latin Intent:	CATHACVS HIC IACIT FILVS TESERN ACVS
Khumric/ Latin English:	Cathacus is here cast down the son of Teithrin the Subtle

King Teithrin the Subtle was a great-grandson of Magnus Maximus, and a grandson of King Arthur I. He was the father of King Teithfallt-Theodosius who was the great-grandfather of King Arthur II. So this is an important inscription. Cathacus would be the Saint Cattwg Doeth who is often confused with St Cadoc son of Gwynlliw.

Chapter 4 - The Discovery of a Mystery

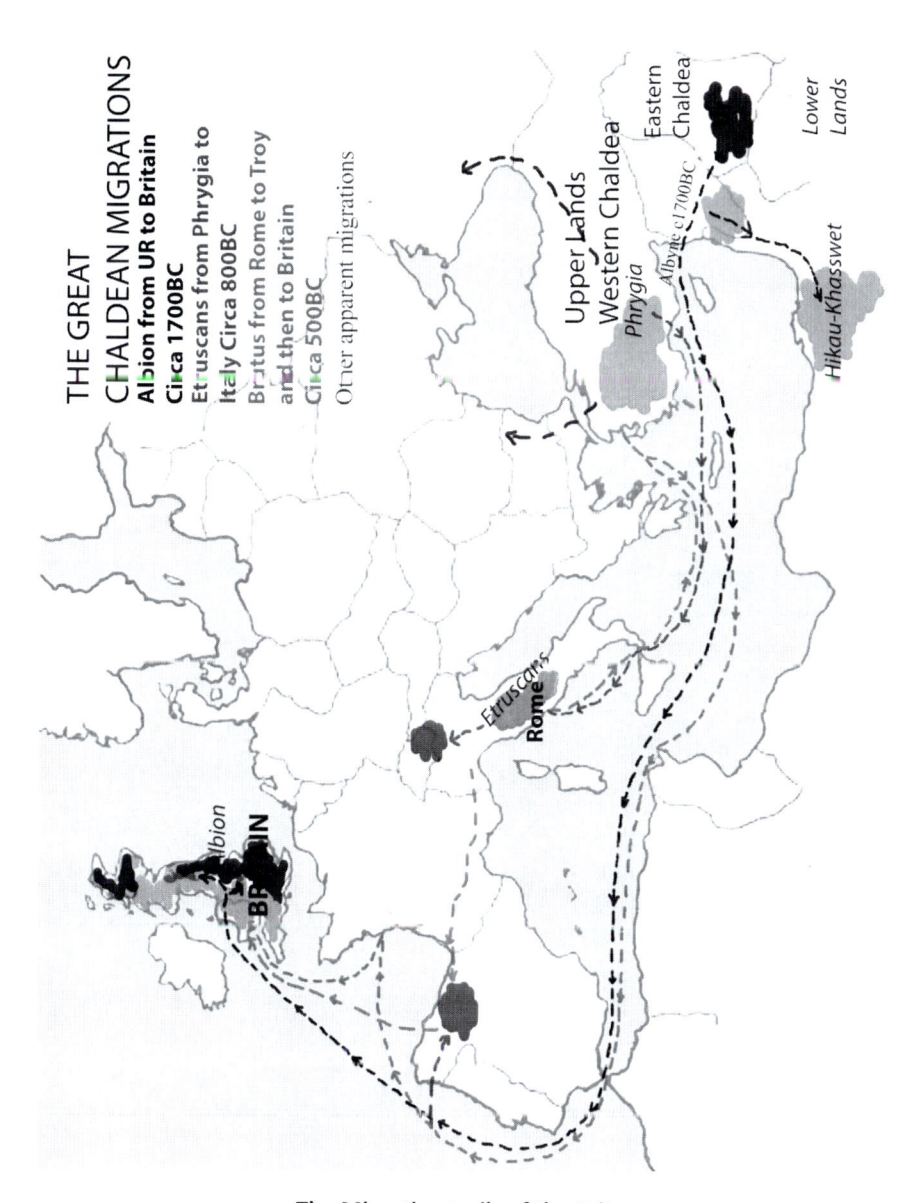

THE GREAT CHALDEAN MIGRATIONS
Albion from UR to Britain Circa 1700BC
Etruscans from Phrygia to Italy Circa 800BC
Brutus from Rome to Troy and then to Britain Circa 500BC
Other apparent migrations

The Migration trails of the Britons

The hypothesis to be investigated was simple. Are there inscribed stones or baked clay tablets, or whatever, which carry the ancient British Coelbren alphabet still surviving or discovered along these historical migration routes? If British history is correct and accurate, then the same alphabet should be found not only in Britain, but also back in time and distance eastwards along the migration trails. The British should logically have been speaking and writing in their same ancient language as they passed along these routes. If the alphabet was found inscribed back along the migration routes, then it should be possible to read these ancient inscriptions directly into Khumric.

Julius Caesar had identified the British alphabet as being similar to that of the Greek, and Ammianus Marcellinus went further and made the same correlation and added that the Greeks got the alphabet from the British. This pointed clearly to an ancient British presence in Western Asia Minor as 'next-door neighbours' to the Greeks. The Khumry had preserved their language in Western Britain, whilst it might have died out in their distant ancient fatherlands, swamped in the eddies and floods of great population movements and invasions. But inscribed stones cut in dim, forgotten ancestral times would still carry messages set down in the same ancient language.

Alan Wilson still remembered the story of Mary Thomas and her ancient book, and his grave doubts about the integrity of the theories of university employees had been reinforced by hearing some vague reports about American inscriptions. The proposed project plan was straightforward enough, and it would either work, and produce results, or it would not. There was the usual problem of lack of time and funds. No support would be forthcoming from any sponsorship sources in Wales as the open hostility of academic and other groups was already violently apparent.

It was however only a matter of a few short weeks before Baram Blackett discovered and purchased a book written in 1846 by John Williams of Oxford, from the same Hayes Antiquarian Bookshop. There, amongst the many quite well-researched records mentioned, John Williams exhibited the complete Coelbren alphabet and the ciphers as preserved by Llewellyn Sion and re-copied by Edward Williams. Below the exhibit of the alphabet was a most remarkable statement:

> 'Is it not a little remarkable, that the above (Alphabet) comprises with four or five exceptions, all the old Etruscan and Pelasgic letters which were probably little different from the Greek characters used in the time of Caesar.'

There then follows a note referring the whole matter to William Owen's volume

Chapter 4 - The Discovery of a Mystery

titled *Bardism*.

So, within weeks Blackett and Wilson had a voice from 1846 telling them that the British Coelbren alphabet was virtually identical with the Etruscan alphabet. The same voice was stating that this near-identicality extended to the 'Pelasgian' alphabet, as the ancient stroke alphabet found in Western Asia Minor had been designated by confused archaeologists. This notation was the first clue that the British and the Etruscans, who both migrated from Phrygian Asia Minor, might have a common language.

Soon afterwards Michael Blackett, the brother of Baram, bought a book by D. Delta Evans published in 1906, and titled *The Ancient Bards of Britain*. On pages 155, 156, and 157, the ancient British alphabet, along with its ciphers, is printed, together with an additional list of variant symbols which were sometimes used.

Edward Williams – 'Iolo Morganwg' had also published the same alphabets, and it was some years later, whilst he was researching in the Cardiff manuscript collection, that Brian Davies found Iolo had also handwritten recorded the British, Etruscan, and Pelasgian identicalities in 1793-4. It must have taken some courage for John Williams to publish what he did at the same time that the bullying Edwin Guest and the strident Bishop Stubbs were dominating the scenes at Cambridge and Oxford Universities, and preaching the new doctrines of Anglo-Saxonism.

Edward Williams – 'Iolo' (pronounced 'Yolo') - noted the ancient links in 1794, and William Owen published this in *Bardism*, then John Williams published this in 1846, and J. Williams ab Ithel published the information comprehensively and in detail in *Barddas* in 1862, and D. Delta Evans also published it in 1906, and yet no one did anything. The Khumric *Triads* unmistakeably link the Coelbren alphabet to the Brutus invasion and to Aedd Mawr-Anchises the Great. No one took an Etruscan-Italian inscription, or a Trojan 'Pelasgian' inscription, or even a British inscription, and attempted to decipher it. With ancient Khumric inscribed stones being broken up and simply disappearing, and the old churches being ruthlessly demolished wholesale to be replaced with new, and the huge all-powerful rampant English Empire inflating the national ego, the nineteenth century was probably not the time to make waves.

The fact that the South East Wales records firmly indicate ancient chronologies, which differ from those favoured by academia, appears to have been sufficient cause to reject them out of hand. These British records placed the Trojan War around 650 BC as did the Romans in Virgil and Horace, the Jews through Flavius Josephus, and the History of the Franks. The fact that these records did not conform with the ludicrous and totally unhistorical blunders and absurdities of Greek mathematicians was in itself an excuse to dismiss them as not worthy of investigation. It did not occur to any academic who researched the Trojan War that the Greeks were chronologically wrong, and that the Romans, the Jews, the Franks, and the British, were all collectively correct. As can be demonstrated absolutely and in detail, the Trojan War did take place around 650 BC, and the evidence was to emerge from these investigations.

Prior to 1982, Alan Wilson and Baram Blackett had attempted to research the histories whilst avoiding anything connected with Edward Williams-Iolo Morganwg. The stridently aggressive allegations constantly made on all sides alleging monstrous forgeries had caused them to be very cautious. They soon discovered that all of those who shouted the allegations so dismissively did not have the slightest clue of what they were actually stating or why. They were simply repeating a meaningless chant.

Looking for the Alphabet

There was an obvious temptation on the part of Alan Wilson and Baram Blackett immediately to seek out stones in Britain which might carry inscriptions in Coelbren. It was an immediate thought that there might be mixed Latin and Coelbren lettering on stones. Whilst they did in fact scan through the volumes where the ancient stones had been photographed and catalogued, they first decided to review the literature on the British Alphabet.

Most British people are instantly familiar with the symbol of the Broad Arrow, /|\ that the Khumry call the Awen. They are however generally unaware that the Broad Arrow is the British Druidic Symbol of the ancient Coelbren alphabet. The alphabet was designed to be cut into wooden sticks or rods using knives or small axes, and so every letter was made from a combination of the three strokes of the Broad Arrow.

English Kings actually adopted the Druidic Awen /|\ Broad Arrow as the royal cipher as early as Richard II (1377-1399). The symbol appears on state documents, it is carved into ancient church pews, and into table tombs. Every state-owned castle, jail, or fort had the Broad Arrow symbol carved into a gate-stone. All army cannons, and indeed all military equipment of every kind, were marked with the Broad Arrow /|\. In 1994, when Alan Wilson was down at Milford Haven with Professor Lee and Dr Joy Pennington from Kentucky, he mentioned this, and a sceptical Lee walked over to a nearby two hundred-years'- old cannon and was surprised to see a very clear Broad Arrow near the firing hole. Right up

Chapter 4 - The Discovery of a Mystery

until our own modern times all government buildings, bridges, and any other property were clearly marked with the /|\ Broad Arrow. All prisoners in British jails wore uniforms marked all over with the Broad Arrow symbol, as did the poor wretches transported to Australia for trivial offences - a motif beloved of cartoonists.

There are several records which tell of the origin of the alphabet, and perhaps one summary statement will be sufficient in the intent of this volume. In the opening lines of Barddas the rhetorical question is asked –

'Pray tell me who was the first that made a letter?'

And this is answered:

'Einiged Gawr (of the Shout), son of Huon (Hu), son of Alser, son of Javen, son of Japheth, son of Noah the aged, after the death of his father, for the purpose of preserving a memorial of what he did, and his praiseworthy actions, warranted in respect of credibility and information. And because it was on wood that such belief was first placed, both the letters, and what they were inscribed on, were called Coelbren.'

The word Coelbren is explained as 'Wood of Credibility'. 'Alser' is usually explained as Elishah as in Genesis 10:4. Hu Gadarn (Huon), meaning 'bold and mighty', is credited as leading the first great migration of the Khumry into Britain, and British chronology in common with other ancient chronology placed the Flood and therefore Noah around 2150 BC. Whether Hu Gadarn is connected with the Albyne migration is not clear. For example:

'According to the calculation of Constantine Manasses, the kingdom of Egypt lasted 1,663 years from its beginning under Misraim the son of Ham, 2188 BC to the conquest of Cambyses, 525 BC.'

The three strokes of the Broad Arrow /|\ are credited to Menw the aged son of Menwyd, which is Intellect the son of Mind. These three strokes are said to mean the letters I O U, which is the Secret Name of God. The rays of the sun slanting down through the clouds are the origin of the three strokes and the holy name. Other records attribute the origin of writing to Adam, or to Seth the third son of Adam. Einigan Gawr, identified as Elishah, took the three rays and the three shouts of Menw, and from these were formed the first three letters and the basic alphabet symbols.

At first there were only ten letters (in some records thirteen), and these were used in combination to make the required sounds. Then the number was expanded to sixteen letters (thirteen in some records and then sixteen), eliminating many clumsy combinations, and this was followed by a further addition of two more letters making eighteen. It was not until the time of the bard Talhaiarn that the alphabet was further expanded to twenty-four letters. Finally, there were thirty-eight letters for cut writing on wood, but only twenty-four in written form in black and white. Whole books have been written on the detail of all this.

The system of Druids, Bards, and Ovates was then established in the time of Dyfnwal Moelmud (Donald the Bald, the great law maker), son of Dyfnfarth, son of Prydain son of Aedd Mawr (Anchises of Troy), probably around 470 BC.

The allegation that the Broad Arrow, and the alphabet emanating from it, was the result of an unproven forgery around 1800 should never ever have been tolerated, if only because lists of ancient writers who alluded to the Coelbren have been many times published in modern times. This is a small selection:

1- Taliesin, c. 520 – 590
I am the depository of song,
I am a reader,
I love the *sprigs* and the compact *watling*.

2- Cadair Ceridwen - Throne of Ceridwen.
Gwydion son of Don
Formed *wood knowledge* upon plagwd

3- Rhys Goch ap Riccert, 1140-1170
The *wooden axe* of an unpolished bard,
Has been *hewing* a song to Gwenllian

4- Cynddelw, 1150-1200
From composing three complete treatises
Of *wood* language – of *wood letters*
Canu i Dduw (a song to God)

5- Dafydd ap Gwilym, 1300-1368
This will address them on *wood*.
If he would have an encomium of gentle character.
Let him go into the *wood to cut* a memorial.
I Ruff Grug.
It is easier to obtain, where the *wood* is poor,

The *carpentry* of a skilful *wright,* then materials.

6- Iolo Goch, 1315-1420
I will bear for Owain,
In metrical words, fresh and slow,
Continually, not the *hewing of alder wood*
By the *chief carpenter of song* – a peacock beneath the *green wood.*

7- Rhys Goch Eyri, 1330-1420
No longer will be seen the mark of the *axe*
Of the flower of the *carpenter's* on a song
Loving and wise one.
Marwnad Gruffydd Llwyd

8- Llewellyn Moel y Pantri, 1400-1430
When I hear, I regret the delay,
The *chief carpenter of song* – a peacock beneath the *green wood.*

9- Gwilym Tew, 1430 – 1470
The form of this person reading *wood.*

10- Ieuan Du'r Bilwg, 1460-1500
May thy praise go – thou art a soldier –
Upon *wood*, as long as day and water continue.

These quotations are more than sufficient to show that there was an ancient straight stroke alphabet in use in Britain continually down the centuries. It was not an invention of around AD 1800 as alleged by Griffith John Williams and others, to the complete delight of the Establishment. Whole books detail the origin of Coelbren.

It remains a historical fact that when in AD 1400-1412 Owain Glyndwr declared Wales to be independent, with himself as Prince, the possession, the use, and the importation of all writing materials were forbidden in Wales by Henry IV. The Khumry simply reverted totally to writing their messages of wood, leaving the English just as baffled as the Germans were in 1914-1918. It is no accident that whilst printing began in London in 1474, when William Caxton set up his printing press, all printing was prohibited in Wales by Act of the London Parliament until 1694. What is meant by the term 'United Kingdom' was never quite clear.

Everywhere they looked, Wilson and Blackett found that they were doing work that should never have been necessary. The entire poem *The Secret*, by Rhys Goch

Eryri (Rhys the Red of Snowdon), of c. 1330- 1420, is devoted to describing the Awen or Broad Arrow and the alphabet cut on wood. So also is *An Ode on Eulogy* by Gytto'r Glyn of around 1450, published in the Iolo manuscripts. References to, and explanations of the /I\ symbol meaning I O U as the Secret Name of God are abundant.

The fact that the Triads deal extensively with the foundation and formulation of the Awen /I\ and the methods of creating records, should have in itself been more than sufficient to silence the ill-educated witch-hunting Griffith J. Williams. The sheer lunacy of the situation lies in the fact that Griffith J. Williams, the poetry freak, had convinced himself that some of the poems published by Iolo Morganwg as being written by the illustrious Daffydd ap Gwilym, who died in AD 1368, were forgeries written by Iolo. To explain this, he alleged that by taking doses of laudnum cough mixture, which contains very small quantities of opium, for a persistent throat and chest problem, old Iolo Morganwg had become a drug addict. Then, whilst in a drugged stupor and under the total influence of drugs, he was able to write the most brilliant poetry, which far transcended the poetry which Iolo wrote whilst not on a drugged 'trip'. Iolo was then alleged to have passed off the very brilliant poetry, which he allegedly produced whilst mentally deranged by opium as the works of the long dead Daffydd ap Gwilym. That the state-controlled monopoly BBC allowed this rubbish to spew out across the airways is indeed sad.

It bothered no one that Griffith J. Williams had no medical training, or that what he was alleging was impossible, or that he had no evidence whatsoever to support his claims. It bothered no one that the very active Iolo lived to be seventy-nine, and none of his family, his friends, or his many literary contemporaries and colleagues, ever thought he was a drug addict. As the HTV television company's programme, which finally de-bunked these idiocies, was entitled *Not Bad for a Junkie*, this sums up the problem. From a totally irrelevant objection over a few ancient poems, the issue spread to contaminate all Iolo's records. It then spread to all records of South East Wales history, and the great forgery paranoia crippled and destroyed all legitimate South East Wales history and most of the remaining British history. Caught up in this disgraceful and pathetic witch-hunt was the ancient British Coelbren alphabet.

The current problem is that the small North Wales universities have raised the idiotic Griffith John Williams onto an academic pedestal in recognition of his accomplishment in destroying all of South East Wales, and most other ancient British history. Institutional reputations are now in peril.

In Percy Enderbie's History titled *Cambria Triumphans, or Brittain in its Perfect*

Lustre Shewing the Origen and Antiquity of that Illustrious Nation, published in 1661, many heraldic coats of arms are depicted. This was a major history in its time, and in amongst the various ancient exhibitions of shields is that of Urien Rheged of the late sixth century AD. The three ravens or crows of Urien Rheged are each shown carrying the Awen /|\ Broad Arrow in their beaks, and again this makes total nonsense of the allegations of forgery some hundred and forty years later around AD 1800. Urien Rheged was one of the three regents appointed when his brother-in-law, King Arthur II ap Meurig, was out of the kingdom from 574-579.

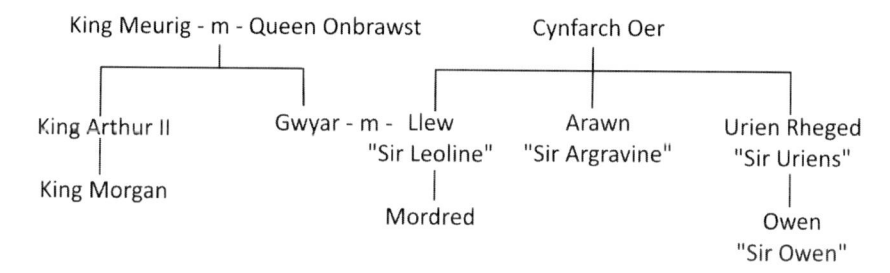

```
King Meurig - m - Queen Onbrawst              Cynfarch Oer
        |                                          |
   ┌────┴────┐                          ┌──────────┼──────────┐
King Arthur II   Gwyar - m - Llew      Arawn            Urien Rheged
   |                  "Sir Leoline"   "Sir Argravine"    "Sir Uriens"
King Morgan              |                                    |
                      Mordred                               Owen
                                                          "Sir Owen"
```

Arthur II died in AD 579; and this simplified genealogy gives a chronological placement for Urien Rheged - of the Gift. As Taliesin, the Chief Bard of Arthur II, moved to the court of Urien Rheged after Arthur II's funeral in *c.* 580, the detailed genealogies serve to tie in numbers of sixth-century personalities.

There are of course objections on the grounds that the Khumry could not possibly have had armorial designs and heraldry centuries before the other nations of Britain and Western Europe. This of course ignores the obvious fact that all the twelve basic heraldic signs originally used are exactly the same as the twelve symbols of the twelve tribes of Israel and Judea as listed in Genesis 49. Reuben has no designated sign in this list, unless it is the raven or crow. It also ignores the fact that the Heraldic colour code follows exactly the ancient British directional colour code, Black for North, White (Silver) for South, Red for West, Yellow (Gold) or Dun for East, Green for Life, and Blue for Death. (Tri + Bran is Three Crows, and Trybaeddiad is 'a wallowing'; descriptive of Reuben's actions.).

The Awen or Broad Arrow is clearly a British - Lloegres and Khumric - property of great antiquity. Whether the records that show that the ancient Hittities of Asia Minor had 'scribes on wood' has any connection is not known. The ancient Hebrews most certainly wrote on wooden rods or staves, as is stated in the Biblical record. The best-known reference is probably that in Numbers 17:1-9.

'The Lord said to Moses, "Tell the people of Israel to give you twelve sticks, one from the leader of each tribe. Write each man's name on his stick and then write Aaron's name on the stick representing Levi. There will be one stick for each tribal leader.'"

In order to write on sticks it is necessary to have a suitable alphabet, but this again appears to have passed un-noticed.

In the 1794 volume *Musical and poetical Relicks of the Welsh Bards* by Edward Jones, the then Bard to the Prince of Wales, which includes much of what was later alleged to be forged by Edward Williams – Iolo, included an entry from an ancient folio manuscript in the Bodleian Library, Oxford, marked KKK. This exhibited examples of ancient alphabets. On page 8 of his book Edward Jones included a note:

'In the time of King Henry VIII there was found at Ambresbury in Wiltshire, a table of metal, which appeared to be of tin and lead intermixed, inscribed with many letters, but in a strange character, that neither Sir Thomas Elliot nor Mr Lily, schoolmaster at St Paul's, could read it, and therefore neglected it. Had it been preserved, probably it might have led to some discovery.' - See Gibbons Notes to Camden.

The fact that there was a metal votive table in the tomb of King Dungi – 'Dioclician' at Ur, and another similar metal votive table in the tomb of King Cynfelyn, at Lexden, is relevant to this find. The difference being that in the case of the Wiltshire find the metal table was inscribed with letters, and it could well have been of monumental importance to British history.

Mixed Coelbren and Latin Inscriptions

The search for Coelbren inscriptions on stones by Wilson and Blackett soon produced late-period mixed Coelbren and Latin inscriptions. This turned out to be fairly common practice in Wales, and a routine format is exhibited on several ancient Welsh memorial stones. Here the standard opening phrase of 'Hic Iacit' - for 'Here is cast down' - is invariably used, as it is on a host of other ancient memorial stones. The names of those who are 'cast down' are however another matter, and these are in a mixture of British Coelbren and Latin scripts. ("Hie Iacit" is frequently mistranslated as 'Here lies.)

A good example of this hybrid type inscription is the memorial stone at Llangorse Church in Brecon, which was found on 9th May 1881. It reads;-

HIC IACIT   G   RD   FILIVS   IVL

Chapter 4 - The Discovery of a Mystery

| Here is cast down | GWIDDETRD | son of | ENIWIOSL |
| Here is cast down | GWLFFERT | son of | ENWYSTYL |

The Charter of Caer Duicil (also referred to as the Castle of Dinduicil) appears in the Llandaff Charters as a grant location in the time of Bishop Nudd. The stony-hearted Enwystyl is said to have been lying ill, and apparently dying when he gave the castle and three modii of land (around twenty-seven acres) to the Bishop of Llandaff in a charter which was witnessed by King Hywel ap Rhys ap Ithael and Bishop Nudd. This places the charter and therefore this stone at around AD 900.

This same Gwlddert or Gwlffert the son of Enwystyl appears in another charter granted to Bishop Nudd. This is listed as the Llandaff Charter of the Martyrs Julius and Aaron. These Julius and Aaron were the two noble martyrs killed in Diocletian's persecutions of the Christians which began on 23rd February in 303, continuing in the West until 306, and lasting to 313 in the East. Alban was the third martyr killed in this pogrom, which had little subsequent effect in Britain.

This Llandaff Charter begins with the statement that Gwlffert had quarrelled with Hewi (Hugh) and Alwystyl (Aristobulus), the sons of Beli, and this then led to conflict between their illustrious families. The resulting warfare was ended by Bishop Nudd, and the peace was sealed by a grant of land made to the church along the upper reaches of the River Usk. After this further identification of Gwlffert and his father Enwystyl, the name of Gwlffert appears on the Church font at Llandefynog, where it appears as SIWVARD + GWLDE(RT). On the opposite side of this same font is another inscription written entirely in Coelbren.

Amongst the names in the list of the noblemen who were witnesses to the Grant of Caer Duicil made by Enwystyl, there is the name of Sauian or Sawiau, who is very likely the Siward coupled with Gwlffert son of Enwystyl on this font. All of this makes perfect chronological and historical sense, and it fits with the general areas described in the Charter Grants and the surviving inscriptions.

The Coelbren inscription on the Llandefynog Font reads as -

SI W DDIAT   or   SIU DDI AT

It may have significance that Sywydd means "star knowledge" and Syweddyd means "an astrologer".

Another well-known Brecon stone also caused the writer to wrestle with the problem of expressing a Khumric name using Latin letters. The standard phrases of 'Hie Iacit' and 'Filivs' appear, and the whole text is:

" CATHACVS HIC IACIT FILIVS TESERN ACVS"

this would read as; -

"CATHACUS HERE IS CAST DOWN THE SON OF TEITHRIN THE SUBTLE"

The most probable explanation of this is that Cathacus is the famous fifth-century saint Cattwg, known as Cattwg Doeth or Cattwg the Wise, who is frequently confused with the sixth-century St Cadoc son of Gwynlliw.

King Teithrin appears in the ancient genealogies in the Brecon Manuscripts and elsewhere as the great grandson of Mascen Wledig - Magnus Maximus, and grandson of Arthun the Black - Arthur I, who conquered all Western Europe in 383-388. Teithrin was the father of King Teithfallt who destroyed Gwrtheyrn-Vortigern. In his turn Teithfallt (Theodosius) was great-grandfather of Arthur II son of King Meurig-Maurice. Teithrin would be Theodorus.

A large body of ancient literature in the form of religious aphorisms is attributed to Cattwg Doeth - the Wise. These have been then loosely attributed to the later St Cadoc without a shred of supporting evidence or justification. That Cattwg is not Cadoc is self-evident, as the same Coelbren symbol meaning 'TH' also appears on the stone of King Teithfallt at Margam Abbey where it has been misread. King Teithrin has also not been identified because of this same error. It would appear to be totally illogical to try to continue deciphering the important Dark Age inscribed stones of South East Wales without proper reference to the royal genealogies which name the rulers who set up these stones. These same rulers are copiously listed in the histories, cathedral charters, genealogies, poetry, lives of saints, and other records.

This brings matters to the stone of the Kings Howell (Houelt) and Rhys (Res) at Llan Illtyd Fawr or Llantwit Major, of the late seventh or early eighth century which clearly exhibits at least one Coelbren letter. The problem can perhaps be illustrated by the fact that a King Erbic (sometimes listed as Erbin) ruled around the year 400 and in the Llandough churchyard there is a remarkable stone column which depicts on one side five busts the central head being crowned, and on another face a crowned horseman, and the inscription is ERBIC. Academia inexplicably refuses to see this as King Erbic although this King is clearly named as Erbic in the Jesus College No. 20 Manuscript and elsewhere.

There is one well-known and indisputable South East Wales story which might

Chapter 4 - The Discovery of a Mystery

bring enlightenment into this academically created unnecessary morass of muddles. In 1855-1856, repairs were being carried out at the old house known as The Court in Merthyr Tydfil and a room 'which had been closed for a time exceeding the memory of men' was opened. Inside were a number of pieces of oak furniture 'of a decidedly Tudor character'. So, furniture of the era 1485-1604. One piece was an oak bedstead, upon which were carved in relief the Coelbren letters, or M C L. Thomas Stephens, author of *The Literature of the Cymry*, lived in Merthyr Tydfil and he examined this oak bedstead and wrote:

> 'As to the age of the letters they are probably, and to all appearance of the same age as the bedstead. Wood carving in England, does not lay claim to any great antiquity. A taste for carving prevailed during the reigns of the Tudors as well as the Stewards; and it seems to me that the bedstead in question may be about two hundred and fifty years old, or perhaps three hundred; but certainly not more. If the true date be ever ascertained, I think it not unlikely that I shall be found to have overstated its age rather than otherwise. This however will be of service in determining the age of the Coelbren to be at least as old as the age of Llewellyn Sion, and in setting aside all imputations upon the character of Iolo Morganwg, as a setter forth of an alphabet of his own invention.'

The important thing to note is that Thomas Stephens was a dedicated sceptic of the traditions of the Bards. He was in fact eating his own words with a vengeance. To his credit, he went further and exhibited the genealogy of the family of Court House. The line traced back to Ifor Bach son of Meurig who in his turn can be traced back to Brutus. Ifor Bach is famous for a midnight attack on Cardiff Castle in 1158 when he captured the Earl William, the first cousin of Henry II, and all his family. The descent is as follows Meurig son Ifor Bach, son Griffith who married Earl William's daughter's son Rhys, son Howel Felyn (Yellow Hair), son Madoc, son Llewellyn, son Llewellyn Fychan (the Younger), son Rhys, son Richert Gwyn, son Lewis, son Edward Lewis, Sheriff Glamorgan 1548, 1555, & 1559, son Thomas Lewis, Sheriff of Glamorgan 1559 - died 2nd

HISTORICAL ACCOUNT OF

Ꮲ ᏞᎩᏚᏚᎬᏙᎨᏁ ᏨᎬᏁᏁᎤᎧ,
Ꮎ ᎧᏍᎨ ᎬᎤᏙ ᏒᏁᏒᏚ ᏒᎩᏒᎧᏗᎨᏁ.

OR

THE FIRST CHAPTER,

OF THE

THREE MEMORIALS OF BRITAIN.

The following curious narrative, describing the principal profession of the *Bards*, is extracted from an ancient folio manuscript, which was pointed out to me in the *Bodleian Library*, Oxford, by the Rev. Mr. *Price*; marked KKK, and page 207, &c. ———— I did not think myself at liberty to make any alterations in this transcript, farther than to modernize the old orthography, so as to make it more intelligible to the generality of readers.

THE office or function, of the British or *Cambrian Bards*, was to keep and preserve *Tri Chôv Ynys Prydain*: that is, the Three Records, or Memorials, of Britain, otherwise called the British Antiquities; which consists of three parts, and are called *Tri Chôv*: for the preservation whereof, when the Bards were graduated at their Commencements, they were trebly rewarded; one reward for every *Côv*, as the ancient Bard *Tudur Aled* recites, and also his reward for the same, at his commencement and graduation at the royal wedding of *Evan ab Davydd ab Ithel Vychan*, of Northop in Inglefield, Flintshire, which he, in the *Cerdd Marwnad* of the said *Evan ab Davydd ab Ithel*, records thus:

Cyntav neuadd i'm grâddwyd,	The first Hall wherein I was initiated,
Vu oror llŷs v' Eryr llwyd;	Was the Court of the Grey Eagle;
Am dri chôv i'm dyrchavodd,	For by the *Tri Chôv* I was elevated,
Yn neithior — llyma 'r tair rhôdd.	In the Nuptial Feast: behold the three gifts!

Which shews that he was exalted, and graduated at that wedding for his knowledge in the said *Tri Chôv*, and was rewarded with three several rewards.

The First of the three *Côv* is the history of the notable acts of the Kings, and Princes of Britain and Cambria.

The Second of the three *Côv* is the language of the Britons, of which the Bards were to give an

Coelbren printed in AD 1794

Chapter 4 - The Discovery of a Mystery

November 1594, which brings matters to the time of the old oak bedstead.

Thomas Lewis had two brothers named William and Edward, and six sisters named Mary, Elizabeth, Margaret, Jane, Blanch, and Cicely. Thomas Lewis himself married Margaret the daughter of Robert Gamage of Coety, who was the uncle of the Countess of Leicester, the great Gamage heiress. Their eldest son was born in 1560 so the marriage may have been in 1559. The bedstead is thought to have been carved with the initials of Margaret Gamage Lewis, with the 'C' being used as a radical, instead of the 'G'. Alternatively, the initials are those of Mary, Margaret, or Cicely Lewis. Either way the bedstead bears Coelbren letters of the era around 1550, the time of Llewellyn Sion who set out the ancient Coelbren alphabets in his manuscript.

Another wooden item, which received much publicity in mid-nineteenth-century Wales, was an ancient font in Powys that was fashioned from the stump of an oak tree. This item was remarkable as it was incised with a Coelbren lettering inscription which read 'Arthrwys', the name of King Arthur II son of Meurig ap Tewdrig. Arthur II died in 579. This also remains invisible to the academic eye.

The Dilemma of the British Stones

In 1982, Alan Wilson and Baram Blackett had already established that there were ancient Coelbren-inscribed British stones throughout Wales, Scotland, and England. This had become obvious to them in their Arthurian researches from 1976, and the stones were crucial to their historical research. Dealing with these stones, which held many important messages, was not easy as the nineteenth-century propaganda wrongly alleged that our ancient British ancestors were illiterate. Dr Goebbels' dictum 'the bigger the lie, the more readily it is believed' certainly applied, and the absolute control of the education system had allowed this falsehood to be enforced.

The result was that whilst it is possible to trace the British stones, they had invariably been first correctly dated, and then, in many cases, subsequently misdated by several centuries to conform to the false requirement of British alleged illiteracy. The mechanism of this exercise in absurdity has been outlined in *The Holy Kingdom*, but needs to be summarised in order to tell this story. There are a number of ancient carved Christian stones in the North of England, and in 1927 a surveyor named W. G. Collingwood published his research into these. He came up with the strange idea that monumental stone carving began in Britain in his native ancient Northumberland. From Northumberland the technique spread to Ireland, and from Ireland it later spread across to his imaginary ignorant, backward, stupid Wales. To state that this 'theory' is incorrect would be a monumental understatement, but Collingwood's absurd theory is consistent with the objectives of Edwin Guest and Bishop Stubbs, and the Establishment in general.

As might be expected, the Collingwood invention has been seized upon eagerly by the academic establishment, and as usual the effect upon British-Khumric history has been catastrophic. The stone found at Ogmore Castle names King Arthmael-Iron Bear, who is undoubtedly King Arthur II, born *c.* 503 and died 579, the son of King Meurig. It also names Nertat, a daughter of his first cousin Brychan II, with Glywys the brother of St Cadoc (another cousin), and Fili the Bishop who is unmistakeably Ufclwyn a grandson of St Gildas and a suffragan bishop of Llandaff. This sixth-century stone was correctly read and dated by Professor MacAlister and others. Now however it is 're-dated' to 900-1000, when no persons so named are to be found. The 're-dating' alleges that part of the badly worn decoration on the side of the stone may resemble similar decoration on a Northumberland stone of around 1000.

This type of anti-Welsh archaeological exercise in absurdity is by no means rare. Where clearly obvious Coelbren letters appear mixed with Latin letters on ancient Welsh stones, these British-Khumric Coelbren letters are hilariously labelled as 'Irish'. At Margam the result is that the accession stone of King Teithfallt - Theodosius - the Em-Rhys Wledig of around 470 is re-identified as the stone of an unknown 'Grutne', who is alleged to be of around 800. Grutne is not a name. Forgetting that it was the kings and major princes who set up stones, the stone that reads for King Tewdrig Uthyrpendragon – Theoderic, successor of Teithfallt, who was killed in 508, is now claimed to identify an 'Einion', and is also re-dated to 800. Actually, the spelling is 'En- ni-ac-un' which is clearly a statement and not any name Einion. The Khumric-Welsh Coelbren letter for 'Th' is being read as an Irish "G".

The persistence of this absurd 're-dating' is extraordinary. The great cross at Margam of 'Cunobelinus' is obviously that of the bishop Cyhylyn, a brother of King Meurig, and therefore of around AD 470-520. This is again 're-dated' to around 850. The Bodvoc stone, which is beyond all doubt the stone of Budic of Amorica who fled to Wales from Brittany around 500, when his brother deposed him in the time of King Tewdrig, is also 're-dated' to around 800. Actually, the Bodvoc - Budic stone names his great-grandfather Eternalis Vedomavus and his father Cato Tigernus, which correctly dates him to the late fifth and early sixth centuries. Only by detailed research tracing Cato into three other ancient manuscript sources, and then identifying Eternalis Vedomavus in several other ancient sources, could this absurdity of misdating be corrected.

The massive nine foot-high and seven-ton weight stone of King Ithael, an immediate successor of King Arthmael - Iron Bear, at Llan-illtyd-fawr names King Ithael, his father Arthmael, and St Illtyd, who was Arthmael's first cousin. All of whom are very clearly sixth century. Again, to conceal the British history this is re-dated to 900 when no such persons can be found. This re-dating is mainly done by the English and Scottish long-stay middle class refugee archaeologists, who dominate the scene in Wales. The persistent determination to obliterate the Arthurian Dynasty is unmistakeable.

That the theories of W. G. Collingwood are incorrect and based on his near-total ignorance of all British history outside his native north-eastern area is obvious. The manner in which his worthless ideas have been uncritically seized upon to 're-date' these priceless Welsh monuments and thus to obliterate and confuse the historical record needs no further comment.

The search for the alphabet was not assisted by the deliberate re-dating and misnaming of ancient royal memorial stones late in the twentieth century. Where it was difficult to express a British sound in the Latin letters it was usual to resort to the inclusion of a British Coelbren letter. The practice, born of ignorance in attempting to identify these British Coelbren letters as 'Irish', has again served to obliterate the Coelbren. It is the customary English practice to persist in seeing the Khumry, and the ancestral Lloegrian people of England, as some form of tribal primitives; the equivalent of Borneo stone-age men, decked with feathers in their hair, paint on their faces, and bones stuck through their noses, despite overwhelming evidence to the contrary. The fact that both the ancient Lloegrian and Khumric peoples were provably culturally far more advanced than the Anglo-Saxons is plainly recorded and this is unacceptable. This is the root cause of the destruction and obliteration of British ancient history.

In the matter of Khumric stones, Wilson and Blackett already had the Gorddyfwn Stone from Llandefaeliog in Brecon. They were also of the opinion that the great stone cross at Nevern in Pembrokeshire has a form of Coelbren. This appears to name a ruler who is named as Higuel Rex or the modern Howell. As this massive stone cross is just a few miles west of Crug Hywel or the Heap of Howell, a grave mound, and this is then just north of Upper Court and Lower Court farms where the court of the King Howell Oda, who died in 948, once was, it is likely that this is the cross of Howell Dda.

Ancient manuscripts present the name of this king as Higuel. Predictably, since this identification was proposed by Wilson and Blackett, a minor prince of around 1150 has been put forward to try to eliminate Howell Dda. The fact remains, however, that the stone states Higuel Rex - Howell the King, and it is an absolute fact that the relatively insignificant Howell of around 1150 was definitely not a king.

Perhaps the most significant stone that was brought to Alan's and Baram's attention was a stone found at Lavernock, just west of Cardiff, in the early 1980s, by the young daughter of Don Tilley. This strange stone is unworked, and resembles a flat-bottomed three-sided low cone. Around the top are incised twelve star-shapes arranged in an oval. One star sign has a descending tail, which splits in two, and attaches to a thirteenth star outside the oval ring. In the centre of the oval formed by these stars are two Coelbren letters. The old Welsh name for Lavernock indicates that it was the place of an observatory.

Coincidently, it was from this spot that George Kemp of Cardiff, with Guglielmo Marconi present in attendance, sent the world's first wireless telephonic signal across water to Echni Island (Flat Holm) in Cardiff Bay, some ten miles away, on the 18th May 1897. This extraordinary stone, owned by Mr Tilley, has to be one of the most incredible ancient artefacts found in Britain.

Chapter Five

The Stones in Britain

Searching out origins requires attention to detail, and Wilson and Blackett had to remind themselves that what is now Scotland was originally Old British territory. This meant that there might well be ancient Coelbren-inscribed stones surviving in Scotland. The logic followed the British line laid down in the traditional British histories, which stated that the British occupied all Britain, and Scotland was once called Albany. At some time around 400-300 BC the Picts are said to have arrived in Britain. Histories of disputed value allege that the British king intercepted people sailing in a Scythian-Pict fleet in the North Sea. These people, who were fleeing from Europe, were allowed to settle in the North-East, to the north of the Firth of Forth. Then, over eight hundred years later, in the aftermath of the great comet disaster of AD 562, the Scots began moving over from Northern Ireland.

So certainly before AD 562, all of Strathclyde, and the west through to Galloway, was Khumric territory, and probably the rest of the entire Scottish Lowlands as well. English Cumberland and Westmoreland (Cumbria, Lancashire, and Cheshire), was also Khumric territory. With King and Saint Ninniaw (alias Ninian) establishing the White Church at Whithorn in Galloway around AD 400, the possibility of Coelbren-inscribed stones was real.

Two friends, Colin and Georgia Games, brought the probable existence of Coelbren-inscribed stones in Scotland to Alan's and Baram's attention. Georgia had a copy of George Bain's book, entitled *Celtic Art*, and in it, Bain records that around 1850, Dr Mill and a Colonel Sykes examined an ancient inscribed stone at Newton in Aberdeenshire. Dr Mill thought that the lettering was Phoenician, and Colonel Sykes was of the opinion that the script resembled the Buddhist 'Lot' alphabets. It occurred to neither of them that an ancient inscribed stone in Britain might bear a British inscription in a British alphabet.

Immediately, everything is again all the way back to the same old political and religious campaign to destroy British heritage, culture, and history. The simple statement made by Julius Caesar, that the British alphabet was similar to the Greek, had constantly been seized upon and misquoted, mistranslated, and misrepresented wholesale. Dr Johnson had assisted in turning everything upside down, inside out, and back to front:

> 'We may suspect that this barbarous custom of this most ancient sodality (training the memory) began at a period when they themselves neither read nor wrote, destitute of an alphabet of their own, for when the Druids had learned from the Greeks their original characters, they adopted them in all their public affairs.'

This is totally contrary to the records as we have seen, and whilst it would exactly fit the illiterate Angles and Saxons, it is emphatically untrue of the British. Then Benjamin Disraeli, a novelist who made a living as a politician, having abandoned his Jewish faith and turned Christian to become Prime Minister in 1862, wrote: 'They (the British) made use of Greek letters', with typically political inaccuracy. Yet Wolfgang Lazius, who actually translated Ammianus Marcellinus, makes the remarkable explanatory statement:

> 'The Greek letters were brought to Athens by Timagenes, who had learned them from the Druids.'

If the sycophantic fawning obsession of the English upper class with all things Greek and Roman is set aside, sense and reality might emerge. The stone at Newton, being British, carries a British alphabetic inscription. George Bain quite understandably went along the academic track when he proceeded to compare the letters of this inscription with Greek, Phoenician, and even Latin letters. Presumably he was seeking for similarities, which might give a clue to the meaning of the message.

Wilson and Blackett read the stone at Newton as Coelbren:

> 'The creative power, hastens to form (or shape), spinning (making) to bestow the woe, in a state of being to you Christ. To give, to follow the path.'

King and Saint Niniaw around AD 400 was followed by numbers of other British holy men, some of whom are obscured, as is St Kentigern Mwngi, or Kentigern the Amiable, who is now St. Mungo of Glasgow. There were also British and Pict intermarriages, and so the survival of an old British Christian inscription in the far North-

Chapter 5 - The Stones in Britain

East of Scotland is not unexpected. There is also an Ogham inscription running down the side of the Newton stone.

The Newton Stone
Photograph- John Romilly Allen and Joseph Anderson – Society of Antiquaries of Scotland 1903

This would appear to be an accession or coronation stone. By this time Wilson and Blackett had ceased to wonder why no one had ever thought to try to read this stone into Old British or Khumric. The fact that British 'Dark Age' records exist in profuse abundance makes it difficult to understand how the term 'Dark Ages' was ever coined.

There is a record in the *Life of St Finnian* that Rioch the son of Meliochon, the greatest and most powerful British king, arrived at Whithorn Abbey in Galloway at some time around AD 560. Arrangements were being made to marry Rioch to Drustice, the daughter of the King of the Picts, and not unnaturally the maiden sought to sleep with Rioch. This was frustrated by St Finnian, who somehow substituted a man from Cork; a strange tale. With correct chronology, Rioch the son of Meliochon is instantly recognisable as the Prince Frioch-Rioch, a son of the mighty King Meurig, son of Tewdrig Uthyrpendragon of the 'Silures' - Essyllwg. It is generally believed that the succession to the Pict throne was matrilinear, so by marrying Drustice a non-Pict prince would automatically become King.

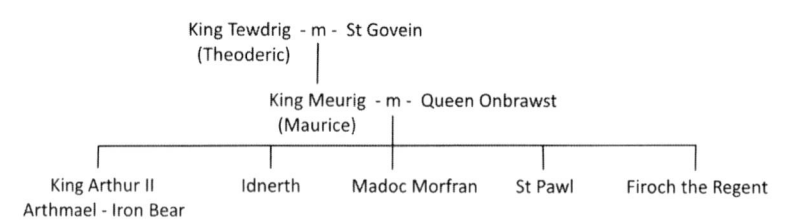

```
            King Tewdrig  - m -  St Govein
             (Theoderic)      |
                              |
                    King Meurig  - m -  Queen Onbrawst
                     (Maurice)        |
    ┌───────────────┬──────────────┼──────────────┬──────────────┐
King Arthur II    Idnerth    Madoc Morfran    St Pawl      Firoch the Regent
Arthmael - Iron Bear
```

Frioch was a regent following the death of his brother, Arthur II ap Meurig, in AD 579, and the Llandaff Charters record how the young Morgan Mwynfawr killed his uncle Frioch to take the throne. Frioch is probably buried in Dyfed in a named mound. There was also another candidate for 'Droster' in a prince named Drustans, the son of March ap Meirchion Gul (the Mad) in the Gewissae (Wessex) area. This March was known in Brittany as Count Comorre of evil repute, as he successively married and murdered heiresses to accumulate land. The Franks knew March as Count Conomurus, and the Mediaeval Romancers styled this Count Comorre - Conomurus, as 'King Mark', a major enemy of Arthur II. The genealogies give detailed accounts of the ancestry of Meirchion Gul, and his son 'King Mark', who may be Count Chanao-Conomurus, who allied himself to Chramn, the eldest son of Lothair I of the Franks, and was killed by his father after a battle in *c.* AD 560.

Wilson and Blackett also noted the stone named for Drustans, the son of March or

Chapter 5 - The Stones in Britain

'King Mark', still standing at Castle Dore at Tywardreath in Cornwall. Also, most students of history are familiar with the popular romance story of 'Sir Tristan' stealing the bride intended for 'King Mark'. Once the correct chronology is in place, with March being killed in *c.* AD 560; King Meurig dying sometime around AD 570; and King Arthur II ap Meurig being assassinated in AD 579, allowing Frioch to act as Regent before Morgan Mwynfawr murdered him, the scholastic mist and fog clears.

Text section of the St Vigean stone

George Bain quoted Professor MacAllister: 'after Caesar's time the Druids abandoned the Greek for the dominant Roman letters', and commented on the inaccuracy of this statement. Bain then proceeded to show that Druid 'Greek' type letters do appear on the Newton and St Vigean stones, and also in various well-known manuscript sources. Then, obviously unaware of both Coelbren and history, he stated that: 'comparisons of Celtic letters of the fourth to sixth centuries will show that A.D.M.N. are derived from Phoenician and Greek.' This is not true; as Wilson and Blackett were to discover.

The basic problem of according a false priority in almost everything to the Greeks causes near total chaos. The Greeks borrowed just about everything from everywhere, Babylonian and Chaldean mathematics and astronomy, from Egypt the theatre and playwriting complete with the chorus, they also borrowed architecture and statuary, from the British they got the alphabet and allegedly philosophy from the Druid Abaris, and so on. To compound everything the Greeks made chaos of ancient chronology in attempts to claim ancient origins.

Statements such as:
'Many of the Celtic letters are derived direct from the Phoenician and early Greek Alphabets, are to be found side by side with Roman letters in the Books of Kells, Durrow, and Lindisfarne' are incorrect.'

They are simply Old British letters of the Coelbren Alphabet, and none of the people were ever 'Celtic'.

Setting aside these 'imaginary' borrowings from distant cultures by the learned British, who had no need to borrow or learn anything from any of them, it was ever clearer that the British Coelbren alphabets had been widely used and had been correctly preserved, which now allowed translation of ancient texts. The information preserved in the ancient inscriptions appears to match with the known historical evidence.

Stones in England

Alan Wilson had tended to regard the Coelbren alphabet as a Khumric, and therefore a Western British, phenomenon. Baram Blackett had a wider view, and he pointed out that the book, *The Holy Blood and The Holy Grail*, discussed paintings by Poussin and Teniers, and somehow related these to a carving on a later monument erected by the Anson family at Shugborough Hall in Staffordshire. This Shugborough Hall monument is actually a mirror-image representation of a painting by Poussin, *Les Bergers d'Arcadie*, but the interesting feature is that it also carries a very clear British Coelbren inscription which is also reversed, or mirror image, as is the painting.

The authors of *The Holy Blood and The Holy Grail* got nowhere with this Coelbren inscription, and declared it indecipherable. This is not correct as it was deciphered over a hundred and fifty years ago and the decipherment was published. Wilson and Blackett found that the selection of papers published in 1841 by Taliesin Williams the son of Edward Williams - Iolo Morganwg - included explanations of the origin of the Broad Arrow or Awen sign. The Welsh Manuscript Society published these. As we have seen the Awen sign meant 'genius', and as such 'original thought'. It is held to be the sign of the Deity, and represents the name of God. In all ancient Triadic record and lore, the Awen is then linked with Menw, which means 'intellect'.

Chapter 5 - The Stones in Britain

Illustration 5-1:The St Vigeans Stone

The offered reading of the inscription on the St Vigean's Stone in Angus is-

dposten:	Droster	Droster = Drystice or Drystans
IPEUORET	Ireidiad (Ireuoet)	is anointed
ETTFOR.	Ettfaw (Ettfed-Etifor)	to inherit
C·U P	Cur	the care (responsibility)

Illustration 5-2: The Newton Stone

	Neif (neifion)	The creative power
	Ffrwst Luyn (ffusgio llun)	Hastens to form (or shape)
	Nyd Low Oce (nyddy loff och-ochi)	spinning to bestow woe (=making)
	Ur Rheydir	pure winds arable land to
	this the agent (to join)	*a variant 'A'
	Roy Olrhewr (rhoi olrhain)	to give, to follow the path

The ancient concept of each individual's life being spun like a thread by a goddess is a well-known motif.

Having achieved some success with the Newton Stone, Wilson and Blackett turned their attention to the St Vigean's stone, in Angus. This appears to read: Line one - 'Droster', Line two - 'Ireidiad' (Ireuonet), Line three - 'Ettfaw' (Etifcdd Etifor), Line four - 'Cur'

This would mean: 'Droster (Drustice) is anointed to inherit the care (responsibility)'.

In the 'Iolo' manuscripts at the end of a long list of Khumric saints there is the following entry:

'I, Edward the son of Edward Williams, took this out of the book of my relative, Mr Thomas Hopkin of Llangrallo, which book was the work of Thomas Evan of Tre Brynn, at the Parish of Llangrallo. Written about the year 1670 from an old manuscript.

And I Taliesin Williams, the son of Iolo Morganwg, *i.e.* Taliesin the son of Edward Williams, retranslated it faithfully, *verbatim et literatim*, from my father's Manuscript, January 4, 1841.'

What Taliesin Williams was exhibiting was an exact replica of the 'indecipherable' Coelbren text on the Shugborough Hall monument, and he translated it. The next chapter of this publication begins with yet another similar notation: -

'From the Long Book of Thomas Trneman, of Pantlliwydd in the Parish of Llansanor in Glamorgan, copied by Iolo Morganwg (me) in the year 1783.'

/|\

The identical inscription at Shugborough Hall appears below the reversed or mirror-image representation of a painting by Nicolas Poussin, born 1595 and died 1665, which further complicates the great faked forgery witch-hunt in Britain as the Anson family are now involved in the alleged forging of the Coelbren alphabets. This much-discussed Poussin painting entitled *Les Bergers d'Arcadie* shows three shepherds and a woman examining a tomb, which also carries an inscription. The inscription in the painting has been read as 'Et in arcadia ego', but it can be read quite differently, and points to a different location, if the instructions in the painting are read. Arcadia was of course the western zone of the Egyptian Delta in Roman and early Christian times. The Ansons knew something, and so did Iolo, but that opens another long story, which can be told elsewhere.

Shugborough Hall was the residence of the Bishop of Lichfield, in the ancient Apostolic Glastonbury area, and it was bought by the Anson family in 1697. George Anson, the brother of Admiral Anson, who circumnavigated the world with a fleet, lived at the Hall, and it was around 1697 that the monument and sculpture were erected. Later research made it obvious that old Iolo Morganwg knew of the significance of the monument at Shugborough and a lot more.

Certainly, Iolo recorded a great deal on the I O V or Secret name of God, and its several other forms of OIV, OIU, OIW, IOU, IOW, IAO, IAU, and so on. One poem attributed to Sion o Ceint or John of Kent, is a series of verses all exhibiting and detailing the many variant secret names of God, mostly of three letters. For example;
-

verse 5
"Pannon ar Gannon ganniad ai gelwir
Dda gelwn cf o'n plaid,
O, I, ar W, yw a gaid,
OIW beunydd i pob enaid."

So the enigmatic OIV emerges again, and if written by Sion o Ceint, this again precedes Iolo by three hundred years. Sion o Ceint lived around AD 1400–1460, and can almost certainly be shown to be Jack Cade who led the forty-thousand strong revolt of AD 1450 against Henry VI. He was almost certainly the Mortimer heir and therefore had powerful claims to both the Welsh and English thrones. See *The Holy Family*.

The secret word appears as the Name of God, when God gave his name to Moses in Exodus 3:15, and this is usually translated in Christian terms as:

'This is my name for ever, and this is my memorial unto all generations.'

Rabbinical tradition, however, states that the word translated as 'forever' should be read correctly as 'secret', giving this translation:

'Let this my name be kept secret, keep this in remembrance for all generations.'

Diodorus Siculus records that the Jews stated that Moses attributed the framing of their laws to God who was named IAO, one on several Khumric appellations. Theodoret, who recorded that the God known to the Jews was called IAO, repeats this. In modern times, Walsh identifies the IAO on Christian coins as meaning Iesu (Jesus), Alpha, and Omega. Taliesin Williams included an appendix on all this, and attributed the IAO to the Greek writing of the Name of God, and he cites ABRAXAS, their talisman name of God and the IAW used by them. The Jews of course simply substituted Adonai and Elohim whenever they encountered the Secret Name.

Around 1842 a small gold plate of about four inches by one inch was found at Llanbeblig, near Caernarfon. On this plate were written in Greek letters the Hebrew words Adonai, Eloai, Iao, Ellion, with other characters thought to be astronomical or even magical. Most of the debate about this was totally irrelevant, and concentrated on the horror of the modern clergy, who recoiled at the thought that their ancestors might somehow have been 'contaminated' with Basilides' early Christian Gnostic related cult.

Printing was, as we have seen, not legal in Wales until 1694, long after its introduction in England, which of course makes mockery of the term 'United Kingdom'. The only way to reproduce old texts was by the traditional manner of copying by hand. As much research has shown, the Glamorgan and Gwent gentry began to have their manuscripts translated into English after 1600, as the pressures from London took effect. Before this their records were ignored as unreadable, and when translated into English they were now 'not original', and again disregarded.

The St Paul's Stone in London (writing on left edge)

Chapter 5 - The Stones in Britain

The Stone Found at St Paul's in London

On August 28th 1852, *The Illustrated London News* reported the discovery of a carved stone in the churchyard of St Paul's in London. This find was made during the course of deep excavations near the end of Watling Street (Gwrtheyrn Strada). The stone was found twenty-eight feet down below the surface, and was clearly of great antiquity. Carved into the face of this stone was a representation of the several-headed and multi-tailed dragon symbol of the ancient comet of AD 562. Around the sides of the stone was carved an inscription.

The inscription on this Watling Street stone quickly became the subject of much correspondence in various publications. In the Cambrian Journal of 1855, No. V. January, one G. H. Beaumont wrote making several propositions.

0. First, he compared the straight line 'runic'-type inscriptions with alphabets preserved in manuscripts in the Bodleian Library, and these he illustrated.

1. Secondly, he claimed a general similarity between the Bodleian manuscript records and the Scandinavian runic alphabets, whilst noting some clearly apparent differences.

2. Thirdly, he proceeded to note that these alphabet symbols bore a distinct similarity to the alphabets recorded by Layard, the contemporary excavator of ancient Nineveh, in his first publication. (ii, p.166 – 177.) No one thought of Albyne from ancient Syria.

3. Fourthly, he stressed that the Watling Street stone inscription was of the same general character as the Scandinavian runic, the Bodleian manuscripts, and the Nineveh alphabets.

In a remarkable display of total illogicality, G. H. Beaumont then ascribed the Watling Street stone to the Scandinavians. He was of the usual English opinion that the ancient British had no scribes or alphabets. Clearly, he had either not bothered to read Caesar, Strabo, Ammianus Marcellinus, or a host of other records, or else he had chosen to forget what he had read. This was the period when through the efforts of Edwin Guest, Bishop Stubbs, and their supporters, all native British records were becoming distrusted regardless of evidence. Beaumont, however, expressed the hope that his ideas might assist in resolving what was only an archaeological argument without foundation. He was in fact prepared to admit to the possibility of the stone being British.

In fact, the possible association with Nineveh alphabets should have washed all Scandinavian ideas out his mind immediately, particularly with the Albyne and Syria histories still well known. Equally the sight of the alphabets in the Bodleian manuscripts should have rendered all such notions as ludicrous.

Remarkably Beaumont recalled 'Arthurian Faith', probably inferring that there were others who would see a stone dug out from deep down in St Paul's churchyard as an indicator of Mallory's *Morte d'Arthur*, and stories of Arthur drawing a sword from a stone in that same churchyard. To quote Beaumont:

> 'The Watling Street inscription forms the margin of emblazonry, in bold outline, depicting a dragon; the two lines omitting in the outer line two figures, which seem panelling, or border, separating on either side three outer letters from the two central are something like this following.'

Fortunately, G. H. Beaumont included a sketch of the letters; otherwise his readers might have had great difficulty in interpreting his description.

The upshot of these observations by Beaumont was a typically vituperative response from another author who preached the false doctrines of alleged British barbarism. The mere suggestion that the stone might be British clearly aroused misplaced anger. It was alleged forcefully that the ancient British had no alphabet or literacy. The script was asserted to be a plagiarising of Roman lettering, and therefore 'this supposed alphabet is surely a spurious one'. Even Nennius, who wrote between AD 800–822, was drawn into the tirade of bile, with assertions that the British were illiterate and therefore Nennius could not have consulted old British records to write his history, as there were none.

> 'Of course the British writer might say this is all a libel on Nennius who did not invent, but merely wrote down the letters of his countrymen, with which he was well acquainted, and thus ingeniously endeavoured to disprove the evidently well-founded charge made by his Anglo-Saxon opponent, that the British possessed no rudiments of letters.'

And so the whole matter degenerated into the age-old racist political vendetta, Anglo-Saxons were a superior race, and the British (Welsh) were inferior. The old

Chapter 5 - The Stones in Britain

Angles and Saxons were illiterates with no history before AD 426AD, and therefore the British had to be worse. The ignorance of the writer of this diatribe is only exceeded by his arrogance.

It is necessary to say something about this, as it is difficult for the modern reader to understand the heat and venom which a supposedly scholarly discussion or debate could generate in the 1850 era. It was, as it still is, an article of faith in many minds that all the inhabitants of pre-Anglo-Saxon England were primitives living in a cultural desert and wasteland. In this climate, everything which should be given to scholarly enquiry and debate degenerated into racist spitting matches and political squabbles. It is all the more strange that, given the huge emphasis which the peculiar English education system placed upon their adopted ancient Greek and Roman ancestors, that they should ignore the Greek and Roman records of the British.

The attitude can easily be illustrated. There were large numbers of Roman-style villas built in what is now England, and very few in Wales, which was generally free of Roman intrusion. So, to illustrate life, in a farce, in an imaginary Roman villa in Britain, the BBC annually parades an Oxford University production set in a fictional villa set in Gwent in Wales, NOT in England. Roman villas are found in large numbers in England, but they are extremely scarce in Wales. In this amazing piece of foolishness, the son of the local Welsh 'chieftain' is depicted as working as a kitchen boy in the Roman lady's villa. The Welsh are deliberately falsely portrayed as primitives and inferiors, just like the Africans, Australians, and Borneo jungle men, whom the English met in their empire-building days. The fact is that any Roman matron would have been lucky if the son of the local Welsh prince allowed her to lick his boots. Why not set this ridiculous farce of a story in England, and show the ancestors of the English cleaning Roman pots and pans?

Wilson and Blackett have no time at all for the aftermath of these appallingly provocative nationalist and racist jingoistic squabbles in which supposedly 'scholarly' debates were, and indeed still are, carried on. The only way to determine the nature of the Watling Street stone is to decipher it. If, as it clearly appears, it carries the Coelbren alphabet, as do other stones already deciphered in Wales, Scotland, and England, then it can be read. This obvious avenue was obstructed in 1855 by the anti-British faction who asserted that if the script was British then the stone was undoubtedly a forgery and a fake. A fake stone buried twenty-eight feet down in an ancient churchyard is another extraordinary concept. In 1855, however, the dominating declaration was that there was no evidence, and if evidence was pointed to, then that evidence was itself also faked and forged.

As the British alphabets were in fact well-known, having been published in 1846 and in 1856, there is no sane reason why they should not have been used to decipher the straightforward inscription on this St Paul's or Watling Street stone.

	Dh		Llu	R	A	U		Ch
Y	H	M	Llu	E	W	E	S	U

The top line reads from right to left, and gives: ChU or CU followed by ARLLuDh, or today's Arlwyd, and so we have Cu-Arlwyd for 'the Beloved Lord'.

In typical ancient fashion the first line reads from right to left (as was later found in both Etruria and the Aegean), while the second line reads from left to right. This is called 'boustrophedon'. First there is 'ymlewesu', which is clearly 'ymlawenau' today. It means that the beloved lord 'gladdened himself', or that he 'celebrated'.

This is therefore a credible statement that 'the beloved lord celebrated', or equally likely 'the celebration of the beloved lord'.

The dragon depicted on the face of the stone is a representation of the great Dragon Comet of *c.* AD 562, which is very clearly described in the *Brut Tysilio* and in the *Brut Gruffydd* ap Arthur (alias Geoffrey of Monmouth) and other Khumric sources.

Whether the message refers to a celebration of the passing and end of the comet is guesswork, but this might be an explanation. Certainly, ancient records refer to Arthur ap Meurig as the Beloved Lord, and he was ruling as Regent at the time of the comet.

That this strange, seven-headed and seven-tailed dragon has a Christian connection is perhaps borne out by the fact that an almost exact replica of the stone found at the St Paul's churchyard is amongst many carvings on a tenth-century Norwegian church, but there is no inscription to accompany the dragon.

There is an almost comic aspect to the antics of those who still indulge in the deliberate destruction of British heritage. In 1585-86 Sir Richard Grenville attempted to found an English colony in North America. The scientific advisor, Thomas Harriot, and John White, the artist, made a written and pictorial record of this failed venture.

Chapter 5 - The Stones in Britain

In 1590, a lunatic Dutchman named Theodor De Bry made a series of woodcuts of John White's drawings of Native American tribesmen for publication in a book. This cultural imbecile had the mad idea that as the Irish and British peoples were furthest west in Europe, and were therefore the closest Europeans to America, then the ancient Irish and British must have been exact replicas of the naked painted savages of North America. De Bry must have been thinking of his own degenerate Dutch ancestors, and he proceeded to also make five woodcuts straight out of his deranged imagination. These showed stark naked, painted, tattooed, clearly primitive, and savage people, closely resembling Stone Age Borneo Man, Native Americans, and Australian aborigines, who he then claimed must have represented the ancient British.

It is amazing how often these grossly insulting bizarre fictions have been reprinted and paraded before an unsuspecting public down the centuries. In a modem reprint of these very objectionable racist distortions a Mr Paul Hulton of the British Museum was 'happy' to write a new introduction to this disgraceful trash.

King Arthur Conspiracy - Wilson & Blackett

Alan Wilson *(left)* with Baram Blackett with the stone of Arthur II, found in the dig at the Church of St Peter's. The stone carries the legend 'REX ARTORVS FILI MAVRICVS'.

The Arthur I, found near Atherstone in Warwickshire.
The fragments on Arthur I's stone 'ARTORIV ... IACIT IN ... MACI ...'

Chapter 5 - The Stones in Britain

The Alphabet in the Bodleian Manuscript No. 572

Alan Wilson and Baram Blackett already knew the Bodleian Library Manuscripts No's 72 and 572, and the existence of Coelbren alphabets in these old manuscripts, which G. H. Beaumont alluded to, should have been more than sufficient to deter detractors of ancient British history. As these alphabets were related to the Watling Street stone found in 1852 by Beaumont it might be well to deal with them.

The letters of the Coelbren shown in the No. 572 Manuscript are all embellished with additional curved marks, which might be described as tails. Some are attached curving upwards to the top of the letters and others curve downwards. Beaumont suggested that the downward curving tails should be disregarded in translation, and in this he was wrong as the tails are inserted to assist with translation. The tails had two functions, as we will demonstrate. Their first use was to indicate the number of letters to be read as a word, and their second function was to point to the sequence of reading those words. Whilst the tails play no part in giving meaning or sound to a letter, they do have a role in reading and translation.

As the illustration shows, there are three lines of symbols. The top line appears to be of numerical significance, with a cross and eight upright stroke symbols, three to the left of the cross and five to the right. These vertical strokes are decorated with varying numbers of upward curving and downward curving tails, and interspersed with varying numbers of dots. The numerical significance of these straight strokes with tails was not immediately clear, but the intention emerged after close examination of lines two and three.

Line two is different from line one in that it is clearly alphabetic. It opens with seven dots placed almost vertically, and then a five-letter word, which ends with five more vertical dots. These first five letters each have one downward curved tail on the left side, which indicate 'first word'. Using this pattern, where the five letters of the second word each have two left downward tails, and the six letters of the third word each have three downward left tails, we can read from the right. There are sixteen letters in this line.

First, however, as noted, there are seven dots before the first letter in the line, so Wilson and Blackett took the seventh letter. There are five dots before the sixth letter, and so they took the fifth letter after the sixth, and finally another four dots before the tenth letter so they took the fourth letter after the tenth. This gave a hidden three-letter word: FF WD DR, which appears to mean 'Ffwdanu'; which means 'to be in a hurry' and perhaps 'to hasten'. Line two ends with a cross of thirteen dots.

Then line three is also followed the same pattern with three dots before the first letter leading to the third letter, then four dots before the fifth letter, leading to the eighth letter, and another two dots before the eighth leading to the tenth, then three dots before the eleventh, leading to the thirteenth, and finally three dots before the fourteenth letter, leading to the sixteenth. Again, by taking the letters directed, which are 3, 8, 10, 13, and 16, Wilson and Blackett again had another hidden word. This is 'W I U FF E',; which only has meaning if read correctly from the right to left as 'effuiw', and probably 'effiath', meaning 'to bring about'. There are sixteen letters in this line.

The message appears to be: 'Hasten to bring about', and the cross would indicate 'Christianity'.

By now it had become obvious that the three vertical strokes to the left of the cross in line one indicated the three words written in line two, and the five vertical strokes to the right of the cross in line one indicated the five words in line three. Once again it was a matter of following dots. The three verticals to the left of the cross give five, then one, and then two reversed dots, which produced 'A H R' or correctly 'R H A', which means 'the power'. Later researches consistently revealed that Rha – 'the power' - routinely refers to the High King. Eight dots in 5 + 1 + 2 = 8.

Five verticals to the right of the cross again had dots, which are 4 - 1 - 1 - 1 -1. Applied to the five words of line three this code produced 'DD - A - I - S – Dh'.

This appears to mean 'dais de', meaning in English 'to wish – right'. The word 'de' can also mean 'to part', and therefore to 'separate right'. Again 4 + 1 + 1 + 1 + 1 = 8.

In this way the dot code produces 'the King wishes right'.

There was then the simple matter of matching the sixteen Coelbren letters in both line two and line three with their modern equivalents to get the whole message.

1- Dot Code 'The King wishes right.' 'Hasten to bring (this) about.'

2- Dot code 'Hasten to bring (this) about.'

3- 'The misfortunes of the elder (ancestor) dead at the cave' (or "tied in a bundle = "embalmed."

4-   Dot Code   "The rottenness of irreverent Judea of necessary in a fallen state."

It is worth noting that these Alphabets were recognized as ancient when they were included in *The Cambrian Journal*, Vol. 1 p. 193, and also in Zeuss' *Celtic Grammar*, where they were unfortunately misidentified as 'Celtic'. This decipherment, in common with almost every other development, now opened up another line of enquiry into who was the ancestor or elder dead and embalmed in a cave, and what did the reference to fallen Judea mean.

Main Text of the Bodleian MS No 572

This ancient British Coelbren alphabet recorded in the Bodleian MS No. 572, was quoted and exhibited by G. H. Beaumont in 1855. The basic alphabet of sixteen symbols or letters is so arranged as to produce words, which then form short sentences. Each alphabet letter is embellished by a series of grouped curving lines that serve to indicate the number of letters in each word, and to select letters to form other words.

We can see this by first viewing the basic alphabet as it appears in the manuscript, and then by stripping away the codes and the curves that are added as guides to reading. At first the top line is complete with the upward curves that identify the number of letters in each word and the downward tails that indicate the sequence of words. The downward tails on the letters of lines two and three merely identify the letters that make up each word.

The first five letters from the right all have one tail, so these are the five letters in word number one, the second group of five letters all have two tails and so these compose word number two, and so on, with the last six letters all having three tails, and so the word has these six letters. In line three this same pattern is repeated. This is how the alphabet and codes appear in MS No. 572 .

Illustration 5-3: The Coelbren alphabet in Bodleian MS No. 572

The exhibit below is what the alphabet looks like when stripped of all its directional and coded curves and tails which do tend to obscure the basic alphabet.

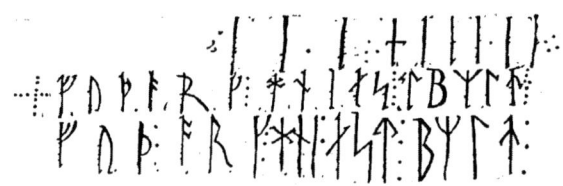

From this stripped exhibit we are then able to read the basic text and to uncover the messages that are written in the Coelbren alphabet and in the Khumric–'Welsh' language. The dots that point to individual letters in the text and which then allow for these letters to be selected to form further words and messages can be seen more clearly.

The ancient British-Khumric tradition holds that at an early era there were only sixteen letters in the Coelbren alphabet. There are only sixteen letters in the alphabet exhibited in the Bodleian MS No. 572.

As shown above, the Bodleian MS No. 572 is by no means a simple exhibition of the alphabet. As can be clearly seen the letters in line two (middle line) form three words whilst the identically arranged letters of line three (bottom line) form five

Chapter 5 - The Stones in Britain

shorter words.

To read this we take the cross in the centre of the signs in line one (top) as a starting point. To the right of the cross, there are five straight vertical strokes. At the top of these five vertical strokes there are from the right respectively 4 - 3 - 3 - 3 - 3 upward curving tails. These tails total sixteen.

The three straight vertical strokes to the left of the cross have respectively 5 - 5 - 6 upward curving tails., which again total sixteen.

These upward curving tails also match the number of the letters in line two (middle) and line three (bottom).

We are being told that the middle line has three words with 5 – 5 – 6 letters in each word reading from the right. The bottom line has five words with 4 - 3 - 3- 3- 3 letters, each word reading from the right.

There are seven dots placed vertically before the first word of line two, followed by five dots before the second word, and four dots before the third word. Again, these dots total 7 + 5 + 4 = 16. From this information we can select the seventh letter after the seven dots, and the fifth letter after the five dots, and the fourth letter after the four dots. From this we get a hidden three-letter word which is 'FF - WD – DR'. This appears to mean "Ffwdanu" meaning "to be in a hurry."

The same practice of inserting groups of dots before the beginning of words occurs in the bottom Line 3. Reading from the right, there are three vertical dots before word 1, then four dots before word 2, two dots before word 3, three dots before word 4, and three dots before word 5. These groups of dots help to locate five letter symbols. These letters then produce W – I - U – FF – E, which only has meaning if read from right to left giving us "effuiw" which is almost certainly the modern "effaith", meaning "to bring about".

This first hidden message appears to be - "hasten to bring about +" or "hasten to bring about Christianity".

If we return to the top of Line 1, there are more dot signals. Before the three vertical strokes to the left of the cross symbol, there are 5 - 1 - 2 reversed dots that refer to the words in the middle of Line 2. These locate the letters A   H   R, that reversed correctly produce "RHA" meaning *'the power'* and a great deal of other research shows consistently that 'the power' intends the High King. These dots number 5 + 1 + 2 = 8.

In the same way there are a series of dots placed before the five vertical strokes to the right of the cross on this top of Line 1. These dots number 4 – 1 – 1 – 1 – 1 = 8. So there are 8 + 8 = 16 dots in total. Applying this 4 – 1 – 1 – 1 – 1 to the beginning of the five words of the bottom Line 3, we find the five letters - "DD - A - I - S - Dh" – that again appears to produce "dais de" meaning "to wish right". The word "de" can also mean "to part right" or "to separate right'.

This dot code produces *'the King wishes right'*. The main point being that all these three and five words on Lines 2 and 3, are directly Khumric words and so are all these hidden coded words.

The Bodleian MS No. 572 holds an ancient British Coelbren alphabet and ciphers that all contain fully intelligible ancient British messages. That these sets of symbols were exhibited together with the St Paul's Cathedral stone inscription, which reads correctly as 'the beloved lord celebrated', and were held to be either foreign Scandinavian or forged is incredible. The entire conspiracy to obliterate all British ancient history is incredible.

The magical number of 16 is everywhere, proclaiming the number of letters in the ancient British alphabet at that time. From what was seen as a simple exhibition of an alphabet we get the following statements by recognizing the alphabet as British Coelbren and the language as Khumric.

1. 'The King wishes right.'
2. 'Hasten to bring (this) about.'
3. 'The misfortunes of the elder (ancestor) dead at the cave (or tied in a bundle = embalmed).'
4. 'The rottenness of irreverent Judea of necessity in a fallen state (dead)'.

That these alphabets were recognised and mislabelled as 'Celtic' and therefore Ancient British, and were included in Zeuss' *Celtic Grammar* and in *The Cambrian Journal* is significant. Once we dispense with the archaeological nonsense of the ancient British being 'Celts'" and restore our correct British ancestral identities we can begin to see daylight.

With the Watling Street Stone, we have the necessary evidence from remote antiquity to prove the accuracy of the ancient British Alphabets. With these decipherments we can start the journey in the past along our ancestral migration trails. The closed and sealed doors that are blocked and obstructed by academic archaeological idiocy about 'Celts' and 'Celtic' inventions will now begin to swing wide open.

The Bridekirk Stone in Cumberland

Around 1600 William Camden visited the area of Cockermouth in Cumberland. This was, as the name shows, anciently Cambrian and therefore Khumric-Welsh territory. As with almost all itinerant antiquarians in England, Camden was Roman-orientated. During what is loosely called 'the Roman period' a fortress was built at Papcastle, which was later used as a quarry for the building of Cockermouth Castle. The result of this, and subsequent robbery of stone for other buildings, is that where stones started out on their journey as building materials or monuments is confused.

At Papworth William Camden noticed a stone, which he illustrated with accompanying notes in his book *Britannia*.

> 'At Papworth in Cumberland which by a number of monuments lays claim to be of Roman antiquity, amongst other monuments was found a broad vessel of a greenish stone artificially engraved with little images which whether it been a laver to wash in, or font, for which purpose it serveth now, at Bridekirk hard by, I dare not say, it is thus inscribed.

> 'But what they mean, and to what nation they belong, let the learned determine, for tis all a mystery to me. The first and eighth are not much unlike that whereby from Constantine the Great's time the Christians expressed the name of Christ.'

So, whilst William Camden acknowledged a mystery in this Bridekirk -Papworth stone, like most others of his time, and later, he was totally unaware of even the existence of ancient British alphabets. Camden having passed the matter over to 'the learned' then proceeded to make guesses. Being English and even though he recognised the stone as being very ancient, he automatically attributed the inscription to foreign sources, and as a result got himself, and doubtless his readers, very confused.

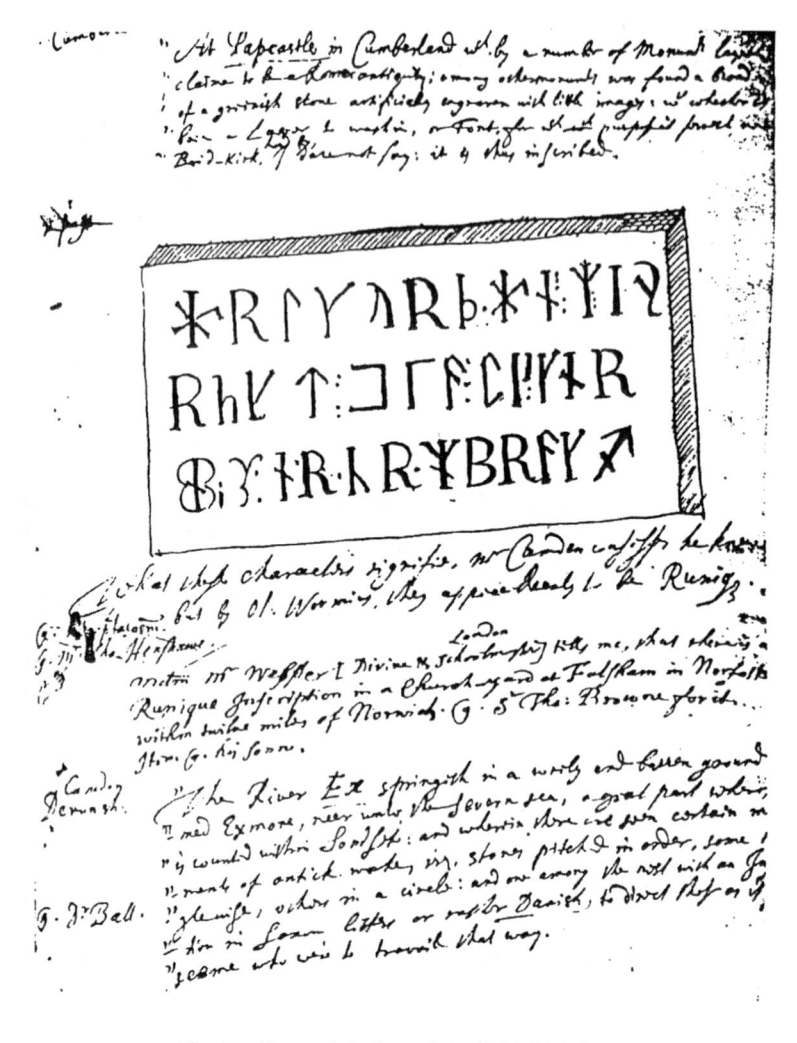

The Coelbren alphabet of the Bridekirk Stone
As illustrated by Camden over 200 years ago

Chapter 5 - The Stones in Britain

'The rest (the symbols) in shape, not in power, come nearest to those upon the tomb of Gorman the Danish King at Jelling in Denmark, which Pettrus Lindeburgus published in the year 1591.'

From this point onwards, the inevitable foreign attribution of all things British took on a life of its own. Thomas Henshaw, F.R.S. (1648-1700) proceeded to compound the problem by referring the stone to Ole Worm's *Danish Monuments*, and stating:

'What these characters signify, Mr Camden confesses he knows not - but in Ole Worm they appear to be runic.'

The fact is that this inscription on this British stone is a very straightforward British Coelbren statement, which reads as follows.

... CHRE	R E	Si A R DD	CHRE	U	WY	I	F
Chresu	Rhe	Ardd (al)	Chresu	Uch	Wyf	I	Fy
Christ		Swifty Speaking	Christ	Above	I am	With	You
		Full of words					

Wilson and Blackett noted that the inscription again has interspersed code dots in the same manner as the Bodleian Manuscript No. 572.

The inscription itself has signs of the tendency to allow Coelbren to be affected by Roman lettering. It appears to commemorate the central theme of Druid thought and Christianity, with the breaking of the bonds of death to rise to the Heaven and create order in the Universe. Why Camden thought that a stone font used in a church, and with Christian inscriptions, might not be an ancient font is hard to understand. At the end of the day, it remains incomprehensible that anyone attempting to research ancient Britain would try to do so without first reading the British historical records.

The evidence of the Lloegres-English stones is vital in many ways. They clearly pre-date the Angle and Saxon infiltrations, and the Mercian-Vandal arrivals. The stones also demonstrate the wide spread of Christianity in the centuries before the Angle and Saxon arrivals. This might appear to be a long way from the muddled attempts of Henry Schoolcraft in deciphering the Grave Creek Tablet, but the gap was closing.

Illustration 5-4: Coelbren on Bridekirk Stone, Cumbria, England

Text								
Coelbren	CH	R E	Si	A R DD	Ch	U WY I		F
Khumric	Chreus	rhe	si	Ardd	Chresu	wyf I		fy
English	Christ	swiftly	a noise	speaking	Christ	I am	with	you

Text						
Coelbren	R H V T	D R E	B U	S I	U R	
Khumric	rhwyt	drefu	bu	si	ur	
English	breaking out from	ties/bonds	he was	whizzing	pure	

Text						
Coelbren	U I DD	U R	Lle R	WY B R E	S I T U	
Khumric	uid	Ur	ller	wybre	sittel	
English	the chief	pure	to satiate	the firmament	to whirl around	

The Book of St Teilo

There are aspects of research into the pandemonium reigning in British historical studies that Alan Wilson and Baram Blackett would prefer to avoid. This is not always possible, however, and as a combination of two neutral British - totally unbiased - they deal with potentially acrimonious matters as fairly and impartially as possible.

The ancient book of St Teilaw is just such a case. This very ancient book is attributed to either St Teilaw (fifth century AD), or St Teilo (sixth century AD), both of whom are associated as early Khumric bishops of Llandaff Cathedral. For many centuries this book remained in Llandaff Cathedral, in Wales, and a letter of 1687 records it still being there. Sometime after 1687, the Book of St Teilaw mysteriously vanished from Llandaff, and later it resurfaced, just as inexplicably, in Lichfield Cathedral in England.

The Welsh story is simple, and it holds that the Book of St Teilo belongs originally to Llandaff Cathedral, in Cardiff. There is much evidence for this, as it was the custom and practice in ancient times to write important grants of charters and statements of accession into the margins, or above and below the main texts, on the pages of holy books.

There are several ancient 'Dark Age' charters of the Khumric-Welsh written in the once clear areas above and below, and around the sides of the text on the pages of the Book of St Teilaw. The Book is entitled for St Teilaw, and was certainly at Llandaff

Chapter 5 - The Stones in Britain

Page from the Book of St Teilo

until 1687.

Not surprisingly, the English story is different. It is claimed that the Book of St Teilaw was, unreported, originally at Lichfield. Then, again unreported or recorded, it was probably stolen from Lichfield by an unknown Welshman at an unknown date. Finally, again unrecorded, the book was re-obtained by persons unknown at an unknown modern date, and brought back to Lichfield. At Lichfield, it was then necessary to disguise the Book of St Teilaw by re-naming it The Book of St Chad - which of course it is not. The presence of the 'Dark Age' Khumric charters in the margins of the book is explained by the claim that the book is that of the seventh - century English St Chad, and that the Khumric charters are all later than this date, after the book was stolen around a thousand years ago by the unknown unrecorded Welsh person at an imprecise time.

Possibly this account should commence with the time-worn phrase 'once upon a time'.

In the 1990s one Welsh cleric raised objections in the press and other media in Wales, seeking support for the return to Wales of the Book of St Teilaw. Predictably, the book, like many other Welsh possessions, remains in England. Sadly, at Lichfield, the new owners of the Book of St Teilo, or St Teilaw, sent the book to a modern bookbinder who discovered that many of the ancient charter entries had been mutilated in a careless cutting and rebinding in 1707. These were ancient Khumric charters and so their loss was deemed irrelevant. They might of course have thrown some light on the old Book's past.

On one single page of this ancient *Book of St Teilaw* there are four charter entries. The one placed immediately above the text is in the position to be the earliest. What is important to this research is that it clearly exhibits a mixture of Coelbren and Latin letters. The entry is of huge significance as it twice names 'Tudfwlch', and there can be no doubt that 'Tudfwlch' is the Khumric spelling of King Teithfallt of *c.* AD 456-480. Tudfwlch was the son of Teithrin, son of Tathal, son of Arthur I (Arthun Ddu, the Black, or 'Andragathius'), son of Magnus Maximus. This of course places the Book in the era of St Teilaw of the fifth century AD about two hundred years before St Chad.

This charter was 'translated', or perhaps to be more precise, mistranslated, around 1700 by Edward Llwyd, known as 'the learned Llwyd', the Keeper of the Ashmolean Museum and Library at Oxford. Wilson and Blackett realised that there

Chapter 5 - The Stones in Britain

were Coelbren letters mixed with the Latin letters of this text, and their interest was increased by recognition of the name of Tudfwlch. The only way to explain what had happened is to set down the effort of 'the learned Llwyd', which is uncritically copied and recopied by generations of publishers, over and over again, and still succeeds in misleading everyone. It misled Wilson and Blackett for over twelve years.

The give-away was Llwyd's translation of the Khumric 'tref uache' as the French 'tres vaches', 'three cows'. The learned Llwyd's version is:

'Tydfwlch the son of Lliwydd arose, and Januarius the hermit, to demand the land of Teilo which was in the hand of Elcu the son of Geibig and his family and to redeem it, together with provisions for the consumption of Januarius and his men, to be raised by a tithesman, and there were given to Elcu one bull, a horse, three oxen, and three milch cows, being, including a mare, nine beasts for his possession. May he be saved henceforth to the day of strict judgement, who will not claim it for Tudfwlch and his family for ever.'

Very peculiar and extremely trivial goings on for a king of all Britain.

What is actually recorded is: -

'The wily one most high Tudfwlch (King Teithfallt) the rash/hasty nation nevertheless came ashore, elevating extremely the country, to make accord, to create humility (in) extremely vexed/pining misery, (in) this place an army in rank/order, the sudden appearance of without an encampment, a moving body without royal covenant of long standing.

Sailing around in an outcast state, choosing learning notwithstanding to make neat/order the Lord (of) the true pure/truth we ourselves the host of battle. Pure/fresh worthy being, to choose the coat of mail, crowned, the gift of what is spread, the religious man, the judge, (at) the place of the spear/lance they to render cause, the order of genealogy, the system of genealogy (descent), what keeps in (preserves) the amazing stream, what is the pure stream of power.'

Given the problem of there still being a monarchy descended from the north-west Wales Tudors, it would perhaps have been unwise for Llwyd to have made a correct translation which mentioned the accession of Tudfwlch - King Teithfallt - and his arrival from Brittany where he had been in a monastery. The account of the raising of a vast army to defeat Hengist and Gwrtheyrn, and the right of succession of Tudfwlch, and therefore of his descendants, would not have been universally well received.

Teithfallt frequently appears in ancient epic poetry as Tudfwlch, the sole surviving royal heir, after the infamous massacre at the Peace Conference at Caer Caradoc in Glamorgan in c. AD 456. He returned to Britain, and came ashore despite the *coup d'état* of Gwrtheyrn (Vortigern) and Hengist the Saxon. The text states that he raised the nation's spirits in the face of sorrow and misery, and chose mail armour instead of the monk's cowl. There is also a statement of his right to rule and lead as a direct result of his correct genealogical descent. The story of how he killed the one (blue-)eyed Hengist, is told clearly in ancient epic poetry.

The mangled mistranslation of Teithfallt's accession stone at Margam Abbey where the Coelbren 'Th' is misread as a foreign Irish 'G', and Thiethell - Teithfallt is mangled into 'Grutne', has already been mentioned. The fact that the Tudfwlch statement in the Book of St Teilaw is one of mixed Coelbren and Latin letters appears to have eluded the notice of scholars. The exploration of this strange affair left Wilson and Blackett wondering what had happened to those two of the Ten Commandments that state 'thou shalt not steal', and 'thou shalt not bear false witness'.

The Stone of King Theoderic - Tewdrig

Another ancient British stone stands amongst many in the rarely visited museum at the rear of Margam Abbey. This has been photographed and published in the relatively obscure academic press, and has been falsified into the 'Stone of Einion'. As might be expected this stone has been mistranslated and misdated to an absurd degree to conform with the politically correct and idiotic theory of W. G. Collingwood. It is yet another example of a disaster caused by archaeological attempts to evaluate data without knowledge or reference to the history of the country to which these artefacts belong.

The text written on the stone in Latin and the translation is:

Line 1 -	CRUX XPI	the cross of Christ
Line 2 -	EN NI AC UN	see / granted / now that / at this same time
Line 3 -	PAC NI MAC	peace / now granted / in honour-worship
Line 4 -	ThUORThOREC	Theoderic (Thuorthorec)

Chapter 5 - The Stones in Britain

Line 5 -   FECIT   made this

That the stone of King Theodosius - Teithfallt the father of King Theoderic - Tewdrig should be mangled into the 'Stone of Grutne' is grotesque, but the contortion and twisting of this equally obvious inscription of King Tewdrig Uthyrpendragon is utterly astonishing.

The importance of this deliberate mangling of evidence is this: first, the great war-king who battered and drove out the German tribes in the era around 456-470 was the Em-Rhys Wledig, 'the Diadem-ed Prince Legate', who was King Teithfallt - Theodosius. If he is identified, then his great-grandson Arthur II is indisputably easily identified.

Second, the Uthyrpendragon, who is named as 'Uther' in the English Bruts and other records, who killed Guinner deu Ffreudwyd *alias* 'Gorlois', at Castle Dameilock in Cornwall, is revealed as King Tewdrig - Theoderic. All this is fully detailed in other volumes written by Wilson and Blackett. Once King Tewdrig is identified as the Uthyr or Natanleod mortally wounded at the battle at Tintern Ford on the Wye in 508 (as set down in the Anglo-Saxon Chronicles and the Llandaff Charters), and who was then buried at Mathern ('ma' = 'place of', and 'teyrn' = monarch, so Place of the Monarch), then the alleged mystery of King Arthur is no more.

That these remarkable stones would have been set up by reigning British kings should surprise no one. That they have been so deliberately misread and alleged to have been set up by untraceable nobodies should amaze everyone. These are accession stones, and that of Teithfallt would probably date from around 470, and that of King Tewdrig at roughly 490. Stone after stone after stone, each carrying fifth- and sixth-century names and valuable historical information, has been deliberately misdated and redacted from around 1950 onwards, in a campaign of obliteration. The stone of King Teithfallt's brother, a bishop, is misdated; the stone of Tewdrig's brother, also a bishop, is misdated; the stone of Arthmael (Iron Bear) Arthur II, at Ogmore, carrying four identifiable sixth-century names is not of the tenth century; nor is the stone at Llantwit Major carrying the name of Arthmael, St Illtyd (his first cousin), and King Ithael (the joint successor with Morgan to Arthur II) of the ninth century, and so on and on and on. The stone of Gwenora the likely Gwenhwyfawr, or the Guinevere of mediæval romance, is another casualty amongst many.

There is a sixth-century cross stone carrying the name of Mevroc-Meurig a few

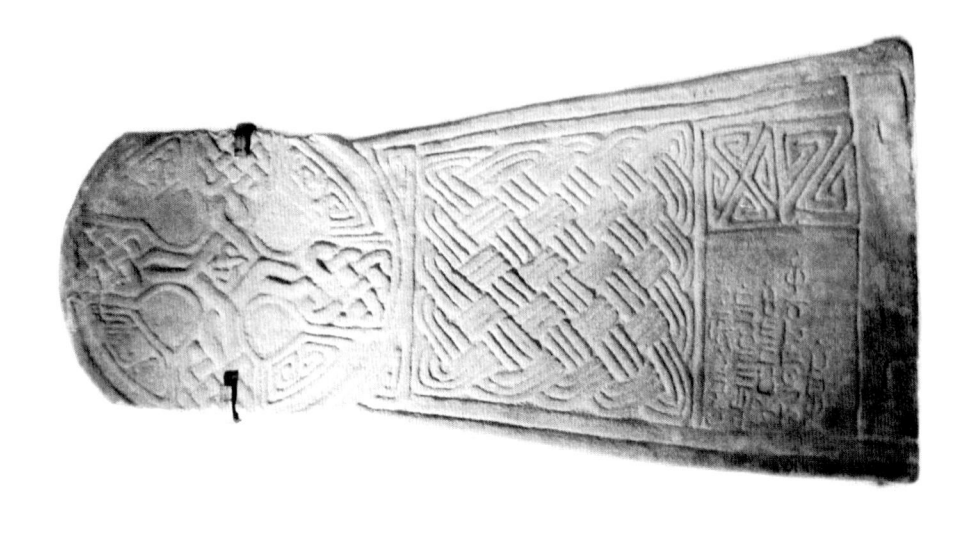

Stones of King Theodosius and King Theoderic
(Currently held at the Margam stone museum

miles from Tintagel in Cornwall, and Meurig was indisputably the father of Arthur II. It has to be recognised that W. G. Collingwood was hopelessly wrong in his ignorant theorising, and the time has come to throw out the political correctness of archaeological comparisons which totally ignore the records, and which distort British heritage and history.

The Cross of King Theodosius - Teithfallt

The audacious lunacy of the theories of W. G. Colllngwood in proclaiming the north-east of England as the birthplace of the art of stone-carving and inscribing in Britain has resulted in the destruction of British Khumric history. All native history is now ignored in the rush to obliterate and to conform with this unfounded theory.

Kings, not any Tom, Dick, or Harry, left inscribed stones; and so it was in Wales. The ancient stone cross of King Teithfallt - Theodosius is preserved at Margam Abbey, but no one notices it. It has been re-labelled as the 'Grutne Cross' in order to conform to the ill-founded and unproven theory of Collingwood. There is no 'Grutne' anywhere in the histories, or in the multitudinous genealogies, or in the mass of ancient poetry, or in cathedral and abbey charters, the lives of the saints, the Triads, or anywhere else. We are entitled to confront this absurdity, and to ask "Who, or what, or where, was Grutne?"

As we get no answer, we should look at the inscription and read it. Predictably, the result is extraordinary when read in the light of the known preserved history. First however, the 'accepted' version of the English translation of the inscription of this priceless ancient British Welsh relic:

> 'In the name of God most high. The cross of Christ which Grutne prepared for the soul of Ahest.'

Needless to say, there is no 'Ahest' traceable listed anywhere in the records either.

If we examine the inscription carefully instead of accepting' this crudity, we get this:

Line 1 -	INOMINE	in the name of.
Line 2 -	DIR	fatal misfortune,/ mischief from "Diritas".
Line 3 -	CIMI	the reproach (of).
Line 4 -	CRUX	the cross

Line 5 -	THITELL	ThhiThell = Teithfallt = Theodosius,
Line 6 -	PROP	prepared
Line 7 -	ATRABIT	clothed in black (Atratus) to go (Bit=Beto = to go.)
Line 8 -	BRUTNE	Brutus, whether or not.
Line 9 -	PROATN	proautor = remote ancestor, in the beginning.
Line 10 -	AHESTI	(he was) an aetheist.

With the reference to Teithfallt (restored with Khumric 'Th' recognised in place of ludicrous Irish 'G') as succeeding to the Glamorgan throne around 456, all this makes sense. All the Glamorgan kings claimed a direct descent from Brutus son of Silvius, son of Aeneas, son of Capys, son of Anchises of Troy. Brutus would have arrived in Britain around 500BC.

The reading would appear to be: -

'In the name of fatal misfortune and the reproach of the cross, Teithfallt prepared to go clothed in black, whether or not Brutus his original remote ancestor was an atheist.'

The reference to 'clothed in black' is very significant. After Gwrtheylin (the Englished 'Vortimer') defeated the Saxons around 456, the Saxons begged for a Peace Conference, to which, by the custom of all nations, not one would come armed. The Saxons then brought concealed weapons, and succeeded in massacring three hundred and sixty-three of the leading British royalty, nobility, generals, and clergy. Teithfallt, who was not present at the Conference, succeeded Cynan and Niniaw as king, but he was not a son of either. So the infamous treachery of the Saxons brought Teithfallt to the throne, and all this is recorded in a plethora of ancient histories and epic poems including *Y Goddodin*.

The reference to Brutus is very necessary, as Teithfallt - Theodosius was affirming his hereditary right to succeed as King of Glamorgan - Gwent, and therefore to the leadership of the British nations.

There were no Grutne' or 'Ahest'; and this cross stone is not tenth-century, but clearly late fifth-century. It is yet another example of an over-reliance on archaeologists and a negation of the study of British history. Archaeologists can no more work independently of historians than forensic scientists can work independently, and usurp the function, of the police. The stone of Teithfallt -

Chapter 5 - The Stones in Britain

Theodosius is a major British historical relic and contemporary record. King Teithfallt is sometimes referred to as Tudfwlch, and is the British version of Theodosius. He was father of King Tewdrig - Theoderic who killed Guinner deu Ffreudwyd at Castle Dameilock five-and-a-half miles from Tintagel, in Cornwall. King Theoderic was then the father of King Meurig - Maurice Utherpendragon, who was the Mailcunos Magnus Rex, or Meliochon, of St Finnian, and who was in turn the father of King Arthur II Uthyrpendragon, *born c.* 503, and *died c.* 579.

The nonsenses of Grutne' and 'Ahest' serve to conceal and obliterate correct British history.

Chapter Six

The Etruscan Challenge

It was with clear feelings of relief that Alan Wilson and Baram Blackett turned away from British ancient history, and addressed the matter of Etruscan inscriptions. They had several times discussed the advisability of abandoning the whole project in the face of growing hostility and vicious dirty tricks campaigns. There was however the possibility of removing the project out of Britain by concentrating on the decipherment of inscriptions in more civilised atmospheres elsewhere. They were already aware of the existence of American inscribed stones, but they reasoned that it was impracticable to attempt decipherments on the North American continent without first restoring the credibility of ancient British history and the Coelbren alphabets.

When their attention was drawn to yet another English stone that carried a very clear long Coelbren message, they decided that the content of the deciphered message was probably so sensitive that it was time to close the chapter on Britain.

Ancient chronology is a problematic matter and it remains so with the Etruscan venture. There is an inevitable logic that the British migration carrying the remnant half of the nation, left Trojan-Phrygian territories in western Asia Minor at some time around 550-500 BC, and perhaps earlier. The first task is however to establish the fact of such a migration, and to date it later. As the Etruscans were said to be half of a nation, which migrated from these same areas around 650 BC, there is the clear probability of the Etruscans and the British being the two halves of the same whole nation. With Edward Williams in 1794, John Williams in 1846, and others pointing to the near identicality of the British and Etruscan alphabets curiosity alone made some attempt inevitable.

Alan Wilson, who had worked in Italy for three years and had visited many museums and ancient sites at weekends, had some clear ideas about the nature of Etruscan artefacts and writing. The decision in 1986 actually to get involved in this next planned stage of the project was triggered by an article in *The Guardian* on 14th November 1985 carrying the headline 'Unravelling the Mummy's Shroud'. The article exhibited a picture of the Perugia Cippus, a large monumental stone carrying a long inscription in Etruscan. The report outlined an attempt being made at Perugia University to decipher the Etruscan language texts using a computer. The Perugia Cippus and the Zagreb Shroud, which carried a number of long inscriptions, were to be used in this strange undertaking. The preliminary examination of the newspaper picture of the Perugia Cippus was sufficient to convince Wilson and Blackett that the script on the Perugia Cippus was undoubtedly Coelbren.

To Alan and Baram, the whole affair was laughable, as there was no way a computer programmer would know even the correct syntax of ancient Etruscan. With a totally unknown word-order of nouns, verbs, adverbs, adjectives, pronouns, prepositions, and so on, the idea was preposterous. Some Khumric words need three or four English words to explain them; others of two letters need two much longer words to translate, and *vice versa*. For example, 'cu' can mean 'mutually together'. All computers have the G.I. and G.O. factor of Garbage In gives Garbage Out, yet amazingly a major international company was sponsoring this attempt with £250,000 ($375,000). The positive side was that there was a definite interest in deciphering Etruscan, as opposed to the British attitude of 'do nothing about everything Welsh' in Wales.

The Zagreb Shroud, to be used in this exercise in futility, is a long wrapping-cloth found by a Croatian explorer in Egypt in 1847, wound around a female mummy. This thirty-two-foot-long shroud has a series of long Etruscan texts painted on it, which some observers have thought might even be from a rolled cloth book of some kind. The Croatian who found the coffin removed the winding-cloth from the mummy and took the cloth back to Zagreb in his native country, where it was deposited in the museum. Apparently, no one noticed the extraordinary inscription until J. Krall found it in 1872, and announced to the world an Etruscan text of some five thousand words.

If we pause but a moment it is necessary to remember that the 'Pelasgian' Western Turkey, or Trojan-area alphabet, and the ancient British Coelbren alphabet, are virtually identical with Etruscan. So, the provenance of this Zagreb Shroud is not indisputably Etrurian.

There are in fact some nine thousand Etruscan texts waiting to be read, most of them brief, and the fact that there was at least one major company willing to sponsor an attempt was in a way encouraging. Modem companies blindly sponsor universities, and forget that were it left to universities, the Earth would still be flat, the Sun would circle the Earth, there would be no aeroplanes, no electric lights, no radio, or a million other things, in fact very little of anything. We would all still dwell in caves, assuming that we had had the sense to come down from the trees to enter the caves. Grotefend, who deciphered cuneiform, was no academic, nor was the army engineer Rawlinson who deciphered Persian cuneiform, and Ventris, who deciphered Cretan Linear B, was an architect, and even Champollion, who attempted to decipher Egyptian hieroglyphics, was a school-teacher, and so it goes on.

Much time was wasted as colleagues in the Maesteg Valley contacted a Yugoslavian man who had lived there for many years, and he wrote letters to the Zagreb Museum. Zagreb was then behind the Iron Curtain, and earlier letters from Wilson and Blackett had produced no response. Many months produced only tiny postcards, which were of no value whatsoever in attempting decipherment. It was not until 1995 that through the good offices of Ms Diane Sawyer, one of America's best known television presenters, that good-quality photographs were obtained.

So, a plan was drawn up whereby decipherment would proceed along a controlled path in successive stages.

First, items which had only one or two Etruscan words would be read.

Then secondly, using the experience gained, items with only short single sentences would be read.

Thirdly, a selection of the longer Etruscan texts would be read.

Scene from Etruscan Tomb of the Orcus

A letter was sent to the named team at Perugia University informing them of the near-identicality not only of the British and Etruscan alphabets but also of the historical traditions. They were offered co-operation and were also advised to feed Khumric into their computer. There was no risk involved in doing this, as predictably, there was no answer. Wilson and Blackett wanted, if possible, two things from Etruscan decipherments.

Chapter 6 - The Etruscan Challenge

Early attempts at tomb inscriptions

Tomb of the Orcus inscription

Amongst the first words attempted was the single three-letter inscription in the Tomb of Orcus. On one wall of the tomb is a painting of a human head, which appears to be the head of a man wearing a laurel wreath. For some reason, which is not apparent, this is thought to represent a woman. Above and to the left of this picture is a three-letter word. This presented an immediate problem as these three letters were reversed, and there was also the problem of whether it would read from left to right, or from right to left. It was established that it can only be read when using reversed Coelbren.

As shown on the illustrations on the following page this reads as -

Khumric	L (Lle)	Fe (Ffe)	B (Ba)
English	this place	outwards from	being in (immersed)

This probably means - Lie - Ffe - Ba - which would mean simply 'this place/room - (to go)' 'outwards from - being in"-which could indicate the soul leaving the tomb to become immersed with the deity. Reading the Lie + Ffe together as 'lief" would give 'to cry out', so 'to cry out - being in (here)'.

Another effort at decipherment was made with the inscription in the Tomb of the Bulls. Here there is a mural of the Knight of the Fountain, which evokes an extraordinary parallel with the Khumric Mabinogi story of Owen and the Knight of the Fountain. The painting depicts an armed knight, complete with lance and shield, riding his horse towards an overflowing fountain. Lurking behind the stone structure of the well of the overflowing fountain is a dark, armed figure, who is presumably the Black Guardian of the Fountain, again exactly paralleling the Mabinogi Tale. In a further exact parallel, there is a tree overshadowing the fountain.

On the painted frieze above this scene there is a short Etruscan inscription. As shown in the illustrations on the following page, in many short Etruscan tomb inscriptions the letters are reversed Coelbren.

The first line (from the "Tomb of Orcus") probably gives – Lle-FFe-Ba – which would mean simply – "this place/room-being in" – which could indicate the soul leaving the tomb to become immersed with the deity. Reading Lle + Ffe together as "Llef" would give "to cry out", and so "to cry out – being in (here)".

ILLUSTRATIONS of ETRUSCAN INSCRIPTIONS

1. Tomb of Orcas
The letters of this inscription as reversed, a common Etruscan practice.

Etruscan			
Coelbren			
Khumric	Le	Ffe	B (ba)
English	(From) this place outwards being in		

Llef =to cry out, a shout, and ba = being in, immersed. The alternative is - "this place, -outwards/from - to be immersed in"

2. Tomb of the Bulls
Again there are reversed letters which caused decipherment problems.

Etruscan							
Coelbren							
Phonetics	Ffo	Mh	ch oo ng	ow(oo)	Ffe	Ffe	Ffe oh
Khumric	Ffe	Mi	chwynog	ow	Ffe	Ffe	Ffeo
English	Outwards me	full of weeds	moaning	outward	demeanour	flight	

Etruscan				
Coelbren				
Phonetics	Raiph = TH	ER	AN (or NA)	AD (or Da)
Khumric	Raith	ER	na (or An)	ad (or Da)
English	Judgement	towads	not(or our)	very (or good)

The inscription appears to read as -'outwards me, full of weeds (= mourning) (my) presence retreats towards judgement our good.

3. Bronze Mirror in Museo Etrusco Gregoriana, Vatican

Etruscan			
Coelbren			
Cipher	CD	A W (wy)	B A W
Khumric	CyD	awy	bawy = bau
English	mutually together	to the sky	the thigh

As the phonetics of Khumric slur a 'D' as 'Dd', it is interesting to note that by inverting the inscription, the inverted version appears to read as A-R-B-E-R-DC, and Arberth means 'sacrifice'. That is exactly what is represented in the scene on the bronze mirror. This fits very well with known Khumtic Bardic practices of coded messages.

Chapter 6 - The Etruscan Challenge

Tomb of the Bulls inscription

Another effort at decipherment was made with the inscription in the "Tomb of the Bulls". Here there is a mural of the "Knight of the Fountain", which evokes an extraordinary parallel with the Khumric story of *Owen and the Knight of the Fountain*. The painting depicts an armed knight, complete with lance and shield, riding his horse towards an overflowing fountain. Lurking behind the stone structure of the well of the overflowing fountain is a dark, armed figure, who is presumably the "Black Guardian of the Fountain", again exactly paralleling the Mabinogi tale. In a further exact parallel, there is a tree overshadowing the fountain.

On the painted frieze above this scene there is a short Etruscan inscription. As in many short Etruscan tomb inscriptions the letters are reversed. As shown in illustration 2, the reading is –

Outwards/demeanour – me – full of weeds=mourning – moaning – outwards/demeanour – flight/retreat.

Judgement / law / jury – towards – GOD – with - good

A first attempt to read this inscription as three long words, instead of ten short words, produced 'to make a transit, sinking down, to cry out'. Something which was later to occur quite regularly in other early decipherments, was the use of words that have dual meanings. Just as in English there are words with identical spellings, but with totally different meanings, the same also occurs in Khumric. For example, 'row' can mean to 'row a boat', to 'have an argument', or 'a straight line of objects'. As has been shown, 'ffe' can mean either 'outwards' or 'demeanour or presence'.

The sense of this inscription in the Tomb of the Bulls appears to be

'outwards I full of weeds (mourning) moaning outwards towards a manner (demeanour) of flight (to) judgement towards God with goodness'.

Another similar statement is written on an alabaster urn, where a dead warrior, who is carrying a broken spear and leading his horse, is shown accompanied by a goddess. The goddess holds the warrior's right hand in hers, and has her other arm around his shoulders. Clearly the deity is enfolding and protecting the warrior. There is an inscription written alongside the goddess' head, and another alongside the warrior's head.

The inscription near the goddess either reads

'the interrogator joined with the carcase', or 'the omnipotent one joined with the carcase'.

The warrior's inscription appears to read

'of whom alas which (was) a son of yours', then 'immersed (baptised?) he closes by, brisk/ active/alert'.

These readings would appear to fit with the funerary urn.

First attempts at deciphering were sometimes hampered by not knowing where a word started or ended. Initially this led to attempts to read quite long single words, which could only be done by taking quite a few liberties with the spellings, and producing phonetic rather than alphabetic similarities. As a growing number of short texts were attempted it became clear that the preference was for using numbers of short root-words in these ancient inscriptions. Invariably the longer inscriptions had dots placed after word endings making reading a very simple matter.

In the mysterious way that things often come together other people were also thinking along the same lines as Blackett and Wilson. In Maesteg, a mechanical engineer, Bill Isaac, was also exploring British Coelbren links with Etruscan. Whilst on holiday in Paris Bill and his wife Jayne visited the Louvre Museum, and there, Bill set about reading and translating Etruscan artefacts on display that had inscriptions. He simply used the Coelbren alphabet and the Khumric language. One of his most remarkable readings was to analyse an Etruscan bronze mirror which showed a man on a river bank with a bellows, from which a pipe or tube (perhaps an animal intestine) descended to the face mask of another man swimming under water whilst wearing a cloak. The word that accompanied this scene was 'Chwyf', and 'chwyfu' means 'to blow' or 'to puff'.

It seems so obvious once it is read and the scene is explained, but like many other things it is not obvious unless first explained. It proves that the Etruscans knew how to blow air through a flexible tube to an underwater swimmer wearing a facemask. It shows how the cloak cast a shadow which might attract sheltering fish, making fishing easier with the pronged fork which the swimmer carried. Above the inscription on this mirror the Broad Arrow or Awen /|\ sign is incised very clearly. This is another very clear British and Etruscan link. The scene is probably the world's oldest picture of diving apparatus.

Bill Isaac also successfully deciphered the scene on a bronze mirror where Venus is shown emerging from the head of her father Zeus - Jupiter.

Chapter 6 - The Etruscan Challenge

universities, the museums, the libraries, the government quangos of the Tourist Board, CADW (Welsh Heritage) and the Wales Arts Council, all resolutely pretend that there is no real history and deny its existence.

Local historians like Terry Witt of Llanharan who set about organizing whist drives, dances, prize draws, and other fund-raising activities, until he had the necessary £10,000 or £16,000, and then he self-published another book on local history. Mr Terry Witt was able to publish five such valuable books, and there are others like him.

The work on Etruscan decipherment by Wilson and Blackett was conducted in considerable secrecy, and knowledge of the real work of decipherment further east and back to 2000 BC was limited to a very small group.

One bronze mirror found at Tuscania which is dated to *c.* 300 BC shows a winged haruspex or prophet priest, rather like the old conventional idea of a winged angel. This being or personage is shown bending over an altar table upon which is an animal thigh. As is well known from a multitude of records the practice throughout ancient world was to devote the left thigh of a sacrificial animal to the god. The Christian Bible tells how Jacob, son of Isaac, spent a solitary night near the River Jabbok, and in a dream, he wrestled with God, who threw him down, injuring his hip. The place was called Peniel, and thereafter the Hebrew people did not eat the corresponding joint of animals. This part belonged to God. See Genesis 32:22-32.

The translation of the bronze mirror in the Musco Etrusco Gregoriano is shown in illustration 3 – it reads-

    Mutually together – to the sky – the thigh.

Some Bardic tracts show how the Coelbren is actually thirteen letters, which when inverted produce the second thirteen letters, making twenty-six. By treating this inscription as a palindrome and inverting it to read the other way (not uncommon), it seems to read A-R-B-E-R-D -C, which would be "aberth dacw', for 'the sacrifice behold'. As Khumric slurs the D and DD, this sounds like 'arberth', 'sacrifice', or 'arberthu', 'to sacrifice', or 'arberthwr', 'sacrificer'.

Every small artefact looked at deciphered

Chapter 6 - The Etruscan Challenge

The Etruscan Fallen Warrior Inscription

Bronze Etruscan Mirror

Chapter 6 - The Etruscan Challenge

The Stelae from Mesocco, Davesco, and Stabio

In Britain, attempting research outside London, Oxford, or Cambridge proved difficult in those pre-internet days. There was very limited access to the necessary documents, artefacts, and information, and the ironic French saying 'Paris and the French desert' applies. Requests for specific photographs made to museums in Athens, Rome, and Berlin were met promptly by return post. Similar requests to the British Museum were time-wasting, and frequently totally abortive. Weeks would go by, and it soon became apparent that the old British privilege and secrecy system was operating. Send a request on university- or college-headed paper and you get co-operation; send a request as ordinary Joe Bloggs and you get ignored. There was also the earlier experience of unanswered letters from the National Library of Wales, which is hidden far away from and is therefore inaccessible to the majority of the population. Alan Wilson and Baram Blackett were also reluctant to let anyone in Britain, and particularly in Wales, guess at what they were doing anyway.

Amongst the thousands of existing inscribed stones and artefacts in Etruria there are several monumental standing stones that are clearly not sepulchral. These have naturally been the subject of much speculation and guesswork, but without knowledge of the language in which they are written, they remain unread. The major effort made by Perugia University to try to decipher the Perugia Cippus demonstrates this. Ideas, mooted by some, that these major stelae are grave markers, were clearly improbable as the Etruscans were the grave mound-builders extraordinary, and there are no graves at the sites where these stelae were found. Cremation burials in urns are found in tomb mounds in the major cemeteries and these indicate that where a soldier died far from home, his ashes, if not his intact corpse, were brought back home in a small urn.

In dealing with the stelae, Wilson and Blackett first chose the Mesocco, Davesco, and Stabio stelae. These stelae all have relatively short inscriptions. The Stabio stelae has two vertical lines of writing inscribed on its face. When set out on the horizontal plane for decipherment the inscriptions were found to read from right to left, as do the vast majority of these ancient inscriptions. The Stabio stone appears to record a battle to repel an invasion, which had been fought and won by Etruscan forces at the place where it was found. Whether or not metal detectors might uncover some remnants of armour or weapons from the site to confirm this remains to been seen in the future.

The literal translation of the Stabio text is:

> 'Mutually together superior, extreme borders to you manifestly the chief power proclaim/shout the agent.'

This may be expressed as:

'With you the superior one extreme, on the borders, to you manifestly the chief power is proclaimed as the agent.'

The Stabio stele seems to record a battle on the borders, and the god is being given the credit for the victory.

The Mesocco stele also bears a message of two vertical lines, following a battle:

'Fetters were sent forth, listen. Lances reached out, sent forth, listen. Chief of the field of battle manifestly the chief of slaughter.'

Whether the chief, who is again credited with victory, is the god or a king is unclear. There are records in Roman ancient history of fetters being sent out by one city to another as a challenge or demand for surrender. Again, this record of a battle records the repulse of some invasion or attack, presumably an attempt to enslave the Etruscans involved, as indicated by the 'fetters'. The site may reveal traces of a conflict.

The Davesco stele is rather different as it may record a treaty instead of a battle. Further specialist research into the Roman historical records may resolve this question. The literal reading of this text of two vertical lines appears to be:

'He, chosen splendid manifestly in motion (/flight/swift) the chief, goods /chattels, utters (says) to inform vigour, to protect extremely, to mutually together what is drawn out mutually.'

This appears to concern an agreement to protect the trade routes in this Northern Etruscan area at Lake Lugano in the southern reaches of the Italian and Swiss Alps. Pliny records that the Etruscans sent out colonies to settle in Rhaetia in Switzerland, so this makes sense.

The first words of the text are 'ai ethel', for 'he the chosen' would also form the name 'Aiethel', which is very close to the Khumric name of Ithael, borne by King Ithael son of Arthur II, and by King Ithael son of King Morgan son of Arthur II. The name Ithael is of course one of the five known names of King Solomon son of David.

In the same way, the probable titular name 'Fe-rhi-o-ch' appears, matching the British name of Frioch, and as we have already seen one of the brothers of Arthur II son of King Meurig was Frioch (modernly contracted to Rioch). This 'Fe-rhi-o-ch' actually produces the titular 'manifestly the chief proclaimed'; and of course Frioch son of Meurig, in late sixth-century AD Britain, was proclaimed Regent after the death of Arthur II. All this is very well known; and from "Ai-ethel' giving Ithael, the Gewissae Kings of England routinely used the 'Ethel' or 'Chosen One' as part of their royal names: Ethelred, Ethelbert, Ethelred, and so on.

Chapter 6 - The Etruscan Challenge

THE BRONZE SITUALA AND WINE JUG FROM ORVIETO c. 400BC

As with every other Etruscan Inscription the texts on these wine vessels deciphers directly into Khumric -'Welsh' through the medium of the Coelbren Alphabet.

Etruscan	ᨆᴧᨉ	I ⌇	ᨆH	Aᨋ	
Coelbren	ᨆᴧ>	I <>	ᨆ◇H	ᴧF	
Khumric	B A D -bad	I CD=cyd	B O Ng=bong=bongam	A F=af	
English	ship's boat	to manually	bandy legged	going on/progress	

Etruscan	ᨋ ᨆ		↑ᨆ	И	Iᨋ ⌇
Coelbren	ᴦ ᨆ		↑ᨆ	И,	I ᴦ<>
Khumric	P E=pe or		Th E=te	Ni	I E C D = iecyd
English	if		spread	not	sanity, sensible

Etruscan	ᨋ I V	◇ I	HA	
Coelbren	ᴦ I V	◇ I	H ᴧ	
Khumric	Rh I W = rhiw	O I = oi	H A = ha	
English	the slope, to run down	the track	of scorn, disdain	

The inscription on these wine vessels is clearly an admonition and warning against over-indulgence of the fruit of the vine. The imbiber may stagger about like a man on a ship with his wobbling legs spread wide, which is not sensible and he will go down the track of scorn and disdain (as an alcoholic.)

The text is not a dedication to any imaginary "Laris Navrenie" any more than the mules-head drinking cup is dedicated to a hilarious "fulfuns Baccus". By abandoning pure guesswork

King Arthur Conspiracy - Wilson & Blackett

Inscription on the bronze statuette from Sarteano - Chiusi

Etruscan	F E P	H	⏀ L ſ	⏀ h	√	
Coelbren	F P P	H	⏀ U M	⏀ h	√	
Khumric	Ff E Pi =field	Mi = Mi	O B R =obr	O Hw	E	
English	Outward appearance	identical/me	beneath/below	from a shout	he	

Etruscan	∧ D	K E L
Coelbren	∧ >	K R L
Khumric	A D=ad	(K)=C E B=ceb=cebyster
English	Going over = dying	tethered

'In outward appearance of me below, from the shouting he going over is tethered.'

Etruscan	L E K	D ∧	√ h	⏀	ſ	L ⏀	H
Coelbren	L E K	> ∧	√ h	⏀	ſ	L ⏀	H
Khumric	B E Ch (bech)	D A(da)	E Hw	O	Rhi	B O(bo)	M I(mi)
English	small	good	he	the shout	from a chief	may be	I am/identical

Etruscan	ſ E F
Coelbren	ſ F F
Khumric	Pl E F (pief - piefr)
English	fine/fair/pure

'Small good the shout of a chief may be, I am fair/pure.'

The strange drinking vessel from Vulci in the shape of a mule's head has been dated around 500 BC. It is inscribed -

Etruscan	F ſ Y	∧ ⏀ T	(∧ ⏀ T)
Coelbren	F ſ Y	ſ ⏀ ↑	(ſ ⏀ ↑)
Khumric	Ff R U=Ffreuo	Rh O T=Rhoth or	P O T = pot
English	to flow, gush out	loose, freely	the pot

The reading is – 'To flow freely' or 'to flow (from) the pot.'

Etruscan	S	∧ 8	ſ L	h ſ	L ⏀ ↑	I E I
Coelbren	< >	∧ ⏀⏀	ſ L	h ſ	L ⏀ ↑	I F I
Khumric	C D=cyd	A OO=aw	PiB=pib	Hw P=hwp	B O T=Bot	I El=ei
English	mutually together	liquid/ fluid	loose/ belly	an effort, push, pull	a round body	to him

'Together the liquid (drink) loosens the belly to push (out) a round body to him.'

Chapter 6 - The Etruscan Challenge

It is worth noting that the Romans, who waged ceaseless wars for five centuries to destroy the Etruscans, made it a practice deliberately to discover the secret names of the gods of other nations, whereupon they conducted religious rites summoning those now vulnerable gods to Rome. These rites then deprived the other nation of the protection of its national god. As previously noted, knowing another man's actual given name could give his enemies the power to harm him. For this reason, the names of rulers such as emperors, kings, or pharaohs (and perhaps all men), were always a secret matter, and a variety of titular descriptions was routinely used.

The immediate importance of all this is that the Mesocco, Stabio, and Davesco stones all decipher and translate in a coherent and straightforward manner, and all three produce credible, meaningful statements by using the British Coelbren alphabets and ciphers, and the Khumric language.

General Etruscan Inscriptions

The Messoco, Stabio, and Davesco,stelae gave a certain impetus to the project, and although Blackett and Wilson were heavily involved in the production of the volume *Artorius Rex Discovered* in 1986, they did find some time to continue with Etruscan decipherment. Whilst the monumental stones with their treaty and battle records were attractive targets, it was decided that it might be more than useful to search the writing in the tombs of the mighty, and to try to examine religious statements, which might give more precise information. It was reasoned that it would be the writings of ordinary people of Etruria as they went about their normal daily life which would place the matter beyond all doubt.

As well as appearing in scenes on bronze mirrors these writings exist on all manner of simple items such as wine bottles, situlas, small statuettes, votive items in tombs, and the various sarcophagi of the dead. The fact that these could be read out logically, coherently, and meaningfully, should now resolve the matter.

The British Museum has amongst its exhibits a bronze situla and a wine jug from Orvieto, which are dated at around 400 BC. Both these vessels are inscribed with the Etruscan alphabet. These texts read out beautifully into Khumric, and are defined in the related British Coelbren alphabet. They are in fact warnings against over indulgence in the juice from the fruit of the vine.

These texts are not dedications to an imaginary 'Laris Navrenie' (whatever that is) as imagined by the inventive scholars with their fertile imaginations, pursuing their totally unscientific methods in archaeology. Nor is the Mule's Head drinking-cup a dedication to the hilarious 'Fufluns Bacchus'. If guesswork and pure invention are avoided, then these texts can be read in their original language and intent. The reading is:

'ship's   boat   towards(/to)   mutually   together   bandy-legged   to   go on(/progress) if not spread, not sanity to run down the slope of the track of scorn(/disdain).'

This simply means that if the drinker gets too closely mutually together with the drinking-cup and the wine, he will stagger along bandy-legged as if on a ship's boat; if he does not spread his drinking out, he will go down the slope of sanity or sense and he will be on the track of scorn and disdain.

The idea of a wine-bibber and alcoholic staggering about like a man on a ship in a rough sea, with his wobbling legs spread wide, and putting himself into a foolishly unwise situation, and thus on a path leading to inevitable disdain and scorn, is made plain.

The Mule's Head drinking-cup comes from Vulci, and has been dated at around 500 BC. This also carries an inscription and is again a pithy admonition and warning against over-indulgence in strong drink. This reads:

'Together the liquid (alcoholic drink) loosens the belly, to push out a round body to him.'

A simple warning about the spreading stomach, or beer-belly, of the heavy drinker!

Another interesting item in the British Museum is a small statuette from Sarteano - Chiusi. The statuette is one of an athlete, who may have once enjoyed the shouts and cheers of the arena. It carries an inscription, which is very cleverly constructed to read from both right to left, and also from left to right. The left to right translation reads:

'In outward appearance of me below, from the shouting, he going over (=dying) is tethered (held fast).'

Then it can be read from right to left:

'Small good to him the shout of a chief may be, I am fair/pure.'

Who the athlete was we do not know.

Chapter 6 - The Etruscan Challenge

Etruscan Sarcophagii in the British Museum

It is not uncommon for Etruscan coffins to have a statue of the owner placed on the lid. For this reason, they are frequently photographed as book illustrations.

The stone coffin from Tuscania, which for inexplicable reasons is known by the name of 'Vipinanna', has a statue of a reclining man on the lid. Given the highly speculative methods of guessing at the text of the inscription that runs around the borders of this sarcophagus lid, this has been attributed to 'Vipinans Sethre'. Again, Etruscan was until now an undeciphered and unknown language, and it is difficult to know how this peculiar attribution could be made.

The inscription is: - See Illustration

Reading right to left these states: -

'Gliding towards what is pervading (= God) not stained, a cry to him what is clear, he from outward appearance assiduous, in flight he to join with tranquillity (/cold), he yea out from with a hood (/shroud) yea it is so, the blow, the oath outwards extremely yoked together, a parting from, gliding (/sailing) together.'

This is undoubtably a funerary statement, and it tells a great deal. It shows a firm belief yet again in one god. It shows a belief in the soul and in a definite form of afterlife. It shows a clear idea of a soul rising to join the deity after death on Earth. The text speaks of the dead man's soul gliding and ascending smoothly to join the deity. There is no trace of any 'Vipinans Sethre', and there is no 'V' in the Khumric alphabet anyway.

Another interesting sarcophagus in the British Museum has been identified as belonging to "Vel Velthur" (they really do like 'V', and there is no 'V' in Khumric or Coelbren), which again is from Tuscania. This stone coffin has a processional scene carved on its side. Leading the procession is a man carrying a bundle of rods and an axe. This would be the 'lictor', to use the Latin name for the person carrying the symbols of judicial rule, which the Romans adopted from the Etruscans. Following the lictor is a horse-drawn chariot driven by one man, and four robed men are shown walking behind the chariot. These four carry bundles of palm fronds which appears to be a Hebrew or Israelite symbol.

Above this scene of an important man, who is probably a judge, riding in his chariot, there is an inscription. This again transfers easily into British Coelbren, and can be read into the British Khumric language using Llewellyn Sion's ciphers. It reads:

'with sorrow (/grief) mutually what is outward (/apparent) amply, the entire inhabited place with hurt is disadvantaged. With the superior god enveloped

(/transformed) father, yea, mutual wonderful (/strange) with proceeding (/what goes) gliding (/smoothly) whirling around, to grow silent, the lord, the journey of the lord.'

The inscribed stelae from Davesco, Mesocco and Stabio

The Mesocco, Stabio and Davesco stelae all have two short lines of writing placed vertically. These are set out in the horizontal plane and the Mesocco stele can be read Right to left.

Crap-fossa da Mesocco   Crap-fossa da Davesco   Crap-fossa de Stabio

Mesocco stele

Line one-

Etruscan	ᴠϝNU	ϝU	ϝV
Coelbren	LϝrV	ϝU	ϝV
Khumric	b-e-r-w=berwy	eb	ew
English	fetters	send forth	listen, attend
Alternate	Ber=lance, pike Wy=reach out	Eb=move out	Ew=listen, attend

Line Two

Etruscan	∩ϝ⋉ϝ	rl	
Coelbren	ΛϝꝞϝ	rl	
Khumric	a-e-rh-fe=aerhfan	r-i=rhi or i r=rhi fe	r-e-a?
English	field of battle	chief to chief manifestly	battle?

Alternate – Ber = lance, pike, Wy = reach out, Eb = move out, Ew = listen, attend. The reading could be Are = slaughter, Fe = manifestly, Rhi = chief.

Chapter 6 - The Etruscan Challenge

Stabio Stele
Right to left

Etruscan	ᐸ	O N	I V	O K L F	(L? R)
Coelbren	< >	O N	I V	O K r F	
Khumric	cyd	on	iw	ochre	
English	mutually	superior	extreme	borders	

Etruscan	I	ᛏ	E	ᴎ		O K	ᴎ F
Coelbren	I	ᛏ	F	ᴎ		O K	ᴎ F
Khumric	i	ti	fe	rh=rhi (rha)		och	mh-e = me
English	to	you	manifestly	chief (power)		woe	(the) agent

The letters F-R-Och can make "froch" and that means "rage".
Davesco Stele

Line One Davesco Stele

Etruscan	A I	F ᴎ F ᴎ	ᴎ K ᛏ		F	ᴎ I	ᐳ		
Coelbren	A I	F ᴎ I	F TH F ᴎ) L F K > V		F	ᴎ I	> >		
Khumric	a i	e-th-e-l	e-ch-dwy=echdwyn	fe		r-irhy	da*		
English	he (who is)	chosen	splendid		manifestly chief	good			

Line Two Davesco Stele

Etruscan	F L F ᴎ	N V F I ᛏ O V I ᴎ I V	ᐳ	I >	<
Coelbren	F L F ᴎ	N Y F I ᛏ O V I ᴎ I V	< >	I >	<
Khumric	eb er	n-wy-f i towil iw	cyd	id*	cu
English	utter in order for sake of	vigour to protect extremely	united together	drawn out ?	mutually stolen

183

The Romanche Inscribed Deerhorns

The Etruscans colonised parts of what is now Switzerland, and their language survived there known as Romanche. Very few inscriptions are known.

Two deerhorns that are inscribed with short Romanche texts survive, however, and these texts are exhibited below:

Again, this is a statement rather than a prayer. It affirms the ascension of the soul of the deceased Lord to glide smoothly to ascend into union with the deity. Viewed from Planet Earth, the heavens appear to whirl around daily as Earth spins on its axis, and this theme of 'whirling around' is expressed in British as well as Etruscan texts.

A third coffin in the British Museum,which interested Wilson and Blackett is one known as the 'Vel Arna' sarcophagus. Again, this has a text that reads immaculately in Khumric. The text again expresses similar sentiments to those found written on the other coffins. Again, there is a belief in the afterlife, and an ascension into heaven to join with the deity. Of course, all this means that all the books previously written about the Etruscan religious ideas are totally wrong, and one can only wait for the demented wrath of the thwarted academics.

> 'Sorrow (/grief) mutually, outward amplitude the entire (/total) inhabitants disadvantaged (/hurt, with the superior god, the father, yea, mutual, wonderful (/strange) imminent with what goes gliding (/smoothly) to whirl around (*i.e.*, in the heavens)'.

There is then an additional phrase at the end of this text thought to read 'sixty-three years'. In Khumric Coelbren it appears to read 'taith rhi', 'a journey of the lord'. Depending on a final descision on the shape of a few signs this could alternatively read 'tawill rhi', 'to grow silent the lord'. Either could fit aptly with the earlier main section of the text.

The only previous ideas concerning the Etruscan religion were those alleged to be of Roman writers, and these are only available in the form of mediaeval copies of around 1200-1400. These time-lapses of twelve to fourteen hundred or even two thousand years between the alleged composition of Roman, Greek, or Jewish documents, and the alleged copies that are now available, seems to bother no one. But British-Khumric historical documents set down two hundred to three hundred years after an event are denounced as not contemporary, and therefore unacceptable. The uneven playing field is all the more uneven as in all cases of battle-fields there are the great mound war-grave cemeteries of the battle and in many cases contemporary inscribed stones for fallen princes. A treaty stone in Wales is unimportant, but not so with Etruscan stones. It might be wise to postpone judgements on the nature and origin of the Etruscan religion until the texts are read.

The little statuette of the Sarteano-Chiusi athlete, the Mule's Head wine jug, and the Situla, along with these inscribed sarcophagi of dead Etruscan lords; all decipher and translate precisely and consistently. Even before any of the longer texts were set out for reading, it had become inescapable that both the British and the Etruscans in their migrations from Trojan Phrygia between 650 -500 BC had spoken the same language and used the same alphabet in their writings.

Once the key to the Etruscan language is known, employing a computer to assist in the work is probably a good idea, but not before the original language and alphabet are known. There are a few variant letters in Etruscan texts, but once these variants are determined and their equivalents established, these remain constants. Work will need to be done fully to explain the vocal sounds which these additional and variant letter forms in Etruscan convey. Basically, these letters that are not found in the British alphabet are combination letters, where the expression of sounds is accomplished by joining two 'o' letters, or of two 'square' letters together to make an '8' or a similar joined double square.

Deciphering Rhaetian

Obviously, all the different fields of opportunity which had opened up in the project were each interesting in their own way. Alan Wilson went down to Swansea and had a meeting with a professor of Classics who was clearly alarmed at the developments, and whilst friendly he had no wish to get involved. This meeting convinced Alan that he and Baram were 100% correct. The proof was piling up, and the Iron Curtain of ignorance protecting the universities remained impregnable, and so things slowed down in the late 1980s.

The decisive factor was that in 1986 Alan Wilson developed cataract problems in both eyes and slowly began to see through an ever-thickening fog. A researcher who cannot see properly is gradually rendered helpless, and Baram Blackett now took over the entire organisation of the project. Alan Wilson jokingly compared himself to the comic cartoon character Mr McGoo, and whilst Baram did all the reading and writing, they were able to develop a slow system of working.

As far as the project of deciphering Etruscan texts using Khumric and Coelbren was concerned - who cares? The double standard employed to censor all meaningful Khumric records was strangling all progress. Nothing which does not fit with the current state-controlled creeds and dogmas of the religious faith of archaeological academics is allowed, and it can never be mentioned. One thing that came along was that S4C, the Welsh Language Television Channel, was co-operating with Swiss Television Companies to make a programme in general terms on the survival of minority languages in Europe. Alan and Baram knew some of the people working on this: a Swiss American lady who had learned Welsh, and a Welsh film editor. Both made themselves very unpopular by mentioning Wilson and Blackett. The interest lay in the fact that Pliny the Elder recorded that the Rhaetians were Etruscan colonies which had migrated northwards out of the Italian Peninsula and through the Alps into what is now the modern Helvetian Republic - Switzerland. The Rhaetian language is known as Romanche in our modern times.

If Etruscan could be deciphered into British-Khumric, then any Rhaetian inscriptions should also decipher into Khumric. It turned out that there were a few surviving Rhaetian, inscriptions which were carved on deerhorns. These were deciphered quite easily, and so these inscribed deerhorns provide a link between the ancient Rhaetians, the Etruscans, and the British. The television programme was made, and whilst both the Swiss-American lady researcher and the Welsh editor knew of the claim that these indecipherable Rhaetian artefacts translated into Khumric, nothing was said. They had careers to protect; and the institutional reputation of the University of Wales and its employees had also to be protected.

Inscribed Deerhorn one

Romanche	Coelbren	Khumric	English
		a n	without
		a le f th = aelaeth	lamentation complaint
		fe- R	frozen solid
		rh = rhi	the prince
		ow	cries out
		i	to
		dwy	the ruler

'Without complaint, the frozen Prince cries out to the supreme one'

Inscribed Deerhorn two

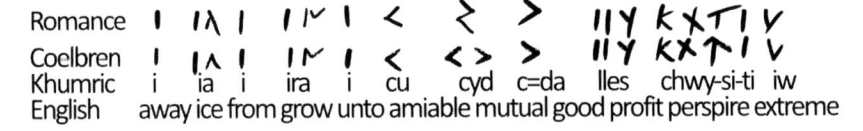

Romance	Coelbren	Khumric	English
		i	away
		ia	ice
		i	from
		ira	grow
		i	unto
		cu	amiable
		cyd	mutual
		c=da	good
		lles	profit
		chwy-si-ti	perspire
		iw	extreme

'To the melting of (the) ice, to the Dog(star) mutual benefit, profitable is hot weather.'

Chapter 6 - The Etruscan Challenge

The rising of Orion bringing the Dog-star Sirius up over the horizon heralds the spring and the coming of summer. This was the watched-for heavenly signal known to all the ancient northern hemisphere nations, and in the Alps, they clearly longed for summer. Whether these deerhorns were used as tools to break the ice covering wells and springs is of course conjecture. Another link had been forged in the chain, and Pliny the Elder had made a contribution.

Etruscan stones in the British Museum

1- Stone Coffin from Tuscania known as "Vipianna".

This coffin with a statue of a reclining man on the lid has been speculatively guessed at as being that of "Vipinans Sethre", and as Etruscan is an un-deciphered language it is difficult to see what justification there is for this attribution.

Etruscan – Coelbren

·⅃ △ ١ ᒫ △⅃ > ∃ ᗯ · ⅆYO ⅄∃⅃ · ∃ ⅆO∃ M: ᛚᛗᎪᛣ|ᎢᎥᎯ
ᒫ:⅃⅃Ꭺ∃⅃:ᒫ|⅃: ᒫ⅃ |⅃ A⅃⅃|⅃↓ᛗᎯO

Reading from Left to Right, this states : -

"Gliding towards what is pervading (= god) not stained, a cry to he what is clear, he from outward appearance assiduous, in flight he to join with tranquillity /cold, he yea out from with a hood (shroud) yea, it is so, the blow/slap oath outwards extremely yolked together, a parting from gliding together."

2- Stone coffin from Tuscania known as "Vel Velthur"

This sarcophagus has a processional scene carved on its side. First comes a 'Lictor' carrying the symbols of judicial rule, followed by a man in a horse-drawn chariot, and behind there are four men carrying palm fronds, a possible Israel custom.

King Arthur Conspiracy - Wilson & Blackett

Reading from left to right the inscription states-

'With sorryow/grief mutually what is outward/apparent amply, the entire inhabited place with hurt is disadvantaged. With the superior god enveloped (transformed) father, yea, mutual wonderful/strange imminent with what goes gliding/smoothly whirling around, to grow silent the lord, the journey of the lord.'

3- Stone coffin known as the "Vel Arna" Sarcophagus

The text again refers to the beliefs written on the other coffins and expresses belief in the soul, an afterlife, and an ascension to heaven to join the deity.

Etruscan – Coelbren

ATHA Z ꓱꓱ ꓥAꙮꓥꓥꓶ Z ꓱAH Z ꓱA Hꓱ AꓱIꓶ
A♡H DꓶꓶꓱA ꓱA⊃ N Z<ꓱꓱTA ⋄ꓱꓶ ꓤ⊃Y TXIII ꓤI

'Sorrow/grief mutually outward, amplitude the total/entire inhabitants hurt/ disadvantaged, with the superior god, the father, yea, mutual wonderful/strange/ imminent with what goes gliding/smoothly to whirl around (i.e. in the heavens).'

There is an additional phrase at the end of this statement, that has been read as "sixty-three years", and in Coelbren and Khumric it appears to read as-"Taith Rhi" meaning "a journey to the lord." Depending on the final decision of the shape of a few signs this could alternatively read as - "Tawill Rhi" meaning "to grow silent the lord."

Chapter 6 - The Etruscan Challenge

The inscription on the "VIPINANA" sarcophagus from Tuscania

The text reads from right to left -

Etruscan	ꗅIT	I	ꖠ Aꖠ	ꖠ Iꗄ Oꗅ	
Coelbren	ꗅiꗈ	I	ꖠ ꖠꖠ	ꖠ I ꗄ ◊>	
Khumric	Ft I T=fith	I	Ni A N LL = anll(w)	Hw I E OD=od	
English	gliding motion towards	not	stained	a cry to he what is clear	

Etruscan	ꗂ ꗅ	ꗅOVꗅ	ꖠꗅ>	ꗅA
Coelbren	ꗄ ꗄ	▶◊Vᗵ	ꖠ ꗄ ᗵ	ꗅ ꖠ
Khumric	E Ff E=ffe	E O W D=eorth	H E D = hedd (hed)	E A
English	he what is outward	diligent, assiduous	transquility (flight)	he with

Etruscan	ᐸ	∕Aꗅ ꗅO	ꗈ ꖠ↓ꗂ	Iꗅ	
Coelbren	<>	∕ꖠ ꗅ◊	ꖠ ꖠ▼ꗄ	Iꗅ	
Khumric	C D = cyd	I A =ia E O	A h w F	IE = iev	
English	junction, coupling	cold, ice he out from	with a hood, shroud	yea, it is so	

Etruscan	V A	ꗂ	Iꗅ	ᐳ̫	ᐳ̫I>
Coelbren	V ꖠ	ꗄ	Iꗅ	<>	<>I>
Khumric	W A = wab	Ffe	I W	D =cyd	C-D-I-D
English	slap, bang, stroke	outwards	extremely	joined	yoked together

Etruscan	>ꗂ A	ꗅꗅ		ᐳ̫
Coelbren	>ꗄ ꖠ	ꗅꗅ		<>
Khumric	D E =de A	E W		C D =cyd
English	a parting from	gliding/smothly		mutually/together

The inferences of this text are that there is one god, and that the human soul ascends into the heavens to enjoy an afterlife. A heavenly union with the god is clearly prayed for and believed in.

King Arthur Conspiracy - Wilson & Blackett

INSCRIPTION ON THE "VEL ARNA" SARCOPHAGUS FROM TUSCANIA.

Etruscan	Coelbren	Khumric	English
ATHA	ΛΤΗΛ	A T H A atha(far)	sorrow, grief
—	< >	C D=cyd	mutually
—	ʃ	Ffe=ffe	outward
√Aჴ⊲A√	√Λჴ>Λ√	E A Ngh D A E	amplitude
>JAH	<>ʃΛH	CD FA N (cyfan)	entire, whole, total

Etruscan	Coelbren	Khumric	English
>JAH⅁	<>ʃΛH⅁	CD F A N E – cyfane	inhabitants
A⅁I√	ΛJI√	A F IE – afies	hurt, disadvantaged
AC	ΛC	A G -ag	with
ⱶI	ⱶI	Th -tha	superior

Etruscan	Coelbren	Khumric	English
ᗞV↓⅁A	>VѴ⅁Λ	D U W FfA = ffa	god enveloped
↑AᗞI√	↑Λ>I√	T A D IE =ie	father yea
>	< >	C D = cyd	mutual
<⅁↑↑	<⅁ⱤT	C E R T = certh	wonderful, strange
A	Λ	A	with

Etruscan	Coelbren	Khumric	English
⊕	⊕	O	proceeding what goes.
⅁↓	⅁↓	E W = ew	glides, smooth
ⱶ>V	ⱶ>V	Si D W = Sidi,	to whirl around ie in the heavens.
↑X₁II	↑ΛV₁II	T A W I LL	to grow silent
ⱶ₁	ⱨ₁	Rh l =rhi	the lord

Sidi = revolving, Sidyll = a whirling around, and Sidydd = the Zodiac.

The text is yet another exhibition of the belief in an afterlife and of the soul ascending to heaven and to a union with the god. The situation where Khumric scholars have identified the identical nature of the Etruscan and the British Alphabets for over two hundred years and where Julius Caesar and Ammianus Marcellinus pointed to its identical nature and possible connections in the Eastern Mediterranean some 2050 and 1600 years ago, and yet nothing was ever attempted is incredible.

There is an additional phrase with this inscription that has been thought to read "sixty-three years". It may read as TAITH RHI or "a journey of the lord". Fitted with the rest of the text this makes sense, and it all depends upon the final decision of some of the shapes of the Sign letters. We have read it as shown above, as TAWILL RHI meaning, "to grow silent the lord."

Chapter 6 - The Etruscan Challenge

The Mystery of Larthia Scianti'

There is a lighter and more comical side to research if one has the wit to see it. One of the earliest ventures into decipherment outside Britain was with an inscription on a rock slab in Val Camonica. This long-hidden valley in Northern Italy is remarkable in that there are some two thousand ancient pictural carvings on its rocks. This valley, difficult to gain access to, remained free from Roman bondage until the year 8 BC, and the vast art gallery on the rocks has somehow also remained almost unknown to the wider world in our modern times of the all-pervading television camera. In 1983 a supporter sent Alan Wilson and Baram Blackett a photograph of a carving on a slab of rock in Val Camonica. The scene shows warriors fighting, some with round shields and others with rectangular shields, but most important there was also writing.

As the writing very clearly resembled Coelbren, the temptation to try to decipher this was great, even if ongoing work was interrupted. The short text did appear to decipher and translate into Khumric, and in 1983 this was something of a wonder, as no serious organised attempt to decipher Coelbren and trace its roots was then envisaged. So, still a little naïve, Alan and Baram wrote to several universities where linguistics were studied, and explained this phenomenon. A reply came from a Professor Glyn Daniel, which magisterially announced that there were no inscriptions on any of the rock-carvings at Val Camonica. So Alan and Baram sent the Professor a copy of the photograph with the inscriptions. They received a reply saying that the professor wished this correspondence to be discontinued. After they stopped laughing, Alan and Baram went out and bought one of the turgid books written by this academic, who had been the assistant to Sir Mortimer Wheeler when young. He should have remained an assistant.

It is necessary to show the dangers inherent in the current situation of fudging alleged decipherments. It is in a way frightening some academics are boasting that the Etruscan language is 50% deciphered. This is a nonsense and comparable with going for a ride on half a horse. To illustrate this pipe-dreaming let us examine the case of the fabled tomb of 'Larthia Scianti'.

In 1836 General Vincenzo Galassi, and Alessandro Bagolini, a priest, began serious excavations at the ancient Sorbo cemetary to the south-west of the Etruscan city of Caere (now known as Cerveteri). Caere is close to the Khumric Caerau = fortresses, as with Caerau in West Cardiff. The digging in the Sorbo cemetary commenced with a series of probes into what seemed to be a large overgrown hill, and very quickly five ancient tombs, which had been robbed long before, were located in one of the great tomb mounds. Another shaft was then dug straight down into the centre of this great man-made mound, and a sixth grave-chamber was located.

This time the perseverance of the two Italian antiquaries was rewarded, for this sixth tomb was untouched. Three undisturbed burials lay in a narrow stone-built chamber. The first, in the entrance of the tomb chamber, was that of a warrior lying on a bronze couch and surrounded by his weapons. The second burial was that of a man, whose cremated remains lay in an urn in a niche, and the third burial was that of a woman. This lady had been buried with a remarkable array of jewels and gold. There was an unmistakeable symbol of her high rank in a golden pectoral (breast plate) placed on the corpse. This pectoral is very similar to a pectoral shown on a statue of the Assyrian city king Ashur-nasir-pal II, depicting him as a priest. It is also similar to a pectoral carved on a winged sphinx found at Nimrud, an Assyrian capital city in antiquity. This may indicate a link between the Etruscan people and Assyria of around 700 BC. As will be shown the Etruscans began their migration from around the region of the northern headwaters of the Tigris and Euphrates rivers around 687 BC.

A mass of funerary gifts lay in this Sorbo tomb, including a four-wheeled cart, presumably the lady's carriage. There was also a warrior's two-wheeled chariot. For the lady there were pendants, necklaces, earrings, and beads. For the warrior there were round shields, cauldrons, bottles, incense burners, fire-dogs, and other items. The most intriguing items were however a set of silver cups and bowls clearly inscribed with Etruscan lettering.

These inscriptions have been 'read', and from these 'readings' it has been guessed that the name of this lady buried in this tomb was 'Larthia Scianti'. As no one in modern times has ever previously been able to decipher Etruscan it is difficult to see how this 'name' could be arrived at. The method seems to be to assume the letters to be Greek equivalents, and then to read them as Greek. Obsession with Greeks and Greek culture generally tends to obscure rather than to enlighten.

The obvious opportunity to translate the messages on these silver cups and bowls was there, and on a wet afternoon when they had time to spare Wilson and Blackett took a close look at 'Larthia Scianti'. At least Baram Blackett got out the notebooks and dictionaries and looked for both of them, first taking the 'Larthia' reading. What appears is 'mi ladhtheia', which is not a name. The 'mi' gives 'I am', while 'lad' means 'gift'; 'the' is from 'techu', meaning 'to lie hid'; and finally 'ia' is simply 'frozen, immobile'. This gives:

'I am the gift to lie hidden immobile'.

The remaining part of the inscription has been read as 'Scianti', but what appears, by reading the Etruscan letters as Coelbren, is 'dychiarit'. This is 'dych-i-ar-it', literally 'a sigh-to-faculty of speech-it'. The import of this is: 'a lament for the ability to speak'. The whole statement would then read:

'I am the gift to lie hidden still, a lament for the faculty to speak'.

Chapter 6 - The Etruscan Challenge

The ancient practice in many cultures of using titular names, and of concealing names, should have been considered. In this way Lucomo - Lucuomo, who was also the great Tarquin Priscus who founded Rome as a city, lies hidden behind a titular screen. Strangely, Virgil describes the founding of the stone-built Rome as distinct from the collection of hut villages of Romulus, and attributes this to Aeneas son of Anchises around 600 BC. Yet Livy and others tell of Lucuomo as Tarquin Priscus building the same city at the same time. Lucuomo appears to be 'Lluchynt' for 'violent onset', with the 'om-o' giving 'what stretches around'.

Even Tarquin, thought to be Tarchon in Etruscan, looks more like 'Tad-dhon', which is 'paternally overspreading'. This Tarquin Priscus had Tanaquil as his queen, and a noble captive Ocrisia as a handmaiden. This young woman conceived a child when sitting near the hearth of the household fire, where a spectral vision of a male organ appeared. A boy was born, and a strange portent occurred as he lay sleeping one day. The child's head burst into flames, which then vanished leaving the baby unharmed. The boy was Servius Tullius, who became King of Rome in a coup d'etat. Servius Tullius appears to be a Latinisation of 'Serfanol Tylu', which is "startling the household". There is a possible alternative in 'Serthu Tylu', which means 'to grow obscenely in the household'. As king, Servius Tullius was also called the Lord Mastarna, and probably this is 'maes taranu', meaning 'from within thunder'; the word 'tar' meaning 'shock' or 'impulse'. (Before the amateurs begin howling 'maes = a field, or a plain', 'maes' as an adverb means 'out' or 'from within', and 'maesa' means 'to eject' or 'to make war').

A great deal more can be written on this area of phonetic translation, and the Latin forms of Etruscan names, and further mention will be made as appropriate. At this time, we can note that the Etruscan King of Clusium, named as Lars Porsenna, dominated central Italy from c. 507-504 BC in the turmoil surrounding the ejection of Tarquinius Superbus from Rome in 507. Lars Porsenna restored order, and he clearly chose not to rule Rome. Instead, he allowed the Roman citizens to develop their own government as a republic on the lines of the Greek democratic models, which were then emerging. The 'name' Lars Porsenna needs to be analysed to understand its titular form, as it deciphers very simply:

Khumric	Lars	Por	senu	na
English	mild/gentle	supreme one	to rule/chide	not

The result is a titular calling affirming 'the mild supreme one who did not govern'.

The answer to the question of the founding of Rome lies in the Tomb of the Tarquins at Caere. Unlike all other major Etruscan tombs, this Tomb of the Tarquins has no painted murals on the walls. Instead, there are only inscriptions, which are of no interest to popular book writers and publishers.

The situation opening up before Wilson and Blackett was very similar to the first steps in ancient Egyptian, where the Egyptian alleged 'Nefer Hotep' paralleled the Khumric 'Nefol Hoffiant', both meaning 'heaven beloved'. As then, the tactics were to take short inscriptions and to run trial comparisons with the Coelbren alphabet, which was not quite as simple as first appeared. The Etruscan texts were producing very slight variations, which was not surprising given a time lapse of between twenty-two hundred and seventeen hundred years from the Etruscan eras of 65 -50 BC to the Llewellyn Sion recordings of the alphabets set out in Britain around 1560.

Chapter Seven

The Longer Etruscan Inscriptions

When approaching the longer Etruscan inscriptions Alan Wilson and Baram Blackett did not so much consider if they would decipher and translate, but simply what they might record. Not being specialists in Etruscan artifacts, they knew of only a limited number of major texts, which fell into three categories.

1- Monumental Stone Stelae.   The Perugia Cippus and the Berlin Stelae

2- Inscribed Metal Tablets.   The Pyrgi Tablets and the Agnone Tablet

3- Cloth or Books.   The Zagreb Shroud

It proved possible to get reasonably good quality photographs of the Perugia Cippus and the Agnone and Pyrgi metal tablets. There was some confusion over the actual existence of the Berlin Cippus and a good picture was not obtained until 1993. Much time was wasted in trying to get photographs of the Zagreb Shroud. Finally, it was decided that getting anything out of Zagreb in Croatia, in what was then Communist Yugoslavia, was more difficult than walking on water, and reluctantly, decipherment was concentrated onto those texts that were available. It was not until 1995 that quality photographs of the Zagreb Shroud were obtained through American efforts. By this time the Project had moved on to other more interesting areas of research.

The three long texts which were available in the mid 1980's were set out and duly deciphered, translated, and were therefore available to be read in English. As had been anticipated these texts gave information that bore no relationship whatsoever to the many guessed and published theories of what they recorded. The information placed the Etruscans into a totally different light, and portrayed them as a very different people from those generally imagined. The only previous source was the scanty, post Etruscan, enemy Roman record, and this seems to be more than muddled.

The Etruscans clearly appear to have worshipped only one god. They do not seem to have worshipped a pantheon of gods in similar fashion to those of the Greeks and Romans.

The Roman accounts of the Druids exhibit the Druids of the southern-European Celts and not the British Druids, yet the same distorted misconceptions and misinterpretations as can be identified and explained.

The Etruscans also left a brief record of their previous history, before they arrived in ancient Italy, to set up their Leagues of Twelve Cities, in the west and later in the east.

As previously expressed, the major historical information may yet lie in the inscriptions on the walls of the tomb of the Tarquins at Cerveteri. These Etruscan kings who founded Rome and provided three kings of Rome before the Roman Republic was established, should prove of great importance to the historical scenario of the ancient world. Wilson and Blackett contemplated visiting Cerveteri several times to see if they could view film, and photograph, these Tarquin tombs, but scarce resources, reports that the tombs were closed to visitors, and the need to spend time and money on more urgent and important parts of the project elsewhere, meant that they never got to go. Communication and co-operation with Italian sources were no better than with Zagreb.

Deciphering and translating ancient inscriptions in more distant areas, and also in more ancient civilizations, proved to be more interesting and more productive spheres. Alan Wilson and Baram Blackett would have attempted the Tarquin tomb inscriptions, if only to prevent academics from creating a shambles of them. Attempts were made to interest universities, colleges, societies, and magazines, that specialized in ancient language studies, but none were interested in *'outsiders.'* Finally, the project on Etruria was *'put on ice'* in 1988, and left in the files.

The Perugia Cippus

The Perugia Cippus is a large monumental standing stone, rather like a typical flat-faced graveyard tomb-stone. Its wide, flat face is inscribed with twenty-four lines of Etruscan writing, which are set out horizontally. These inscriptions fall into three well-defined sections or paragraphs, and begins with each line reading from right to left.

Even unread, the bulk and style and general appearance of this monumental stelae has long been recognized as making it an important record. The technique

Chapter 7 - The Longer Etruscan Inscriptions

employed by Wilson and Blackett in deciphering this Perugia Cippus was their simple standard format followed in all decipherments. The Etruscan letters were set down line by line in reversed order so that the text could be read from left to right in the conventional modern manner. Then, line by line, and one letter at a time, the matching British Coelbren alphabet symbol was set immediately underneath its matching Etruscan counterpart, thus producing a line of matching Coelbren letters. The preserved cipher of Llewellyn Sion was then used to identify each modern letter represented by the Coelbren letters. These rows of modern letters then made up Khumric words, and for the Khumric speaker, the task would end there. The next and final stage was to translate the Khumric statements into English.

There was a certain hilarity in all this, as Alan Wilson with his failing eyesight was prone to frequently mistake letters or miss out letters, or even duplicate them, much to the amused exasperation of Baram Blackett, who got it all right in the end. It does not matter if a letter or word has been used five hundred times, it is always necessary to follow the same unvarying, slow routine. Large numbers of Khumric words have archaic dual and treble meanings, just as English words do, and nothing whatsoever can be taken for granted. Archaic words, and sometimes the archaic meanings, are produced and the older dictionaries have to be carefully searched.

The Perugia text concerns an agreement by a confederation of states to set up a union. This union was to act in concert as a confederation in which the states would co-operate with each other peacefully. It is rather like the *Declaration of Independence* document of the United States of America. The text defines that the land is to be cleared and cultivated. Ditches are to be dug, and drainage is to be organized and controlled. Water conservation is to be part of the drainage objectives, and irrigation techniques are to be employed. The objective is then to grow corn and other crops.

Provisions are made in the pact to set up a code of conduct in the event that cold weather might ruin or severely limit the crops, and what should be done in these circumstances. It seems that the implication is that "federal aid" would be given to disaster-stricken areas.

The Perugia Cippus text immediately struck Alan Wilson and Baram Blackett as an account that was reminiscent of the division of lands between the Hebrew tribes after they succeeded in the conquest of most of Old Canaan.

The peculiarity of the text is that the first section of eight lines reads from right to left, but then the second section of four lines reads from left to right. Finally, the third section of twelve lines reverts to reading from right to left in the same manner as the first section, completing this strange boustrophedon pattern by paragraphs. Once the basic mechanical task of drafting out of the lines of Etruscan and the corresponding Coelbren symbols had been laid out, and everything prepared, it took about seven hours to make a careful first reading.

Experience had shown that it was best to put this aside and forget about it for a while, and then to return to re-do and recheck the entire text from scratch, looking for possible misinterpretations and any alternative readings.

It was extraordinary to realize that the Perugia University Project, involving staff and an expensive computer, was variously reported to be costing either £250,000 or up to £500,000 (depending on which newspaper was carrying the story), and would take up to three years to complete. Wilson and Blackett simply used technical expertise and analysis.

The Pyrgi Tablets

Etruscan texts of any reasonable length are in fact few in number. In this context it is necessary to look further afield for inscriptions. One of the few Etruscan texts of any length and one of the best known is held in the famous Pyrgi Tablets. These Tablets are three, small, gold plates, which are inscribed. One plate is covered with what has been identified as either Phoenician or Punic Carthaginian. The other two plates are covered with what is clearly the script of the Etruscan alphabet.

One of the greatest and earliest Etruscan citadels was the fortress city of Caere, to the north west of Rome. Caere had three ports, Alisum (near Palo), Punicum (S.Marinella), and Pyrgi now Santa Severa. Punicum implies that there were ancient Phoenician and Carthaginian trade connections, and at around 600 BC there was reportedly a Greek colony at Pyrgi. That the Etruscans were trading with both the Carthaginians and the Greeks is an accepted historical fact. Caere is thought to have been one of the great cities of the world in this era. The scenario was interesting as Caere is only the Khumric "Caer" meaning fortress or 'Careau' for multiple fortifications. 'Pyr' means 'Lords', and 'Aliwn' (Alisum) means 'aliens'.

On the 8th July 1964, three small rectangular sheets of thin gold were found between the foundations of two ancient temples at Pyrgi. One in a Phoenician-type script, and the other two in the Etruscan Coelbren type script. In 1966 a similar Phoenician inscribed bronze tablet was found, and the fact that all four tablets had small holes around their edges indicates that they might have been nailed up on doors or on a wall. The strata in which they were found made the archaeologists date them at around 600 BC.

The fact that two different alphabets and two different languages are involved on these tablets implies that there might be some form of treaty or agreement between the Etruscans and the Carthaginians. The Phoenician or Punic text has been '*read*' as a statement recording that *'Thefarie Velianus'*, the ruler of Caere gave a place sacred to Astarte within these temples.

As Astarte was a major female Phoenician deity, this appears to point towards a provision of a place of worship for these foreign sailors. In this context of a possible religious aspect on at least some of the tablets, it may be necessary to state a few basic facts about what is reported about the Etruscan religion. All that is known about Etruscan religion comes from Roman writers, which means that everything must be approached with extreme caution.

The Roman notion was that the supreme creator god of the Etruscans was one *'Tages,'* and that the Etruscans were under the protection of a power which the Romans called *'Tinia'* and identified as Jupiter. More can be said of *'Tages,'* and "Tinia" later. Like Judaism and Christianity, the Etruscan religion was said to be a revealed religion, and the Roman writer Cicero wrote down some part of this for posterity. Cicero wrote that the Etruscan legend held that one day, a strange phenomenon occurred in a field near the river Marta in Etruria. A divine being rose up from the freshly ploughed furrows in the guise of a child, but speaking with the authority and wisdom of an old man. The shouts of the ploughman brought the priests of Etruria to the place in great haste. There the divine child chanted the sacred doctrines to these *'lucumones'*, or priest kings, whilst they reverently listened and wrote down these precious doctrines. When all was done, the divine being fell down as if dead and vanished into the field.

The divine child was said to have been be called *'Tages'*, which seems to be the Khumric *'tades'*, meaning *'the father a shoot from.'* In English syntax, *'a shoot from the father'*.

The Khumric *'Tulcus'* means *'complete'*. This *'Tages'* was said to be the grandson of the god *'Tinia'*, and the son of the power known as Genius, or Thought. This entire story is a good parallel to the British Druidic record of Finigan Gawr dying and being buried and then the three shoots of the Awen/Broad-Arrow, are found sprouting and growing from his mouth. These were found by Menw son of,

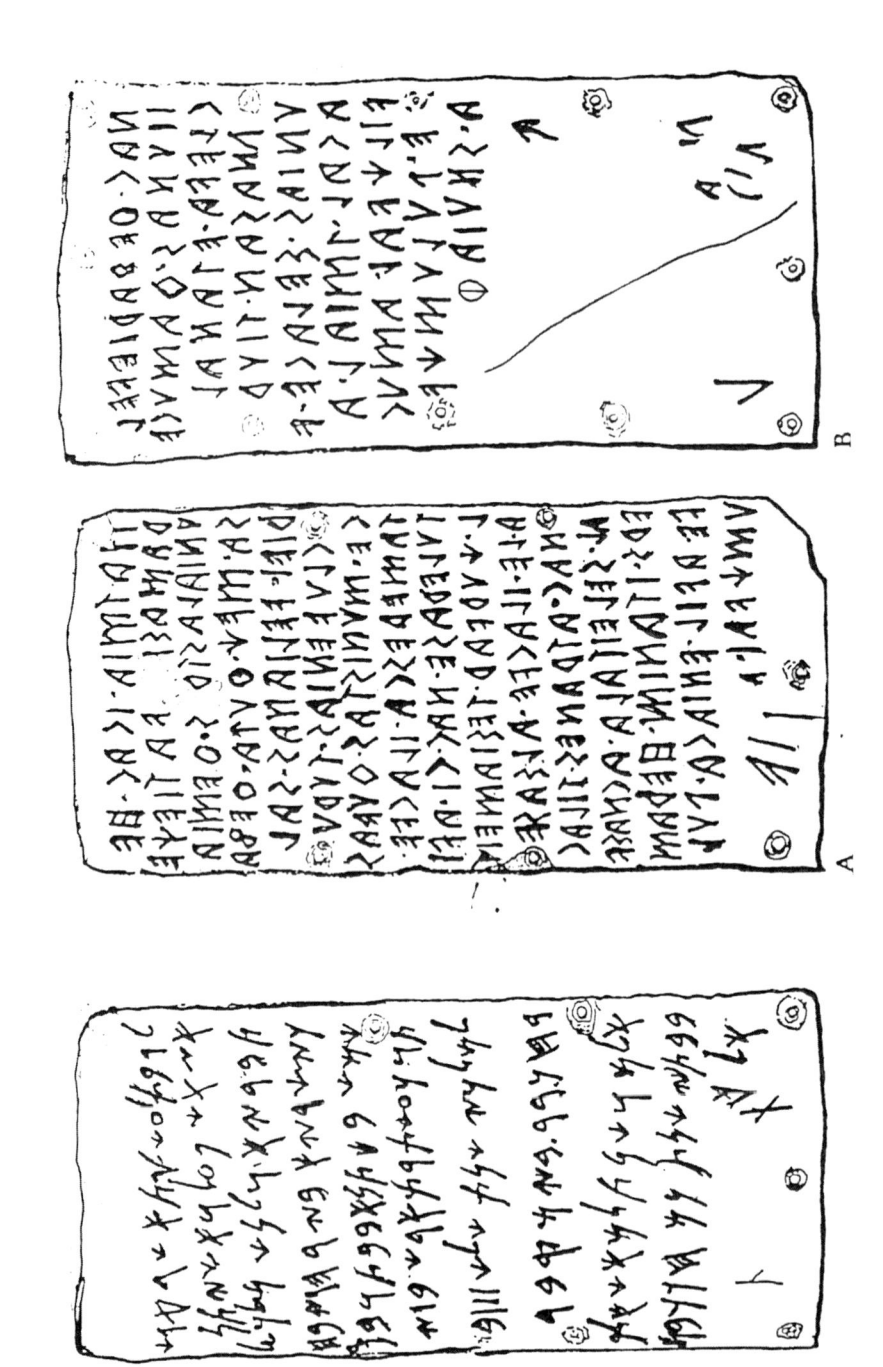

The Pyrgi tablets

Chapter 7- The Longer Etruscan Inscriptions

Menwyd, who is Intellect, the son of Mind.

There is then an Etruscan bronze mirror with a scene carved upon it, which is much used as an illustration. It is believed to show the seated god *'Tinia'*, from whose head *'Genius'* is springing newborn. Alongside this scene is an inscription which has been read as *'Tinia'*. Just how this can be *'read'*, we have already queried. As these readers invariably confuse a Coelbren *'R'*, as an *'N'*, what we actually have is *'Tiria'* or *'Airit'*, and this is a palindrome that reads both ways. First there is 'Airit', meaning-'*his/her-appearance*', and then in reverse we have- *'Tiria'*, which means *'Land I am'*, or even *-'Land-sound I whole,/ healthy'* from Iach.

The words Tirio for *'to come ashore'* and Tiriad as *'freshening'* and also Tirioni for *'to render pleasant'* may be involved, as the Etruscans were migrating into the country by sea in the era around 650 BC. Possibly the god of the Etruscans was identifying with the new land that the people had settled into. The city of Tarquinia was then built on the spot where the Divine Child had appeared, which again points to a land claiming or foundation ceremony. The sacred writings, which were revealed by the Divine Child, were then preserved as the revealed faith of Etruria.

It is conjecture whether *'Tages"*, who seems to be associated with the fertility of corn or grain, is the child of the weather god of heaven, or the god of crafts and invention. Certainly, there appears to be an association with the annual sprouting, growing, and dying back, of the crops.

What Wilson and Blackett found intriguing was the series of poems written in Britain down the long centuries which deal with *'The Divine Child'*. These are preserved, although little published, presumably to avoid offending the sensitivities of the dominant Establishment.

The text of the Pyrgi Tablets appears to read, (note that the syntax/word order makes this seem clumsy in English – whereas it matches Welsh/Khumric syntax.)

<u>Tablet No.I:</u>
Grain/corn towards to loiter/wait for what is drawn out/produced going on for ever mutually in goodness he reduplicates.
in this place to confess?
Strengthening towards what is drawn out (of) thee mutually together what is drawn out away from hypocrisy/dissimulation.
Join together to nourish to state/proclaim superior sacred safe/secure (from)enemies.

Saviour (salvation) to join together.

To wed together region/area tribe/clan one's own quickly to mutually protect (Tadu-Tadcu) boundaries enveloped mutually.

Calm what is outward/manifestly mutual act joined together good pure.

Tablet No.2. reads.:

What overspreads outwardly mutually to acknowledge co-operative not disadvantage/ hurt.

The that what is produced most important/uppermost to spread (with) assurance Tumult good mutual extremity call yours to battle.

Power spreading dividing/parting to spread defence sailing.

Weapons grievous he who is outward (Greeks) to denounce mutually. Not opposition outwardly mutually the land and (what is).

Above mutually outward power effective force to hew (=hew them down). To expose mutually burn violent also singe/blast

To move to battle sailing to the seas.

To adorn oneself with ? who is ejected.?

Not from outward/abroad going on forcibly ejected arouse.

To freshly refuse of conformity.

To produce/trade outward he that is outward (=Greeks) whence upon hindering ventures.

Close towards that mutual waters which outward he.

Going on surface cause of identical faculty of speech (complaint/statement) Towards trade/barter forget contention extremely to acknowledge.

To co-existence.

There can be absolutely no doubt that this Treaty on the Pyrgi Tablets refers directly to the arrival of the barbarian Greek Phoenician pirates in Corsica in circa 545BC.

History and the Pyrgi Tablets.

Archaeologists have dated the Pyrgi Tablets to sometime around 500 BC. This rough dating accords with the translation of this treaty between Etruria and Carthage.

Herodotus tells us how, when Cyrus was establishing the Persian Empire, his Mede General Harpagus attacked cities along the coast of Asia Minor. Harpagus arrived at the promontory near Smyrna where the Greek city of Phocaea stood

Chapter 7- The Longer Etruscan Inscriptions

(today Poca). Here Harpagus stated that he would not destroy the city, but would be content if the Phoceans pulled down one tower of their fortifications, and set aside one house for Cyrus the King.

The Phoceans feared slavery, and so they asked for one day to deliberate these proposals made by Harpagus. This was agreed to, and Harpagus withdrew from the city to allow them to debate freely without duress. That night the Phoceans put their women and children, and all their sacred objects and moveable goods, aboard their galleys, and sailed away to Chios. Harpagus was left with an empty, useless, untanable city.

The Phoceans first tried to buy an island group from the Chians, who refused to sell. So, they set sail westwards across the Mediterranean, south around Greece, on past Sicily, and north to Corsica. Here they founded their new city named Alalia, complete with temples and a civic area. They then proceeded to carry out organized piracy and attacked the merchant shipping fleets of the Etruscans and Carthaginians, which thronged these Tyrrhenian seas. Inevitably, the Phoceans rapidly became a pirate menace of intolerable proportions to the economies of both Etruria and Carthage.

The reaction of the Etruscans and Carthaginians was to agree to a Treaty to form an alliance to crush the Phocean menace. Each state provided sixty warships to put an end to the pillage and plunder of the Phoceans. All this was recorded by Herodotus, and the alliance is referred to in his *Politics*.

> 'A state is also something more than a pact for mutual protection or an agreement to exchange goods and services; for in that one case Etruscans and Carthaginians, and all others with contracted obligations to each other, would be citizens of a single state'.

This is the meaning of the Pyrgi Tablets and the provision for the sailors of Carthage to worship their own god at temples in Pyrgi, following the arrival in Corsica of the barbarian Greek Phoceans around 545 BC. This treaty was brokered between the power bases of Carthage and Caere, and the ports of Pyrgi, Punicum, and Alsium, probably served as the naval bases.

Around 535 BC, the Phocean fleet was sighted off Sardinia, and the combined one-hundred-and-twenty strong, warship task force of Carthage and Etruria put to sea to engage them. The Phoceans sent out a further fleet of sixty ships to assist those off Sardinia, and a major sea battle was fought for the first time in recorded history. It is not impossible that the smaller Phocean fleet at sea off Sardinia was sent out to lure the allied Carthaginian-Etrurian fleet out into a battle. In the event, the outnumbered Phocean fleet was destroyed, with forty ships sunk and twenty very badly damaged with their rams wrenched askew, rendering them unfit for further service.

The surviving Phoceans had no option but to embark in what merchant or smaller vessels they still had, and they were compelled to leave Corsica. They went south to Rhegium near the toe of Italy. There, at what is now Reggio di Calabria, near the Straits of Messina, they settled, and they later established Oenotria at Elea or Velia, now Castell-e-mare di Bruce.

The shock of the total defeat of a powerful barbarian Greek fleet resounded across the ancient world, making a huge impression. It was the first great naval battle in known history. Thucydides records the only other such conflict was between Greek Corinth and Greek Corfu. Never before had the civilized nations defeated so large an armada of barbarian Greeks. The western Mediterranean and the Tyrrhenian seas were free for trade and commerce. The treaty between Etruria and Carthage was renewed and the alliance made even closer.

This then is the significance of the golden tablets from Pyrgi, with their record in Coelbren and Carthaginian Phoenician allowing the foundation of a place of worship for the goddess Astarte at Pyrgi. Elsewhere in Etruria treaties of alliance stand preserved on monuments of stone. These are also decipherable.

The Agnone Tablet.

The artefact known as the Agnone Tablet is a large rectangular bronze plate, which carries a medium length incised inscription in Etruscan on both sides. It is now in the British Museum.

It has been speculatively described as a *'menu'* with a listing of items. The Agnone Tablet may well be one of the world's most important ancient documents yet discovered. It does decipher using the matching Llewellyn Sion Coelbren alphabets and the ciphers. Needless to say, the reading that emerges bears no resemblance whatsoever to the fabricated version brazenly advertised without knowledge of the language.

The text of the Agnone Tablet outlines the history of a people who have experienced three migrations. Two of these migrations were voluntary and one enforced. The longer text, on what we shall call the front or No.1 side of the Tablet, describes the long journey of the people under a Prince, fleeing from a devastated, plague-ridden land. The people follow a little cabinet, which rides in a cart, and this record is unavoidably matching the Hebrew Exodus from Egypt under Moses, a Prince of Egypt and of the Hebrews, where they followed the cart carrying the Ark of the Covenant. This around 1360BC. The people finally arrive in a pleasant land where they are content and happy. This then appears to match the Hebrew arrival in Canaan as their *'promised land'*.

The text on the reverse, or the No.2 side of the tablet, records how the people are taken away to a land where they are unhappy. This then matches the deportations of huge numbers of the Ten Tribes of Israel by the Assyrian Emperor Tiglathpileser III, and his successors Shalmaneser V and Sargon II. These unhappy people were removed northwards towards Armenia and the Caucasus, back to the ancestral lands of Abraham who had moved south from the northern Chaldean Ur. This around 722BC.

Then the people set off again in search of a new homeland, and again they follow the little cabinet riding in its cart. They are led to the sea-shore where they build ships and sail to their present lands in Etruria.

In this Agnone Tablet text, the Etruscans are clearly identified as part of the migrating Ten Tribes of Israel, who took off, going west from Armenia and northern Assyria around 687BC. They probably set off when, the Emperor, Sennacherib was murdered by two of his sons, and the chaos of civil war reigned in the Assyrian Empire. The heir Esarhaddon pursued and fought with his two patricide brothers, and finally established himself on the throne. The fact is that in the archives of the Assyrian Emperors, Tiglathpileser III, Shalmaneser V, Sargon II and Sennacherib, the Ten Tribes of Israel are discussed and named. In these records they are indisputably called the Khumry. The twenty-five thousand clay tablets in these archives were found in the ruins of Nineveh by Austin Layard, and were brought to London in 1846.

When these tablets arrived in London in 1846, it was remarked by several scholars that some of the tablets appeared to be written in the Old British alphabet. With the political and religious-correctness campaign gathering speed this was not a good time for these observations to have been made. These are the same archives from which Layard exhibits alphabets, which were seen to be remarkably similar to the ancient British Coelbren. So, we have a nation called the Khumry heading west out of the region between the Caucasus and northern Assyria around 687 BC. These same people are mentioned in the *Second Book of Esdras* in the *Apocrypha* as going west across both the branches of the "Y" shaped upper Euphrates.

II Esdras 14:39-50.

'And whereas thou sawest that he gathered unto him another multitude that were peaceable; these were the ten tribes, which were led away out of their own land in the time of Osea the king, whom Shalmaneser the king of the Assyrians led away captive, and he carried them beyond the River, and they were carried into another land. But they took counsel among themselves, that they would leave the multitude of the heathen, and go forth into a further country, where never mankind dwelt, that they might there keep their statutes, which they had not kept in their own land. And they entered by the narrow passages of the river Euphrates. For the Most High then wrought signs for them, and stayed the springs of the River, till they were passed over. For through that country there was a great way to go, namely a year and a half; and the same region is called Arzareth. Then dwelt they thee until the latter time; and now when they begin to come again, the Most High stayeth the springs of the River again, that they may go through; therefore sawest thou the multitude gathered together in peace. But those that be left behind of thy people are they that are found within my holy border.'

It is very clear that the Khumry were moving west slowly, first across the eastern branch of the River Euphrates, the Arsanias Fl., and camping for eighteen months before moving on across the second upper branch. The Arzareth, where they paused, is almost certainly the Arzanene region immediately south west of the lake Arsissa Paulus, now the Van Golu, where the main ancient city was Arzen.

The Khumry migrating west from northern Assyria -Iran, were next identified by Herodotus writing his *'Histories'* around 450 BC. Herodotus calls the Khumry the Kimmerians, and the Kimmeroi, and he dates their migration clear across Asia Minor to the Dardanelles as from circa 690 BC to 650 BC. That the people the Assyrians called the Khumry are those the Greek called Kimmeroi, is surely not disputed. This long march to the sea at the Dardanelles brings the Assyrian-Greek Khumry-Kimmeroi, to exactly the place where the British Khumry claimed their ancient origin in Trojan Western Asia Minor was.

The main body of these Kimmerians are reported by Herodotus to be called the Treres, and it is not difficult to see the Treres - meaning *'travelling homes'* people - as the Y-Treres and so the Etruscans *('y' means 'the')*. That these migrating multitudes were a powerful problem is clear from the fact that they attacked Sardis, the western capital city of Asia Minor. They captured the city but were unable to take the stronghold castle citadel in the centre. There is further evidence

Chapter 7- The Longer Etruscan Inscriptions

in Herodotus of the influx of this migrating multitude in Western Asia Minor, where he recounts a story told to him by a Phrygian prince of how the land could not support the number of people there, and so it was agreed that half should emigrate elsewhere around 650 BC.

That there was a common heritage, language, alphabet, and religion, in Britain, Etruria, and Trojan western Asia Minor, became ever clearer, as the researches of Wilson and Blackett progressed. One interesting point that had emerged was that the Ten Tribes took the Ark of the Covenant with them when they were deported to northern Assyria around 734 - 700 BC. They then followed the Ark westwards through Asia Minor to the Dardanelles, from 687 - 650 BC, and so the Ark was at the Dardanelles by 650 BC. This meant that the Ark either went to Etruria with the first half of the people, or it came to Britain with the second half of the people under Drutus at a later date.

The Text of The Agnone Tablet.

Even the first rough draft of the translation of the Agnone Tablet makes it very clear that this is an historical, religious document. The content of the text makes this evident. There are also evident the clear and unmistakable signs of poetry, or of a chant. Lines 2 to 15 on the front, or No.1 side of the tablet, all end in a near identical phrase or statement of six letters. The variations are that the fourth letter appears on thirteen lines as a '*T*' and once as an '*I*' and the fifth letter appears variously as '*Z*' or ' *T* '. The most common form of this repetitive phrase is,- T T See Illustration.

The letters for - HW- followed by varying endings also appear seven times in central sections of Lines 2 to 13. Other letter groups with similar phonetics appear in lines 2, 8, and 11.

This repetitive rhyming effect is enhanced throughout the entire text of the Agnone Tablet by a peculiar choice of alterative words based upon the " HW" sound. We constantly find '*HW*' – '*HWF*' – '*HWM*' – '*HWI*' – '*HWCH*' – '*HWP*' – '*HWR*'- and so on.

The actual content of the Text of the Tablet then appears to support this obvious arrangement of poetic meter, rhyme, and alliteration, as being a poem, song, or psalm. As Baram Blackett put it – '*This may be the oldest original version of a psalm*'. As with some old Welsh poetry there are words which may have two or even three meanings, and the answer to '*which one,*'? is simply '*both or all.*'

Agnone / "Oscan" tablet text

Chapter 7- The Longer Etruscan Inscriptions

The decipherment of the Agnone Tablet
Front Side reading Right to Left

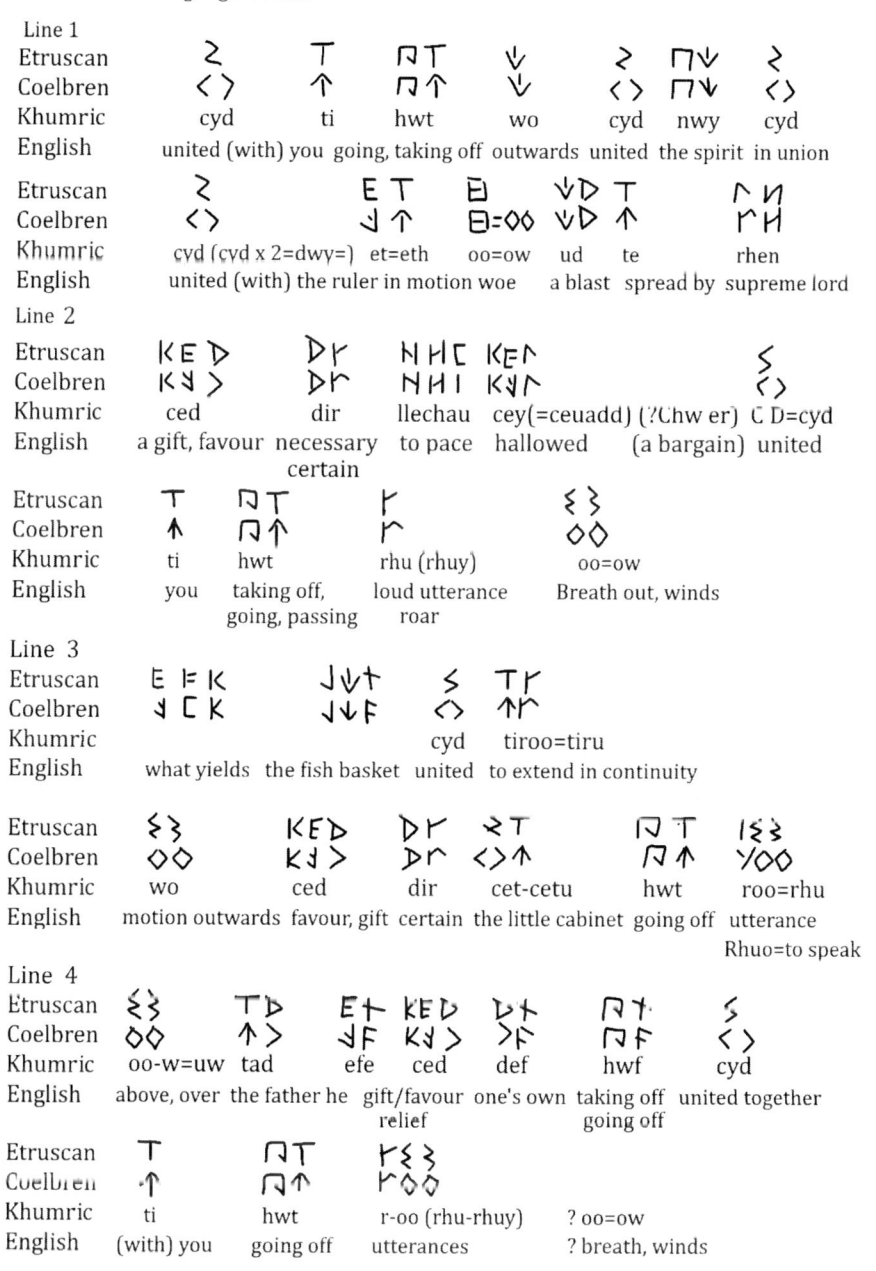

Line 1

Etruscan	⌇	T	∩T	↓↓	⌇	∩↓	⌇
Coelbren	<>	↑	∩↑	↓↓	<>	∩↓	<>
Khumric	cyd	ti	hwt	wo	cyd	nwy	cyd
English	united (with)	you	going, taking off	outwards	united	the spirit	in union

Etruscan	⌇	ET	ㅂ	↓ᗡT		∩ᴎ
Coelbren	<>	↲↑	ㅂ=◊◊	↓ᗡ↑		ᴦH
Khumric	cyd (cyd x 2=dwy=)	et=eth	oo=ow	ud	te	rhen
English	united (with)	the ruler in motion	woe	a blast	spread by	supreme lord

Line 2

Etruscan	KEᗡ	ᗡᴦ	NHC	KEᴧ		⌇
Coelbren	K↲>	ᗡᴦ	NHI	K↲ᴧ		<>
Khumric	ced	dir	llechau	cey(=ceuadd)	(?Chw er) C D=cyd	
English	a gift, favour	necessary certain	to pace	hallowed	(a bargain)	united

Etruscan	T	∩T	ᴦ	⌇⌇
Coelbren	↑	∩↑	ᴦ	◊◊
Khumric	ti	hwt	rhu (rhuy)	oo=ow
English	you	taking off, going, passing	loud utterance roar	Breath out, winds

Line 3

Etruscan	E F K	↲↓†	⌇	Tᴦ
Coelbren	↲ ᴄ K	↲↓F	<>	↑ᴦ
Khumric			cyd	tiroo=tiru
English	what yields	the fish basket	united	to extend in continuity

Etruscan	⌇⌇	KEᗡ	ᗡᴦ	⌇T	∩T	I⌇⌇
Coelbren	◊◊	K↲>	ᗡᴦ	<>↑	∩↑	Y◊◊
Khumric	wo	ced	dir	cet-cetu	hwt	roo=rhu
English	motion outwards	favour, gift	certain	the little cabinet	going off	utterance Rhuo=to speak

Line 4

Etruscan	⌇⌇	Tᗡ	E†	KEᗡ	ᗡ†	∩T·	⌇
Coelbren	◊◊	↑>	↲F	K↲>	>F	∩F	<>
Khumric	oo-w=uw	tad	efe	ced	def	hwf	cyd
English	above, over	the father	he	gift/favour relief	one's own	taking off going off	united together

Etruscan	T	∩T	ᴦ⌇⌇	
Coelbren	↑	∩↑	ᴦ◊◊	
Khumric	ti	hwt	r-oo (rhu-rhuy)	? oo=ow
English	(with) you	going off	utterances	? breath, winds

209

Line 5

Etruscan	⊓HT	E▷	≷	T△	T	⊓†
Coelbren	⊓ԻΙ↑	↓>	<>	↑∧	↑	⊓Ի
Khumric	hwnt	ed	cyd	ta	ti	hwff
English	foreign, outward, at a distance	velocity	united with	superior	what is	hood, cowl

Etruscan	≷	T	⊓T	Ի⧏⧐		✝⧏⧐
Coelbren	<>	↑	⊓↑	Ի◊◊		F◊◊
Khumric	cyd	ti	hwt	rhu-rhuy	or	foo = ffu
English	united	with you	going off taking off	utterances		a fleeting state, passing

Line 6

Etruscan	⊓НΙ	НΙΛΙ	KE▷	▷Ի	I	ΛԻ
Coelbren	⊓НΙ	НΙΛΙ	KJ>	>Ի	I	↑Ի
Khumric	hwm	mai	ced	dir	y	ar
English	sinking	the field	gift/favour	necessary	the	ploughland

Etruscan	≷	T	⊓T	Ի⧏⧐
Coelbren	<>	↑	⊓↑	Ի◊◊
Khumric	cyd	ti	hwt	rh-oo rhu
English	united with	you	going off	the utterances

Line 7

Etruscan	RIV	НΙН	ΛԻ	≷	KE▷	▷Ի
Coelbren	ГIV	НН	↑Ի	<>	KJ>	>Ի
Khumric	rhyw	meh (mehin)	ar	cyd	ced	dir
English	race, lineage	prosperous, fat	ploughland	united with	gift, favour	necessary

Etruscan	I	⊓T	≷	≷	T	⊓	Ի⧏⧐
Coelbren	Y	⊓↑	<>	<>	↑	⊓	Ի◊◊
Khumric	y	hwt	cyd	cyd	ti	hwy	r-oo = rhu
English	the	going off	united,	united with	you	a long time	the utterances

Line 8

Etruscan	Ի>	⊓Н	⊓K	R	Ի	KEԻ
Coelbren	Ի>	⊓Н(ph)	⊓K	Ի	L	KJԻ
Khumric	rhad	hwt	hwch	rha	se	chwer (chwerfu)
English	race, favour	of hood, cowl, hooded one	to push thrust	the power	established	with violence

Etruscan	EН	T▷	⊓Ի	≷	T	Ի⧏⧐
Coelbren	JН	↑>	⊓Ի	<>	↑	Ի◊◊
Khumric	en	tud	hwre	cyd	ti	r-oo = rhu
English	the spirit	the region	accepted	united	(with) you	the utterances

Chapter 7- The Longer Etruscan Inscriptions

Line 9
Etruscan	⌐⌐	⌐⌐≷≷	▷Γ	≷	≷	KE▷
Coelbren	⌐⌐	⌐⌐◊◊	＞Γ	<>	<>	K⨆>
Khumric	ha	hw-oo = hwy	dir	cyd	cyd	ced
English	well done	a long time, them	necessary	united	united with	gift, favour, relief

Etruscan	▷+	I∨	⟨	≷	≷	T⌐⌐
Coelbren	＞⊦	I∨	⟨	<>	<>	↑⌐⌐
Khumric	def	iw	si	cyd	cyd	ti-hw tefu	teghau
English	one's own,	that is	established	in unity	united	to spread	to beautify

Line 10
Etruscan	⋕ ⌐⌐	⌐⌐T	∨+	≷	KE▷	KE▷
Coelbren	⋕ ⌐⌐	⌐⌐↑	∨⊦	<>	K⨆>h	K⨆>
Khumric	m+hw mehyn	hwt	wff	cyd	chwedl	ced
English	on a cart	going off	out from	in unity	the legends, myths	(of) gifts, favour

Etruscan	▷+	⨆∨	↓E	≷	≷	T	⌐⌐
Coelbren	＞⊦	I∨	⊦⨆	<>	<>	↑	⌐⌐
Khumric	def	iw	ffe	cyd	cyd	ti	hw tefu teghau
English	one's own	that is	outwards	in unity,	united	you cry	to spread, beautify

Etruscan	TΓ	≷≷
Coelbren	↑Γ	◊◊
Khumric	tir	oo - ow
English	the land	a motion outwards

Line 11
Etruscan	R I∨		F F T	[E ▷	(E) E B	⌐⌐	≷
Coelbren	Γ I∨		[⨆ ↑	<⨆>	(⨆) E◊◊	⌐⌐	<>
Khumric	rhiw		cet	ced	e-oo-hw = ewch	cyd
English	stock, race, lineage	the little cabinet	gift, favour	(he) weak	united

Etruscan	I∨	Γ	≷≷	T	⌐⌐	T+
Coelbren	I∨	Γ	<>	↑	⌐⌐	↑⊦
Khumric	yw	rha	cyd	ti	hw	t-ffe = tefu
English	it is	the power	united with	(with) you	to cry out	to spread out

Line 12
Etruscan	R I∨	[E T	▷ E [	⌐⌐T	T∨▷	E+
Coelbren	Γ I∨	< E ↑	＞⨆<	⌐⌐↑	↑∨＞	⨆⊦
Khumric	rhyw	cet	dec (dechru)	hwt	tud	ef
English	race, lineage (of)	little cabinet	in the beginning	taking off,	the land	he

King Arthur Conspiracy - Wilson & Blackett

Etruscan				
Coebren				
Khumric	cyd	ti-hw = teghau		incontinuity
English	united	to beauty		

Line 13
Etruscan						
Coebren						
Khumric	oedi ech	wr	ced	dir	yw	ffe
English	in time, what is	in being	gift, favour	necessary	what exists	outwards

Etruscan			
Coebren			
Khumric	cyd	ti-hw (teghau)	ti-r-oo = tiro
English	united	to beautify	to extend in continuity

Line 14
Etruscan					
Coebren	a hat	hwm ar	hir + cyd hyrcyd	t-ffe = tefu	hwr/hwf
Khumric	with cover	this ploughland	to drive with force	to spread out	hidden one
English					

Etruscan			
Coebren	cyd	ti	hwt	ffe-oo = ffu
Khumric	united	distinctly	taking off	fleeting, passing state

Line 15
Etruscan					
Coebren					
Khumric	r-e =rhe	si-c =sech	hw-fe = hwf	c-e-n-e-t =cenedl	hwr
English	swiftly, to run	dry, parched	going, taking off	the nation	going taking off

Etruscan				
Coebren				
Khumric	cyd	t=ta ?	hw-t = hwt	r-oo = rhu
English	united	superior	hooded one	utterances

Line 16
Etruscan							
Coebren							
Khumric	hw	cyd	hwf	aw	da	cyd	y	hwf
English	to cry	united	hooded one	fluid, liquid	good	united	to	hooded one

212

Chapter 7- The Longer Etruscan Inscriptions

Line 17
Etruscan
Coelbren
Khumric   cyd   hw   oo=wy   tw   mi   te-oo = tew   dwm dyma
English   united   to cry out   of him   rising up identical   prosporous, fat   here

Etruscan
Coelbren
Khumric   hwb   ti   tid   e   ffe
English   push, effort   you   an anchor chain   he   outwards

Line 18
Etruscan
Coelbren
Khumric   aw   ti   edef   ph-si-r=pesychu   hwch   en   er
English   fluid, liquid   you   in the   to force out   to push, living impulse
           = water   dimness   thrust   spirit   forward

Line 19
Etruscan
Coelbren
Khumric   cyd   di-ch-hw=dichell   oo wffi   ted
English   with, united   a trick   push off, flight from   stretch, distend

Line 20
Etruscan
Coelbren
Khumric   oo=ow   i=y ?   ww=wy   cyd   hw-cyd=hwch+hwch   i
English   breath   to/the   of him   united with   to begin + to thrust   to

Etruscan
Coelbren
Khumric   hw-fe=hwf   cyd   a1=a'l   cyd   oo-w-d=oerwydd   t-w-m=twm
English   hidden one   united with him   united   washorses   torn,rent, broke

Line 21
Etruscan
Coelbren
Khumric   cyd   hwch   hw   de   hwt   ed
English   united   to thrust   begin   a parting   taking off   with velocity

Line 22
Etruscan
Coelbren
Khumric   nedd   pa   ffe   ced   dry   ar   cyd
English   grasp the hand which   outward   gift,   forward   (to)ploughland   united
                                                        favour

213

Etruscan	✗	⊓T	r⟨⟩				
Coelbren	⊦	⊓∧	r◊◊				
Khumric	ffe	hwt	r-oo = rhu				
English	outward	taking off	the utterances				

Line 23

Etruscan	⊓Ш	Ш	⊓ř	KE⊳	⊳	ЬI	⋈ř
Coelbren	⊓Ш	Ш	⊓r	KJ>	>	ЬI	∧r
Khumric	hwm	mi	hwr	ced	de	si-y=sych	ar
English	apt to sink down	me	taken off	gift, favour	a parting	a dought	ploughland

Etruscan	⟨	✗	⊓T	✗	⟨⟩
Coelbren	⟨⟩	⊦	⊓∧	⊦	◊◊
Khumric	cyd	ffe	hwt	ffe	oo = yw
English	united	outward	away	outward	it is

Line 24

Etruscan	⟨⟩	⟨	VV	⊓ř KE⊳ ⊳⊦|⊓			
Coelbren	◊◊	⟨⟩	W	⊓r KJ> >⊦|⊓			
Khumric	oo-yw	cyd	ewy(br)	hwr ced de-f-r-hw-y deffnoi, def + rhwy		
English	it is united	quickly	away	gift, favour awake, one's own prince		

Etruscan	⟨	T	⊓T	✗	⟨⟩
Coelbren	⟨⟩	∧	⊓∧	⊦	◊◊
Khumric	cyd	ti	hwt	ffe	oo = yw
English	united (with)	you	away, get hence	outwards	it is

Line 25

Etruscan	ECK	KJ∨r	H	⊓T
Coelbren	J<K	K∨r	H	⊓∧
Khumric	e-c-ch	chw-w-r=chwa	ph=ffu	hwt
English	whay yields	gale of wind	a fleeting state	away, taking off

Etruscan	E⊳E✗	⟨	T	⊓T	r⟨⟩
Coelbren	J>JF	⟨⟩	∧	⊓∧	r◊◊
Khumric	e def	cyd	ti	hwt	r-oo=rhu
English	he one's own	united together	(with) you	taking off, away	the utterances

214

Chapter 7- The Longer Etruscan Inscriptions

The Agnone Tablet Decipherment
Rear side-reading from right to left

Line 1
Etruscan	ᑎᑎ	⋛	ᑎ	⋛	EKᑎ		⋛
Coelbren	ᑎᑎ	<>	ᑎ	<>	ᒎKᑎ		<>
Khumric	hw-hw	cyd	hw	cyd	ech	(or) echw	cyd
English	hooting	united	cry out	united	what yields	having motion	united

Etruscan	KEE	⋛	Tᖉ	H T
Coelbren	KᒎᒎB	<>	ʌᖉ	H ʌ
Khumric	chw-e-e-chweio	cyd	ti-r=tir	pli=ffa-t-ffat
English	to move briskly	united	the land	a smart blow

Line 2
Etruscan	ᗺ	ᕝ ᐅ	T ᕝ
Coelbren	◇◇	ᕝ >	ʌ ᕝ
Khumric	oo=ow	wyd	twr
English	a moan, breathing out	you are	towering (tower, heap, pile)

Line 3
Etruscan	ᑌEI	KEᖉ
Coelbren	<ᒎI	KᒎᖉB
Khumric	c-e-y ceulo/ceuo	cer
English	to congeal/to excavate	furniture/tools

Line 4
Etruscan	ECK	ᒎᕝᖉ
Coelbren	ᒎ<K	ᒎᕝᖉB
Khumric	ech	d-w-r=dwr or h-w-r=bwr or eur = gold
English	what yields/pervades	water

Line 5
Etruscan	⋛⋛	WT	ᐅEᖉ
Coelbren	◇◇	WWʌ	>ᒎᖉB
Khumric	oo-yw	wwt=wyt	der
English	it is	you are	hard, stubborn

Line 6
Etruscan	ᑎHT	Eᐅ
Coelbren	ᑎHʌ	ᒎ>
Khumric	h-w-n-t =hwnt	ed
English	foreign, at a distance	with velocity, speed

215

Line 7
Etruscan	KED	D⊢
Coelbren	K↲>	>⊢
Khumric	ced	d-si=des
English	gift, favour	system, order, rule

Line 8
Etruscan	⊓⊞	⊞	⊓⊢
Coelbren	⊓⊞	⊞	⊓⊢
Khumric	hwm	mi	hw-si = hws
English	to sink down	I, me	covering

Line 9
Etruscan	RIV	⊞	H	⊓⊢	≷
Coelbren	⌐IV	⊞	H	⊓⌐	<>
Khumric	rhyw	mi	na (a)	hwr	cyd
English	natural	me, I	a state of going	away, taking off	united

Line 10
Etruscan	⌶⊢>⊓	H ⊓K	R⊢		
Coelbren	⌶⌐>⊓	H ⊓K	⌐⊢		
Khumric	b-d-r-hw =briduw	ni hwch	rh-ll=rhyll	(rh-si-rhys)	
English	covenant with baptism	we thin skin	cleft	(the lord)	

Etruscan	KE⊢	EH	T D	⊓⊢
Coelbren	K↲⌐	↲H	↑>	⊓⌐
Khumric	cer	en	tod (ted)	(tedd) hwr
English	furniture, tools	livimg spirit	to cover over	(display) going, taking off

Line 11
Etruscan	KED	D	⊢I	⊓⊢
Coelbren	K↲>	D	⌐I	⊓⌐
Khumric	ced	de	rh-i=rhya	hwr
English	the gift	parting	the lord	taking off, going

Line 12
Etruscan	⊓H	⊓≷	D⊢	≷	≷	DV
Coelbren	⊓H	⊓◊◊	>⌐	<>	<>	>V
Khumric	hw-ph=hwp	hw-oo=hwyl?	der	cyd	cyd	dwy
English	effort, push	sail of a ship	hard, doggedly	mutual	united	(with the lord)

Line 13
Etruscan	⊞	⊓	⊓T	V⊢	≷
Coelbren	⊞	⊓	⊓↑	V⌐	<>
Khumric	mi	hw	hwt	wt	cyd
English	me (we)	shout, cry	taking off, going	being on, at	united

Chapter 7- The Longer Etruscan Inscriptions

Line 14

Etruscan	R I V	C E ʞ	C E ▷	E	ᗷ
Coelbren	r I V	⟨ ᖷ r	⟨ ᖷ ⟩	ᖷ	◊◊
Khumric	rh-y-w=rhyw	cer	ced	e	oo=oow
English	of a sort, some	tools, furniture	gift, favour	he	breathing out (blowing = winds)

Etruscan	⊓	≷	I V
Coelbren	⊓	⟨⟩	I V
Khumric	hw	cyd	yw
English	to carry out	united, together	it is

Line 15

Etruscan	R I V	C E r	∩ I r	ʞ E ▷ E
Coelbren	r I V	⟨ ᖷ r	∧ I r	ʇ ᖷ ⟩ ᖷ
Khumric	rh-y-w	cer	a-y-r=awyr	ffede
English	of a sort, some	tools, furniture	the air, sky	outside presence

Etruscan	ᗷ	I V r	▷ E ⟨	⊓ T	V ▷	E
Coelbren	◊◊	I V r	⟩ ᖷ ⟨	⊓ ↑	V ⟩	ᖷ
Khumric	oo = ow	ywr	dec (hre)	hwt	wd	e
English	winds, blow	in proportion	origin, beginning	going away,	blast, howl	he

Line 16

Etruscan	⊔ E ▷		ᖷ V r		K E ▷	▷ I
Coelbren	◊◊ ᖷ ⟩		ᖷ V r		k ᖷ ⟩	⟩ I
Khumric	oo-c-d = oed	ech	bwr (bwriad)or(dwr)		ced	dy
English	ancient, ages	that pervades	intending (water)		gift, relief favour	you, yours

Etruscan	I V	r
Coelbren	I V	r
Khumric	iw	rh = rha
English	that extreme	the power

Line 17

Etruscan	ʇ	⊓ T	⊓ H	⊓ ʞ	∩	И	≷	T r	⊓ r
Coelbren	∧	⊓ ↑	⊓ H	⊓ ʞ	∧	И	⟨⟩	↑ r	⊓ r
Khumric	a	hwt	hwn	hwg	a	ni	cyd	ti-r=tiur	hwr
English	with	taking off, going	this	covering with = protection		we	united	the land	covering

Line 18

Etruscan	R E	ʇ A r	⟨ E И E T		⊓ r
Coelbren	r ᖷ	ʇ ∧ r	⟨ ᖷ И ᖷ ∧		⊓ r
Khumric	rh-el	ff-a-r=ffar	c-e-n-e-t cenedl		hwr
English	a trail	extends out	the tribe, nation, kindred		taking off, going

217

Line 19

Etruscan							
Coelbren							
Khumric	hw	hw	cyd	hwr	awd	hw	cyd
English	shout	shout	united	taking off, going	opportunity	cry	united

Etruscan		
Coelbren		
Khumric	i	hwr
English	to	going away, taking off

Line 20

Etruscan							
Coelbren							
Khumric	cyd	hw	hw	oo=yw	twnn-twm	t-e-cow -teulu	d-w-nn
English	united	to cry	to cry	it is	broken, rent, torn	tribe, family	murmer

Line 21

Etruscan						
Coelbren						
Khumric	hw-b	ti	ti	der	pyw	ted=tedu
English	push, effort	distinctly	you are	stubborn, hard	complete, in order	to stretch out

Etruscan		
Coelbren		
Khumric	ef	affr
English	he, him	flowing principle = water

Line 22

Etruscan					
Coelbren					
Khumric	hwch	en	er	oo-yw	di=dy
English	thrush, push	liviving principle, spirit	impulse forward	it is	you, yours

Etruscan						
Coelbren						
Khumric	r-e=rhe	mi	hw	ni	n-y-w=nyw	r=rha	cyd
English	swift motion	I, we	cry out	we	with vigour	the power	united together

Line 23

Etruscan				
Coelbren				
Khumric	cyd	ti	hwr	ffe
English	united	you, yours	taking off	outwards

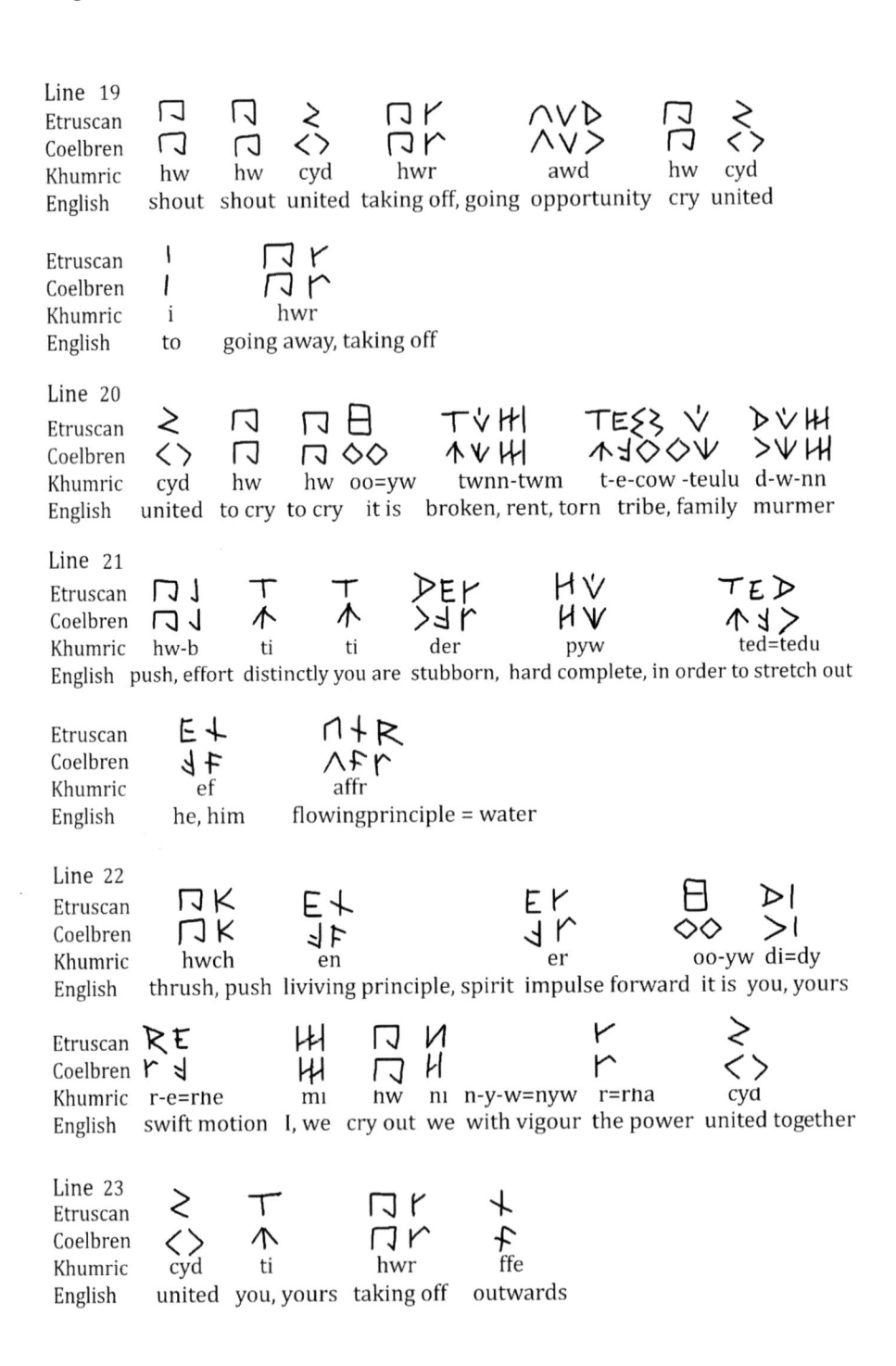

Chapter 7- The Longer Etruscan Inscriptions

The Text Front Side, No.1.

1-   united with the united with thee (superior?) going off outwards (in motion) united with the spirit (flowing) united with the ruler, in motion a cry a blast spread by the supreme lord.

2-   a gift/favour a place hallowed necessary, united (to) spread out, going off, the utterances (roar - breath of winds),

3-   what yields (is given of) the fish basket (= Moses) united to extend in continuity (of) motion outwards the gift/favour/relief of certain united with thee, going off (with) the utterances

4-   above the father, he the gift/favour/relief of one's own taking off/going united stronger/superior, going off with the utterances, (or "with the chief").

5-   foreign/at a distance with velocity united with superior what is hooded/cowled (=hidden) united with thee going off the utterances.

6-   apt to sink the place is (inundations) the gift/favour certain to the ploughland united with thee, going off the utterances.

7-   the race/lineage the fat/prosperous ploughland, united with the gift/favour certain the going off united, united with thee a long time the utterances.

8-   the grace/favour of the hooded/cowled one to push/thrust the power established with violence, the spirit/living principal, the region accepted, united superior with thee.

9-   well done a long time necessary united with the ruler, a gift/favour of one's own outwards, what is established united together, united to beautify, to spread.

10- on a cart going off out from united/together the legends/myths a gift/favour/relief of one's own that is outwards (= a foreign place) united, united to beautify the land (= or a beautiful land) the land a motion/movement outwards.

11- the stock/race/lineage of the little cabinet, weak, united it is powerful/enveloped united thee to cry (to) to spread out.

12- the stock/ race favour(ed) the little cabinet in the beginning taking off/away the earth he united together to beautify, to extend in continuity.

13- In process of time the story/fable being the gift/favour necessary/certain what exists (i.e. god) outwards united together to beautify to extend in continuity.

14- the covered one shouts/calls the ploughland to drive with force to spread out, the hooded/cowled (i.e hidden one) united (with) distinctly taking off in fleeting/passing state.

15- swiftly to run, the dry/parched (places) taking off/going united superior-spread out the hooded one in fleeting state (or utterances).

16- to cry out the ruler united (with) the hooded/cowled one fluid/liquid (waters) good united (with) the hooded one.

17- united/together to cry for what is of him/ produced the rising up/driving away the fat/prosperous (one), the push/effort thou an anchor chain, he outwards.

18- the waters (/fluid/liquid) thou (in the) dimness to force out, to push/thrust living.

19- spirit, the impulse forward, united with (thee) a trick flight to stretch(/distend)

20- the winds, he of him united with to push/thrust the hooded/cowled one united with him united, warhorses torn/rent/broken.

21- united to push/thrust, to begin a parting taking off/going uff (with) velocity.

22- to grasp the hand which outwards the gift/favour forward (to the) ploughland, united outwards taking off (with) the utterances.

23- apt to sink down me taken off, the gift/favour/relief of a parting, a drought united outward, away outward it is.

24- it is united quickly going away/taking off the gift/favour/relief, one's own prince united with thee, to get hence/away outwards it is.

25- what yields/produces a gale of wind as tools, in a fleeting state taking off/ away, he one's own (god) united together (with) thee in taking off/away to the cultivated area/ or region (alliterative to the spelling of "utterances").

The Text Back Side, No.2.

1- hooting of an owl, united cry united with what is in motion (or what yields) united/together, to move briskly united the land (to give) a smart blow.

2- breathing out (the winds) thou art towering, the column of smoke.

3- to congeal furniture tools.

4- what yields gold

5- it is, thou art stubborn.

6- foreign/ at a distance with velocity/speed.

7- the gift/favour of order/rule

8- to sink down me covering.

9- natural to me a state of going taking off/away (nomadic?) united

10- a covenant with baptism we thin skin cleft from the Lord the tools/furniture of the living spirit to cover over (when) taking off/going.

11- the gift of parting the Lord taking

12- the push of the sail of ship hard/doggedly mutually united.

13- we shout/cry (when) taking off/going being united (syntax = being taken off

Chapter 7- The Longer Etruscan Inscriptions

together).
14- of a sort of tool a gift/favour (from) he breathing out(winds) to cry out united/together it is.
15- of a sort, some to make haste, the sky/air breathing out (to blow) in opposition the origin going away blasting/howling he.
16- ancient what pervades, (god) intending a gift/favour thee that extreme the power (you that are the extreme power)
17- with taking off/going this covering(? darkness or protection) we us the land ...... covering.
18- a trail extends out the tribe/kindred/nation going/taking off.
19- shout united taking off/going the opportunity cry united, the going away
20- united together to cry to cry, it is broken/rent/torn the tribe/kindred/nation-family murmur.
21- a push /effort distinctly, thou art hard/stubborn in order to stretch out/distend he the flowing principle (water). (crossing the Euphrates).
22- the push/thrust of the spirit/living principal the impulse forward.
23 it is your swift action we cry out we with vigour the power/what forces united together. (Rha implies "the ruling power").
24- united (with) thee taking off/going outwards.

This account clearly specifies two flights by the Etruscan forefathers. The prince leading the first migration is recognizably Moses who is united to the national god. The little cabinet riding in a cart is unique to the Hebrew people as the Ark of Covenant. The god Yahweh, who is now doctored into Jehovah, to make him acceptable to western minds, is the 'hidden' or 'cowled', 'concealed' god. The mention of the blast and the great winds driving back waters in one account, are reminiscent of the Red Sea crossing of the Exodus, and the limiting of waters, or perhaps freezing them, in the second account would fit the crossing of the upper Euphrates. Then there is mention of ships, and the hidden god provides winds to blow the sails, which would have brought the people from Western Asia Minor to Etruria.

Golden tools and furniture are to be made for the travelling hidden god, and this again matches Hebrew and Biblical record. There is also a constant stream of references to the gift or favour granted of a land to spread out in, to live in, and to beautify. These would seem to be references to *'a promised land'*, and that would again indicate the Hebrew traditions. That this hidden god provided rules by which the people should live, is also made apparent in this Agnone Text and this again parallels Hebrew record. Ea the great Weather god of Heaven, the lord of all winds, storms, water, and rain, became Aa, and then Yah and Jah, and finally Yahweh alias Jehovah.

Above all the unity of this people with their one god is constantly expressed. There is first the flight from Egypt around 1360 BC, under the Prince Moses. Second, there is the deportation of the Israel Ten Tribes by the Assyrians between 740 – 710 BC. And third, there is the flight from Assyria starting around 700 -690 BC, which took these Khumry- *'Kimmeroi'* through Asia Minor to the Dardanelles and on by ship to Etruria.

The whole text fits remarkably well with known facts. The Khumry took the great city of Sardis in 660 BC and began migrating to Italy around 650 BC. Any Biblical student can see the similarity of these Agnone Tablet statements and the account in Exodus. Drought and parched dry places indicate Sinai, and the passage where the action of powerful winds upon the waters, and the rending and breaking of warhorses, is described, must surely match with the destruction of the Pharoah Timaeus - Thoum, and his chariots when he attempted to pursue the fleeing tribes across the Red Sea. The story of a united group of tribes fleeing a stricken land towards a country gifted to them by favour, whilst obeying the Utterances of a Hidden god who rides in a small cabinet in a cart, an Ark, can only logically refer to the Exodus under Moses.

The Ark of the Covenant.

The fact of the Khumry being identified by the ancient Assyrians as the Israel Ten Tribes, as distinct from the Judean Two Tribes, and then as the Kimmeroi by the Greeks, leads to a momentous situation. Half of these Khumry known as the Treres (Y Treres) sailed to Italy around 650 BC, and the other half remained in Trojan Western Asia Minor for perhaps a hundred to a hundred-and-fifty years, before sailing to Britain under Brwth-Brutus. The question then is which of these two groups took the Ark of Covenant with them as it appears certain that the little cabinet being followed across the Euphrates was the Ark? Did the Ark go to Etruria, or did it come to Britain? This little puzzle attracted Blackett and Wilson, and they looked into it.

The story begins at Mount Sinai where the Hebrew encamped after their escape across the Red Sea, when the seas withdrew only to return with a tremendous rush to engulf and destroy the pursuing Egyptian Pharoah with his army. This would have been around 1360 BC. At Sinai, Moses having twice been given tablets of laws by the god Yahweh, was instructed to make an Ark to contain these tablets. Biblical record details the pattern dictated by Yahweh to Moses and passed on to the artisans. From the very outset of its construction, this Ark, or its contents, proved to be a very dangerous object.

Exodus 37: 1-9

> 'Bezaleel made the Covenant Box out of acacia wood, 45 inches long, 27 inches wide, and 27 inches high. He covered it with pure gold inside and out, and put a gold border all around it. He made four carrying rings of gold for it, and attached them to its four feet, with two rings on each side. He made carrying poles of acacia wood, covered them with gold and put them through the rings on each side of the box. He made a lid of pure gold 45 inches long, 27 inches wide, (and 9 inches thick). He made two winged creatures of hammered gold, one for each end of the lid. He made them so that they formed one piece with the lid. He made them so that the winged creatures faced each other across the lid, and their outspread wings covered it.'

Several other Biblical references describe this Ark, in *Leviticus*, in *Deuteronomy*, in the *Book of Numbers*, in *Chronicles*, *Exodus*, and in *Kings*. The main feature of the Ark was that it was an extremely dangerous piece of sacred equipment. It is recorded as causing the death of numbers of people on several occasions, and it maimed or burned Moses. It caused leprosy, or something very like it, and could cause physical damage as when it was carried around the walls of Jericho before the walls collapsed.

For these and other reasons, the Ark, with its dangerous contents was kept behind screens in a specially made tent set up in a specially screened compound, and this was sited well away from the camps of the Hebrews as they slowly migrated from Egypt to their final destination in Canaan. Only chosen and trained priestly families were allowed to go near the Ark, and they had to wear protective layers of thick clothing, and then leather, and then again, more clothing. All that is recorded as being contained in the Ark are the two tablets bearing inscriptions, which were given to Moses by God. These two tablets are described in Deuteronomy 10:5 and in Exodus 34:30.

> 'Aaron and all the people looked at Moses and saw that his face was shining and they were afraid to go near him. But Moses called hem, and Aaron and all the leaders of the community went to him, and Moses spoke to him.'

After this Moses never removed a veil from his face unless he was either in his own tent, or in the holy tent with the Ark communicating with God.

'And he would put the veil back on until the next time when he spoke with the Lord.'

Within a few weeks of the tablets being placed inside the newly made Ark and the travelling tent shrine being erected, the Ark killed two priests.'

Leviticus 16:1-2, and 10:1.

'Aaron's sons Nadab and Ahihu each took his fire-pan, put live coals in it, added incense, and presented it to the Lord. But this fire was not holy and the Lord had not commanded them to present it. Suddenly the Lord sent fire and burnt them to death in the presence of the Lord.'

The bodies of Nadab and Abihu, who had approached the Ark with unholy fire, were hastily buried well away from the main Hebrew camp. The Lord then told Moses, who in turn told his brother Aaron,

'Tell your brother Aaron that only at the proper time is he to go behind the curtain into the holy place, where I live/appear in a cloud above the lid of the Covenant Box, if he disobeys he will be killed.'

Moses seems to have used the Ark as a terrifying weapon to enforce obedience. When brother Aaron, and his wife Miriam, criticized Moses' marriage to a Cushite woman the Lord blasted Miriam with *'leprosy'*. He then removed this terrifying condition after seven days, after Miriam was suitably frightened and punished. Numbers 12:1-16. Korab of the Levite clan of Kohath, with three men from the Reuben tribe and two-hundred-and-fifty supporters, then challenged the authority of Moses. All those men were killed at an Ark ceremony arranged by Moses. Numbers 16:1-35. It may be that the Ark deity was worried by metal incense burners, and when over six-hundred-years later the King Uzziah went into the Jerusalem temple with a metal incense burner, he was immediately stricken down with what was diagnosed as *'leprosy.'* II Chronicles 26:16-23.

So dangerous was the Ark that only men from the clan of Kohath of Levi were allowed to carry it from the temple tent to the ox cart in which it travelled. The ox cart led the way, and the people followed on at a safe distance behind. The Etruscan Agnone Tablet records just such journeys, with the little cabinet, or Ark, riding in its cart and leading two successive migrations. One under Moses out of Egypt around 1360 BC, and the other out of the north of Assyria in circa 690 BC.

When the Hebrews finally settled in old Canaan the Covenant Box was kept at Shiloh, as in II Samuel 3:3-4. Throughout its history until this time the Ark had

Chapter 7- The Longer Etruscan Inscriptions

served as a potent military talisman, and it was believed to guarantee Hebrew victory. In the time of the Judge Eli, unauthorized soldiers took the Ark into battle against the Phillistines at Ebenezer and were defeated. The Ark was captured by the Philistines, and the old Judge Eli died of shock, bringing Samuel to power.

The Philistines put the Ark in the temple of the god Dagan at Ashdod, and the statue of Dagan promptly collapsed. The statue was re-erected, and the next day it fell again, and its head and arms were shattered causing much alarm. Then a plague of tumours broke out in Ashdod, and the Ark was quickly removed to Gath where the people also began to develop tumours. The same thing happened at Ekron, and after seven months the Philistine Kings, on the advice of their Magi, decided to return the Ark. So, the Ark was put on a brand-new ox cart drawn by two never-previously-yoked oxen, along with suitable offerings and gifts, and it trundled off down the road to Beth Shemesh unattended.

At Beth Shemesh the Ark caused further trouble and killed seventy, excited men of Israel. It was then taken to Kiriath Jearim, and Abinadab, son of Eleazar, who was (taught) consecrated to take charge of it. At Kiriath Jearim it brought good fortune to everyone and twenty-years later, when David became King, he decided to have it brought to Jerusalem. At the threshing floor of Nacon' the oxen drawing the cart stumbled, and the Ark was in danger of falling from the swaying cart. In haste a man named Uzzah reached out to prevent the Ark from falling and was immediately struck dead.

After this further demonstration of trouble, King David changed his mind, and he sent the Ark to the house of Obed Edom in Gath, and there was tranquillity. The family of Obed Edom are listed as one of the families originally chosen to take care of the Ark and Tent or Pavilion, and this name later becomes an important clue. Three months later the Ark was brought to Jerusalem and installed in its tent there. Biblical history relates how Solomon, son of David, built a temple in Jerusalem, and at its core he erected a strong vault in which he installed the Ark.

Immediately after Solomon's death, his Kingdom split into two separate parts. The tribes of Judah and Benjammin were ruled by Rehoboam, as Judea, and the Ten Tribes of Israel were ruled by Jeroboam. Five years later the Pharaoh, Shishack, entered Judea with his armies. Solomon's richly furnished temple in Jerusalem was stripped of its wealth by the Pharaoh Shishak, around 930 BC, but it is unlikely that Shishak made any attempt to remove the Ark from its sanctuary. No such mention is made, and Shishak would have been aware of the fearsome reputation of the Covenant Box.

It seems that Rehoboam handed over the valuable gold and silver implements of the temple, and its accumulated wealth, as the price of Shishak leaving the city of Jerusalem undamaged. Everything points to the Ark remaining at Jerusalem after Shisack's raid, and in Kings: 12 & 13, the story is told of King Jeroboam being concerned over the dictate that the people of the Ten Tribes of Israel should go to worship god in the rival Kingdom of Judea. His solution was to set up an alternative religious site at Beth-El in Israel, and the Jerusalem priests, who saw a vast source of wealth vanishing from their grasp, were furious.

Over a century later, King Joash of Judea took the funds and treasures of the Jerusalem temple for his own treasury. Then his son Amaziah became a pagan and worshipped Edomite idols, and this brings us to the important Biblical story. King Amaziah the pagan, whose father, Joash, had robbed the Jerusalem temple, planned to make war on the King Jehoash of Israel, and foolishly refused to listen to warnings. The story is in II Kings 14:11-14, and in II Chronicles 25:21-24.

> 'King Jehoash of Israel went into battle against King Amaziah of Judea. They met at Beth Shemesh in Judea. The Judean army was defeated and the soldiers fled to their homes. Jehoash captured Amaziah and took him to Jerusalem. There he tore down the city wall from the Ephraim Gate to the Corner Gate, a distance of two hundred meters (220 yards.) He took back to Samaria as loot, all the gold and silver in the temple, <u>and the temple equipment guarded by the descendants of Obed Edom and the palace treasures. He also took hostages with him.</u>'

As the family of Obed Edom were the officially appointed guardians of the Ark of the Covenant, it is obvious that by taking them and the temple equipment they guarded, King Jehoash took the Ark to the city of Samaria around 790 BC. It becomes equally obvious that when at the request of King Ahaz of Judea, supported by a huge tribe, the Assyrian Emperor Tiglathpileser III-Pul, attacked Israel around 740 BC, the Ark was in Samaria. When Tiglathpileser and his successors deported the Israelite Ten Tribes far to the north towards Armenia and the Caucasus, they took their religious furniture, including the Ark of the Covenant, and the priests with them. Therefore, the Ark would have been up north in Armenia or Northern Iran from around 740 to 690 BC when the people began their westwards migration towards the distant Dardanelles.

It was a few years after the victory of Jehoash of Israel in circa 790 BC, that Uzziah-Azariah of Judea, attempted to enter the *'holy of holies'* vault in the Jerusalem temple, to see if the Ark was still there. He only got as far as an altar

Chapter 7 - The Longer Etruscan Inscriptions

outside the vault before being very badly burned. As only one man, the High Priest, was allowed to enter the room of the Ark on a few days a year, no one else knew if the room was empty or not. King Uzziah was prevented from finding out whether Jehoash of Israel had removed the Ark or not. There must have been more than rumours flying about to cause Uzziah to take the action he did. Everything points to the Jerusalem Priests refusing to admit and acknowledge that the Ark was in Samaria, and the '*holy of holies*' vault was in fact empty.

Significantly, King Uzziah was standing by the incense altar and was not in, or near, the chamber of the Ark when he was badly burned. Equally, the records show a certain panic on the part of the priest, Azariah, and eighty others, to keep Uzziah out of the temple. Whatever the cause, Uzziah was badly burned and his disfigurements caused him to remain inside his house for the rest of his life, whilst his son Jotham ruled over Judea as Regent. 2. Kings15 and 2 Chronicles 26.

Later Pekah of Israel, a successor of Jehoash defeated Ahaz of Judaea, around 734 BC, and 2 Chronicles 28 records that Pekah killed a hundred-and-twenty-thousand Judean soldiers and deported two-hundred-thousand women and children. The Israelite army seized vast amounts of loot, and one soldier Zichri, killed Masseiah, the son of Ahaz, the King's deputy Elkanah, and the palace administrator Azrikam. It appears certain therefore that Jerusalem, the King's palace, and the temple, was once again looted. The possibilities of the Ark remaining in Jerusalem whilst the family of Obed Edom were seized and taken to Samaria, are virtually zero. In this situation of King Jehoash and then King Pekah of Israel, both taking everything they could from Judea, along with the vital family of Obed Edom, the official attendants and keepers of the Ark, they undoubtedly took the Ark of Covenant.

Following these catastrophes, Judea was invaded by the Edomites, and the desperate King Ahaz made the fatal mistake of asking the Assyrian Emperor Tiglathpileser III for aid. So, Judea became a client ally of Assyria, whilst Israel remained allied to Syria and several other states as an opponent of Assyrian domination. From around 734 – 700 BC, the majority of the Ten Tribes of Israel were then deported hundreds of miles to the northern borders of the Assyrian Empire.

If King Jehoash took the family of Obed Edom, then he took the Ark. It is that simple. This makes the unexpected, and surprising statement on the Agnone Tablet in Etruria as a perfectly logical account. The Ark went north with the Israelite deportations to Armenia, and then it was used to lead the people on their long trek westwards all the way through several lands and mountain chains to the distant Dardanelles.

The Ark of the Covenant somehow caught the public imagination in the later part of the twentieth century, with numbers of fundamentally flawed books and films being produced. The Agnone Tablet throws some light on the matter and breaks the mind-set or rigid thought-mould that the Ark has to have vanished into some remote, distant, unexplored, exotic, region. Ancient Britain looms into focus.

This was how, after much thought, Blackett and Wilson set up their biggest and most complex plan to erect a project to examine evidence for the Ark in Britain. As usual no one else had ever thought to look at British records and seek out the mass of detailed information locked away in them.

They noted that much is made of the statement attributed to King Josiah of Judea in c. 622 BC when he made a request to the Levite teachers, as in 2 Chronicles 35:3.

> 'Put the sacred Covenant Box in the temple that King Solomon built, the son of David. You are no longer to carry it from place to place, but are to serve the Lord your God and his people Israel'.

In short, the Ark was very definitely not in the temple, which Josiah was trying to repair and rebuild, and he wanted it returned, if the Levites had it. The prophet Jeremiah makes it very clear that not only were the Ten Tribes far away to the North, but also that they had the Ark with them.

> Jeremiah 2:16 'Then when you have become numerous in that land, people will no longer talk about any Covenant Box. They will no longer think about it or remember it, they will not even need it. Nor will they make another one.'

> Jeremiah 2:18 'Israel will join with Judah and together they will come from exile in the country in the North, and will return to the land that I (God) gave to your ancestors.'

Jeremiah got things wrong, because people still do remember the Covenant Box, and the Israel Ten Tribes did not return south to join Judea, but instead they went west.

Jeremiah proved useful however, as the Maccabees Book II in the *Apocrypha* tells how he took the Tent used to surround the Ark, and went to a strange land with it. There he buried it in a cave, and although others followed him, they were never able to find it. Amongst the five sealed caves so far located by Blackett and

Chapter 7- The Longer Etruscan Inscriptions

Wilson in their systematic following of the records trail, is one named as "The Cave of the Tent" or the "Pavilion". Whether or not there is anything inside remains to be seen, but the name is correct.

The Ark is interesting as there are parallels with the Holy Greal of Britain. A Greal is a set of records, or laws, and Moses came down the mountain with a Greal. The Koran could be described as a Greal, so could the Bible, or in modern times the Constitution of the United States. Both the Ark and the Greal are thought to be very dangerous, and can kill the unwelcome. Both need specially qualified and selected attendants, both emit blinding light and cannot be looked upon, both are hidden, covered over, wrapped in cloth. Both are very sacred objects, and the Agnone Tablet makes perfect sense.

All this is another story, but it is interesting that some people in North Cardiff areas still spend sunny summer days out searching for a traditional treasure with metal detectors. They are looking for a great wooden chest that contains a fabulous treasure. This box is guarded by two Giant Ravens, Cig-fran-gawr (flesh eating crows, giants), and it is not difficult to imagine these guardians Cigfrangawr as the golden Cherubim on the lid of the Ark with their wings outstretched across the box.

Other Long Etruscan Texts.

There are several other long Etruscan Texts amongst the thousands of very short statements. One is a clay tablet from Santa Maria di Capua which is dated from the fifth century and is estimated to contain three-hundred words, and which has not yet been approached.

There is the famous bronze liver from Piacenza, which is marked out in a number of sections which each have a written statement. This would guide the augurs in divining the portents revealed by the liver of a sacrificial animal. Then there is the Berlin Cippus which is a long text on a stele, and of course there is the, more than interesting, leaden tablet from Magliano, which has a text of around seventy words arranged in a spiral on both sides.

The remarkable Zagreb shroud, from Agram in Egypt, has already been mentioned. The academics have got themselves into a muddle over Etruscan because they have wrongly assumed that the Etruscans got their alphabet from the Greeks, and that everything is Greek related. We can quote Ernst Doblhofer who expresses the general misconceptions: -

'A discovery made in 1944 aroused the interests of students of the epigraphic problems of Ancient Italy. At Gubbio, the Ancient Umbrian Iguvium, were found by chance in a vaulted cave, seven bronze tablets partly engraved on both sides, which were subsequently preserved in the local town hall. Five of these tablets were incised in the Umbrian script and language. The writing, like other Italic alphabets bequeathed by the Etruscans, is of Greek origin and does not deny this affiliation. The language is closely akin to Latin.'

This goes on to claim that Richard Lepius and others, deciphered Etruscan (claims to have identified all the letters), but no one knows how to read the language. This is a nonsense. There is no beloved "V", no X, no Z, no J, and no Q. Neither the Etruscan Alphabet, nor the language, has anything to do with either Greek or Latin, nor was anything acquired from the Greeks. Then the puzzled Ernst Doblhofer expresses the general bewilderment in the hiatus, which has been created.

Pliny the Elder, and his contemporaries had it right two-thousand years ago.

Chapter Eight

In Search of Brutus

To leave Italian Etruria and to go cast in search of the legendary Brutus, the founding King of Britain, was not as quixotic a venture as might first appear. In the Musei Capitolini, in Rome, there is an ancient Etruscan statue of Brutus, variously dated between 500-300 BC. Around the plinth of the statue runs another Etruscan-Coelbren inscription. The foundation stone of Rome, known as the Lapis Niger, is a short, square, rough pillar which again has Etruscan-Coelbren inscriptions on all four sides.

Edwin Guest, Bishops Stubbs, J. Gwenogfran Evans, Griffith J. Williams, and a host of others, would have the British people believe Brutus to be a mythical figure, yet this mythical personage has an inscribed statue proclaiming Brutus' humanity and reality. Significantly, reputable Arab historians of *c.* 1050 were referring to Britain as Brutus-land, and this was a hundred years before Griffith ap Arthur (alias Geoffrey of Monmouth is alleged to have invented the Brutus story.

In 1862, the Rev. Robert Williams 'translated' a number of old Welsh documents, and W. H. Skene published them. Amongst these was *The Songs of the Graves*, and in the total hash made by Robert Williams, it was claimed that some one hundred and eighty to two hundred ancient kings and princes were variously briefly named. This complete nonsense was exposed in 1958 by W. H. Thomas, who showed that there were, in his opinion, no more than some eighty names. These warnings were disregarded, and detailed research designed to trace these graves, shows that there are fewer than thirty named kings and princes in *The Songs of the Graves*. These all have detailed grave references, rather than vague notices, and once the adverbs, verbs, adjectives, nouns, etc., are seen not to be names' they can be traced.

The grave of the 'first ruler' is described, and a visit to the specified site brings one to a massive tomb mound, right on target as specified. The 'first ruler' is undoubtedly Brutus, and it is curious that a mythical figure should be affirmed to be real in veritable multitudes of ancient British records, and should then also have a statue and a grave mound. At the very core of the British Brutus histories is the story of Brutus gathering the people and the fleets in Trojan Western Asia

Minor, and sailing for Britain in the era c. 550-500 BC. It was to seek evidence of this that Baram Blackett and Alan Wilson turned their attention eastwards to the Aegean and Turkey.

The Brutus History

The majority of the British people will not know of their own historical and cultural heritage, and a brief account of Brutus will allow the reader to follow Blackett and Wilson on their journey back along the British ancestral trail.

If we take the account in *the Aeneid*, by Virgil, written just before the dawn of the Christian era, we find that Virgil describes the Trojan Prince Aeneas gathering many of his people after the destruction of Troy, and sailing in search of a new homeland. The first destination was to the African coast, near newly founded Carthage, and from there Aeneas led his people in their migration to Italy. It was at this time, around 650 BC, that Aeneas participated in the founding or building of Rome.

The tale begins with Aeneas tempted to kill Helen of Troy, but desisting on the advice of his grandmother Venus. Aeneas then took his son Ilus-Ascanius (the Welsh Ancwn), his father Anchises (Welsh Aedd Mawr), and his grandfather Capys, and led their combined fleets towards Carthage in North Africa. At Carthage Queen Dido made desperate attempts to persuade Aeneas to marry her, but failed. Reference to the genealogies that Flavius Josephus exhibited in his work *Against Apion* places these events around 650 BC.

Various Roman accounts describe the founding of Rome, and Brutus son of Silvius became the first consul of the new Republic after the expulsion of the Tarquin Dynasty. In the Roman account, Brutus could not avoid condemning his sons to death for participating in a conspiracy to restore the Tarquin monarchy, and in this way, he was responsible for the deaths of near members of his family. Livy then states that Brutus was killed in the front line of battle, which would be a most unlikely position for the First Consul of Rome.

In the British versions of the Brutus story, Capys, Anchises, and Aeneas gather their fleets and people and again sail to Italy *via* Carthage. This Trojan arrival in Italy then causes a war to erupt, just as in the Roman versions. Aeneas first negotiates with King Latinus, which arouses the anger of Turnus, King of the Rutuli, who starts the war. Aeneas kills Turnus, and by seizing and marrying Lavinia, the daughter of Latinus, he finally gains control over both kingdoms. In the British historical version, the subsequent events take a very different and less glorious Republican course than those recorded by the politically motivated Livy.

Aeneas was ultimately succeeded by his son Ascanius, who in turn was to be succeeded by his son Silvius - Selys Hen (the Aged). Silvius has an illicit affair with a niece of Lavinia, who was Aeneas' second wife. This prompts Ascanius to consult the diviners and soothsayers, who tell him that the child will be a boy who will cause the death of both his mother and father. The boy will become a wanderer and he will achieve the highest honours.

Inevitably the mother dies in childbirth, and so the infant Brutus fulfils the first part of the awesome prophecy. Then, when he was fifteen, young Brutus was out hunting with his father Silvius and he shot an arrow which accidentally killed his father Silvius. This fulfils the prophecy, and the tragic youth is then banished from Italy. The Livy story is different, with Lucius Junius Brutus as the first Consul of Rome, and responsible for driving out the Tarquins and their adherents. There are two different but equally tragic versions of the story. One is of a youth who inadvertently kills both his parents, and the other of a Consul forced to execute two of his own sons, and in doing so sets the pattern of the superior virtue of inflexible and unquestioning loyalty to the Republic. The Livy version is redolent of much similar Republican propaganda that enveloped several totalitarian regimes in the twentieth century.

The general chronology of the British versions appears to place Brutus around 570-500 BC, and chronological record places his decisive actions late in life, at around 504 BC. Tacitus, the first-century AD Roman historian, dates the expulsion of the Tarquins at 510 BC, and this again brings Aeneas and the Trojan War down to the 650BC era. Tacitus also credits Lucius Junius Brutus with the overthrow of the Tarquins. Modern archaeology dates the foundation of Rome as a proper city at circa 550 BC and all this leaves Livy floundering at around 725 BC.

The Brut Tyssilio contains what is probably the oldest British version of the Brutus story, with St Tyssilio dying around AD 684. Copies of this Brut dating from c. 1100 still exist, and it is highly likely that this is the older history, which the much-abused Gruffydd ap Arthur (Geoffrey of Monmouth) took much of his information. Brutus is alluded to in the Triads, in ancient poetry, the royal genealogies, and in several other sources, including the great *Historia Brittonum* of Nennius, c. 800-822, and also in *De Excideo Brittaniae*, by Gildas.

As with the story of Albyne from Syria, there are strange echoing ancient correlations with the British Brutus story. After leaving Italy, Brutus returns to the remnant half of the Trojans who had remained in Western Asia Minor near Byzantium, and around the Dardanelles. Here he found that the Greeks had made war upon his kinsmen and were oppressing them. This parallels the Greek histories of a war around 510 to 500 BC, which led to Greek domination of the same area around Byzantium, as the British histories specify. Brutus quickly becomes a rallying point for his beleaguered nation, and is opposed by the Greek commander named 'Pandrassus'. Historically the Greek historians named their commanding general as Pausanius the Spartan.

Brutus then finds an able ally in Assaracus, who is half Greek and half Trojan, and the fortresses of Assaracus provide Brutus with the necessary military bases. By means of a series of military stratagems Brutus is able to ambush and capture Antigonus the brother of Pandrassus. By using Antigonus as a pawn, Brutus is able to plot the capture of the Greek general Pandrassus himself. This then allows Brutus to exact a threefold ransom from the helpless Pandrassus. He is given Pandrassus' daughter in marriage; he is allowed to collect three hundred and twenty-four ships; and he is given gold and silver and also an agreement allowing him to depart peacefully with his fleets.

The Greek accounts, which are vague, contain stories of Pausanius the Spartan being disgraced in an affair involving the misuse of large quantities of gold and silver, and also of being involved with a young woman. He is also recorded as overseeing a military disaster in the occupation and control of Byzantium. Certainly, this very real Greek general was brought down in disgrace by his failures. Exactly why is not stated anywhere other than in the British records.

After two days and one night of sailing, Brutus arrives with his fleets at an island named as Leogotia. The island is uninhabited as the native population had been slaughtered by pirates. On Leogotia Brutus finds a deserted temple of the goddess Diana, where he makes the correct offerings. The oracle then directs Brutus to sail beyond the place of the setting sun, past the realm of Gaul, to the great island in the sea, which was once occupied by Geauntes (Gutians).

'Now it is ready for you and your folk. Down the years it will provide an abode suited for you and to your people, and for your descendants, it will be a second Troy. A race of Kings will be born there of your stock, and the round circle of the whole Earth will be subject to them.'

Thus advised Brutus set sail to North Africa where he arrives at the Altars of the Phillistines and the Salt Pan Lake. From this point he proceeds to Russicada and the mountains of Zarec. Then the story takes Brutus and his fleets past the River Malva, to a landing place in Mauritania, where he ravages the country. Then the fleet passes on west through the Pillars of Hercules-Straits of Gibraltar, and on to the West coast of Iberia-Spain. This journey and its stopping points, is still traceable.

At this Iberian landing, Brutus and his six thousand warriors are joined by another westward migrating group of Trojans led by Corineus, who are fourth generation migrants who left Troy under Antenor. Corineus and his people now join with Brutus swelling his armada, and the combined fleets sail to Acquitane, and anchor in the Loire estuary. Here the fleet lies at anchor for seven days, presumably to gather food and water and to re-fit the ships. Messengers arrive from Goffar the Pict, who rules this land, and enquire into the intentions of Brutus. Then a fight erupts and Himbert, the ambassador sent by Goffar, is killed by Corineus.

Chapter 8 - In search of Brutus

This results in Goffar launching an attack on Brutus, and after a ferocious battle the Pictish king is routed. Goffar then appeals to the other eleven kings who rule over Gaul to assist him. In the fighting which follows, Brutus is victorious in several battles, but sees his forces dwindle as the enemy continues to arrive in ever-increasing numbers. The only sensible thing to do is to leave, and so once again the sea-worn fleets set sail to seek out the island kingdom promised to them by the oracle.

Finally, Brutus arrives in Britain, where a party of his soldiers is ambushed by one Gog Magog, the local Geauntes king. After a resulting battle Gog is captured, and then, in a wrestling match with Corineus, Gog is thrown down a slope and killed. Tracing this site is actually possible, with the *Top of the Throw* and *Bottom of the Throw* still so named in Khumric, as are other sites. Amidst all this, in the account of 1135 there is mention of Corineus having earlier fought against Geauntes in Italy.

There are a number of obvious parallels in the British, Greek, and Roman accounts. Significantly the British manuscripts pre-date the later alleged Renaissance copies of Roman and Greek accounts. Perhaps university employees would baulk at the idea of testing out the reality of Brutus in the Aegean and Western Turkey on this evidence. But it was on just such ancient evidence that Heinrich Schliemann discovered Troy in 1876, whilst they dithered and hesitated. There is an old Welsh saying: 'Fear knocked on the door, Faith answered the door, and there was no one there.'

It is perhaps important that British accounts include what appears to be an elder brother of Aeneas, who is named Prydain. This Prydain would fit with Tarquinius Priscus, and this will probably be the vital in unravelling the early history of Rome. Prydain means 'of delicate aspect', and might well match Tarquinius Priscus. The Khumric 'ap' can mean 'son of' and 'successor to', and this can cause problems when family succession goes from brother to brother, or reverts from uncle to nephew or *vice versa*.

The Lemnos Stele

After much deliberation, Alan Wilson and Baram Blackett decided that their best chance of finding some traces of the British migration from Troy might be on the island of Leogotia. Brutus and his people might only have stayed on the island for a few days, but there was clear reference to a temple of Diana, which just might be traceable. The first problem was to locate Leogotia, under its modern name, and this meant slogging through the ancient names of the Aegean islands. Finally, they decided that the most probable place known as Leogotia was the island of Lemnos.

Enquiries about Lemnos brought an almost immediate piece of possible information when they read that in 1876 an inscribed stele had been found on the island. There was no mention of what script or language was used in this inscription, but they did learn that it had been taken to the Athens Museum. There was no mention of what this stele recorded or whom it named, and this aroused their curiosity. So, with mixed feelings of hope, pessimism, apprehension, and impatience, they typed a letter to the Curator of the Athens Museum requesting a photograph.

If this stele from Lemnos remained unread, it was because once again the scholars who publish voluminous tomes claiming to identify all the known alphabets of the world had once again omitted to mention the British Coelbren. They know all the alphabets, except one - the British Coelbren.

This is exactly how things turned out. The reply from Athens came within days rather than weeks, and they sat down to open the letter. The anticipation of Wilson and Blackett was something like that of a boxer before an important fight, or a footballer before a big game. Would the Lemnos stele be in the anticipated Coelbren alphabet and would it be decipherable? Or would it be Latin, or simply Greek, or whatever? If the stele was inscribed in Coelbren, then it might provide the final nail to drive into the lid of the coffin of bogus British 'Celticism', which had been deliberately invented to obliterate the correct Chaldean and Trojan inheritance of the British.

For three thousand six hundred years, the British had preserved the story of the Albyne migration, and for two thousand five hundred years they had firmly remembered Brutus and his line of descendants. The question was whether this Lemnos Stele would provide further conclusive proof and evidence to overthrow the idiotic, unsubstantiated, unproven invention that the old British were ludicrously 'Celtic'.

Their first sight of the photograph of the Lemnos Stele from the Athens Museum was an electric moment. There was no doubt whatsoever that the alphabet used to inscribe the Lemnos Stele was virtually identical with British Coelbren. The texts were actually written over and around the figure of a powerfully built man holding a spear. It seemed even more incredible than ever that no one had ever tried to compare this inscribed stone with the British Alphabets. For centuries the English universities and public schools had taught nothing much else other than Greek and Latin as 'Classics'. Thousands, perhaps even millions, of bored students must have read the statements of Julius Caesar, of Ammianus Marcellinus, of Strabo, and others, giving British origins to the Greek alphabet. They must have known something of the connection with the Byzantiun and Trojan area by virtue of the Brutus legend.

The British histories, and other associated records, are firm and clear in tracing the Trojan origins, and about a gathering of the fleets at an Aegean Island, which

Chapter 8 - In search of Brutus

6th Century BC Steele from Lemnos
Athens National Museuem

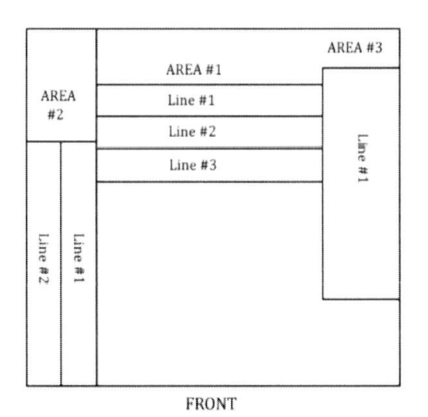

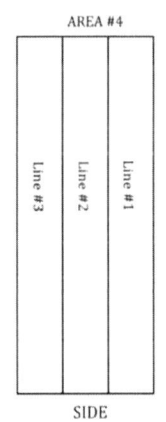

237

King Arthur Conspiracy - Wilson & Blackett

The Lemnos Stele now in the Athens Museum

Area No.1 Line No.1
Text	ꓱᴧꓴ	ꓱ	ᴧ ꓥ ᴧꓱ ꓲ ꓴᴧ ꓲ ꓴ
Intent	F A R	E B	A Ph A R I Ch A I Ch
Khumric	ffar	eb	afar iachiad, iach
English	what extends out Large/ample "ffaraon" = high powers	faith	grief/sadness saviour, sound/healthy

Area No. 1 Line No. 2
Text	ꓢ	I F ᴧ	ꓢ	I E F ꓯ ꓩ ᴧ ꓱ
Intent	Cy	I F A	(Cy)	C I E F Y R A I D D
Khumric	cu	iff	cu	cyfeiriadd
English	together/ mutually	forcibly/ejected	to join together (mutually)	direction

Area No . 1 Line No. 3
Text	ꓱꓶ	I ꓫ	⊕		ꓴꓩꓯꓳꓩᴧꓲ		
Intent	E Ef	I Dd	Croes Cant	Can	Cy E Ph O R	A I	Croes Cant
Khumric	eff	idd	Croes Cant	Cant	Cyflor	Ai au	Croes Cant
English	he	towards	across circle horizon	the borders			to go across the circle

Area No. 2 Line No. 1 reading from right bottom to left top.
Text	ᴧꓹꓱꓩ	ꓔᴧꓲᴧꓯ ꓴ ꓲ		O
Intent	A Ch E Ff (ph)	T A E A Ff (ph) I		Cylch, cant
Khumric	achef	taen, taeanadwy, taenellu		cylch, cant
English	genealogy/pedigree	spreading out		the circle, horizon

Area No.2 Line No. 2
Text	ꓱᴧꓴ	ᴧꓔᴧ	ꓨ ꓲᴧꓔ	ꓴꓩꓯꓳꓩᴧꓲꓯꓳꓯ ꓲꓯᴧꓲ			
Intent	E A R	A Th A	Dd I A Th	Ch E Th O R A I R O Th I R A I
Khumric	ea, ear	Athafa	Diath	ceth orai rhoti rai
English	free, at large Extends out	sorrow/ grief	clamour, dias - direct diathal - unimpeded	fiends to cry furies often ruthriad breaking out attack

Area No. 3 Line 1
Text	ꓭoꓲᴧꓲꓱ	ꓴ	ꓯᴧꓰ	O	⊕		
Intent	H O LI A I E	Cy	Rh A EO	cylch, cant	Croes	Cant
Khumric	hollallu	cu	rhea	cylch, cant	croes	the earth
English	all powerful	together mutually	in battle	the circle	across	horizon

238

Chapter 8 - In search of Brutus

Area No 4. Line No. 1 reading from right to left.
Text   iⵏⵔOⵏ   ʃIFⵏ   ⵔLⵏPⵏⵔ ʃIFψⵔⵏ   IϚ
Intent   I A R O A   Ch I E A   Rh Wy A Ff A R Cy I F U Y Th A I CD
Khumric   iarew   cyfiaw   Rhwyfadur   Cyfeithrin
English   a pilot   make, equal directing   to nurse together
          what directs   Rhywyfan - to lead away to nurse together

Area No.4 Line No. 1 continuation
Text   ʃ IFⵏ   IⵏFIʃ
Intent   Th E I F A   I A F I Ch (cy)
Khumric   theithiad   iaffu, iach, ieith
English   travelling   pedigree
                       lachadur = saviour

Area No.4 Line No.2 reading from right to left
Text   ⵋ   Oⵍ   BⵏⵇⵏHo   ZIⵍAI   ⴵITⴵZIO
Intent   Th = Ff O R Ysg A N A Ph O   Th I E A I   E S T E Ch I O
Khumric   Ffor   Ysgarano = ysgaradde thieai = pieau estrichio
English   escape/flee a scattering/dispersion to worn, possess to haste, to battle

Area No. 4 Line No.2 continuation
Text   ⵏⵋ ⵏI   TIⵂ   ⬜◻⋊ⴵ
Intent   A Th (ph) A I   T I WY   All O Ch E
Khumric   aeth   tiws   alltud
English   He has gone pleasant   foreign land
          he went

Area No. 4 Line No. 3 reading from left to right
Text   ⵏⵍo ⵇ   ⴵⴵoTo B ϟ Iⴵⴵ   B IⵏZOⵇⴵZ
Intent   A R O Th (ph) E F O T O OLI Dd I F E   OLI I A Ch O Th E Ch
Khumric   arofyn   efo   ti o olladdifaol   olliach   offech = offern
English   intent, design   him   you from all consuming   almighty   sacred service

Area No. 4 Line No.3 continuation
Text   ⴵTⵏIϟⵏ   IZo⬚   IZTIⵏToↄ
Intent   E Th A I S A   I Ch O OoL   I Ch Th I A Th O G
Khumric   ethais   a   iachaol   iachaethog = iachaedigaeth
English   what spreads out healing quality   the act of healing

239

they call Leogotia, just off the western coasts of Asia Minor - Turkey. Here was a large inscribed stone on what was the most likely island for this gathering, where Brutus was elected as leader. This is where the decision was made to sail from Troy forever, and to head for the great green island in the western ocean, which can only be Britain. Yet no one thought to check the British alphabets and this inscription.

Perhaps there were those who might have considered checking out the Lemnos Stele and the British Coelbren alphabet. But they may have had second thoughts and considered their careers, their reputations and social standing, and of course their personal safety. Either way, no one had ever made such thoughts known. Strange as it was, at this very same time the Welsh university departments, which had viciously attacked and vilified Wilson and Blackett, were doing another standing triple somersault, and they were now stating that the Khumric Language was at least four thousand years old. This was published without giving any reason for the changes successively from (a) it developed after *c.* AD 500 to (b) changed to 500 BC (c) and now changed to 2000 BC.

In the strange way of 'feast or famine' and nothing in between, Alan Wilson and Baram Blackett actually located a good-quality line drawing of the Lemnos Stele and its unread inscriptions in a little red book a few days after receiving the photograph from the Athens Museum.

The texts on the Lemnos Stele were copied and laid out carefully, and the work of deciphering and translating using Llewellyn Sion's Coelbren and ciphers began. The texts translated with very little difficulty, and the content of the inscriptions did in fact record the meeting and the decision to sail for Britain. The figure of the man holding a spear carved on this style can only be intended to represent Brutus. These were the remnant of the people, the other groups having left heading for Etruria and elsewhere long before. The Lemnos Stele proves this record absolutely. The stele records how the god was consulted by oracle to assist in directing the fortunes and the course of action the people should take. The god at the Lemnos temple directed that they should sail west.

The most frequent spelling of the island name in the many manuscripts of Gruffydd ap Arthur and Tyssilio is 'Leogotia'. The Jesus College Manuscript gives us 'Legetta' which analyses as

'Lie' - for 'the place', - 'cetyn' - for 'the little cabinet', and 'ta', which is 'superior'. The strange Khumric word Lleoldeb may also supply an answer with 'Lie' for 'a place', and 'ol' meaning 'everyone', and 'eb' meaning 'to set forth'.

The clear intention however seems to be 'the place of the little cabinet'.

The literal reading of the text is -

'Large ample/what extends out a friend a saviour mutually together forcibly ejected to join together to make a compact to be moving (to) the Earth's circle of borders to go the Earth a refuge in urgent state/ spreading out (=migrating) the encircled large grief unimpeded terrible to cry out often breaking out. The all-powerful (one) with us mutually together in battle to the circle (horizon) of the four quarters of the Earth.'

'A pilot a wanderer to lead (us) away to nurse together travelling of the lineage/a saviour.'

'To escape scattering to possess/own to battle he is going to a pleasant foreign land. The intent of him all consuming (? or to proceed outwards the gift towards?) (for) everyone's good to proceed from to lie hid. He the journey to remain (in a fixed state) to the rotundity (horizon of the Earth) everyone towards casting off good a covering/a generation.'

There can be no doubt that the Lemnos Stele records the decision of the people to assemble under the leadership of the 'wanderer', who is Brutus. It is equally clear that they have 'the little cabinet' with them, and they decide to set out on a journey to sail to the limits of the known world, to escape from the oppression of Greek barbarians. That they set out for this 'pleasant foreign land' at the ends of their Earth, is exactly what the British histories say.

Some very serious questions now need to be asked and some straight answers are required for a change. Where do 'Celts' enter this situation? Hopefully we can now deport all those uninvited imported legions of foreign 'Celtic' ghosts back to their homelands in Southern France, and along the German and French banks of the Rhine. Perhaps all our displaced British ancestors can be re-issued with their own rightful passports, their birth and death certificates, and identity cards. It is not impossible that able and well-directed research will replace speculation, theorising, inventive guesswork, and simple falsehoods. There is, sadly, little hope that proper authorities will do anything to stop the criminal activities and dirty tricks campaigns aimed at honest researchers.

As for Brutus, the doubly-exiled king, well, he has his British grave mound: he has a Coelbren-inscribed statue in Rome; he appears on the Lemnos Stele; every ancient British history acknowledges him; a British king of around AD 500 names him as his ancestor on his accession stone; all the British Glamorgan-Gwent kings trace their descent from him; innumerable poetic, Triad, and other references name him; and he did found New Troy, now London.

Archaeologists found monumental walls some thirty feet down in London, well below the 'Roman' records, and close to the neglected foundation stone of London. But these obviously pre-Roman walls 'cannot be British'. Why not, what are they - Chinese? They found remains of a huge ancient monumental arch at the bottom of Ludgate Hill, precisely where the British histories state that King Lludd built a huge monumental arch, but these ruins 'cannot be British'. Why not? They found other obviously pre-Roman ruins, and amphorae dated at AD 37, and again they plastered 'Romans only' labels on them. How can relics dating at AD 37 be Roman in Britain? The Claudian invasion of the south coast did not take place until mid-AD 42, and was followed by decades of conflict. The Romans could not have and did not build London in such a short space of time.

Alan Wilson and Baram Blackett believe that it will take generations to re-educate the archaeological community, for whom British history seems to have neither value nor meaning. Looking at things positively, however, the priceless Lemnos Stele places 'a little cabinet" on the island of Lemnos around 504 BC, and so Etruria can be ruled out as a possible destination for 'the little cabinet'.

The Asia Minor Evidence

After the wonder of the Lemnos Stele most other things were something of an anti-climax. In Asia Minor there are an estimated hundred and twenty inscriptions of the same script that have been dated between 650 to 500 BC. These have been labelled as 'Pelasgian' or Phrygian. The assignment of 'Pelasgian' is simply a classification as the first known inhabitants of ancient Greece are thought to be the Pelasgi people. They first inhabited Argolis, then they spread to Aemonia, and then to Crete, Epirus, Italy, and Lesbos. All Greeks were apparently indiscriminately referred to as Pelasgians and their country as Pelasgia. It may be that the alphabet was thought to be a Greek original and so it was termed Pelasgian, and because it was found in Asia Minor it was labelled as Phrygian.

There is another much larger group of inscriptions in the same alphabet, which have been dated to sometime around 200 to 100 BC. These probably belong to the 'Gauls', some of whom resettled in Gallatia after crossing western Europe in 284 BC to attack both Greece and Macedonia, to seize the treasures of the Persian Empire which Alexander had won. The British Triads relate how Erb Llwydawg, sometimes Urb the Levyer of Hosts, raised the armies to go on this incredible venture. That they ravaged Macedonia and robbed and despoiled Delphi is well known. The fact that ancient British records state who they were and who led the armies is, like everything else, concealed.

It should be no surprise that these armies marching from Britain across Europe to Greece, probably using the rivers like the Danube, and then on into Asia Minor, brought the same ancient British Coelbren alphabet back to Asia Minor with them. This demonstration of the military power and the capabilities of the literate ancient British does not however conform to the necessary politically correct propaganda, and this evidence of it is very unwelcome. No ancient Khumric Triad, or any other reference, must ever be allowed to be proved to be true.

Chapter 8 - In search of Brutus

The Eski-Sher Temple in Turkey

Illustration

The inscription on the Temple of Eski-Sher in Asia Minor

The inscription seems to be a form of prayer or statement of intent that asks to be granted by the deity. There is more than a hint of the regular passing of the seasons and possibly a wish that the regular seasons prevailing this will assist the supplicants to enjoy freedom.

Pelasgian					
Coelbren					
Intent	ateb - atres	adchi	a Fe E A Dd	A Ch	
Khumric	ateb atre	adchwi	a Ffead	ach	
English	return reply	revolve, circumvolution	to drive away	fluid, water	

Pelasgian					
Coelbren					
Intent	Fe R A R	O O	P A E	C D	A I
Khumric	Fferadwy	o	pae	cyd	a i
English	congealing	from	constrain from	mutually	with

Pelasgian					
Coelbren					
Intent	R Y D A I	P A E	A P	T A P	Fe D A E
Khumric	rhydai / rhydef	pae	ap	tap	Ffedae
English	overspreading	constrain	the son	covering	driving away

Pelasgian				
Coelbren				
Intent	C D	E A R	A Ch	Te Fe I
Khumric	cyd	ea (ng)	ach	teffei (+ tefu)
English	together	free, ample	the fluid	to spread

It is reasonable to propose that this inscription was set up by the migrating Ten Tribes of Israel on their way from Armenia to the Dardanelles in the 687 – 650 BC era. It is not impossible that they carved out this rock temple in the cliff face.

This inscription indicates that the Eski Sher Monument is a temple rather than an empty tomb as supposed. The temple appears to be dedicated to the Weather God of Heaven and in the Israel Ten Tribes context this would be their god Yahweh. The text appears to ask that the winter ice and snows that cover everything should melt and spread and run away and that the revolution of the heavens should bring a return of the Sun or Weather god.

Chapter 8 - In search of Brutus

Illustration
The inscription on the right side of the Eski Sher Temple

Pelasgian	Coelbren	Intent	Khumric	English
		LL A H W D I	llawdi (llawdhi)	to seek fertility
		I O I	ioli	to worship
		E	e	he
		Cy d	cyd	mutually together
		E	e	he
		A I L	ail	return again

Pelasgian	Coelbren	Intent	Khumric	English
		C*	cy	as
		P O I T	poit	to wax hot
		A E	aed	going
		O I	oi	to come forward
		Fe Th	ffeth	to cause
		P A R	par	state of readiness

Pelasgian	Coelbren	Intent	Khumric	English
		A E Th (P)	aeth	he has gone
		P O I	poi (polio)	to fix poles
		H W	Hw	mighty
		C + D	cyd	together
		Ch	chwa	blast
		Ch R	chwym	to whirl

Pelasgian	Coelbren	Intent	Khumric	English
		A Ee	ael	nigh, near borders
		Fe D	ffedu	intention purpose with
		A	a	with
		E I	ei	him
		(A E I)	(ael)	(going, proceeding)

'To seek fertility, he to worship together, he once again waxes hot a proceeding to come forward to cause a state of readiness he has gone to fix: poles, mighty with blast (wind) to whirl near his intention of proceeding.'

The Eski Sher monument, although traditionally known as "The Tomb of Midas", appears as the shrine of the weather god of heaven. The phonetic sound in Khumric might be 'Wag y Siaff' or the "Waters of the Lord". The concept was of there being a great weather god of the oceans, of the distant heavens up on which the stars sailed and his son as the weather god ruling the terrestrial skies of the earth.

Some of the letters are variants and give some minor difficulties. The "/" is a variant that can only be read as a 'Y', and the triangle sign is another variant. No words can be found to allow these signs to be read in any other way than as 'Y' and 'DD'.

The ancient inscriptions do not lie however. As Omar Khayam, the Court Poet of the Caliph Haroun al Rashid, wrote around AD 800: -

'The moving finger writes,
And having writ moves on.
Not all your piety or wit can cancel half a line.
Nor all your tears wash out a word of it.'

As the decipherment of these texts opens up a huge can of worms for academia, the subject can be left for a future date, as it plays no part in the drive back eastwards and back past the era of 605 to 500 BC. Previous experience has taught Wilson and Blackett not to go near or step on snakes when there is no necessity. Alan Wilson had a long-term interest in Hittite histories and warned of the dangers. After making a further survey of the histories it was decided just to prove the point and put the rest on file. The chaos reigning in these Asia Minor histories is a direct knock-on effect of scholars unthinkingly matching these chronologies with the known-to-be-defective ancient Egyptian chronology, which they employ as a yardstick.

The problems can be solved but is not worth the effort to publish this. Some of these Asia Minor inscriptions of *c.* 650 BC, which were unmistakeably in a Coelbren alphabet, were selected and deciphered. Attempts were made to contact some of the university groups working in Asia Minor, but these predictably proved abortive.

The Eski Sher Inscriptions

There is a remarkable monument at Eski Sher which is reminiscent of the rock-carved tombs and temples of the city of Petra. The giant façade of a monumental building has been carved out of a living rock face, with all the appearance of a great temple. There is a carved doorway, but there is no vast temple within.

This strange monument has of course been 'labelled', and it is known as the 'Tomb of Midas', the immensely wealthy, semi-legendary King of Phrygia. Running right across the top of this façade, and all down the left side, is a long inscription. This script is distinctly Coelbren and was therefore an attractive proposition for decipherment. The text might settle the matter of it being a temple or a tomb or whatever, and there was also the consideration that the persons who were responsible for carving this rock façade might not be the same people who wrote the inscription.

Even the most cursory view of a clear photograph of the Eski Sher inscription makes it immediately apparent that the alphabet used is near identical with the British Coelbren and Etruscan-Rhaetian. There was therefore every possibility that the EskI Sher letters would match with the Coelbren alphabet, and that the modern letters produced would form recognisable words in Khumric. These should then decipher into meaningful and logical statements. If this were to happen then the Khumric tongue and the British Coelbren alphabet being already identified all over Britain, all over Etruria, and in Rhaetia, and also on Lemnos,

Chapter 8 - In search of Brutus

would be shown further back along the migration trail in Asia Minor. This would conclusively support the continuing accuracy of British and Khumric correct ancient history and chronology.

As things turned out the Eski Sher inscription was capable of decipherment and translation, and it appears to be an invocation to a god, and a form of a harvest prayer. The prayer which emerges from the text appears to be directed at an unnamed deity who would be the Great Weather God of Heaven, and in Chaldean terms this would be Ea, or Aa, Yah or Jah, and Yahweh, and so on.

The text reads:

> 'Respond/reply revolve to drive away the liquid (water) from congealing together (winter ice), from overspreading the sun, covering, driving (it) away with large power, spread out the liquid (waters).'

This seems to ask that the snows and ice of winter, perhaps on the mountains, be melted slowly by the spring and summer sun to avoid floods, and that the rains should augment these waters from the melting snow and ice. This would indicate that the Eski Sher rock building is a temple and not a tomb. There is no evidence that King Midas carved it out either as a temple or a tomb. There are no human or animal figures carved anywhere on this building, which again points to a people who avoided this practice of making living representations.

Whilst the transient Khumry when passing through this region may have carved this inscription, it is conjectural whether or not they carved the great ornamental façade. Alan and Baram would dearly like to know what George Bain would have made of the distinctly 'Celtic' ornamentation cut into this building frontage.

From this moment when the Eski Sher inscription was read, Wilson and Blackett both had a great feeling of relief and inward satisfaction. Both knew that this decipherment marked a decisive point in the tracing of our British ancestors, and in demonstrating the unfailing truthful accuracy of British-Khumric histories. They knew that they were absolutely correct. From this moment on masses of historical dilemmas and puzzles, which bedevil historical and less important archaeological studies, evaporated and vanished.

The problem does not lie with the histories. The problem lies with the adulation and near-worship of the hasty, ill-conceived theories of the long-dead 'great' eighteenth- and nineteenth-century publicity-hunters. The gibbering grey ghosts of these 'pioneers' that still haunt the corridors, lecture halls, and libraries of the universities, are still the main problem. Archaeology is more prone to beatifying these ghosts as in its rigid religious pantheon, than to doing true history justice. Once a 'pioneer' is dead for fifty years he becomes a holy great 'authority', and when he is dead a hundred years, he then rises to become an untouchable 'great authority'. The longer he is dead, the higher he will rise in the archaeological religious pantheon, and the harder it becomes to demonstrate his fabrications and obvious errors.

Fighting ghosts is a difficult and dangerous business. Their followers feel safe, secure, and comfortable, by simply adhering to their dictates; rather like children endlessly repeating nursery rhymes. Not for them the dangerous arena of uncertainties. Yet it remains a fact that you have to dig out and erect firm foundations before you can paint the walls and put on the roof, and most eighteenth- and nineteenth-century academic structures are firmly founded on very wet quicksand.

The Gordium Stone

Deciphering texts that no one has read for around two thousand years and more can become addictive, and other inscriptions in Asia Minor were read as they became available. The danger in this book is however that historical matters in Asia Minor are too muddled and too complex, as emerges from decipherments elsewhere, and should be reserved for another volume.

One of the better-known Asia Minor inscriptions, said to be Phrygian, was found at the site of the ruined city of Gordium. This inscribed stone is now kept in the Pennsylvania University Museum in Philadelphia, in the U.S.A., having been found by members of an archaeological expedition from Pennsylvania University. The stone is not large, but it carries a reasonably long inscription. The alphabet used to write this inscription is immediately identifiable as being very similar to, if not identical with, the Etruscan and British Coelbren letters. This obvious similarity was taken by Blackett and Wilson as offering the distinct possibility that the language used in this inscription is again Khumric.

Another simple decipherment and translation exercise was again set up to test this possibility. The same routine was followed: of first setting out the letters of the Gordium inscription and then matching them with the British-Etruscan letters. Then the British ciphers were used to identify the modern alphabet equivalent letters. There are of course no 'J', 'Q', 'V', 'X' or 'Z', and the modern quirk is to express 'K' as a hard 'C'. There are Ch, Chwy, Dd, Ll, Th, Ngh, Ng, and other letters and sounds. The matching and the automatic modern equivalent production process then produces a series of letters that form words in Khumric (Cymraeg). For Khumric speakers the process would end here, and any further steps would be unnecessary. F or the wider public these Khumric words can be translated into English or any other modern language.

A clear, coherent, sensible, logical statement emerges from the Gordium stone, which appears to be of a religious nature. The layout of the inscriptions and carvings on the stone are peculiar. On the right-hand side there are cut the shapes of two sandals, feet, or shoes. No toes are shown, and what might at first sight appear to be footprints may in fact be sandals or shoes. Two vertical inscriptions run along the left side of each foot shape. On the left side of the stone a horizontal inscription runs along the top of the flat face. Another horizontal inscription runs along the bottom of the left-hand area.

This creates a rectangular area on the left side of the stone, which appears to be free of inscriptions. A further vertical inscription intrudes slightly into the right-hand side of this uninscribed area.

It is almost as if a map is being created in this clear area, using the inscriptions running vertically and horizontally to make a frame. Alan Wilson and Baram Blackett were working from photographs, and these were perfectly adequate for dealing with the inscriptions, but inadequate to allow them to look for a star chart map, or less likely a ground map.

The Gordium Stone text appears to read: -

Top left horizontal.
'(in) preparation I to listen/to wait'.

Bottom left horizontal.
'the keep/shutting in the support (of) what preserves/keeps in'.

Centre vertical.
'the flowing principle (= liquid = waters) (in) a standing/fixed state'.

Left Sandal vertical.
'to bid to seek out to augment heaven.

Right Sandal vertical.
'I the private god/secret god whirl'.

The correct order of reading the Gordium message is obviously not certain because of the scattered arrangement of the inscriptions in various small horizontal and vertical sections. An offered arrangement is: -

'I prepare to wait/listen for a bidding to seek out to augment/increase (from) heaven.' 'The stronghold the support encourages and preserves he the waters/flowing in a regular

(fixed/standing) condition (state).'

'I the unseen (secret) and private god whirl.'

Once again there is a reference to the unseen god and the promise of the waters being delivered and controlled, with neither droughts nor floods. Ea was the Chaldean and Babylonian Great Weather God of Heaven, and Ea became Yah, and then Yahweh or Jehovah. The Weather God was the Water God and the Wind God and as the wind he was invisible, and everywhere, and all-seeing. The heavens

Illustration.

The inscribed stone from Gordium in Asia Monor

An inscribed stone was found at Gordium, the site of the great ruined city of antiquity in the South West of modern Turkey. The stone is now in the University Museum of Philadelphia in the U.S.A. This remarkable stone has five short inscriptions in the ancient Coelbren alphabet carved into its surface. Alan Wilson and Baram Blackett deciphered and translated these inscriptions.

On the right-hand side of the Gordium Stone are the carved outlines of two show prints. Set against the left side of each shoeprint is an inscription. In the centre of the stone there is a shape, which appears to be a phallic symbol, and this also has a third inscription running along its length. A fourth short inscription runs horizontally across the top of the stone and heads from the left-hand side, whilst a fifth inscription runs parallel to this along the bottom of the stone again beginning at the left-hand side.

Gordium: Phrygian inscription

These Inscriptions translate quite correctly into understandable Khumric-'Welsh', and they appear to carry a religious statement.

1- Top horizontal reading from the Left.
'Prepare to from an eminence to keep/ holding.'
2- Bottom horizontal reading from the left.
'Keep/ holding to treat kindly encourages the greater/ more.'
3- Centre vertical
'Flowing principle, a standing state, condition.'
4- Left shoe vertical
'To bid to seek out, to augment heaven.'
5- Right shoe vertical
'To the deity whirling.' Or 'I the secret (private) god whirl.'
This appears to mean:
'I prepare to listen to a bidding to seek out to augment heaven. The stronghold the support encourages and preserves the flowing principle in a standing still state. I the unseen/secret god whirl' (or 'to the deity whirling').

Chapter 8 - In search of Brutus

Illustration
The Gordion inscription in Asia Minor

1. Top horizontal reading from the left

Pelasgian	ᐃᎱᏉY	I	◊	ᏞᗩᎱ		I
Coelbren	ᐃᎱᏉY	I	◊	ᏞᗩᎱ		I
Intent	A R L W Y	I	O	B A N		I
Khumric	arlwy	i	o	ban		i
English	prepare	to	from	an eminence		to

2. Bottom horizontal, reading from the left

Pelasgian	Kᗩ	K◊I◊	11◊KC	P◊
Coelbren	Kᗩ	K◊I◊	11◊KC	P◊
Intent	C (K) A	(K) C O I O	L L O Ch C	P O
Khumric	ca	colof	llochi	po
English	keep, holding shutting in	stem, support treat kindly	encourages the more	the greater

3. Left shoe vertical

Pelasgian	ᖴᎱK	KᖴIᎱI◊	Iᖴ	Ꮋᒍᖴ◊ᖴ
Coelbren	ᖴᎱK	KᖴIᎱI◊	Iᖴ	ᑎᒍᖴ◊ᖴ
Intent	E R Ch	C E I S I O	I L	N E F O L
Khumric	erch	ceisio	il	nefol
English	to bid	to seek out	to augment	heaven

4. Right shoe vertical

Pelasgian	I	<ᎩILI	ᎱITᐱ	
Coelbren	I	<ᎩILI	ᎱIᐱ	
Intent	I	C Y I L I	S I T A	
Khumric	i	cyili = celli	sita (sitio)	Ceilli or Ceilliad
English	to	the deity	whirl	private or secret

5. Centre vertical

Pelasgian	ᐃᎻᎱ	Ꮁᐱ
Intent	A F R	S A
Khumric	affr	sa
English	flowing principle	a standing state, condition

The sketch of No 5 is a phallic symbol of an erect male sex organ, hence the 'standing state' and the 'flowing principle'.

The inscription may be one dedicated to the Weather God of heaven, and it has some similarity of expression to that on the monument at Eski Sher.

seen from Earth do whirl around, and the winds whirl, eddy, and twist. Desert winds spiral around, as do tornados. There is also the cult of the Whirling Dervishes in still surviving in modern Turkey.

Everything arrives back at Ea, the protector god of mankind, who saved mankind from total destruction. There may be fertility implications in the inscription, with the desire for renewal and continuance of the established seasons, bringing the annual cycles of crop germination, growth, and then harvest. All of which are then followed by the annual dying away before the next year's re-growth.

The Gordium inscription does appear to have a similar expression of sentiment as that which emerges from the Eski-Sher inscription.

Predictably, there is much confusion over the origin of the people who founded the ancient city of Gordium, thought to be a capital city of Phrygia and founded around 900-850 BC. Very little is known for certain. The Assyrian records name two kings in this same western-central area of Asia Minor, both of whom are named as Mita, which may be a version of Midas. Around 717 BC a King Mita supported the eastern Asia Minor and Syrian Hittites against the Assyrians. In 709 BC, Sargon II of Assyria sent a general against Mita of the Mushki, and Mita was defeated and parts of his kingdom were despoiled.

Everyone forgets that Abraham was a Chaldean and that his Chaldean close kinsmen were dominant in these areas. The name of Labarna, the first Hittite king, the name which was subsequently adopted by all succeeding Hittite kings, and its similarity to Laban, the close kinsman of Abraham, has been previously noted. One version of 'Hittite' origins places them as moving from areas around Armenia to the east. The Greeks thought the Phrygians came from Europe, and were perhaps confusing them with the western European Galatians of 284 BC.

Sufficient decipherment of Asia Minor inscriptions had been done, and a wealth of other work supported the results, and therefore the primary objective of this part of the project had been achieved. As Baram Blackett always puts it: "Don't waste time hunting down and killing all the individual snakes and alligators with a stick, just drain the swamp."

Chaldean links

Before moving on with this alphabet trail, some indication of what needs to be done may be in order. During the nineteenth century a number of Khumric scholars conducted large-scale exercises in language comparisons. They collected the place names of Asia Minor, of areas south of the Caucasus, across Northern Iraq and Iran, and through Syria, and then they analysed them. They took the names of the mountains, hills, valleys, plains, rivers, streams, lakes, and shorelines, in fact the calling of any named feature. They took the names of the ancient nations and tribes, and those of the cities and towns. The objective was to try to discover

Chapter 8 - In search of Brutus

whether or not these names had corrected direct meanings in Khumric.

Time and again the names fitted, and gave accurate correlations with the geographical nature of things and places, and also of the people. Names indicated jagged rocks or rocky mountains when they are so, or smooth hills and steep mountains when they are so. Names meant 'fast-flowing', or 'slow', or 'turgid', or tumbling streams, when they are so. Names stated that waters were bitter or sweet, and they are so. Names identified people as mountain men, or shoreline people, or plainsmen, and they were so. The fitting of names to the areas of ancient Chaldea was remarkable. But none of this was politically correct.

This working back through migration areas went on through Italy and Switzerland, and even in Macedonia. It also applied all through Britain; and this patient linguistic study of transliteration applied to ancient names, piled up. Names rarely change beyond recognition, and the evidence that a mass of place names have clear, identifiable descriptive meanings in Khumric is overwhelming.

Wilson and Blackett decided to amuse themselves and to carry this line of analysis into a previously untouched area. If the Chaldean tongue had been preserved in Egypt, and then taken from Egypt into Canaan in the Exodus, and from there to Upper Assyria and Armenia, and finally through Asia Minor on to Etruria and Britain, then the ancient Chaldean names of Kings and Gods might have literal descriptive meanings directly into Khumric.

The most important Gods of Chaldea (with Roman equivalents) were: Bel Merodach (Jupiter), Bel Enlil (Saturn), Nergal (Mars), Nabo/Nebo (Mercury), Ishtar (Venus), Shamash (the Sun), Eresh-ki-gal or Allatu (Queen of Hell), Anu (the Sky), and Ea (the Creator and Great Weather God of Heaven).

The well-known Nabopolassar and his son Nabochadrezzar (the terrifying Biblical ogre Nebuchadnezzar) both used the name of the god Nabo or Nebu, who we would see as Mercury. The brother of Nebuchadnezzar was Nergilassar, and he used the god name of Nergal, thought to be Mars. Nebuchadnezzar's son Evil-Merodach (Amel Marduk) used the name of the great god Baal Marduk or Bel Merodach. Other Chaldean kings were Shamash-shumukin, who used Shamash the Sun god; and there is old Merodach Baladan, who appears in the Bible, and Enlil-rabi who used the name of the god Enlil or Saturn.

The question was whether the names of these Chaldean gods and kings had direct equivalent meanings in Khumric. Allatu, the fearsome goddess of Hell, is retained as 'Aleathu' (the verb 'to mourn, to grieve, to wail'), and as 'Aleath' for 'sorrow, wailing, grief'. The other name for Allatu was Eresh-ki-gal, and again Khumric still preserves 'erchyll' for 'ghastly' and 'crchyllu' meaning 'to make ghastly'. 'Gal' still means 'mourning'. It is obvious that Erchyll-Gal matches Ereshki-Gal with very appropriate meanings.

The consort of the terrifying Eresh-ki-gal was Nergal the War God. Analysis of Nergal produces 'ner' meaning 'lord god', while 'gal' as we have seen is 'mourning'. This gives Nergal simply as 'the lord god of mourning'.

Nabo or Nebo, recognised as Mercury, is remembered in the word 'nabod', which means 'to know', and Mercury or Nebo was the messenger of the gods, who knew their will. The word 'neges' means 'message', and 'negessa' means 'to carry messages'.

Anu was the Chaldean Sky god of the Great Deep or the Abyss, as the vast expanses of the universe was known. For Anu we have Annwfn, which can mean 'the great deep', whilst Annwn means 'the other world'. Llachmu was an important god in the Chaldean creation legend, and correctly 'llach' means a 'ray of light", and the idea of 'let there be light' in Western Christian ideology and Gnostic Christian expressions of the great void of black nothingness, in which there came a Thought which was Light, both mirror this idea. 'Llachar' means 'gleaming', whilst 'llachau' translates as 'gleams'.

Bel-Merodach appears in the Khumric Triads as Menw, which means 'intellectual' or 'blessed', which is appropriate for the great god Bel Merodach. The word 'menwedig' also means 'mind or intellect'. Bel and Beli mean 'war, tumult, havoc', which is appropriate for the heroic warrior Bel-Merodach and for Bel-Enlil the War God of Chaldea. En-lil appears to be 'En' for 'spirit', and 'llill' means 'goat-like' or 'bearded'. Goats do have beards, and Capricorn the Goat constellation is frequently identified as bearded. The Chaldean Bull god of Heaven is also described as bearded.

The Storm God of Earth, as opposed to the beneficent Ea of the Heavens, was Adad, and he is remembered in 'Addawd' or 'Adaddewiad', and associated words, all meaning 'the repeat, or returning of a promise'. This is associated with 'awd' meaning 'seasonal', and we have the rain or storm god Adad returning annually after the dry season as 'promised'.

Anu was the God of the Abyss, and the abyss was the great unending depths of the heavens, which were seen as vast oceans upon which the stars floated, and was called Apsu. The Chaldean Apsu matches the Khumric 'aflun', which is 'devoid of form', and 'afwys', meaning 'the precipice or steep'.

The Chaldean Aya, thought to mean 'the dawn', who was married to Shamash the Sun god, looks very like 'awyr' meaning 'air or sky'. Then there is 'y wawr' meaning 'the dawn', and 'gwawio' for 'to dawn'.

So, we can move through the Chaldean pantheon of powers with a constant stream of previously unnoticed parallels. The goddess Arum, responsible for the creation of Enkidu, the companion of Gilgamesh, may be seen as 'arythrol' for 'wonder and amazement', and in 'aruchel' for 'very high, or lofty'. The myth of

Chapter 8 - In search of Brutus

Enuma Elish involving the Abyss and the mingling of sweet and bitter waters (the sea) and from this presumably the clouds as the third form of water, may also have meaning. 'Enuma' is perhaps the Khumric for 'cow', meaning 'name', and then extended to 'enwog' for 'renowned or famous', and 'elish' is certainly 'elusen' and 'elus', which mean 'charity' and 'bounty'. Blessed rain in a dry, hot climate, in fact in any climate, was seen as the bounteous gift of charity from the great water and creator god Ea.

Like all well-organised institutions, the Chaldean gods had their scribe, who was 'Belit Sheri'. Here there are the very obvious Khumric words of 'beili yscrifenu', which literally mean 'the court writer'. In the same way the temple precincts of the ancient city of Chaldean Uruk were known as 'eanna', which may be 'y annadl'; 'the dwelling place'. Ea-anaf would simply be Ea the Lame. This particular place was the dwelling of Ishtar and Anu.

The listing goes on with the dread spirits of the ancient underworld, who were known as En-du-kugga and Nin-du-kugga. In Khumric 'En-dychryn' and 'En-dychrynadwy' mean respectively 'the spirit of terror' and 'the terrible spirit'. Following this there is 'Ninau-dychryn', which means 'we also are terror'.

There may be some minor rethinking wanted in some areas of these readings, as it seems that 'n-n' is simply 'm'. An example is with the god of irrigation, an absolutely vital entity in the lands of the Euphrates valley, who is currently known as 'Ennugi'. If the 'n-n' is read as an 'm', this makes perfect sense. In Khumric 'E-Mwydo' is simply 'he who moistens or soaks'. And the function of 'E-nnugi' or 'E-mugi' was to moisten, soak, and soften the sun-dried land. Some identifications are made difficult because the Germans and the English who have made attempts at decipherment have been unaware that some sounds, and therefore some letters, do not even exist in Khumric. There is a zealous over-use of 'Z' and 'Q' by translators, and the gods associated with the germination and growth of crops are listed as 'Tammuz' and 'Dumuzi'. 'Tammuz' actually appears to be both 'Tyfiant' and 'Tyfedig', for 'vegetation' and 'growth', whilst 'Dumuzi' appears to be 'dychrau' meaning 'to rise up'.

In this same manner the goddess known as 'Nin-Hursag' is credited with the feat of raising all crops and vegetation by sprinkling water, and if the Khumric 'ni' ('not') and 'hys buddu', ('dried out' or 'barren' are used, we get 'not dried out/barren in 'Ni-Hysbuddu'.

Blackett and Wilson recognize that this is no idle matter, and it is of huge importance, for it means that most people in Britain, Australia, New Zealand, Canada, and large numbers elsewhere can trace their ancestry directly back to the greatest of the high civilisations of antiquity. The name of the great ancient city of Ur of the Chaldees, as distinct from the Southern Ur in Babylonia simply means 'ur' or 'the pure place' The dominant ruling city of Uruk is probably Uruch, and with 'ur' added to 'uwch', this is Uruwch, which means the place which is above or over'. For a capital city this makes sense.

The cattle-god Samquan is probably Samchwan, and would be a combination of 'sant' and 'ychain'. 'Sant' means either 'holy' or 'saint', so Samquan is simply 'the saint of oxen'. 'Nisaba', the goddess who protected the grain crops, would be 'Ni-sathru', which means 'not trampled'. 'Nisir', or 'the mountain of salvation', turns out to be 'ni-sarhadd', for 'not disgraced'; and anyone who is not disgraced, or who has not fallen from grace, is fairly described as being in a state of salvation.

Some of these direct translations are hilariously simple. Pap-sukal was the Chaldean messenger of the gods, and 'papreath' in Khumric means a chatterer, or a babbler. The spirit of nightmares was Alu, and as most nightmares follow over-eating or drinking, it seems obvious that the frightening Alu was the Khumric 'alaru', meaning 'surfeit' or 'loathing'. Adapa the son of Ea was the ocean god, and the Khumric word 'Jaw' means 'chief of waters', an equivalent of Neptune. The wife of Ea was the Lady Damkina, and 'Damchweinio' means 'fate' or 'to happen'. The original creatrix goddess was 'Mama' and 'Marni', words still in use in Wales for 'Mother', for no self-respecting Welsh person uses the English 'Mum'. The elder goddess figure was 'Nana', and again this is the normal term for 'Grandmother'.

Ea, the great lord of all waters, had a wife named Damkina and she had a secondary name was 'Ia', which is simply 'ice' in Khumric. Ice is simply water as a solid instead of in its fluid form, and the link is obvious with the Ice Queen and the Water Lord. Adapa, the son of Ea, was a fisherman. When he was out fishing one day, Shutu the South Wind Storm Demon upset his boat. Adapa immediately attacked Shutu and he broke off the Storm Demon's wings, and then calmed the waters. This offended Anu the Sky god, but Adapa appeared before the assembly of the gods wearing mourning dress, and he was offered the water and bread of life, which would make him immortal. Adapa had been warned that this was actually the bread and water of death, and so he refused to eat or drink. In this way he was never to be immortal.

Adapa son of Ea appears to be 'the promised one', with 'addaw' meaning 'promise', 'addawl' 'to worship', and 'addawiad' for 'a promising'. There is also a group of words stemming from 'adanfon', meaning 'to send again', and 'adanofonol' for 'sending again'. There are some obvious parallels to be drawn with Adapa, going out in a boat, fishing, being caught in a storm, stopping the storm, calming the waters, putting down demons, having to stand trial in a rigged corrupt court, the bread-and-water-of-life motif, and so on.

The matter would fill whole books, and the Chaldean Lilithu is probably Lilith, the first wife of Adam before Eve. She appears in Khumric as 'Lithio' meaning 'to entice' or 'to attract', as 'Lithiol' meaning 'alluring' and 'Lithiwr' for 'one who allures'. The shadowy partner of Merodach was named Beltu, who may be 'bel-tu' or 'bel-du', with meanings of 'the region of war' and 'black havoc'. 'Beltu' is probably the original Black Hag of Khumric, Irish, and Scots folklore. The dreaded

Chapter 8 - In search of Brutus

Demon of the South wind sandstorms was Shutu, who could devastate lands. He seems to survive as 'Swtrws', meaning 'bruised mass' or a mashed or crushed mass.

There is much, much more, and the simple fact that the names of many ancient Chaldean city begin with 'Car' should alert some people. Car-chemish, Car-duniash, and Car-desh, to name a few, match with British Khumric names beginning with 'Caer', meaning a fortified place. 'Caer' names are peppered all across the British landscape, from Car-lisle and Car-hampton in England to Car-diff and Caer-melyn in South East Wales, Car-marthen, Car-digan, and Caer-narvon, and hosts of others in the West and North.

Is it just coincidence that the Khumry-Kimmeroi attacked and seized the great capital city of Sardis in western Asia Minor around 660 BC, and there are Sardis names on the South Pembrokeshire coast, also near Llanelli, and at Pontypridd?

The Lord of the annual rebirth and re-growth of vegetation, which germinates, rises, flourishes, and then dies away, was 'the child-lord Gishzida', which in Khumric is 'gist-chwyl-droi', meaning 'the revolving Earth'. This 'child-lord Gishzida' matches the Etruscan child springing from a field, and the many Khumric 'Crowned Babe' poems. Shamash the Sun god was as Apollo the Archer in Greek terms, the Shooter, and the Khumric archer or shooter is 'Saethydd'.

We can finish of this brief excursion into part of the British and Chaldean links with those Biblical heroes Shadrach, Meshack, and Abednego, who seem to be none other than Shadrach as Shamash the Sun god, Meshack as Merodach, and Abednego as Nebo or Mercury, the messenger of the gods. Nego corresponds with Khumric 'neges' for 'message', while 'negessa' means 'to go on errands'. The 'Abed' name may be the Khumric ' AJ-berth', meaning 'to transmigrate' or 'to move around in migrations'. The god Mercury flitted not only among the various gods, but also between the Heavens and Earth. These three appear to match the gods who were the joint progenitors of Orion (Urion), who sprang from the Earth from a buried ox-hide filled with the urine of these three gods.

It is no longer a matter of academic professors pretending to analyse the facts fairly whilst actually defending their own lost theories and publications. Their strongest card is always to sit silent and do nothing, which invariably misleads the media into thinking that no progress can be made. Hopefully not all will do so. The matter is not one of any 'learned opinions', and it now resolves itself into one of mathematics and statistics, for it is properly one of odds and probabilities. What is the likelihood of all this - and much more - being mere chance and a mass of coincidences? Several million typists working for several hundred years would be required to type out the zeros on the odds of this being such an improbable coincidence or fluke.

A few writers have noted the similarity of town layouts and foundation and other ritual in Chaldea and Etruria. All manner of research remains to be done beside these initial probes into comparative layouts of town and temple. The systems of jurisprudence, customs, and measurements, and ancient stories of origins, and so on, need to be examined. Wilson and Blackett have made inroads into these areas, but they believe that positive university involvement might be required.

Researches in America in 1994

In 1994 Alan Wilson was flown out to Boston by Dan Dimancescu to deliver the prestigious annual Bemis Lecture. Dan had taken an interest in the researches of Wilson and Blackett for two years and was convinced that there was truth in what was emerging from the relentless probing of the recorded histories. During his week's stay in Boston, Dan arranged for Alan to meet a group lawyer from a major Boston law company to discuss the possibility of getting Alan and Baram political asylum in the U.S.A. The sad consensus opinion was that American officialdom would be unable to comprehend and accept the reality of the endless campaigns of illegal dirty tricks waged against them in Britain; and the false propaganda images of Britain would prevail.

From Boston, Alan went south-west with Jim Michael, and whilst in Kentucky he was able to spend some time with the eminent Dr Ray Hayes. Ray had long been one of those many unsung researchers who, unrewarded, put in time and money to search out truths. He had converted the basement of his home into a large office area lined with bookshelves and surrounded with worktables and a desk. Sadly, Ray had had a triple by-pass heart operation, and he had also had other previous surgery and was in a very frail condition. His lady wife guarded him like some friendly dragon, watching over him anxiously to see that he did nothing to exert or excite himself.

The drill was for Ray and Alan to talk for a while, and Ray put over his ideas and offered his notes and references to entries in books. Then, whilst Alan sat quietly working at Ray's desk, Ray lay down on his bed and rested quietly and slept for a while. Their major topic was Gnostic Christian writings, which Alan and Baram had been exploring to check possible similarities with Apostolic British Christianity. Both Gnostic record and British record affirmed that Jesus the Nazarene survived the crucifixion of *c.* AD 34 - 36, and this comparative research might indicate other links.

In 1945 an Arab named Mohammed Ali had been searching for firewood near his home at Nag Hammadi, also known as Chenoboskion, when he found a large clay jar. This clay jar, reportedly some five feet high, contained fourteen leather satchels, inside which was a whole Gnostic Christian library. Mr Ali had no idea

Chapter 8 - In search of Brutus

what he had found, and he actually burned some parts of some of the documents in this very ancient library collection before realizing that they might be valuable. The majority of the Gnostic Christian library was rescued, however, and added to knowledge obtained from the first Gnostic document, found in 1896. This is now the *Berlinensis 8502* manuscript, which contains the *Gospel of Mary*, *The Secret Book of John*, *The Sophia of Jesus Christ* and the *Acts of Peter*. Previously, all that had been known of the Gnostics was what their sworn enemies in the Roman and Greek Orthodox churches had written. Now there was a flood of Gnostic Gospels and other writings available. The situation parallelled that of the Welsh in Britain, where all that has been allowed to be published of their histories is the version of what their enemies say.

The clay jar is believed to have been buried around AD 400, and the dating of the actual writing of the various books and gospels in the leather satchels is a matter of much debate. Naturally, the mainstream Christian writers try to date their composition as late as possible, and as far removed from events in Judea around AD 33-36 as can be achieved. The texts may be very early documents, however, or at least copies of very early documents; and they make uncomfortable reading for religionists, as some deny the crucifixion in Jerusalem, and allege the sacrifice of a substitute, and so on.

These texts did not get much publicity: in fact they received very little, and perhaps this is because predominantly Egypt is a Moslem country with no great national interest in early Christianity in any form. Perhaps it was because 1945 was the year in which World War II ended, leaving in its aftermath a plethora of more urgently pressing economic and political problems of recovery in the affairs most nations; much more likely the near silence was because these Gnostic Christian documents contained statements which were totally contrary to the 'orthodox' church doctrines. In the perverse way of fate, the religious scholars who went rushing to study these newly discovered records were committed 'orthodox' Christians. These men had no interest in seeing, or a desire to see, a wide publication of these very ancient records, which made ancient statements totally contrary to their own religious ideas. They wanted discoveries that supported their theories and belief systems. The first rule of religion is always to attack and to destroy the opposition, or at least to deny it publicity and condemn it to silence, no matter what.

Alan and Baram could not help but notice the significant indications in the old British records of ancient Egyptian connections, and since 1984 they had been developing a major project following the direction of these ancient British statements. They had, in common with Dr Ray Hayes, taken an interest in these Gnostic discoveries and the early ancient commentaries on the Gnostics, once it was apparent that early British Christianity was markedly different from the versions that later emanated from Rome and Constantinople. What Alan and Ray were interested in was the record found in the *Book of Manasses*, which describes an alphabet; and, along with Baram, both were convinced that they were looking at a very clear description of the ancient British Coelbren alphabet.

If this is correct, and it certainly appears to be, then the hazardous and destructive anti-British position invented by Edwin Guest and Bishop Stubbs and company as a substitute for history is even more untenable than ever before. Documents written in Egypt before AD 400, and buried for some fifteen hundred and fifty years before being accidentally discovered in 1945, and which contain a description of the British Coelbren alphabet, again indisputably proves that the alphabet cannot have been an invention forged in Wales around 1800. There was now yet another large time-bomb to plant under the hugely incompetent Griffith J. Williams and his mendacious deranged mentor J. Gwenogfran Evans.

This again opened up a whole new area of research and also gave clues as how to read certain ancient Welsh texts. It again demonstrates the tremendous loss resulting from the abandonment and obliteration of the continuous historical records of the nations, which have dwelt in Britain since the migrations *of c.* 1600 BC and 500 BC. The major achievement of Guest and Stubbs and their determinedly blind followers has been the creation of a powerful anti-Welsh mind set in Britain. The result is that the problems of carrying out the research are insignificant when compared with the insurmountable difficulties which confront the researcher who dares to attempt to publish anything appearing to offer even the tiniest threat to the most gigantic ego-system in the universe.

By 1994, however, Alan Wilson and Baram Blackett had turned their attention in British Arthurian History as preserved in the authentic British-Welsh manuscripts, to follow the clues and directions given in the ancient British records concerning Egypt, with astonishing success.

Assyrian Records of the Khumry

A theory has been developed in our times that the 'People of Omri' were called the 'People of Ghomri', by themselves (the Israelites), and were known as the 'People of Khumri' by the Assyrians. The reasoning is that the Hebrew name 'Omri' begins with the consonant 'ayin', pronounced as a guttural 'H', which gives a sound like 'Ghomri'. This then transliterates as 'Kh' in ancient Assyrian. So it is held that 'Omri' was pronounced as 'Ghomri' by the Israelites, and as 'Khumri' or 'Khumry' by the Assyrians.

Strangely none of the many authors on this subject ever mention the British Khumry, and indeed it appears that they are not even aware of the existence of the Khumry.

This Assyrian style name of Khumri is used in the Annals of the Assyrian

Chapter 8 - In search of Brutus

Emperor Tiglathpileser III, which describe his invasion of Israel around 740 BC and the removal of large numbers of the people from there to Northern Assyria:

> 'The cities of Gilead and Abel Beth Maacah on the borders of the land of Khumri, and the widespread lands of Hazael to its entire extent, I brought within the territories of Assyria.'

His successor, Sargon II, makes another mention of these Khumri people in his Annals, which record the subjugation of Samaria. He styles himself as the conqueror of the Tribe of Omri, and states that 'Bit-Khumri' are the conquered people. This is supplemented by the record carved onto a large black stone known as the Black Obelisk, which depicts the ruler Jehu kneeling in homage before the Emperor Shalmaneser V. The writing on this stele identifies the defeated Prince of the Syrian and Israelite territories as 'the son of Omri'.

In 1846 the Englishman Austin Layard, who was an attaché at the British Embassy in Constantinople, conducted amateur archaeology on a grand scale by the excavation of a huge mound known as Kiyunjik. Layard, like Henry Rawlinson, the army engineer who deciphered Persian cuneiform, was no college academic. In his amateur expedition however, Austin Layard uncovered the walls of the buried palace of the Emperor Sennacherib, who succeeded Shalmaneser V. There amongst the great treasures, in the form of huge animalistic statues and magnificent carved wall reliefs, along with all manner of effigies and pictures, Layard found something even more valuable. In two small storerooms he found great piles of baked clay tablets inscribed with the writing known as cuneiform. Later, a second storeroom of tablets was discovered by Mr Rassam, who was assisting Austin Layard.

Over twenty-three thousand baked clay tablets were found, and these were carefully packed up and shipped off to the British Museum. Consensus opinion is that these libraries of written clay tablets were collected by the Emperor Asshurbanipal (669-627 BC), and that they represented the accumulations of his predecessors Tiglath-Pileser III, Sargon II, Shalmaneser V, Sennacherib, and Esarhaddon, as well as Asshurbanipal's own archives. All manner of subjects are dealt with in these Assyrian royal archives, including historical records, the correspondence of the kings, religious texts, business transactions, and a mass of astronomical data with planetary observations, along with mathematical records and calculations.

The fact that some of these baked clay tablets appeared to carry the ancient British Coelbren alphabet interested no one in London, Oxford, or Cambridge, in 1846.

What emerges from the study of the painstaking decipherments and translations of these historical texts by scholars is the near-certainty that the

People of Khumri are referred to as the Gimira or Gamera, and finally as the Kimmerians, in these early contemporary Assyrian records. These Gimira-Gamera people are said to occupy the same territories as those where the deported Israel Ten Tribe Khumri people were placed. E. Raymond Capt, in his *Missing Links Discovered in Assyrian Texts*, makes a detailed case, which stands up to examination, in identifying the Khumri-Khumry as these Gimira-Gamera people.

This tracing of the deported Ten Tribes of Israel to lands north of Assyria, and therefore, their highly probable identification as the Kimmerians, or Kimmeroi, of the Greek writers, and as we now know them the Khumry, brings us to the Second Book of Esdras.

The Apocryphal Books of Esdras, along with the other ancient Books of the Apocrypha, were not included in the collection of documents selected as the Bible. This was simply because they were not amongst the collection at Lyons, which was chosen as the basic Bible grouping. In II Esdras, 13:39-47, there is a description of the migration of the deported Ten Tribe Kimmerian people westwards away from Assyria. This is said to have happened around 687 BC, when the Emperor Sennacherib was assassinated by two of his sons, and a bitter civil war erupted which tore apart the Assyrian Empire until the heir to the throne, Esarhaddon, finally killed his two half-brothers:

> 'And whereas thou sawest that he gathered another peaceable multitude unto him; those are the ten tribes, which were carried away prisoners out of their own land in the time of Osea the king, whom Salmanasar, the king Assyria led away captive, and he carried them over the waters, and so came they into another land. But they took this counsel among themselves, that they would leave the multitude of the heathen, and go forth into a further country, where never mankind dwelt, That they might there keep their statutes, which they never kept in their own land.

> 'And they entered into Euphrates by the narrow passages of the river. For the Most High then shewed signs for them, and held still the flood, till they were passed over. For through that country there was a great way to go, namely of a year and a half: and the same region is called Arsareth. Then dwelt they there until the latter time; and now when they shall begin to come, The Highest shall stay the springs of the stream again, that they may go through...'

The text goes on to relate that some of these people remained within God's holy borders, which appears to mean between the 'Y' of the twin upper branches of the Euphrates. The narrative accurately describes the need to cross the Euphrates twice, as the great river is -shaped, having two great northern tributaries.

Some researchers have theorised that these same people are those of the powerful but short-lived kingdom of Urartu, a state of high civilisation which

Chapter 8 - In search of Brutus

emerged very suddenly, and flourished briefly in these northern regions. These questions may possibly be sorted out once ancient chronology is arranged into a more correct order, and the chronological chaos of the eras before 600 BC is removed.

Wilson and Blackett examined the published notations and records of the elusive Kimmerians-Kimmeroi-Khumry to see what conclusions had been reached on these people who appeared and disappeared so rapidly from the scenario of ancient history. Most historians hold firmly that the Assyrian Gimmirai are identical with the Khumry, and with the Kimmerians, and it becomes amazing that these Assyrian-recorded Khumri-Khumry people have never been investigated as the possible ancestors of the present day Khumry in Britain who claim an arrival *c.* 500 BC.

The Assyrian records of these Gimmirai begin with their inflicting a terrible defeat upon Argistis son of Rusas, king of Musasir, around 708 BC. A few years later Sargon II of Assyria was forced to go north himself to fight these Gimmirai at Tabal under their King Eshpai. Then in the reign of Sennacherib these Kimmerians-Gimmirai are recorded as moving through the southern parts of the Kingdom of Van, and these records follow numerous letters sent by the local Assyrian governors to their king during the reign of Sargon II *c.* 722-705 BC.

The Emperor Esarhaddon had continuing trouble with these Gimmirai-Kimmerians during his reign *from c.* 681-669 BC. Again, a serious battle was fought between the forces of the local Assyrian governors of the north and the Gimmirai (Khumry) allied with the Daae (Dacians? Dan?) and others at Khubishna in Tabal in 679 BC. It appears from all this that the Gimmirai-Kimmerians were on the move and unsettling everything and everyone in the area. Finally, the Emperor Esarhaddon called in his traditional allies, the Scythians, and sent them after the migrating Gimmirai who were clearly moving westwards towards Asia Minor.

Alan Wilson and Baram Blackett, along with a great many others, consider that the conventional ancient chronology before 600 BC is more than suspect. These dating inaccuracies arise because the ramshackle muddle of ancient Egyptian history is used as the chronological yardstick against which all other ancient histories are organised. As the ancient Egyptian chronology is easily demonstrable in chaos, with a mass of confusions, inaccuracies, and misreadings, this practice is generally as useful as employing a long strip of highly elastic rubber as a measuring tape.

However, the conventional chronologies place the Kimmerians on the borders of Lydia in 687 BC. Strabo states that the Lycian people assisted the Kimmerians, and he identified the Treres as the main tribe of the Kimmerian people. What appears to be certain is that King Gyges, who also needs re-identification, was attacked in Lydia by these people. Unable to hold off the Kimmerian onslaught, Gyges wrote to Asshurbanipal of Assyria asking him for help, and Gyges was compelled to place himself under Asshurbanipal's protection. The king of the Kimmerians is named as Lydamme, sometimes expressed as Tugdamme, and in Greek as Lygdamis. This is probably from Khumric 'Lluganu' meaning 'to dress in armour', and 'damuno' meaning 'request', and these armed Kimmerians were certainly military and making requests for a passage through to the west.

It is probably at the request of Gyges-Gugu that the Emperor Asshurbanipal fought with Sandakhshatra the son of Lygdamme, and the Assyrian claimed a victory. This did not halt the Kimmerian march westwards, however, and they proceeded to capture the great city of Sardis-Sardes, the capital of King Gyges. They may not have succeeded in capturing the central fortified citadel castle known as Hyde. Sardis is generally thought to have been captured in 652 BC, and some Greek sources allege that King Gyges was killed by the Kimmerians, which does not however fit with the emerging scenario.

Whilst at least half of the Kimmerians led by the Y-Treres – 'the travelling homes' people - left for Italy around 650 BC to become the 'Y-Truscans' - Etruscans, very substantial numbers remained in Western Asia Minor for a considerable period of time. They lived in the cities of Antandrus, just south of Troy, and at Sinope. Alyattes the son and successor to Gyges is recorded as fighting with these Kimmerians, who kept up a correspondence with kinsmen in the Crimea on the north coast of the Black Sea. Not surprisingly an inscription, which appears to be in Coelbren, has turned up in the Crimea.

What is encapsulated in these records is the story of a people who were transplanted from Israel to regions on the northern borders of the Assyrian Empire as frontier guards, and who refused to settle in these lands where they were ordered to dwell. Taking advantage of the assassination of the Emperor Sennacherib, they began moving westwards with the clear notion, as expressed in II Esdras, of going far west to lands unoccupied by anyone else. This caused upheavals in the regions to the north of present-day Iran and Iraq, and further collisions occurred as the horde moved slowly west. Only the Lycians appear to have had the good sense to allow them free passage, and the kingdom of Midas fell before them, as did Gyges' Lydian kingdom, and other states including Cappadocia. The plans of the Assyrian emperors to place these people as a northern defensive buffer to their own lands fell apart. The combined efforts of Assyrian governors failed to stop them from moving, and so did the attempt of the Emperor Esarhaddon. Too late the Assyrians asked for Scythian horsemen to try to turn the Kimmerians back, and even Asshurbanipal was unable to prevent their march through Asia Minor to the sea at the Dardanelles.

The fact that many of these Kimmerians, or Khumry, left for Italy around 650 BC, and the remainder stayed in known locations in Antandrus, Sinope, and elsewhere, until around 500 BC, when Brutus led the great migration to Britain, fits with the British traditional records and historical patterns.

Chapter Nine

The Arthurian Dynasty

The Arthurian Dynasty in Britain is arguably the best recorded in Western Europe. It is copiously identifiable with surviving royal tombstones, accession stones, and other tangible monuments. Small armies of descendants of these Arthurian Kings are still traceable today. Yet the vast majority of the British people know absolutely nothing of the existence of this ancient founding Dynasty of Britain.

Outlines of the Arthurian Dynasty have been published in the other works of Wilson and Blackett, and a further detailed history is planned. At this time, it is only necessary to deal with the kings of the era between AD 383 and AD 600. In doing this, the power structure in Britain needs to be explained. There was first the line of dynastic Brutus kings in Essyllwg – 'Abounding in Prospects' - in the Fortress Kingdom in South-east Wales. Alongside these senior kings there seems to have been the intermarried Imperial Line which generally held sway in Warwickshire and the English Midlands, and the capital at Uriconium -Wroxeter- Viroconium.

Scattered across Britain were other sub-branches of the royal lines, whose leaders usually claimed the title of king, and they were in fact Sub-reguli, or local kings. The best way to describe the situation is to explain that Essyllwg – 'Siluria' was a fortress kingdom with a vast ring of connected hill-forts surrounding its borders. This immense demonstration of military engineering is still largely visible. The basic system is the building of fort groups resembling giant cartwheels, with the main fortresses at the hub of the cartwheel. The ring of outer forts surrounding the centre fort is linked by lines of sight to it, and to their neighbouring outer forts. Each giant cartwheel system joins on to the next system, with some outer forts being common to each adjoining wheel system. In this way signals of an enemy approach could be flashed and signalled around the entire kingdom in minutes, and the military leaders of the centre or hub forts could be informed.

The enclosed area of the Fortress Kingdom surrounded Glamorgan, Gwent,

Chapter 9 - The Arthurian Dynasty

Brecon, Herefordshire, Western Gloucestershire (the Red Cantrefs), and much of present-day Carmarthen. This represented a formidable kingdom. It appears that 'Siluria' in Britain enjoyed a similar position to the Macedonia of Phillip II and Alexander III the Great, and held a dominant military position over all the other various states of ancient Britain, just as Macedonia dominated all of ancient Greece.

Where the king was also the military commander he was often titled as a Dragon or as an Uthyrpendragon, the 'Wonderful Head of Dragons'. When the military command was designated to another more militarily experienced or capable Prince, then that Prince held the title of Wledig, which is 'the Legate'. The senior king was the Teyrn, or the Monarch, and the regional kings were styled as Brenin - King. In this scenario, the Teyrn called King Carawn, who was also the Western Emperor of Britain and most of Gaul, and known as the Emperor Carausius, was a Dragon (*c.* AD 282-293). His British military successor was Casnar Wledig, who was in Latin terms Crysanthus the Legate, and Casnar was not the Teyrn or Monarch, and so he was simply styled as the Wledig.

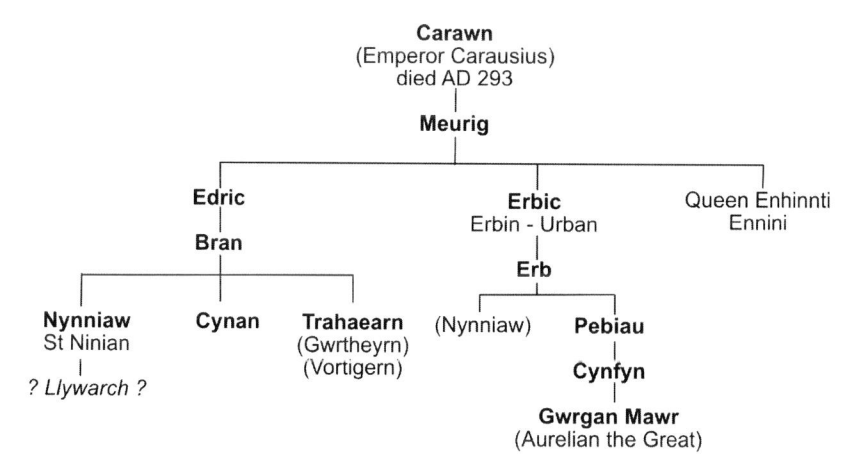

```
                         Carawn
                    (Emperor Carausius)
                       died AD 293
                            |
                         Meurig
                            |
    ┌───────────────────────┼─────────────────────────┐
   Edric                  Erbic                Queen Enhinnti
    |                  Erbin - Urban                Ennini
   Bran                     |
    |                      Erb
    ┌──────────┬──────────┐ |
                           ┌──────────┐
 Nynniaw    Cynan   Trahaearn (Nynniaw) Pebiau
 St Ninian          (Gwrtheyrn)           |
    |               (Vortigern)         Cynfyn
 ? Llywarch ?                             |
                                      Gwrgan Mawr
                                   (Aurelian the Great)
```

In this way Magnus Maximus, the Emperor of the West (383 - 388), was styled Mascen Wledig as he was not the senior Brutus Dynasty King in Britain. Owain Vinddu, a son of Magnus Maximus, was killed in AD 434, and command of the armies against the Irish passed to one Cuneda Wledig, who is Lord (Cun) of the Restoration (Edau) the Legate. His real name was Eternalis Vedomavus. These simple rules exhibited in the titles and designations allow for clarity to be perceived in what might otherwise be a tangled situation. Alan Wilson and Baram Blackett wondered at the failure of earlier writers to establish these very basic ground rules, and it can only be a direct result of the British preference for literary style in place of factual accuracy. In the inevitable way of the aristocracy and nobility, all the major families were heavily intermarried, and almost everyone claimed Brutus, Imperial, and Arimathean descents in various degrees of the devolved pecking order.

ILLUSTRATION - The Basic Genealogy of Arthur I and Arthur II

Evidence in several of the most reputable British Manuscripts, including the British Museum Vespasian A XIV, the Harleian 4181, the illustrious Harleian 3859, the Llandaff Cathedral Charters, the Jesus College MSS 20, numbers of other manuscripts (including the Historical Bruts, Epic Poetry, and Roman genealogical sources.

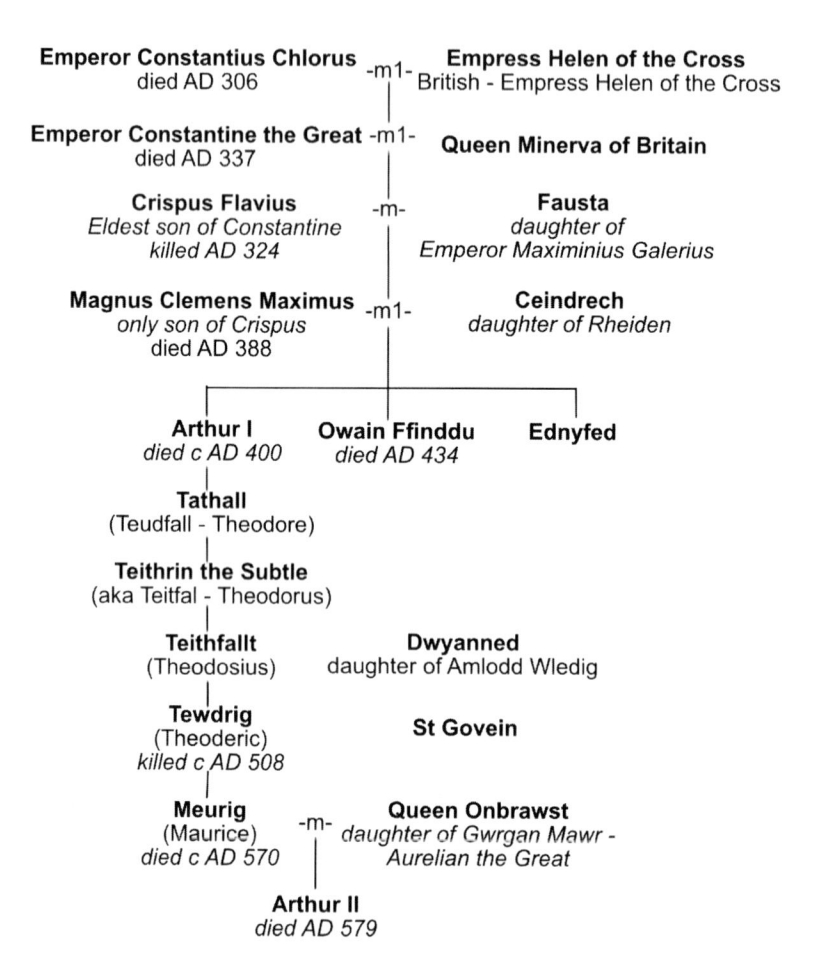

```
Emperor Constantius Chlorus    -m1-   Empress Helen of the Cross
    died AD 306                        British - Empress Helen of the Cross
                                  |
Emperor Constantine the Great -m1-   Queen Minerva of Britain
    died AD 337                   |
                                  |
        Crispus Flavius          -m-         Fausta
    Eldest son of Constantine              daughter of
        killed AD 324              Emperor Maximinius Galerius
                                  |
    Magnus Clemens Maximus    -m1-      Ceindrech
       only son of Crispus              daughter of Rheiden
         died AD 388
                                  |
      ┌───────────────┬───────────────┐
    Arthur I       Owain Ffinddu     Ednyfed
  died c AD 400    died AD 434
      |
    Tathall
  (Teudfall - Theodore)
      |
  Teithrin the Subtle
  (aka Teitfal - Theodorus)
      |
    Teithfallt              Dwyanned
   (Theodosius)       daughter of Amlodd Wledig
      |
    Tewdrig
   (Theoderic)              St Govein
  killed c AD 508
      |
     Meurig         -m-     Queen Onbrawst
    (Maurice)              daughter of Gwrgan Mawr -
   died c AD 570              Aurelian the Great
                     |
                  Arthur II
                 died AD 579
```

The many descendants of Arthur I and Arthur II are all very well recorded and known down to this present time. It is a conspiracy and not a mystery.

Chapter 9 - The Arthurian Dynasty

It took some time and patience on the part of Alan Wilson and Baram Blackett to get anything like a clear picture of the descents and relationships of the kings of the era. In their earlier attempts they frequently found it necessary to revise their presentations.

Brothers of Meurig were Brochwael and Maelgwn of Llandaff, and sister Queen Marchell. Other sons of King Meurig and Queen Onbrawst - Idnerth, St Pawl, Ffrioc, Madoc Morfran Daughters of King Meurig and Queen Onbrawst -Anna married Amwn Ddu, Affrella married Umbraefel, Gwyar married Liew, Gwenonwy married Gwyndaf Hen.

King Erbic left a memorial stone which bears his name at Llandough[?] Church in Glamorgan. The stone has five busts carved on one face, the central one wearing a crown, and presumably King Erbic. Another face shows a carving of a crowned man with a raised sword and riding a horse. Odd as it must be to any sane man, the academics insist that 'this cannot be' King Erbic of Glamorgan, without saying why this 'cannot be'. Yet King Erbic is named in many genealogical sources including the Jesus College Manuscript 20.

The gravestone of King Carawn-Carausius the Emperor was found at Penmachno and is in a Welsh Museum. Remarkably the BBC 2 Timewatch series made a programme, which insisted that there was no stone in Britain that named Carausius of Menevia, the St David's area in Dyfed. Not surprisingly, the obvious Welsh district of Menevia, and a host of other Welsh sources, are routinely ignored, and so Carausius, or Carawn of Menevia, becomes Carausius of the Menapii, a continental Belgian Tribe in the time of Julius Caesar and a mere three hundred and fifty years out of date. If it were not so tragic then it might be comical. Several manuscripts list Carausius as King Carawn or King Crair, and he routinely appears in all representations of the South East Wales King Lists. Some quantities of coins minted by Carawn-Carausius exist, and the ruin of his palace residence at Caer Mead is irrefutable mute evidence.

The treacherous Trahaearn was killed at Nant Gwrtheyrn in North Wales, and his grave was excavated there in AD 1776, to reveal skeleton of a tall man. An effigy of King Pebiau Glafoerog, the Dribbler, with two attendants, was in a Herefordshire church until our modern times. King & Saint Ninian is of course best known for founding Whithorn Abbey in Galloway. There is other evidence, but this is enough to show that these are not imagined or invented shadow figures. King Pebiau, Gwrgan Mawr, Cynfyn, and Erbin, and the Queen Enhinnti, all appear in ancient Cathedral and Abbey Charters, and none of these ancestral figures are ghosts or phantoms resulting from historical forgeries.

The main lines of the Brutus Dynasty were decimated at the infamous massacre at Caer Caradoc in *c.* AD 456. The Saxons had been defeated in the war of their revolt, and had sued for a Peace Conference. Both sides were to come unarmed, and Trahaearn alias Vortigern-Gwrtheyrn, who was largely responsible for the war, was a key figure in persuading the British to hold the Conference instead of simply eliminating the Saxons.

Trahaearn was a debauched drunk who committed incest with his own thirteen-year old daughter. He engaged in civil war with his brother the King, and had in his youth first married Servilla, a daughter of Magnus Maximus and Helen. Then, aged and dissolute, he had married Rowena, the reputedly beautiful daughter of the one-blue-eyed Hengist the Saxon, and they had a son named Gotta who survived into in adult life by becoming a monk. Hengist and his Jutes and Saxons were hired, and placed in Ceint-Kent as coastguards to warn against a channel crossing from Brittany by Amlodd Wledig (Ambrosius the Legate), a grandson of Magnus Maximus. Hengist was obviously intended to try oppose any invasion by Amlodd Wledig and to give early warning to Trahaearn-Vortigern-Gwrtheyrn.

At the Peace Conference the Saxons, true to their nature, brought concealed weapons, and when considerable quantities of alcohol had been consumed, at a given signal from Hengist they murdered some three hundred and sixty-three unarmed British leaders. This brought about the death of the aged British King Cynan ap Bran (as in the poem *Gwarchan Maelderw*, by Taliesin), and Llywarch, the shadowy son of King & St Ninian. Trahaearn remained, and Hengist put his aged dissolute drunkard of a son-in-law into chains. Hengist claimed the crown for Trahaearn, and clearly entertained the mad idea that when old Trahaearn died or was killed, then Hengist's grandson Gotta would be the King.

Hengist clearly thought he would control his daughter as Queen Rowena and his grandson, the child Gotta. These plans were doomed from the start as no King had ever married a non-British Queen, and matters began to go astray when Amlodd Wledig-Ambrosius the Legate, from Brittany, threatened Trahaearn-Vortigern. There was also the looming problem of the Prince Teithfallt-Theodosius, the senior legitimate surviving British heir. This Prince Teithfallt was the son of Teithrin the Subtle. Teithrin had married Dwyaned the daughter of Amlodd Wledig-Ambrosius of Brittany, and Teithfallt's father, Teithrin, was also a grandson of Arthur I son of Magnus Maximus. At the time of the massacre Teithfallt-Theodosius was spending time in a monastery, which was a safe place for a young Prince with claims to the throne to be in the middle of a civil war.

Hengist's rosy little plan was punctured when this last surviving member of the British royal family, Teithfallt-Theodosius, arrived back in Britain. Teithfallt was now the Em-Rhys Wledig, or the Jewelled or Crown Prince Legate, and a great-grandson of King Arthur I, the eldest son of the Emperor Magnus Maximus-Mascen

Chapter 9 - The Arthurian Dynasty

Wledig. A massive army was raised under Teithfallt and the Saxons were hunted down. Hengist was captured and executed, and Trahaearn was pursued to his hideaway castle in Nant Gwrtheyrn, which was burned down, and Trahaearn himself was killed. Teithfallt, sometimes recorded as Tudfwlch, became King, and his accession stone is at Margam Abbey. This stone is predictably concealed by deliberate, crude, misdating and misnaming. The Welsh Coelbren 'Th' is misread as an Irish 'G' and so on, and the whole text is ludicrously mistranslated.

The three hundred and sixty-three noblemen killed in the peace conference massacre were buried by King Teithfallt in the circular monument at Mynwent y Milwyr (Grave Monument of the Military = Soldiers), which he built on the second highest point of Mynydd-y-Gaer at Caer Caradoc, and the revived and now deeply Christian British dynasty ruled with an iron fist.

This first great British disaster of the massacre at Caer Caradoc in Mid-Glamorgan was a memory, which was burned deep into the Khumric psyche. Down through the ages, generation upon generation was taught the tale of the hideous murder of the king, the sub-kings, the generals, bishops, and leading Princes. The Saesneg-Saxons had again broken the laws and customs of the nations, and they were never ever again to be trusted. This then became one of the three great British catastrophes in a triad.

As stated, King Teithfallt or Tudfwlch, who in Latin would be Theodosius, had married Dwyaned the daughter of Amlodd Wledig of Brittany, who was a grandson of Magnus Maximus. His successor was King Tewdrig-Theoderic, who was the Uthyr-pen-dragon who was mortally wounded at the ford at Tintern (Din-Teyrn) in AD 508. The story is told in the Llandaff Charters, of the aged retired Tewdrig blocking the Tintern ford to prevent the fleeing Saxon army from escaping back across into Lloegres, so as to gain time for his son King Meurig-Maurice, to come up with the army and destroy the Saxons. Tewdrig also left a misread misdated stone. He was well recorded as buried at Mathern Church, and his stone coffin has twice been exhumed, in 1609 and 1881, to examine the corpse with its head wound. King Tewdrig married St Govein, the interior of whose little chapel was still standing, and excavated in the late 1980's, when a small female skeleton was found under the altar.

Next came King Meurig son of Tewdrig, who married Onbrawst the daughter of Gwrgan Mawr-Aurelian the Great, who also descended by another line from Magnus Maximus through Cystennhyn Lydaw - Constantine of Lydaw (later Normandy). King Meurig is, like Teithfallt and Tewdrig, copiously recorded in Cathedral Charters and histories. He is probably the Uthyr-pen-dragon associated with legends, as he was the father of the celebrated Arthmael-Iron Bear, also recorded as Athwys, Arthwys, Arthrwys, and finally Arthur II. As it was the prerogative of the kings and major princes to erect stones, it may be relevant that there is a sixth-century stone set up naming a Meurig in Cornwall, about six miles from Tintagel.

The most important of dynastic marriages was now planned. The importance lies in the fact that King Meurig was the senior British King descended from Magnus and Arthur I, and Gwrgan Mawr-Aurelian the Great was the leading descendant of the Brutus line, through his grandfather King Pebiau. By marrying Meurig the son of King Tewdrig to Onbrawst the daughter of Gwrgan Mawr, these senior lines were united together in harmony. There were a number of children born of this marriage, and the eldest son was variously known as Arthmael, (Iron Bear) Arthrwys, Athwys, and Arthur. This prince was also the senior descendant of the First Holy Family of King Bran.

It was late in the reign of King Meurig and when his eldest son Arthmael was the Ail-teyrn or Regent, that the second great catastrophe befell Britain. In AD 562 débris from a comet is recorded as falling in a scatter across Britain, causing tremendous devastations and vast conflagrations. At a stroke much of the great island kingdom lay in total ruins. The cities, the towns, the monasteries, and the villas, were shattered; the buildings were shaken to their foundations and the roofs slid or were blown off. The forests and the crops burned, the rivers were polluted, wildlife, animals, birds, fish, and reptiles, all perished. Humans and their domesticated livestock were killed in innumerable multitudes. Terrifying clouds darkened the land and the droplets raining down from these clouds caused certain death. Those who could fled to areas which had escaped devastation, to Cornwall, to Brittany, to parts of the far north of Britain, and to scattered inland areas.

This was the destruction of the powerful Arthurian British state. Fourteen hundred years ago the neighbouring nations did not send aid to a stricken nation, as we might today. Instead, the Irish, the Picts, and Angles, Saxons, and others, along the Western coasts of Europe, seized their opportunity to attack and try to plunder the devastated British state. Like hyenas stalking a wounded buffalo, they raided. Many areas were totally uninhabitable, and for seven to eleven years it was death to enter them. So was born the story in the later mediaeval Romances of the Great Wastelands which none dare to enter, as all who had entered had died. This motif will be familiar to all who have read the mediaeval Arthurian Romances. At the onset of this catastrophe King Arthur II, son of Meurig, removed the British army to Brittany and brought it back to Britain after seven years.

Just as he had destroyed the infiltrating Angles and Saxons before the comet strike had shattered the Kingdom, Arthur II now set about the annihilation of invaders who were pushing into Britain. He had foreseen the need to preserve the army, and now he used it. Mentions in epic poetry show that he firmly believed in deterring these invaders, and he bound his Irish prisoners and threw them into

Chapter 9 - The Arthurian Dynasty

lime pits, which should have been a fair warning to anyone, whilst the lucky ones were burnt alive. Arthur II's cousin, King Howell of Brittany, brought his cavalry army into Britain to aid his near relatives, and peace and order were restored.

In the midst of the reconstruction and reorganization of the badly damaged British state, there was an amazing happening. The Prince Madoc Morfran-the Cormorant, a son of King Meurig ap Tewdrig, and a brother of Arthur II, arrived home after being ten years away at sea. No ship could stay afloat for that long, nor could the crew survive without fresh food and water. Prince Madoc explained that he had been in the vast territories across the Western Ocean, which they called The Other World. Whether Madoc Morfran sailed in an expedition to try to find new lands 'as told of by the ancients', or whether he was at sea when the comet débris devastated Britain and caused vast storms driving him far westwards out across the Atlantic is uncertain. It is however very well recorded that he found the great Other World across the Atlantic Ocean. Madoc's return would have been in AD 572.

The Admiral Gwenon was despatched by Arthur II, presumably in 573, to check out Madoc's star readings and reckonings, which were doubted as he was taking sightings of the heavens from unprecedented positions. The Admiral Gwenon later returned and confirmed Madoc's discoveries. Budic then also made a voyage, and Arthur II held a long conference with Lliwlod (brown-skinned person) a son of Madoc. Then, almost certainly in AD 574, Arthur II summoned an army and assembled a fleet of seven hundred ships at Deu Gleddyf-Milford Haven. He sailed for *The Other World*, which the Spanish called The *New World*, and was away for five years, until Taliesin and six others returned with his embalmed corpse in a ship in 579.

This was regarded as the third great catastrophe to strike Britain. It is on this basis of these three great disasters that most of the content of the epic poetry which describes these events is constructed. First, there was the Civil War and the importing of the Saxons by Trahaearn to aid his forces, and the Saxon revolt and their defeat around 456, and how victory was almost thrown away at the Caer Caradoc Peace Conference. Then came the almost unbelievable and overwhelming disaster of the comet, as the second tragedy in 562. Finally, there came the third act of the drama, with the loss of many soldiers and the death of King Arthur II in The Other World of the Americas.

Urien Rheged was the Northern Regent left behind by Arthur II, in what is now Northern England and Southern Scotland. Frioch or Rioch, another brother of Arthur II, was Regent in the South, and it seems that Maelgwn Gwynedd may have been a Regent in north Wales. The throne actually went to King Morgan Mwynfawr and to King Ithael, who were brothers, and Morgan killed his uncle Frioch to clear him out of his path, as recounted in the Llandaff Charters. Maelgwn Gwynedd attempted to seize the crown of Britain by an election rigged by Ugnach in 580, and Urien Rheged, the Northern Regent, was murdered by Morcant a brother of

Rhydderch Hael of the Edinburgh region around 596.

Morgan Mwynfawr seems to be the titular Cadfan-Prominent in Battle, or Many Battles, and Iliad 25 of Series I, and Triad 9 of Series II, and Triad 31 of Series III, all point to this. King Morgan is listed as second only to Arthur in battle and blood, and also in the ready willingness of warriors to flock to his banners. Predictably, and also unsurprisingly, this warrior King appears nowhere in the modern 'politically correct' histories. His son Gwaednerth is again certainly the Caswallon-Ruler of a Separated State, a Viceroy in Lloegres, and both Gwaednerth and the Caswallon have identical life stories and lived and ruled simultaneously. Gwaednerth means 'mighty in blood', and this fearsome Prince caused major concern to his own people. Finally, Gwaednerth was compelled by a Council of the Church of Britain to abdicate, and leave Britain for good. Shortly afterwards however Gwaednerth became restive of living abroad, and returned to Britain after a short absence, and resumed his terrifying activities. This then leaves King Ithael II son of Morgan, as the Cadwallader-Battle Sovereign, under whom everything finally began to collapse c. 684.

Political correctness has demanded that these three Titular Princes who were identified under the titles of Cadfan, Caswallon, and Cadwallader, were from Gwynedd. This would allow them to be Tudor ancestors and to conform with the necessary English political requirements. The Gwynedd Princes of the era are in fact well known, and they do not fit with any of these three major seventh-century rulers, who are amongst the last of the major Kings of the British Arthurian Dynasty to rule over Britain. The Princes of Gwynedd of this era were-

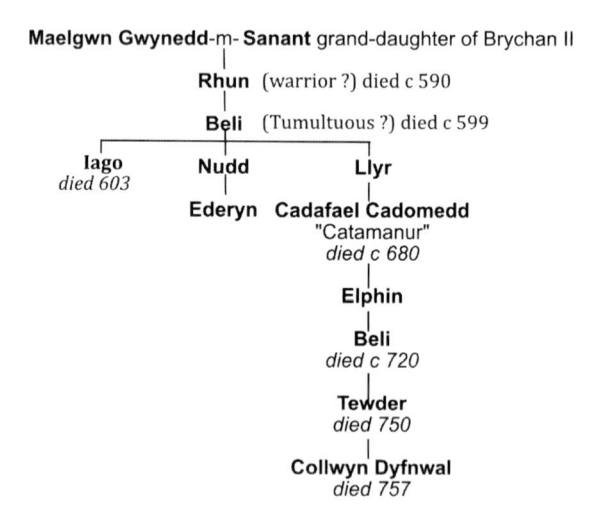

```
        Maelgwn Gwynedd-m- Sanant grand-daughter of Brychan II
                          |
                Rhun  (warrior ?) died c 590
                          |
                Beli  (Tumultuous ?) died c 599
                          |
        ┌─────────────────┼─────────────────┐
       Iago            Nudd               Llyr
     died 603            |                  |
                      Ederyn    Cadafael Cadomedd
                                  "Catamanur"
                                  died c 680
                                      |
                                   Elphin
                                      |
                                    Beli
                                  died c 720
                                      |
                                   Tewder
                                  died 750
                                      |
                              Collwyn Dyfnwal
                                  died 757
```

Cadafael Cadomedd is famous for fomenting a battle and then withdrawing his army from the danger and leaving his allies stranded. This would be the Catamanus whose grossly mistranslated stone is at Llangadwallader in Gwynedd, and who is wrongly identified as 'Cadfan'. He is far too late to be the Cadfan of the histories.

The result of simply restoring the invisible dynasty of South East Wales to the general historical scenario is that we have a perfectly clear and credible history for what is alleged to be a confused and mysterious era from AD 450 to 600.

Dynastic Chronology

Huge problems in chronology have been deliberately created in desperate attempts to obscure the Brutus and Arthurian Dynasty in Britain. What is precise and clear has been distorted to match political inventions, and then the totally confused historical scenario that emerges from these deliberate distortions has been held up to ridicule.

A prime example is the ridiculous 'identification' of King Teithfallt-Theodosius by one Egerton Phillimore, who actually stated that King Teithfallt was an alias or alter ego of King Athelbald of Mercia. This breath-taking absurdity has been seized upon and used and requoted *ad nauseum* for over a century, causing historical chaos. To confuse King Teithfallt-Tudfwlch who was probably born around AD 430, and died around 480-490, with Athelbald of Mercia who ruled the English Midlands from AD 716 to 757, has to be as Alan Wilson puts it 'a major prize winner'. A two hundred and fifty- years' error, which should have been immediately dismissed as rubbish, was allowed to prevail. Egerton Phillimore apparently could not tell the difference between King Teithfallt son of Teithrin the Subtle, and a minor Teithfallt who was a grandson of Llywarch Hen, who was himself a great-great-grandson of King Teithfallt. This extraordinary piece of historical buffoonery was actually published by the Honourable Society of Cymmrodorion. It has to be deliberate.

If King Teithfallt is displaced by two hundred and fifty years to the era of Athelbald of Mercia, then automatically his son King Tewdrig is confused and obliterated. In a domino effect, the son of Tewdrig who was King Meurig, and his grandson Arthur II, are cast into limbo.

If three records of the same event are brought together sanity can return. The Anglo-Saxon Chronicle records that the 'chiefmost King of the British' was killed in fighting at a ford of a river *circa* AD 509, and the name of this King is given as Natanleod. The death of King Tewdrig is detailed in the Llandaff Charters, and the aged and infirm King was mortally wounded in a battle with the Saxons at Tintern Ford. He was taken in a special cart drawn by stags to Mathern well, where he died and was buried. The *Brut Tyssilio* and the *Brut Gruffydd* ap Arthur both describe the death of an aged 'Uthyrpendragon' who is also old and infirm, who is similarly mortally wounded, and who also dies at a well early in the sixth century AD.

The genealogies support Tewdrig as being old and probably dying around AD 509, and the evidence in the Charters support this also. A Prince Brochwael is named, who fits as a son of King.

Tewdrig and a brother of King Meurig, and in Cornwall there is a sixth-century stone inscribed for Brocagnus fili Natanleod. The South East Wales records constantly affirm Cornwall to be a sister state, and several senior Kings abdicated in favour of their sons and retired to Cornwall. Caradoc II is one such King and there is a stone of Caractacus in Cornwall. Arthur II's father was King Meurig Uthyrpendragon the son of Tewdrig, and Meurig left no stone yet discovered in South East Wales. But there is a sixth-century stone named for a Meurig just six miles from Tintagel. There is other earlier significant evidence of some importance in Cornwall, which is also passed by and unrecognised. It was the Kings who set up stones and not lesser men.

Some entries in *The Lives of the Saints* name Anna, the mother of St Samson of Dol, as the daughter of King Meurig. Other entries name this same Anna as the daughter of the Uthyrpendragon. Obviously Meurig and Uthyrpendragon are one. As Samson signed the papers of the Second Council of Paris *circa* 556-7, it is extremely difficult to see how his great grandfather King Teithfallt could be identical with Athelbald of Mercia two hundred years later. It is equally impossible to displace his maternal uncle, King Arthur II ap Meurig, from the era of AD 503- 579, and into the period 600- 660. Ideas of St Samson's great-grandfather being buried at Mathern around AD 600 are patently obviously mistaken. The reason for misdating King Tewdrig at Mathern is simply one where the Church of England remains reluctant to acknowledge a Church being built over the tomb of a Christian Welsh King in AD 509 some eighty-eight years before the Monk Austin (Augustine) arrived in Kent from Rome in 597.

Whilst Alan and Baram were patiently sorting out the pandemonium of the problems of the three St Patricks, the two St Samsons, the three Uriens, and the fiasco of the three Prince Brychans, the two Modreds (or Medrawds), and much more, the Establishment was busily erecting its defences. At the time, the Welsh Arts Council had been running for sixteen years, and after polite enquiries met with open hostility, Alan and Baram visited the Welsh Office in Cardiff where they were refused access to the library. They then wrote and asked to see the library, and there a stony-faced librarian assured them that the Welsh Office, which annually handed over many millions of Public Funds to the Welsh Arts Council, did not have any of the Welsh Arts Council's annual reports. The Cardiff Central Library did have fourteen years of these reports however, and these made

Chapter 9 - The Arthurian Dynasty

interesting reading.

Grants were made to promote book publishing in Wales, and there was a committee consisting mainly of University of Wales employees, and the recipients of grants were named, the amount of cash received was stated, the name of the book was listed, and the publisher was named. All looked all right, but when these reports were laid out in a row, strange facts emerged. Committee members sometimes illegally received grants, and dubious organizations in which Arts Council employees were involved received fat annual grants. A game of musical chairs was being played, and grant recipients moved over to become committee members, whilst ex-committee members moved over and became grant recipients. Whereas the rules stated that completed manuscripts had to be submitted for grant consideration, this seemed not to apply to university employees.

So, Alan and Baram approached a respectable religious publishing house and asked them to submit a manuscript to the Welsh Arts Council for a publishing grant. They knew that they would get nowhere, and so Baram carefully spot-glued over a hundred of the manuscript pages together before it was passed to the publishing house for dispatch, with the required Reader's Fee. Predictably the manuscript came back with a raging vitriolic negative review of its contents. Extraordinary, as the pages were still all firmly spot-glued together and so the manuscript could not have been read. Alan and Baram proceeded to take the Welsh Arts Council to Court, as they had accepted a Readers' Fee but had not actually read the manuscript. They won the case, and were pleased and amazed when the Western Mail of 12th August 1994 carried a front-page article "Arts Council gets stuck in Authors' glue trap", along with a cartoon which showed a blind gentleman at a cocktail party explaining to a lady in evening dress - "I'm a proof reader for the Welsh Arts Council".

Less than four months later the South Wales Echo of 05/12/94 carried the headline "Lottery Cash Up For Grabs" and stated that "A massive £25 million of National Lottery money is waiting in the bank for deserving causes. But South Wales people have been slow to bid for the cash. So far, the Millenium Commission has had just one bid from South Wales." Not surprising, as Welsh people know well that no one is going to get any grants for anything apart from the same old Taffia-Mafia gangs. Another more gruesome press report announced that a further £7 million was allocated annually to the Welsh Arts Council.

For those who may not know, the river Taff runs down the Rhondda Valley and through Cardiff to meet the great Severn Estuary. Welshmen are referred to as Taff or Taffy, in the same way as Irishmen are called Paddy or Mick, and Scots are referred to as Jock. So, the crooked ruling Junta and their adherents are referred to as the Taffia, a pun on Mafia.

With Alan and Baram attempting to release British History from bondage, a

Rhondda university employee was given £45,000 by the Welsh Office to write a history book. This predictably turned out to be yet a another turgid, boring, reiteration of the same old misleading nineteenth-century humbug, which has been strangling British History for the past few centuries. Seventeen university employees were also each given £2,500 each to write an essay on sections of what is alleged to be Welsh history.

The year following this Court victory, which the Welsh Office desperately attempted to cover up with a series of falsehoods, saw the Welsh Arts Council's annual report alter. It simply stated that some seventeen unnamed authors had been allocated unspecified grants, from a gross total of cash, to bring out untitled books that were to be published by unnamed publishers, and no detail of anything whatsoever was published. Who got how much for what and why was kept secret. Welsh politicians again predictably did absolutely nothing when approached, over this monstrous lack of accountability.

In one peculiar exercise, academics formed what they called The Welsh Academy, and the Welsh Arts Council funded this organisation, and then also donated a further sum of £50,000 to it, to enable an anthology to be written. The Academy then immediately gave the same £50,000 back to the Secretary of the Book Division of the Welsh Arts Council to write the anthology. This action disregarded the rules that Arts Council employees are not to receive Arts Council Grants. It also disregarded the very clear Arts Council's rules whereby a finished manuscript has to be submitted to be read, in order to qualify for Grant consideration. Alan and Baram pointed this out to the Welsh Office, and also that some eight books had been published which had no authors, but simply an Editor who was an Arts Council employee. Alan and Baram also pointed out a lot more, particularly where large annual Grants were going into similar purpose-built organizations. They were outsiders and they had nothing to lose by exposing the Welsh Arts Council, even though nothing would be done in the lunatic world of Quangoland.

In the mayhem of Khumric History there are three St Patricks named. The St Patrick selected to be the Patrick who was Ireland's favourite missionary, was predictably the only Patrick from North West Wales-Gwynedd. This Patrick son of Alfred was firmly avowed in the new born Academy's Anthology. Yet this Patrick is recorded as being at the Bangor Monastery in the time of Bishop Elvod. Here we have the doctrines of the political correctness of the establishment meddling again, for the Bangor Monastery was not founded by St Deiniol (Daniel) until the second half of the sixth century, with a grant from Maelgwn Gwynedd. It is difficult to see how St Patrick who went to Ireland in AD 434 could have attended a monastic college that was founded some hundred and thirty years later, after about AD 550

Chapter 9 - The Arthurian Dynasty

or even later. Matters get worse as the Bishop Elfodd or Elvod is well known to have lived around AD 780 - 820 in the time of Nennius, and Patrick son of Alfred was at the same monastery at the same time as Bishop Elfodd.

This nonsense persists everywhere. When Llewellyn the Last of Gwynedd was killed in AD 1282, his severed head was taken to London and stuck onto a spear on London Bridge in a display of primitive barbarism. Monasteries and churches in North Wales were afraid to offer burial to the headless corpse because of the wrath of the English King Edward I, and it finally arrived at a small monastery in Glamorgan. After the dissolution of the monasteries in 1536, this became Llanrumney Hall in East Cardiff, and later the home of Henry Morgan of piratical fame. When excavations to modify the old building were carried out, a stone coffin, which contained a headless corpse, was discovered buried in a wall. This strange discovery would be regarded as evidence elsewhere, but not in Quangoland. CADW posing as 'Welsh Heritage', but more accurately the Commission Arranging Destruction in Wales, then spent several million on an archaeological exercise at an abbey in North Wales speculatively alleging that this is where Llewellyn the Last of Gwynedd was buried. Not a penny is spent on the Kings in the South East.

The other two Patricks were earlier. One from Dyfed is too late to be the Patrick of Ireland, but the one from Tair Onen-Three Ash Trees at Cowbridge In Glamorgan is a perfect chronological match. Not only this, but the story of St Patrick and all the places and place names fit perfectly, with Patrick attending the Caerworgorn monastic college, founded by the Princess Eurgain, daughter of Caradoc I, in the first century AD, and just six miles from Tair Onen on the coast at Llan-illtyd Fawr. To paraphrase Shakespeare 'there is something rotten in the State of Wales'.

These nonsenses are endless, with the highly regarded poet Dafydd ap Gwilym, who died *circa* AD 1367, having two alleged graves, one in South Wales where he was born and where he lived, and the other in North Wales. The rules of the game are that nothing must ever be allowed to be associated with South East Wales. The City Hall in Cardiff in South East Wales has, on the first-floor entrance balcony, twelve heroic statues, which supposedly represent illustrious Welsh historical figures, and all are from North Wales. South East Wales is markedly non-existent.

As Alan Wilson says, 'a blind man on a galloping horse would be able to see more detail in Khumric history'. The classic case is probably that of the Prince Brychan, who is in fact three quite separate noblemen spread over a period in excess of two hundred years. This is so obvious as to be a well-nigh unbelievable nonsense. Tired academic dogma propounds just one Brychan with three wives, twenty-four daughters, and twelve sons. In addition, the Lives of Saints allot Brychan a mistress and an additional illegitimate son. This does not explain the three graves of 'Brychan', and one manuscript lists two of these graves in succession. This muddle had Alan and Baram going in ever decreasing circles for years.

The 'Brychan' disaster is a serious one, as in many cases the husbands and wives of his alleged multitude of daughters and sons are known, along with their fathers, mothers, and grandfathers, and so on. If there was only Brychan II of around 500 - 560, then there is chronological pandemonium. First, there was Brychan I of Brittany, a brother of Conan Meriadauc who was made King of Brittany by Magnus Maximus in AD 383. This would be the Brychan who married the Visigoth (Spanish) Princess Poestri. Many of the twenty-four daughters and twelve sons are his. Second, there was Brychan the son of Queen Marchell, a daughter of King Tewdrig and sister to King Meurig. She married Enllech Coronog (the crowned) son of Hydwn Dwn, son of Ceredic, son of Cuneda, and Ceredic had seized lands in Ireland. St Patrick is recorded as rebuking Ceredic for his harsh treatment of the Irish. Not surprisingly a 'Roman'-style fort was discovered a few years ago near Dublin. This second Brychan of Brecon would be the husband of his first cousin Eurbrawst, a daughter of King Meurig. He would have been active around AD 500 - 560. Third, there was Brychan, a grandson of Llywarch Hen, who would have been active around 600 - 650.

Attempts to correlate the families named in the many marriages of the progeny of one 'Brychan' have resulted in historical chaos. When the three Princes are identified, then the nightmare goes away. One grave of Brychan is in Brittany, and it would logically suit Brychan I brother of King Conan. A second Brychan grave is at Mur Castell, and would match with Brychan II son of Marchell and Enllech Coronog. The third grave recorded for Brychan is on the Calf of Man, which is the small island just south of the Isle of Man, and the Isle of Man was the territory of the family of Llywarch Hen. As Brychan III was a grandson of Llywarch Hen, this makes sense.

All that is happening is that the complaints that the ancient histories are confused are being dispelled, and instead it is the university employees who are confused and not the records. The old adage is 'A bad workman always blames his tools', and there is nothing wrong with our ancient British records, which are clear and precise. There is no doubt at all that the records do not match with the imaginary scenarios of Edwin Guest and Bishop Stubbs, and their adherents, but how can reality match the modern political and religious fantasy?

Arthur II

The story of 'King Arthur' really begins with the British Constantine the Great, for both Arthur I and Arthur II were his direct descendants. Constantine's first wife was Minerva by whom he had his eldest son Flavius Julius Crispus Caesar. In turn the young Crispus married Fausta and they had one son who was Magnus Clemens Maximus. Tragedy struck young Crispus and Fausta when Constantine the Great's second wife poisoned his mind, and he had his own eldest son and daughter-in-law murdered. The child Magnus Clemens Maximus, then an infant in his first year, was taken to Spain by his guardian the Spanish Christian Knight named Aelius Severus.

When grown to manhood Magnus Maximus first appeared on the stage of history with his acknowledged uncle, the Emperor Julian the Apostate, and by this time the extensive families of Constantine the Great and his brother Julius Constantius had succeeded in all but annihilating each other. Magnus must have removed himself earlier to his British patrimony where he married Ceindrech the daughter of Rheiden and had children.

If we take all the evidence that is available to us from the many sources it is possible to reconstruct the Family Tree of King Arthur I and King Arthur II. In the case of Arthur I, he was the eldest son of Magnus Maximus or Mascen Wledig. His mother was Ceindrech a daughter of Rheiden, the first wife of Magnus Maximus, and Arthur I had two brothers in Owain Vinddu and Ednyfed. All three brothers left many traceable descendants.

This would be the Arthur I, traditionally known to have been active in the Midlands, in Chester and up North to Carlisle, and across into North Wales. He would have been the King Arthur I who killed the Irish invader Reueth at Snowdon in AD 367. He would also have been the Arthur, who as the Latinised 'Andragathius' led the sixty-two thousand strong armies of Magnus Maximus across the Channel to invade Gaul in 383. That this 'King Arthur' besieged Paris in France is true, and he captured the city held by the Lady St Genevieve. This siege of Paris in AD 383 is commemorated in a carving at Modena Cathedral, which was made before the Arthurian Legends swept out of South Wales in around 1135, in the writing of *The History of the Kings of Britain* by Gruffydd ap Arthur. This same Arthur son of Magnus would be the King Arthur who defeated the massed armies of the Emperor Gratian at Soissons, 'the battle of Sassy', in AD 383. The victorious Arthur I pursued the pretender Gratian to Lugdunum-Lyons, where he executed him.

Arthur I, and his father Magnus Maximus, moved south through Switzerland and some Welsh writers thought that the pass of Arthur's Cat or Cat d'Arthur, is simply "cad" for "battle", so the Pass of Arthur's Battle. He seized Italy, and a mosaic in the Cathedral of Taranto, in Southern Italy, depicts Arthur I. He then moved his armies across into Greece and the Balkans, to meet the threat from Theodosius of Constantinople. Here he acquired the title King of Greece, as stated in British Manuscripts. In 388 two major battles were fought in what is now Yugoslavia, the first at Poetovio, and the second at Sisica on the Sica river. The outnumbered forces of Arthur I were defeated and he was forced to flee back to Britain. Tradition in Warwickshire held that he lived out his life in quiet. This is a simple synopsis of what occurred.

This History, including Arthur I son of Magnus Maximus, makes sense of the traditional records of a King Arthur holding court at Carlisle, and it explains the ancient corpus of Mediaeval poetry from the Midlands of England which tells of a King Arthur in the Midlands. In these poems Arthur is described as fighting abroad in Italy, at Milan to be precise, and of warring in Europe in general. In the Midlands regional folklore Arthur I became Guy of Warwick, or in Khumric terms simply "Gwyr o Caerwythelin". Gwyr is "the Man", and Caer is "Castle", and "Gwythelin" may be from Gwyth = wrathful, and Thelin apears to be a corruption of Teulu for "Military retinue".

That Guy of Warwick and Arthur I son of Magnus Maximus were identical was noted by Edward Lluyd writing around AD 1700, and this was noticed by Alan Wilson and Baram Blackett in 1994, long after they had made their own dual identifications. They were looking at a brief notice of the Lords of Coed y Mwstyr, made by Edward Lluyd, and saw that Lluyd also matched Guy of Warwick with Arthur I son of Magnus on the same pages. Lluyd also identified this prince as Arthur, and not as Andragathius. The ancient group of texts known as the Brecon Manuscripts are amongst many which clearly identify the Imperial Line in Britain in this particular era, and there can be no doubt about the message they carry.

These one-thousand-year-old Manuscripts of the Harleian MSS 4181 and British Museum Vespasian A.XIV, tell the story of the Princess Marchell, the daughter of Tewdrig son of King Teithfallt, being escorted by three hundred soldiers to a port in South East Wales, in the middle of the fighting which followed the Saxon revolt and the massacre at Caer Caradoc in Glamorgan. The Princess Marchell was a sister of the future King Meurig, the son of Tewdrig, and after three severe conflicts with roving bands of Saxons, she was put aboard a ship for Ireland at the Great Port at Cardiff. In Ireland Marchell was married to Enllech the Crowned son of Hydwn Dwn, son of Ceredig, son of Cuneda Wledig. King Ceredig was of course the ruler castigated by St Patrick for his harsh treatment of the Irish. A son named Brychan was later born in Ireland to the Queen Marchell and Enllech Coronog.

This marriage and the descents of Brychan and his own children figure prominently in these Manuscripts. In the section De Situ Brecheniauc, Part 10 the listing is-

> 'Hec est genealogia sancti Kynauc filii Brachan, Brachan filius Marchell, Marchell filia Teuderic, Teuderic filius Teudfall, Teudfall filius Tewder, (Tewder) filius Teudfal, Teudfal filius Annhun rex Grecorum.'

> "Here is the genealogy of Saint Kynauc son of Brychan, Brychan son of

Marchell, Marchell daughter of Tewdrig, Tewdrig son of Teithfallt, Teithfallt son of Teithrin, Teithrin son of Teudfal (Tathal), Teudfal son of Arthur I King of Greece."

The 'King of Greece' title clearly applies to Arthur I son of Magnus Maximus and his exploits in Greece and the Balkans in the war of AD 388 against Theodosius of Constantinople. In the Mabinogi of The Dream of Rhonabwy, there is an episode near the end of the Tale where men with twenty-four donkeys laden with treasure arrive bringing tribute to King Arthur from Greece.

In Ach Kynaus Sant" there is the same type of listing:
'Mam Vrachan oed Marchell, merch Tewdric, m. Teidfallt, m Teidtheyrn, m Thathal, m Annwn Du vrenhin Groce.'

The mother of Brychan was Marchell, the daughter of Tewdrig (Theoderic), son of Theithfallt (Theodosius), son of Teithrin (Theodorus), son of Tathal (Theodore), son of Arthur I, the Black, King of Greece."

A third listing appears in "Cognacio Brychan", and again there is the same type of descent.

It begins with: -
'Hee geneologia eius : Kynaucus filius Brachan, filii Anlach, (Enlech), filii Gornuc (Coronog = the Crowned), filii Eurbre (Eurbefr = (with) Bright Gold), of Hibernia (Ireland), et hoc ex parte patris.'

The matriarchal genealogy then follows: -
'Ex parte matris, Brichan filius Marchell, filie Teudric, filii Teithphal, filii Teithrin, filii Tathal, filii Annum nigri, regis Grecorum.'

'Enllech Crowned with Bright Gold of Hibernia' is not a genealogy but a specific identification.

So once more we finish up with *Arthur the Black* who has to be Arthur I son of Magnus Maximus, known to the Romans as Andragathius. Whichever way this is examined King Tewdrig, who was mortally wounded in AD 508 at Tintern in the Wye Valley, and buried at Mathern on the Gwent Coast, had a daughter named Marchell and a son named Meurig. This makes Brychan II of Garthmathrin (Brecon) a son of Queen Marchell, a first cousin of Arthur II son of King Meurig. This then is the simple answer to the supposed mystery of 'King Arthur', with two Kings who were both to become Arthur and welded into one gigantic figure.

The Llandaff Charters are peppered with references to King Meurig ap Tewdrig and his progeny as are the royal genealogies, the ancient poetry, the Triads, and a host of Manuscripts. Several hundred Welsh authors, between 1760 and 1920, all nominated Arthur son of Meurig son of Tewdrig, as the Arthur of Round Table legends. Some actually identified both Arthur I and Arthur II, but no one East of the Border over in England was ever prepared to listen.

The difficulty may have arisen with the Welsh 'ap' which can mean 'son of', and also 'the successor to''. If a son succeeded his father to the Throne, he was for example 'Hywel ap Rhys' - or 'Howell the son of Rhys'. If however a brother succeeded his sibling to the Throne the same 'ap' was used, as in 'Caradoc ap Caid' for Caradoc I successor to Caid ap Arch, his brother, and both were sons of Arch. In turn there was 'Ceri Longsword ap Caradoc', but Ceri was a son of Caid, and he succeeded his uncle Caradoc I. This brings in the matter of the infamous massacre at Caer Caradoc in *circa* AD 456 when the majority of the royal clan were murdered. King Teithfallt certainly succeeded the murdered Llywarch ap Cynan, and King Cynan ap Bran II, but he was neither son nor brother. The King lists might sometimes simply state 'Teithfallt ap Llywarch ap Cynan ap Bran, etc.', but this actually means 'Teithfallt the successor to Llywarch', and Teithfallt was the son of Teithrin, and descended directly from Arthur I son of Magnus Maximus.

There is no more to the Arthurian dilemma or mystery than this. Two Kings named Arthur meant that there were two graves to be sought for these Kings, just as the three Brychans required three graves, one in Wales, one on Man, and one in Brittany. It is a fact that once the person being traced is clearly identified into his family and correct chronological era, the tracking down of graves and habitations becomes very much easier.

The Politics of the Orwellian 1984 Nightmare

There are difficulties in researching and displaying the History of South East Wales that are unique to that area. These are the grotesque political and commercial offspring spawned by the falsifications of Bishop Stubbs, Edwin Guest, J.G. Evans, and the blind followers of these inventors. There is no History anywhere on planet Earth which has so many powerful enemies. This of course was unknown to Alan Wilson and Baram Blackett when they set out to write a few books on the strangely neglected History of the Welsh kings in their major territory of South East Wales.

The British Universities do not want these British Histories in any way shape or form because they are the unmistakeable proof and evidence of their past Institutional and individual wrongdoing and failures. The current generation of older academics do not want these histories as they themselves have signally failed to do anything to remedy an obviously catastrophic legacy from the eighteenth and nineteenth centuries. Academic and other pseudo-researchers are frightened of these historical truths, as their own fragile reputations and publications will be generally seen as ridiculous, and reputations will pop and crumble like balloons at a New Year's party.

The university employees close ranks and stand silently in a circle like a frightened herd of prehistoric musk oxen. As Americans would say they 'circled the wagons'. Silence is the major academic weapon in modern times as many frustrated researchers are discovering. The media and publishing worlds wrongly persist in interpreting these defensive silences as some form of superior knowledge or disproof. The truth is that not one university employee has ever accepted the challenge to civilized open public debate with Wilson and Blackett. Probably the spectre of the battering that the Bishop of Oxford received which he challenged the theories of Charles Darwin still haunts them. If they know more and know better, why then do they skulk in silence instead of publicly demolishing the upstarts? The truth is that the colleges have put themselves into a dead-end blind alley of unquestioning repetition. They only know what their own misguided tutors taught them, and what is written in the blundering books which line their library shelves. The books of their predecessors in the libraries are their arsenals; if the books are taken away as false, forged, faked, and just plain wrong, then they are stripped as bare as the naked Emperor whose non-existent and invisible clothes were made by the two Thieving Tailors.

The most virulent opposition to any approach to ancient Welsh History came out from the University of Wales. As John Dudley Jones, the then Manager of the Welsh Book Council Warehouse, situated just outside Aberystwyth, said to Wilson and Blackett: "I could sell four times as many of your books than I do, if it were not for the opposition coming out of Aberystwyth University." In 1986, one academic from Bangor University and another from Cardiff, actually wrote disgraceful libellous 'confidential' letters on University headed paper, to local councils in Wales, which falsely alleged that Alan Wilson and Baram Blackett were awaiting trial in the Criminal Courts on unspecified charges. These were widely distributed.

All totally untrue, and in response Wilson and Blackett wrote to the University Chancellor, Prince Charles, who passed the matter to his vice-Chancellor, who passed on this hot-potato by stating that these were matters for the individual colleges. So, Alan and Baram wrote to the College Principals at Cardiff and Bangor, and were told that these were not College matters, but instead they were matters for the individuals concerned. This made the combat more equal and Alan and Baram began Court proceedings against Dr N. Edwards of Bangor University. The immediate result was that the University of Wales did a standing somersault and their lawyers stepped in and Alan and Baram were faced with an enormously wealthy and very corrupt institution, with millions of Public Funds at its disposal, in the prohibitively expensive English Courts.

Life is strange however, and in 1988 Mrs Margaret Thatcher, then Prime Minister, demanded the resignation of the principal and the entire Senate of the

University College of Cardiff. They refused to resign and Mrs Thatcher bluntly told them that she would close down the entire twelve thousand student college completely if they did not resign. The excuse was that over £20,000,000 had gone missing from college funds. This extraordinary saga got banner headlines locally in South Wales, and was totally ignored in the London-British national press. All sorts of rumours circulated and it emerged that loans were granted by college staff to each other, with no interest charged and no schedule of repayments laid down.

Cardiff University employees had a massive dislike of Arthurian Research in South East Wales and of this there is no doubt. In the 1930's, the archaeologist Mortimer Wheeler was at the College and he was for many years later the great panjandrum or guru of the archaeology trade in Britain as 'Sir Mortimer'. Just around the time of the outbreak of World War II, he was digging up the ancient city of Mohenjo Daro, in the Indus Valley. A young Second Lieutenant in the Indian Army heard of the excavations and took three weeks' leave, and rode over to the site on his pony. This was Leslie Alcock, who after the end of the war in 1945 appeared at Cardiff University on the strength of his 'experience' at Mohenjo Daro with the great Sir Mortimer.

The publicly-funded Welsh Book Council publishes a quarterly magazine in which it is obliged to review all books published in Wales. Predictably this North Wales-based quango declined to publish any reviews of Wilson and Blackett's first three books. This absurd stance was challenged and an alleged review of the fourth book was printed. As anticipated, this was written by a seventy-two year old retired academic from Aberystwyth College in the North, who had a reputation for frustrated sarcasm and offensive wit. He simply wrote a vile personal attack upon Alan Wilson and Baram Blackett, and made only one comment on the book, that was factually incorrect, untrue, and designed to be damaging. So, Wilson and Blackett commenced legal proceedings for Libel and Defamation against the Welsh Book Council, who immediately backed down and apologised, and offered equal space for a review in their next issue. This was of no value as the damage had already been done.

The Taffia Mafia mob are very tightly knit bunch in Wales, and they are confident of their own mutual protection. They do 'gang up' against any outsider or any perceived threat to their monopoly and control of huge amounts of cash in Government Grants and Public Funds. The National Library of Wales is also staffed by the same breed, and again it is located as far away as is possible from the majority population of Wales. Some 90 % of the Welsh live in Glamorgan and Gwent in the South East, and so the National Library is placed one hundred and forty miles away, out in the sticks in the tiny village of Aberystwyth (population around five thousand.) It is like the French putting their library in Monte Carlo

Chapter 9 - The Arthurian Dynasty

instead of Paris, or the English locating their Library out of London and putting it in Land's End in Cornwall where as few people as possible could get at it. Alan Wilson wrote five times to try to get certain information from the Welsh National Library, and he even sent stamped self-addressed envelopes three times, but never ever got an answer.

The Church of Rome does not want these British Histories, which it acknowledges but not too loudly or too often, because Western Christianity originated in Britain in AD 35-37 and not in Rome. The Church of England, the rudderless splinter of the Church of Rome, does not want these Histories because they preach the arrival of Christianity in England with Austin in AD 597 some 560 years later, and try to pretend that the truth is not the truth. These are powerful opposing influences.

The London Government does not want these Histories because they are the major villains of the piece. The London Parliament committed "the treachery of the Blue Books" in 1846 and passed an Act that deliberately destroyed the entire Welsh schools system.

In Wales a very rich English businessman collected politicians. Julian Hodge recruited James Callaghan, an Englishman who was successively Home Secretary, Foreign Secretary, Chancellor, and Prime Minister, and also George Thomas - Bible George - who was Secretary of State for Wales and then Speaker of the House of Commons, as Directors of his Bank of Wales. They also indulged in land acquisition, and by a most remarkable coincidence when the Labour Government decided to build a new modem Royal Mint, the only suitable location for this vast enterprise was on poor quality land owned by their company at Llantrisant in South East Wales. Various Government departments and offices were located in Cardiff buildings owned by Hodge.

Most important however was the Ryan company set up by Hodge to remove coal tips which littered Wales, and to recover the large percentages of useable coal discarded in the frantic hey-day of early nineteenth-century anthracite production. This however was a finite business for when there are no more suitable coal rich slag tips left, then business is at an end. This came in the early 1980's, and surprisingly Ryan, with near worthless shares, was purchased by South African Open Cast Coal Mining interests. The company bought Crouch Open Cast Mining, and another major politician was recruited as a director in the then Secretary of State for Wales, Nicholas Edwards.

So suddenly Alan Wilson and Baram Blackett found themselves in a major political war zone in the mid 1980's. The plan was very clear, and the London Government intended to smash the Miners Unions with their power base in the deep shaft mines. Deep coal production was to be replaced with the dirty anti social Open Cast mining techniques. Caught in the middle of what proved to be a very bitter and nasty social and political struggle, Wilson and Blackett found themselves publicising scores of immensely important Welsh Historical cultural heritage sites all across vast coalfields earmarked for Open Cast Mining by the Government of the day and its business adherents.

Nicholas Edwards set up CADW, ostensibly 'Welsh Heritage', but whereas English Heritage is directed and run by English persons, and Irish and Scottish Heritage by Irish and Scots persons respectively, Welsh Heritage was directed and manned by English people. In the same way the National Museum of Wales and numerous other Welsh agencies were all English Directed. The CADW Quango immediately usurped the Statutory Authority of the Royal Commission for Ancient Monuments in Wales, and also announced the policy of 'Your Industrial Heritage', which in effect means that South East Wales is prevented from having any History before AD 1760. All that is allowed are the ruined archaeological sites of iron works, canals, mills, coal mines, and so on. South East Wales with a magnificent provable history almost unparalleled in Western Europe set back to at least 504 BC is alleged not to have any Ancient History.

A business and political group formed a company that bought near useless land in South East Wales, and lo and behold, when the Government decided to relocate the massive Royal Mint out of its overcrowded site in London, the only place to relocate the Royal Mint was right on the useless land bought by this company. Later James Callaghan and Bible George Thomas got up in the House of Commons very late one night amidst a small group of supporters, and apologised to the House over this farce. Once the apology was accepted it meant that the matter could never again be debated in the House of Commons.

Not every battle was lost and casualties were inflicted on the enemy. The Cold War however remains unresolved. Why did Nicholas Edwards resign at the pinnacle of his political career? Was it because he announced a government-funded drive of £500 million to revitalise much of South East Wales to be 'spearheaded' by the Ryan Open Cast Coal company of which he was a director? Well, it may be that the letters sent to the Prime Minister and others concerning his activities had some effect. Why did the Chief Constable of South Wales, David East, suddenly resign with five years still to run on his contract? Well, maybe the letters sprayed around by an enraged Alan Wilson and Baram Blackett had some effect.

There is an almost hilarious side to Taffia antics. In one case John Evans, a resident of Blaenavon, took an interest in the history of the defunct Blaenavon Ironworks. He studied and he delved; he collected plans and photographs, and compiled notes. He made some of this available for an exhibition in the Ebbw Vale library. This was then seen by an English employee of the Royal Commission for

Chapter 9 - The Arthurian Dynasty

Ancient Monuments in Wales and a by CADW employee. Recognising that this fitted the Nicholas Edwards dictat of "Your Industrial Heritage", and that life in Wales began around AD 1760, they took these exhibits without consulting the owner, and set up a larger, better-funded exhibition. Next there was an archaeological excavation at the Blaenavon Ironworks, and John Evans was one of the locals employed as labour in this area of high unemployment. During this work, the archaeologists decided to demolish a certain structure that they thought was relatively modern and of no importance, but John Evans argued and showed it was original and important. This made the archaeologists angry and so they sacked the real expert. The other casual workers then went on strike and picketed this archaeological site. This caused the sponsoring body to demand an explanation, and the archaeologists then claimed that John Evans had been sacked for a breach of the Official Secrets Act.

Again, as usual, the British media failed to pick up on the Pickwickian absurdity of casual workers on strike and picketing an archaeological dig, and the totally hilarious claim by the archaeologists that there was a breach of the Official Secrets Act.

Another Taffia piece of buffoonery took place at the 1986 British Tourist Exhibition at Olympia in London. Councillor Clayton Jones of Mid-Glamorgan County Council had taken a keen interest in Wilson and Blackett's researches, and it took no time at all for this Taffia-wise politician to discover that a hatchet job was going on. Clayton owned a Bus company and a Travel Agency, and he set up a King Arthur Company with Wilson and Blackett to attempt to promote Tourism based on their discoveries. So, this Company hired space - a table, four chairs, and racks for promotional literature - on the Wales Tourist Board stand at the 1986 Olympia exhibition. CADW agreed to assist in financing Clayton's promotional brochures on the strange condition that the names King Arthur, Alan Wilson, and Baram Blackett, did not appear anywhere. Nor were any photographs of Welsh Arthurian sites to be shown in this promotion of the real Welsh King Arthur.

The routine was for all exhibitors to deliver their packs of printed literature to the Wales Tourist Board in Cardiff, and for the whole lot to be taken in a truck to the Olympia exhibition halls. Early on the morning of the opening day of the show, Clayton Jones, Alan Wilson, Baram Blackett, Gerald Edwards (a Taff Ely Borough Councillor) and Michael Blackett, all set off from their Bayswater hotel for Olympia.

The large Welsh Tourist Board stand had a dummy Welsh cottage in the centre that was the office. All promotional literature was delivered to the Wales Tourist Board Offices in Cardiff and transported to the Olympia site in a truck. These brochures sent up from Cardiff were securely locked inside, and when Tourist Board Staff arrived everyone got their literature. Well, not everyone, as surprise, surprise, the Clayton Jones, Wilson, and Blackett, brochures were missing. A miracle had occurred at the Olympia Halls, and four large heavy brown paper wrapped parcels had got up and had succeeded in escaping from a securely locked office.

Frantic telephone calls made by Clayton to the Tourist Board in Cardiff got absolutely nowhere, as only the cleaners were there, and everyone else was up at Olympia for a week of bingeing. Alan Wilson is streetwise on the Taffia however, and it was past 9.30 a.m., and so he stood back from the turmoil and watched as the hundreds of various workmen cut and hammered and banged on the rows of stands, making the last hours rush to have the exhibition read for the 10 a.m. official opening. There were several large waste-material skips in the area, and trucks were starting to lift and remove these huge metal bins filled with off-cuts of timber, boards, fabrics, and so on. One large skip stood full on the far side of the Wales Tourist Board stand.

Alan Wilson walked over to the full skip and started to pull out the larger pieces of débris that had been thrown into the skip. When he had enough space Alan climbed into the skip and threw out everything he could. Amazed onlookers stopped to watch this well-dressed man emptying the skip. Alan paused for a moment and saw Clayton, Baram, Gerald, and Michael, watching him in wonderment, and he also saw four very anxious and worried Tourist Board employees looking out through the windows of their little Cottage office. There, deep down in the bottom of the rubbish skip, were the four neatly wrapped heavy brown paper parcels that had somehow escaped from the securely locked Wales Tourist Board office on their Olympia exhibition stand. Alan called the others over and they heaved the parcels out, while an irritated truck driver arrived to try to remove a half empty skip surrounded by a pile of rubbish.

Clayton, Gerald, Baram, and Michael, began hastily stacking the racks on the stand with brochures whilst Alan tried to brush himself down. When you are in deep trouble, it is sometimes best to attack. It was no surprise when a large, dark-haired, bearded man emerged from the Wales Tourist Board office and marched over to Clayton Jones. This individual turned out to be the British Sales Manager of the Wales Tourist Board, and he glared at Clayton, and said loudly: "I'll give you two minutes to get these two off this stand or I will throw them off", gesturing towards Alan and Baram. So Alan said: "If you want to throw me off, come and try it." The bearded one then retreated back inside the office and locked the door. Actually, Alan Wilson and Baram Blackett were directors of the King Arthur Company set up by Clayton Jones and they had every right to be on the space that their company had hired.

Alan Wilson later wrote to the Chairman of the Wales Tourist Board, one Gordon Parry, to complain about this affair, and predictably nothing happened.

Chapter 9 - The Arthurian Dynasty

Gordon Parry was famous as standing for Parliamentary election three times in a row as the Labour candidate in a safe Labour seat, and losing every time. The Party rewarded the political unpopularity of this journalist by making him Chairman of the Wales Tourist Board.

The stories of Taffia Mafia-dominated Quangoland would fill a large volume, and would make Lewis Carroll's *Alice in Wonderland* appear as a dry- as-dust tome on economic policies, and as this is a serious book these few illustrations must suffice.

The dirty tricks campaigns conducted against Alan Wilson and Baram Blackett are too sordid to detail here. The plain truth is that it is unwise to do anything that might in any way obstruct the plans and intentions of Big Business in South East Wales. This may he illustrated by the fact that a long criminal record was forged in the name and address of Alan Wilson, and placed on the Cardiff Police Computer. This supposedly confidential bogus record was then widely disseminated throughout Wales, causing huge damage to the Arthurian Research Projects. This certainly began in 1981, but it was not proved until 1990 when an English Police Force discovered this vicious fraud. Needless to say, Alan Wilson has never ever been convicted of any crime in any court, anywhere. A similar attack was made upon Baram Blackett and his brother, which would result in jail sentences for several police officers in any civilized society.

Another sordid matter occurred when Alan Wilson and Baram Blackett laid evidence against named persons before the Cardiff Police Fraud Squad. Predictably the Crown Prosecution Service refused to take any action. The Files then vanished from the Rumney Cardiff Police Station, and resurfaced in Bridgend some twenty-five miles away. Here a travesty of a summary report was written by a Senior Police Officer that alleged that Alan Wilson and Baram Blackett (who made complaint), had been the persons investigated, and that there was insufficient evidence to proceed against them. The complaint was stood on its head and turned around against the innocent injured complainants.

These are but a few of the multitude of nefarious activities practised to destroy the Arthurian Research Project. As a finale to this brief excursion into the perils of trying to do anything constructive in Quango-land there is a tale of a Fax. Frightened employees of the University of Wales have been responsible for a great deal of the harm inflicted on the Arthurian Research Project, and they seem to know no moral limit to their illegitimate activities. In late 1998 a newspaper features writer wrote an article in which he commented favourably on the work of Wilson and Blackett. The day after the article appeared in the press, an anonymous Fax slid out of his Fax machine onto his desk. This unsigned Fax was a libel that Alan Wilson was a criminal. Fortunately, the newspaper writer knew Alan Wilson and Baram Blackett. Now letters may be anonymous, but Fax machines are not, and all have identification numbers. The newspaper had very little trouble in tracing the Fax machine used to send this libel to an office in the University College of Cardiff. As a graduate of the University Alan Wilson wrote to the College Principal, Sir Brian Smith, who did not respond.

Chapter Ten

The Myth of Celtic and Roman Britain

In order even to begin to understand ancient British history it is first necessary to slay some fearful dragons that terrorise and bewilder the academic mind. The myth of the dragon of the Celts and the myth of the Roman dragon must be put down.

Without even a cursory examination of any of the evidence available British university employees routinely propound that the ancient Welsh, the Scots, and even the Irish were Celts. In 1994 Professor John Collis, of the Sheffield University Archaeology Department, spoke at a Conference on 'Celts in Europe' in Cardiff, and stated that none of these people were Celts, which is precisely what Alan Wilson and Baram Blackett have been saying for many years.

'There is a widespread assumption that in the Iron Age, much of northern and central Europe was occupied by the Celts. It is assumed that they shared a culture, and were a people.

'It is also widely assumed that today remnants of this ancient Celtic people survive in the modern societies of Scotland, Ireland, Wales, and Brittany.

'These assumptions are flawed in every respect. There were no pan-European Celtic people. There was no broad-based Celtic art, society, or religion. And there never were any Celts in Britain.'

A brief correspondence with Professor Collis brought his expressions of regret that he had broached the subject, as it had proved to be extremely unpopular news to other university employees. Wilson and Blackett could well imagine how this revelation of truth must have shaken their revered creeds and dogmas of the static, moribund, and stagnant religion of archaeology to its very foundations. Fortunately, Professor Collis persisted and published a book in 1999.

In December of 1993 Collins said:

'No ancient author ever referred to the inhabitants of Britain - the Brittani - as Celts. It was not until the eighteenth century that the term was applied to Britain, and then it was used to denote a group of languages spoken in western Britain and Brittany.

Then later in his lecture he stated:

'... by the nineteenth century the concept of the "national Celts" was well developed and applied to Britain. This extension is confused and illogical, and brings us into direct conflict with the ancient sources.'

As is being demonstrated in this volume, to identify the British-Khumry as 'Celts' is both confused and illogical, and as Professor Collis put it:

'The archaeological basis for claiming a cross-European Celtic society is equally illogical. Indeed, the whole notion of an archaeological "culture" defined by material remains is, in my view, flawed.'

The ideology of a pan-Celtic ancient Europe is nothing more than an ill-founded and baseless theory. Where ancient artefacts - pots, swords, and whatever - have been discovered in one area and carelessly labelled as being of 'Celtic' origin, these items have then been matched and related to similar ancient artefacts found in diverse areas all across Europe, and the whole corpus of material has been branded as 'Celtic.' From this loose classification procedure, it has then been theorised that all the various people who owned these ancient artefacts scattered right across Europe were all therefore 'Celtic'.

It boils down to the completely different objectives of archaeologists and the historians, and their totally different mental approaches to the same situations. Gordon Childe is quoted by Professor Collis to illustrate this:

'We find certain types of remains - pots, implements, ornaments, burial rites, house forms - constantly recurring together. Such a complex of regularly associated traits we shall term a "cultural group" or just a "culture". We assume that such a complex is the material expression of what today would be called a people.'

This is the core of the matter, an <u>assumed</u> homogeneity of ancient peoples, through a process of arbitrary selection of objects. Professor Collis went on:

Chapter 10 - The Myth of Celtic and Roman Britain

'The theories of Celtic expansion are accepted dogma on the continent. Yet the whole methodology is suspect...' and '...The extent to which cultures *can* be interpreted ethnically has never been adequately discussed in this context."

While this slow, grinding process of years wasted in breaking down the barriers of intransigence went on there were episodes of hilarity to lighten the gloom. Clayton Jones, who had backed Wilson and Blackett in the tourism venture at Olympia, had now become a target. In true Taffia fashion the bus routes operated by Clayton Jones in the South Wales Valleys came under attack. It is only a slight exaggeration to say that every bus owned by Clayton Jones was constantly boarded by inspectors on almost every run as his business came under attack. Clayton was reluctantly forced to draw clear of Wilson and Blackett in the same way as two experienced television people and two press reporters had been forced to as their jobs were threatened. The Taffia onslaught brought problems however, and eventually there was a court action against Clayton's business operation.

Clayton Jones, who was a county councillor and businessman, and is a very well-known figure in the Pontypridd area, marched down the street to the court wearing only a white shirt wide open to the waist, black trousers with the right leg rolled up above the knee, shoes, and the apron of a Master Freemason. He is not a Freemason, but the attire was the ridiculous garb of a Novice Freemason at initiation, and Clayton was making a very clear anti Taffia-Mafia statement. The photographs duly appeared in the Press and Clayton won his case as the Taffia retreated.

In May of 1999, Dr Simon James, of the Durham University Archaeology Department, published a book *The Atlantic Celts* - sub-titled *Ancient People or Modern Invention?* Again, he like Professor John Collis was breaking ranks and stated that "British history needs to be re-written". Again, he places the origin of the strange idea of the Welsh, Scots, and Irish being Celts and Celtic into the eighteenth century, and attributes the birth of this crude deformation of British history to Edward Lhuyd in 1707. It does not alter the fact that Alan Wilson and Baram Blackett have been viciously abused for twenty years for making these same comments, and perhaps there is a crack in the Iron Curtain of ignorance.

Like other archaeologists, Dr Simon James totally fails to appreciate that there is no need to invent a new hypothesis for the scenario and structure of ancient British history as he proposes. By inventing a new hypothesis, he is simply replacing one incorrect imaginative ideology with another. He fails to understand that we already have our own real accurate British history, and we have no need of alternative speculation to replace that British history.

The idiotic dogma of an ancient pan-Celtic Europe is not confined to the European continent, for like any other plague it has spread to become an article of faith amongst the members of the archaeological religion in America. It is this absurdly pathetic and amateur assumption that the Khumry 'Welsh' are Celts and Celtic, which bedevils and obstructs all intelligent efforts to research the ancient history and origins of the British peoples. It acts as a well-guarded Iron Curtain to obstruct any clear view of our priceless histories.

The Myth of the Romans

The second blight which obscures our British histories is of the same breed as the 'Celtic Dragon' which never was. Again, both archaeologists and historians are prone to make sweeping, generalised un-researched statements. It was once popular to conform by writing of an illusory four-hundred-and-fifty-year Roman occupation of Britain. Now it has become popular to conform by citing an alleged four hundred-years' period of Roman domination and occupation of Britain. Not true, and contrary to the recorded facts and evidence. In fact, to speak of 'Roman Britain' is as inaccurate as describing the British as 'Celts'.

If we summarise the facts, we find Julius Caesar invading Britain in 55 BC and being forced to evacuate. He came back in 54 BC and was totally defeated. The Caswallon allowed Caesar to march inland virtually unopposed, and to cross the Thames and to move northwards towards the Midlands. Unfortunately for Julius Caesar the British had evacuated all their people, and their flocks and herds, ahead of his advance, and left his army nothing to eat. The Caswallon confidently disbanded most of his army and sent them off to winter quarters, whilst keeping only four thousand chariots with which to harass and prevent the Roman foraging parties from Caesar's forty thousand-strong army from gathering any food.

Then Julius Caesar, stranded and starving up in the Midlands, got the really bad news that a British army was attacking his base where his ships had landed his army, and another British army was moving to block his passage back across the Thames. It all ended up in an early version of Napoleon's retreat from Moscow, with a British army 'escorting' Julius Caesar and his rabble back to their ships. In his own account in *De Bello Gallico*, Caesar tells of the scramble to get aboard with each ship carrying three times the normal number of soldiers. So much for Julius Caesar's 'conquest' of Britain. Even this clear Roman humiliation is given an extraordinary explanation, as it is claimed that the British army which surrounded Caesar and escorted him back to his ships in great haste where his soldiers tumbled aboard in disarray with three times as many men per ship as would be normal, was performing a servile ceremonial escort duty.

The second invasion, in the time of Claudius, was much more carefully planned, and it was assisted by the initial refusal of the legions to board their ships in Gaul. The British army got tired of waiting, and concluded that the Romans, as with Caligula, were not coming, and they dispersed to their homes. When the Romans did finally sail, they arrived almost unopposed. They brought elephants, the smell of which rendered the horses of the British cavalry and chariot armies unmanageable, and so began the piecemeal occupation of Britain. Some of the peoples along the south-east coast were non-British Belgic tribes and the Romans profited from their disaffection.

Without going into the unnecessary detail of the subsequent wars, we can summarise that King Caradoc I ap Arch led the British opposition to Rome for nine years, from AD 42-51. Tacitus records that of eighty battles with his Trojan 'Silures' the British won sixty. A whole legion was obliterated fighting the Southern Khumry and a similar fate befell another legion in what is now Lancashire. Finally, the Romans got their longed-for big battle, and here there is a problem as the Romans claimed that they won, and the Southern Khumry claimed that they won. All the evidence points to a British victory, or at worst a drawn battle. The Romans having celebrated the triumphs of the conquest of Britain in AD 43 could hardly admit that they were losing the on-going war in AD 51. It is not surprising that no one has ever questioned or challenged Roman claims, which are obviously flawed.

What is fact is that King Caradoc I ap Arch went north to Aregwedd Voedawg, *alias* Cartismandua, the Queen of the Brigantes, to try to persuade her to join in the fighting against the Romans. He would hardly have done this if he had lost the AD 51 battle. Aregwedd Voedawg, however, earned herself undying infamy in Britain by seizing Caradoc and handing him over to the Romans in chains. It is also a fact the Romans were unable to penetrate the south Khumry territory after the AD 51 battle, where they claimed victory, and where King Ceri Longsword, the nephew of Caradoc I, ruled. Not until twenty-three years later in AD 74 were the Romans able to penetrate this supposedly 'conquered' area.

So, there was a partial conquest of some southern and eastern areas of Britain. In the truce in the period around AD 44, Claudius adopted King Caradoc's daughter Eurgain, and she had married a relative of Claudius, Rufus Pudens. A sister of Caradoc I had then married Aulus Plautius, the Roman governor of southern Britain, and it is difficult to imagine these imperial intermarriages if the British were even one tenth as primitive as Edwin Guest and Bishop Stubbs and their adherents would have us believe. Boudicca's rising of AD 56 and the rapid slaughter of some hundred-thousand Romans saw the beginning of new and different policies in Britain as the Romans finally realised how precarious and dangerous their position in Britain actually was.

Then in AD 80 the Romans record that 'Bonassus usurped the Empire in Britain', which means that Bonassus threw the Romans out of Britain. The Romans remained ejected from Britain for thirty-four years. One would think this should be a major point of interest to historians, but not so, for dogma demands worship of the barbaric Roman aliens. No one even asks the question, who was Bonassus? To do so would raise the spectre of the British kings in south-east Wales, for Bonassus was King Baram the son of Ceri Longsword. The last Roman governor of south-east Britain was Sallustus, and he was executed by Domitian around AD 80. After Sallustus there are no Roman officials recorded for Britain for over thirty-four years, proving that once again the British kings ruled independently, and matching British historical records of independence in this period.

Roman records prove that their new policy, even before their ejection in AD 80, was to persuade the British kings and princes to use their own wealth to build Roman-style towns, markets, villas, temples, and forums, and to continue to trade with Romans. The value of the cross-Channel trade in the ancient Bronze Age, the Iron Age, and in Roman times has been underestimated, and the Romans saw the value of controlling this lucrative trade on the Continental side at least. If they could hold both sides of the Channel by controlling south-east Britain, they might in fact tax both exports and imports.

The situation was similar to that of our own times, with the western nations building palaces, houses, hotels complexes, and so on for the Saudi Arabian oil magnates, and trading with them for their oil. The buildings may be western designed and built, but the Eastern peoples own then and live in them. The Roman armies massed along the Rhine needed grain, corn, leather, metals, woollen cloth, horses, cattle, and sheep, and Britain could supply these.

It was not until the diplomatic visit of Hadrian to Britain in AD 124 that an accord was reached with the British, and it certainly was not a conquest. It was the forging of trading agreements, which brought Britain back towards the Roman orbit. It is also a fact that intermarriages of the Claudian period had placed the British royalty in the position of carrying the Imperial blood- line, and Hadrian had no heirs. So, by AD 124 the false notion of four hundred years of 'Roman Britain' is demolished. Hadrian did not build a wall across northern Britain. He built a

Chapter 10 - The Myth of Celtic and Roman Britain

string of forts connected by a road, and for much of the way the road was fronted by an earth bank and ditch. Septimus Severus built the wall around AD 210 in very different political circumstances.

Is it an accident that the paramount or senior British king dwelt in Glamorgan along the banks of the Severn? Is it an accident that Cardiff, where the fortress was founded in AD 74, is properly Caer Dydd, and the archaic meaning of Dydd is 'agreement'? Might it not be that it was here that the agreement was struck between the British king and Hadrian, at the 'Castle of the Agreement'?

Next there is a statistical phenomenon. All the Roman emperors from Hadrian's death in AD 138 until AD 235 are close matches with leading British princes: the same names, and the same characteristics. Old British king or prince - old Roman emperor; young prince - young emperor; violent prince - violent emperor; religiously inclined scholar prince - religiously inclined scholar emperor; good prince - good emperor; cruel sadist prince - cruel sadist emperor. Successions of father to son, or uncles to nephews, and so on, can also be matched. If, however, the unsubstantiated dictates of Edwin Guest, Bishop Stubbs, J. Gwenogfran Evans, and their ilk are followed, then the records have to be ignored, and there were no British kings and princes, and so this comparison cannot be made. All the ancient records, and the ancient memorial stones and named grave mounds become meaningless.

The question is whether, in order to persuade the powerful British state and its stable lines of rulers to enter the Roman Empire, a deal was struck. The Romans got Britain into their vast imperial trading consortium, for that is all that it was, and in return the British gave to Hadrian and the Empire with the much-needed legitimate emperors. It is a remarkable fact that in the fifty-one-year period from AD 235 to 286 there were no fewer than nineteen short-lived usurping non-British emperors. There was chaos in the Roman Empire, which effectively collapsed. Also, right through this period Britain remained outside the Roman Empire, and for that era Britain was part of a separate Western Empire of Britain, Gaul, and Spain. Tombstones of some of the more prominent of these Western Emperors have been found near grave mounds in South Wales, which anywhere else would be regarded as evidence.

The murder of the British Emperor Carausius - King Carawn, in 293, who had for many years ruled Britain and most of Gaul independently and then as equal imperial co-partner with the Emperors Diocletian and Maximinus from 283, saw the beginning of a short-lived reunification with Rome. The new Western Emperor living in Britain from AD 296-306, was Constantius Chlorus, the husband of the British Queen Helen of the Cross. Their son, Constantine the Great, re-established British rule over the entire empire, and made himself head of the entire Christian Church which he formally legitimised in Rome and Constantinople. Constantine was a British Apostolic Church Christian, and he therefore believed that God used the Sun as a dwelling place. The Sun was not God, but the Sun was the home of God.

Britain again split off from the Roman Empire when Constantine left to conquer the rest of the Roman world. King Euddaf-Octavius, a grandson of the Western Emperor Victorinus, fought a war from AD 310 to 322 and finally defeated and ejected Constantine the Great's lieutenants from Britain. Once again, Britain was independent under King Euddaf from 322 until 367, and these are the facts. After this there was a brief excursion into Britain by the general Theodosius, and then Britain was off and away again under the next of the British Imperial line in Mascen Wledig, or Magnus Maximus the son of Crispus, the eldest son of Constantine the Great.

Magnus Maximus and his son Arthur I - Andragathius invaded Gaul in 383 and seized the entire Western Empire, until 388. Then there was another brief Roman foray into Britain, before independence was again established. The British elected three kings in rapid succession, and in 406 Constantine Coronog 'the Crowned' (whose genealogy is well attested) and the British army invaded Gaul and held it, threatening Honorius in Rome until 411. Quite obviously the election of Constantine Coronog to be King in 406, after Arthur I son of Magnus Maximus, gave rise to the mediaeval notion that after the death of 'King Arthur' his cousin Constantine became King.

This brings us to the crowning glory of duplicity and invented history. In Rome the beleaguered Honorius was unable to prevent the German King Alaric from ravaging Italy, as Alaric and his hordes moved southwards towards Sicily, Honorius then wrote a letter to the citizens of Rhegium, the local capital of the region of Brittium, on the toe of Italy opposite the Straits of Messina. In his letter Honorius advised these Italian citizens of Rhegium in Brittium that he could offer them no aid against Alaric.

In an astonishing piece of effrontery and trickery the anti-British academics have time and again claimed that this letter of 411 was sent to the allegedly helpless British in Britain, 'allowing' these allegedly weak and primitive British to go their own way without the friendly protection of Rome. So, at the same time that powerful British armies had once again seized Western Europe in 406-411, and had totally defeated the confederation of German Vandals, Sueves, and Alans

Chapter 10 - The Myth of Celtic and Roman Britain

which had over-run the weak Romans in Gaul, their sworn enemy Honorius is exhibited as being no longer able to protect these same British. In fact, the British general Geraint, who blocked the passes of the Pyrenees, set up his own puppet emperor in a rage against King Constantine the Crowned, because of his indolence in not moving to attack and destroy Honorius.

It is hilarious that with King Constantine III sitting in Trèves in France, and controlling all Britain, France, and Spain after having defeated the Vandals, Sueves, and Alans, to keep them away from the Channel and Britain, that Honorius cowering in Rome should be allowed to write a letter to the British telling them that he could no longer defend them.

The academics in Britain stand utterly condemned for this duplicity in lying wholesale to the British nation. The letter went to the city of Rhegium in Brittium in the far south of Italy and not to the powerful and independent people of Britain.

In short, the periods of Roman control over parts of Britain were brief, and the theory of four hundred years of 'Roman Britain' is an illusion. There is, therefore, a total confrontation between the facts as recorded, known, and provable, and the ridiculous academic theories relating to Britain. In recent years the rapid expansion of progress made in identification of ancient sites in Britain has forced them to move from a position of postulating the population of ancient Britain to have been around five hundred thousand, to a revised estimate of around ten million, which should give some indication of their capability, and their reliability, or perhaps more correctly their lack of ability and their inaccuracy. They even ignored Julius Caesar, who stated that Britain's population was huge.

Magnus Maximus is routinely misrepresented as (a) a usurper, and (b) as Spanish. In fact, he was neither. The reign of the Emperor Julian the Apostate, the last surviving son of Julius Constantius, the brother of Constantine the Great, which saw the restoration of the old gods of Rome, had shaken and alarmed the newly legitimised Christian Church in Rome. The reaction was quickly to set up a confirmed Christian emperor in the totally illegitimate Jovian son of Varrovian, when Julian died in 364. The legitimate heir to the empire was Magnus Maximus, the only son of Flavius Julius Crispus Caesar, the eldest son of Constantine the Great. As a baby, Magnus Maximus had been hurriedly taken to Spain by the Spanish knight Severus Aelius in 326, when his parents were murdered through the machinations of Fausta, anxious second wife of Constantine the Great.

The illegitimate Jovian died in 364, and was followed by his equally illegitimate nephew Flavius Valentinianus I. When Magnus Maximus and his British family invaded Gaul in 383 to fight Gratian the son of Flavius Valentinianus, it was Gratian who was the illegitimate Emperor of Rome, and not Magnus Clemens Flavius Maximus, who was clearly the rightful heir as the son of Crispus, the eldest son of Constantine the Great.

The university theorists have been looking through the wrong end of the historical telescope, and minimising and distorting the British past beyond all recognition. Some are guilty of looking through the wrong end of the telescope with a Nelsonian blind eye. There is no need for the university employees of today to inhabit the ramshackle, deluded and unsafe theoretical edifices of the previous centuries. A detailed History of Britain in the era is written and will be published.

Dating by guesswork

It cannot be overestimated and overstated that all those who seek to discover the truth of ancient British history find themselves hostages and prisoners of the centuries'-long cold war of embittered politics and bigoted religious strife which distorts the entire scenario. The racist and religious politics of the past pollute the atmosphere of rational logical research in every quarter, and make reasoned argument and debate virtually impossible.

Solutions to problems are only acceptable in academic quarters if they are the required politically correct solutions. Alan Wilson often tells the story of the academic at a seaside resort in stormy weather, who was washed from the promenade by huge wave. A passer-by saw him struggling in the storm-tossed water, and as he went beneath the waves, the would-be rescuer rushed to throw a bright yellow lifebelt to him. Despite being in great danger of drowning, the academic made no attempt to take hold of the yellow lifebelt as he sank. The drowning academic resurfaced and despite pleas he made no attempt to take hold of the yellow lifebelt as he again sank. Finally, as he surfaced and began sinking for the third time, the rescuer cried out : "Why don't you save yourself and grab the yellow lIfebelt?" And Just as he drowned the academic shouted back: "I want a blue one."

This encapsulates what is happening, and the attitudes which all patient detailed research encounters. In 1973 Professor John Morris wrote a thick book titled *The Age of Arthur*. The title appears to include the magic name of 'Arthur' as a sales draw or bait, as the contents of this weighty volume say little or nothing about either of the Arthurs. In fact, of six hundred and sixty-five pages, Wales, where the evidence lies in abundance, gets fifty-seven negative and destructive pages. This much-heralded hook was accorded much acclaim, but it was simply just another large serving of the same old anti-British nineteenth-century stew. Sadly, Morris was simply an academic reincarnation of Edwin Guest and Bishop Stubbs, rising again like a dreaded Dracula to suck the lifeblood from our tired and battered authentic British history.

Professor Morris totally failed to recognise the comet disaster that destroyed Britain in the mid-sixth century, and loosely ascribed the catastrophe to 'a plague'. He described the mass exodus of priests and monks from Britain to Brittany and Ireland, and did not even pause to wonder that they did not carry this plague with them. His scant mentions of south-east Wales history are remarkable for their total inaccuracy and confusions. What he actually did was to give an extra churning to an already swirling muddy pond. He first guessed that the Gildas manuscript might be authentic, and then he went on to guess that Gildas wrote around AD 540 and not after his return from Ireland in circa 570. From this tottering and unstable position, he then postulated that the Battle of Baedan fought by Arthur II, took place around AD 496. In one fell swoop 'King Arthur' was removed from the sixth century to the fifth, and the battle of Baedan was dislocated from close to AD 550 to an impossible c. AD 495.

This is hugely important, for the dating of the Battle of Baedan had always previously been wrongly placed too early at around AD 517. This date had also been fixed by a superb piece of illogic. The *Welsh Annals* list the great Battle of Baedan Hill, and also the Battle of Camlann, both of which involved Arthur II. The problem of the *Welsh Annals,* however, was that no dates as we might recognise them are given. All we have is a Listing of Years and major events in those Years. So, the Annals begin with Year 1, Year 2, Year 3, and so on. This means that it is vitally important to try to fix Year 1, to establish the chronology. This was done by trying to date a much-discussed letter sent from Britain to a powerful ruler in Gaul in the fifth century. In fact, several statements made in the *Gildas Manuscript* cast great doubt upon its authenticity as a sixth-century document. At best it has been much tampered with. Although the Gildas text names the ruler as Agitus, which is obviously the powerful King Aegidius in northern Gaul, the English academic choice is instead, predictably and absurdly, the Roman Aetius.

This selection of Aetius, rather than the obvious Aegidius, is all the more peculiar as both the *Brut Tysilio* and the *Brut Gruffydd ap Arthur* name the ruler in Gaul, who was the recipient of the letter, as Aganypus, and Acanypys, which is undoubtedly Aegidius. These British-Khumric texts pre-date the much-vaunted Gildas text, which is only an alleged fourteenth-century copy, and therefore they should be accorded more weight. The matter is important because a letter sent to

Aetius would have to be sent around AD 444-446, and a letter sent to Aegidius would be sent around 474 or later. If the sending of this letter influenced the setting of Year 1 of the Welsh Annals, then every subsequent dating could be some thirty plus years wrong. These misdatings would include those of the battles of Baedan and Camlann, which in turn misdate Arthur II. It also requires a considerable re-writing of history to account for a British appeal to their hated Roman enemies.

Flavius Afranius Syagrius Aegidius was King of the Seven Cities of northern Gaul, and for eight years he was elected King of the Franks in place of the dissolute Frank King Childeric, who had outraged his subjects by wantonly seducing their daughters. The reign of Aegidius over the Franks was from *c.* AD 457-465, and Aegidius remained as King of the Seven Cities until his death around 480. King Aegidius was succeeded briefly by Duke Victorius, and then by his own son Syagrius, who went on to become the comic Romance figure of 'Sir Sagremore the Foolish'.

As the famous letter from Britain must have been sent to the illustrious Flavius Afranius Syagrius Aegidius, King of the Seven Cities of Northern Gaul, then it must have been sent around AD 474 or later. This would make the actual date given for the Battle of Baedan in the *Welsh Annals* to be around AD 550 or later. With Morris giving a totally conjectural AD 495 he casually and ineptly created chaos.

Mynydd Baedan is still in the Maesteg Valley in Glamorgan, in sight of the Severn as specified in records, and its fields are still Maes Cad Lawr, 'the Fields of Battle Area', and the inevitable huge grave mounds of the war cemeteries of dead soldiers of both sides killed in the battle still stand there. The road from the shore to Mynydd Baedan is Ffordd y Gyfraith – 'road to the tumult', and the army gathering grounds are traceable. A plethora of other place names supports the identification of this well-known great battle site, which has to be 'close to the banks of the Severn'. Astonishingly, Professor Morris nominates a bare hill near Bath as the site, but nowhere near the Severn.

In the same way, Professor Morris nominates Portchester near Portsmouth as the site of the battle of Llongborth, where Arthur II and Geraint fought their way ashore from Brittany to attack Modred ap Llew. Prince Geraint of Dumnonia was mortally wounded in the fighting and a stone coffin was brought from Brittany for him. Strange, as Llongborth is still named in Cardigan Bay, and place- and field-names abound there. (The ancient Llongborth Farm near the beach was re-named as Llanborth Farm in 1926.) The Bloody Pool, the Field of Blood, the Place of Slaughter, and so on. There is also the stone of Bledri son of Meurig of Dyfed there,

Chapter 10 - The Myth of Celtic and Roman Britain

and Bledri became 'Sir Bleoberis' of Romance stories. More important however is the farm named Bedd Geraint Farm just four miles inland. This means 'The Grave of Geraint' Farm, and there is a very large ancient grave mound there right on target.

Geraint is named as from Dumnonia, which is now still Domnonée in Brittany, yet this guessing professor nominates Devon as the patrimony of Geraint. Why then did he sail from Brittany, and why was a coffin brought from there for Geraint?

The Llongborth battle on the beaches in Cardigan Bay was the prelude to the epic Battle of Mynydd Camlann, and inland from Llongborth the main route to North Wales passes through the narrowing, twisting, tumbled passes of Camlann Valley below Camlann Mountain, some ten miles south of Dollgelly. Here the ancient war grave mounds litter the valley, where the hastily retreating Modred ap Llew fought his Thermopylae-style rearguard battle to stave off the pursuit of Arthur II. The names are clear on the modern O.S. (Ordnance Survey) maps published by the British Government, and so officialdom knows where Baedan and Camlann were fought. Any competent researcher with mind and eyes open could find these clearly-named battle sites. The mute grave mounds are there, and many local supporting place-names and traditions abound. Yet Professor Morris ignored the government O.S. maps and came up with the Roman fort at Birdoswald on Hadrian's Wall some four hundred miles away, which has to be ludicrous by any standards.

In our modern times it is no great problem to look for place names on maps, and the problem is clearly one where any mention of any connection with Wales is unwelcome to the point of there being a prohibition, which amounts to a deliberate policy and an unnatural phobia. The idea of Baedan being fought around AD 497 automatically means that the Camlann and Llongborth battles would have been in 517. This would mean that Modred ap Llew and his wife Gwyar daughter of King Meurig had two grown sons by 517, which distorts all Welsh genealogy and every form of historical record wholesale. As Morris then misdates King Meurig 'Mourioc' to around 580 his chronological scenario is shapeless to the point of being chaotic. Also, a battle of Baedan in 497 would mean that it took place in the reign of King Tewdrig-Theoderic (the grandfather of Arthur II), who died in 508-509.

By using the very suspect fourteenth-century alleged copy of the Gildas manuscript, that no longer exists, and by attempting to date the writing of Gildas' treatise *The Ruin of Britain* at around AD 540 and using the notation in Section

26.1 to somehow date the Battle of Baedan at around 497, John Morris re-created a total confusion automatically requiring that all Welsh history should be abandoned. The alleged Gildas text states:

> 'That was the year of my birth as I know, one month of the forty-fourth year since then has already passed."

which plainly indicates that the battle of Baedan was around forty-three years before he wrote.

Not surprisingly Professor Morris makes absolutely no mention whatsoever of the great catastrophe of the comet débris striking Britain. Gildas is alternatively known in the genealogies as Aneurin y Coed Aur, or Aneurin of the Golden Woods. What we do know about St Gildas was that he made bells at Llancarfan Abbey in the time of St Cadoc son of Gwynlliw, and was a contemporary of St Illtyd and St David, to whom he sent a bell. He is also said to have fled to Ireland at the time of the comet disaster and Welsh scholars place his return around AD 570, when a famous meeting of reconciliation was held between Gildas and Arthur at Llancarfan Abbey. A brother of Gildas, named Hueil (Huail), had rebelled against Arthur II, and Arthur executed Hueil on a stone block still standing in the town square at Ruthin, which seems to have upset Gildas.

Significantly Gildas-Aneurin writes of Maglocunos as a King, and it can be shown comprehensively that Maglocunos, *alias* Maelgwn Gwynedd, became king in AD 580. This alone rules out any possibility that *The Ruin of Britain* was penned before the AD 562 comet disaster, and makes it virtually certain that it was composed after 580. The disaster is clearly described in Gildas' epistle, as Dr Victor Clube pointed out in making a parallel with evidence from astrophysics, and most of Britain was rendered completely uninhabitable from AD 562 to 569. This makes it most unlikely that Gildas could have written before AD 570, as he certainly describes the 562 catastrophes. His mentions of Maglocunos demonstrate that he was certainly writing during Maelgwn's reign, which began in 580. This means that a Battle of Baedan dating of around 550, in the year when Gildas-Aneurin son of Caw was born, is more than likely, and he may have been writing as late as *c.* 593.

As St Cadoc was a son of Gwynlliw and Gwladys a daughter of Brychan II of Brecon, and the marriage of Gwynlliw and Gwladys was arranged by Arthur II, who was a first cousin of Brychan II, there is a linked chronology. As Arthur II brought St Cadoc before the judges at Usk over the matter of giving absolution and sanctuary to the murderer of Arthur's brother Idnerth, there is further chronological link as Gildas resided at St Cadoc's Llancarfan Monastery after his return from Ireland in 570, and made bells there. Gildas and his bells were contemporary with the older Saints Illtyd and Dewi, and Dewi had removed his church from Caerleon to Menevia (St David's in Dyfed) after the cometary catastrophe, when Gildas sent him a bell. Arthur met Gildas at Llancarfan in 570, after his return.

Professor Morris' solution to the problems of numerous mentions of King Arthur II in the obvious sixth-century Welsh *Lives of the Saints* is simple and audacious. He simply states that all these records are false and written a hundred years after Arthur lived. Three times he dismisses a whole separate corpus of Welsh evidence in this same cavalier fashion. If anything fails to match his notions, then he simply throws the whole lot out.

Alan Wilson and Baram Blackett rarely attack other writers, but the generalisations and assertions of Professor Morris have been virtually adopted as renewed articles of faith, as were the fabrications of Guest and Stubbs, by British academics. What the professor did was to write a volume using the drawing power of Arthur's name in the title, but in which he made no attempt whatsoever to research either King Arthur. The idea of a Battle of Baedan around 497 has introduced another major source of distortions into general thinking on Arthurian topics, and it has to be debunked. Suffice it to say that Professor Morris's weird ideas about the ancient British, and particularly the Welsh and their language, are probably the most absurd nonsenses ever written. Yet his book, which is a model of political correctness, has inevitably become a 'standard work'. We cite:

> Page 424: 'Its (Ireland's) contribution to other lands was its aim and method, the recording of the past and the present and, above all, the gift to the Welsh and the English of the ability to write in their own spoken language' etc.
>
> Page 422: 'The Irish, unlike the Welsh and English, inherited an immensity of ancient tradition.'
>
> Page 417: 'The Welsh story-teller had greater need of foreign borrowings than the Irish. The principal collection of tales is grouped in the text commonly called the *Mabinogion*. [Actually, it is correctly *Mabinogi* and not Mabinogion, and this '-ion' stems from Lady Charlotte Guest.] It comprises a mythical cycle, the 'Four Branches of the Mabinogi', properly so-called whose form and content are heavily indebted to Irish mythological tales."

There is a great deal more of this insanity, and suffice it to say that Wilson and Blackett's researches into written Khumric in Coelbren are back to well over three thousand years. Also, *The Mabinogi* are definitely not 'mythological tales' when the keys for reading them, which are hidden in the Coelbren, are understood, and they owe nothing whatsoever to Ireland. They are solar tales of origin and represent a record that is a form of Genesis. They are carefully coded messages and give precise and accurate directions to hidden sites. In common with most others, the professor forgot that the St Patrick of Ireland was an educated British-Welshman.

The views expressed by Morris in his incongruously misnamed *Age of Arthur* are nothing short of a travesty.

> Page 407, 'The pens used for writing on wax tablets, called styli, are found in numbers in towns, but are not uncommon in the countryside; they are evidence not only of Literacy, but of Latin, for British (Khumric) was unwritten.'

A masterpiece of misleading inaccuracy. Imagine it, a pen that would only write in Latin.

The chaos re-born by Morris resulted in some extraordinary theorising, and an outburst of even greater confusion. Geoffrey Ashe published an alleged *Discovery of Arthur* in 1986, claiming to have discovered the fourteenth-century *Life of St Genovesius*, which E.K. Chambers of Cambridge part-published and commentated upon in 1922. In it, Genovesius is recorded as working on dykes along with two thousand, four hundred other monks, under the supervision of St Illtyd 'in the land of Arthur'. These many miles of ancient dykes are still there holding back the high tides along the banks of the Severn in Glamorgan and Gwent, where Illtyd spent all his adult life before fleeing for his life to Breconshire. The 'land of Arthur' where Illtyd built the dykes is correctly Gwent and Glamorgan. Not so, said the Canadian Ashe, and then he proceeded to 'identify' King Arthur as Prince Rhiotafwys-Rhiothamus, who is almost certainly the Breton prince Rhun Dremrud (Red-Eyed Warrior), son of Rhun, son of Brychan I (Frachan) of Brittany. Brychan I (Frachan) was the brother of Conan Meriadauc who invaded Gaul with Magnus Maximus in AD 383, and was set up as King of Brittany by Magnus.

In an amazing set of Canadian assertions, Arthur, now transformed into Rhiotafwys, was declared not to be a king, but a French or Breton mercenary. He did not fight the Romans as Arthur I the Black, and the Angles, Saxons, Irish, and Picts as Arthur II, but instead he hired out, with twelve thousand Breton marines, to fight against the Visigoths for the Roman Emperor Anthemius in AD 467. This newly invented Arthur is now alleged to have fought in France for a Roman emperor instead of killing one, and on the River Loire instead of at Soissons – 'Sassy', and not in Britain near the banks of the Severn. He lost his battles instead of winning them, and he fled to die in Germany. The lunatics had finally taken over the asylum. It was forgotten that Rhun Dremrud had a career matching that of Rhiotafwys, and finished up East of the Rhine as a King in Germany.

Dating the reign of Arthur II

Dating the era of Arthur I is comparatively simple. His father, Magnus Maximus, as the son of Flavius Julius Crispus Caesar, was born in AD 324. Magnus Maximus married his first wife Ceindrech daughter of Rheiden in the safety of Britain, and Arthur I is recorded as killing the Irish Prince Reueth, near Snowdon in AD 367, and presumably he was in his early twenties at that time. So, he was probably born around 344. The Irish Prince Reueth appears in Welsh traditional tales as Rhitta Gawr, and in romance stories as 'King Ryons'. Arthur I, as Andragathius in the Latin texts, was the general of the armies of his father, Magnus Maximus, in the invasion of Gaul in 383, when Paris was stormed, as depicted on the carved mural in Modena Cathedral, and the illegitimate Emperor Gratian was defeated at Soissons –'Sassy'. Five years later in 388, Arthur I was defeated by the massed armies of Theodosius at Poetovio, and at Sisica in Yugoslavia, and he retired to Britain and lived out his life in Warwickshire.

We know from numbers of genealogies that Arthur II was a sixth-generation direct male descendant of Arthur I son of Magnus Maximus, and the Llandaff Charters offer a date of AD 503 for his birth. The *Bruts of England* offer no other early date apart from Arthur II's death '546 years after the Incarnation of the Lord'. This would be the year 33 + 546 = AD 579 in accord with British religious ideas. The incarnation would be at the time of the crucifixion around AD 33, and not at the time of the birth of Jesus the Nazarene, which is in itself uncertain. Some twelfth-century romance stories and historical traditions, place Arthur as seventy-six years old when he died, and again the date of AD 503 in the Llandaff Charters gives 503 + 76 = AD 579.

There is then the Glamorgan record of the aged Owain Vinddu the brother of Arthur I being killed fighting the Irish in AD 434. The ever-reliable *Songs of the Graves* place Owain Vinddu as buried near St Illtyd's church at Llanhilleth in Gwent, and there, right on target, south west of the ancient church, is a very large grave mound, and Owain Vinddu was succeeded in the military command by Cuneda Wledig. Amongst several accurate dating calculations, Nennius places Maelgwn Gwynedd's accession to the throne at a hundred and forty-six years after

Cuneda, and again 434 + 146 brings Maelgwn's accession to AD 580, matching with Arthur II being dead in 579.

In his *History of the Franks*, the then living Gregory of Tours, a contemporary writer, records that the two islands in the sea - Britain and Ireland - were on fire from end to end at a date which is easily fixed at AD 562. This would be the disaster resulting from the comet débris striking large areas of Britain and Ireland. The Gwarchan Maelderw and other records place Prince Madoc being at sea for ten years, so from 562 to 572. Then Admiral Gwenon sailed on a checking voyage in 573, and when he returned, confirming Madoc's star reckonings, Arthur II sailed with his fleet of seven hundred ships in 574. Arthur is said by Taliesin to have been in Er- Yr ('towards that which is beyond' America) for four years. This brings us to 578 when he was assassinated. Then his body was kept under an overhang for the winter and brought home in the spring to summer of 579. Maelgwn was then elected in 580. Everything fits into place from data in these records.

It is only when this chronology is in place, along with the two Arthurs, the three Prince Brychans, the two St Samsons, the three Uriens, the two King Caradocs and the two Modreds, and so on, that the thousands of genealogical relationships which form the solid skeleton of the British histories come together in complete harmony.

If Professor Morris and others are right, and the Irish-spelled king list genealogies in MSS Bodleian Laud 610 and MSS Bodleian Rawlinson B.502 are the originals, and the same king lists in the Welsh-spelled genealogies in MSS Harleian 3859, MSS Bodleian Rawlinson B.466, MSS Cardiff 25, MSS Jesus College 20, and others, are the copies, then it follows that Magnus Maximus, and his sons Arthur I, Owain Vinddu, and Ednyfed, and all their myriads of descendants, along with Amlodd Wledig-Ambrosius and a host of others, are all Irish. No further comment is necessary.

Chapter 10 - The Myth of Celtic and Roman Britain

The Genealogy of Flavius Africanus Syagrius Aegidius

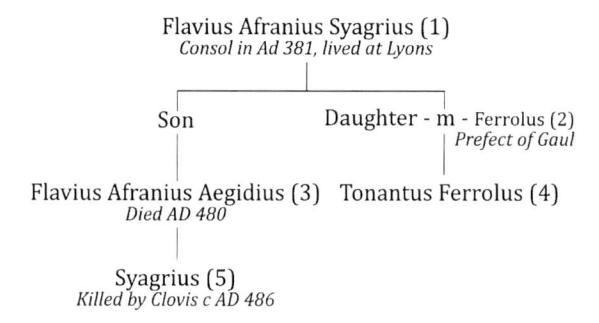

```
            Flavius Afranius Syagrius (1)
              Consol in Ad 381, lived at Lyons
         ┌──────────────┴──────────────┐
        Son                  Daughter - m - Ferrolus (2)
         │                                 Prefect of Gaul
   Flavius Afranius Aegidius (3)   Tonantus Ferrolus (4)
              Died AD 480
              │
          Syagrius (5)
        Killed by Clovis c AD 486
```

1- Flavius Afranius Aegidius (3) was a personal friend of the Emperor Avitus (Flavius Maecelius Eparchus Avitus) AD 455-456. He was also a friend of Sidonius and a first cousin of Tonantus Ferrolus. (4)

2- Syagrius (5) the son of Flavius Afranius Aegidius was a friend of the writers Symmachus and Ausonius. He fought against King Clovis I of the Franks in AD 486. Syagrius became secretary to King Gundobald of the Burgundians. His tomb is recorded as being at Lyons in the fifth century. In legend he became 'Sir Sagremore the foolish'.

3- Flavius Afranius Syagrius the Consul, (1) is recorded in Ammianus Marcellinus. see Arnm Mars. xxxviii, - 2 - 9.

4- Other references are: Symmachus CX, Ranshen Jarhle p. 85, Sidonius Epistolae vi, 17. 'conditorum Syagrii consoles'. Epistolae I, 7. 'Afranii Syagrii consoles et filia nepos', also in Epistolae ii, 9. and vii, 12.

5- Sidonius Apollinaris, who was made Bishop of Clermont Ferrand from c. 472-488, recorded his visit to the villa of Tonantus Ferrolus (5) near Neves on the bank of the Gardon Prusianam.

6- The Consul Flavius Afranius Syagrius (1) was clearly a contemporary of King Arthur I son of Magnus Maximus, who invaded Gaul in AD 383. Ferrolus (2) the Prefect of Gaul who married Consul Syagrius's daughter fits very neatly as the Roman ambassador who the British knew as Frollo, and who visited Magnus Maximus and Arthur I in Britain before they invaded Gaul.

7- Gregory of Tours mentions Aegidius in his *History of the Franks*, where he describes the powerful Aegidius who lived at Soissons, as the King of the Seven Cities of Gaul, and also as the King of the Franks for eight years, c. AD 457 -465.

8- There can be little doubt that the famous letter sent from Britain to Gaul was addressed Agitus/Aganypus/Acanypys was sent to King Aegidius around AD 474, and not to the barbarian 'Roman' General Aetius at some time near AD 444. The thirty-years chronological blunder of misidentifying Aetius instead of Aegidius has caused havoc in British historical studies.

The effect was to drag the real dates of historical events in Britain into an incorrect and chaotic era some thirty to thirty-five years out of their correct context, and this caused the clearly recorded history of sixth-century Britain to be distorted out of all recognition.

The British Druids and the Celtic Druids

It should be more than apparent at this stage of the account of the alphabet and the British people, that these ancient British were not Celts or Celtic. This then brings to the fore the religion of ancient Britain. All ancient cultures are structured around their religious beliefs, as is clearly obvious in the most cursory study of ancient Egypt and its pantheon arranged around the myths of Osiris, Isis, Horus, and Seth, and the supporting cast of gods led by Atum, Amun, Ra, Thoth, Ptah, and so on. The same basic pattern of pantheons is traceable through ancient Sumeria, Akkad, and Chaldea, and these near-identical arrangements persist through ancient Greece where Zeus and Hera lead the cast, and Rome where the identical Jupiter and Juno head the list. Therefore, the religion of the ancient British is also intrinsically bound to their history and culture.

The British stem from two major ancient migrations. The first from Chaldean Syria around 1600 BC, and the second from Israel *via* Assyria and Asia Minor, embarking in *c.* 504 BC. It follows that the British were not and are not 'Celtic.' Therefore, it becomes equally logical that the ancient British religion has nothing whatsoever to do with the religion of the Celts who dwelt in Southern France. The importance of recognising this disassociation and complete dislocation lies in the fact that of eleven Roman and Greek writers who described the Druid religion of the Celts of Southern Gaul, only one had even minimal knowledge of Britain. Yet another catastrophic British disaster has ensued because English historians and archaeologists have wrongly assumed that there were identical customs, culture, and religion between the Celts of Southern Gaul and the non-Celtic British. This assumption is incorrect.

The Celts were a people who lived in Southern Gaul between the rivers Sequanna and Garumna, now called respectively the Seine and the Garonne. There is no evidence whatsoever of any common link of blood, culture, or religion, with the British. The Roman and Greek writers who described the Celts of Gaul were Strabo, *c.* 51 BC, Julius Caesar around 53 BC, Diodorus Siculus, *c.* 44 BC, Cicero Pere 43 BC, Pliny born AD 23, Pomponius Mela AD 45, Suetonius Tranquillus *c.* AD 120, Diogenes Laertius, who died in AD 222, and Ammianus Marcellinus, *c.* AD 380. None of them knew anything of the British religion. The only writer in antiquity to deal specifically with Britain was Cornellius Tacitus, writing *c.* AD 80 to 100, who never came to Britain and who relied upon the vague soldier's tales of his father-in-law Agricola, who was the Roman governor of those parts of South Eastern Britain seized by Rome.

Tacitus is not a pillar of integrity and his honesty in his writings as has been frequently commented upon. He claimed that the Jews or Iudaei received their name from Mount Ida, and that they fled from the Isle of Crete into Egypt. Tacitus stated that the Jews religiously preserved images of a wild ass in their homes, and that this stemmed from a grateful memory of Moses obtaining water in the wilderness by following a herd of wild asses. Whether this is true or not, there was a firm ancient Jewish prohibition on any representation or image of a living creature. As there were large numbers of Jews in Rome during Tacitus' life from the time of Nero to Hadrian, there would appear to be no justification for these remarkable and dubious statements. So if Tacitus could be so glaringly incorrect about the Jews, then his lurid second-hand propaganda accounts of the British desperately defending Mona-Anglesey against Suetonius Paulinus fall into a less than reliable category. The Roman indignation that the British should dare to desperately defend their homes, their territories, and their religious centres, is itself ludicrous.

It is worth noting the remarks of Suetonius, who tells us that Ausinius Pollio (a contemporary of Caesar), held the opinion that the assertions of Julius Caesar are not always reliable:

- Asinius Pollio thinks that -

'...they (Caesar's works) were composed with little accuracy, and little truth, since Caesar used to believe rashly concerning the deeds done by other men, and also to relate erroneously the things done by himself, either of set purpose, or through failure of memory, and he is of the opinion that he intended to re-write or correct them.'

In short, the truth came a poor second to the needs of political and military propaganda.

Wilson and Blackett seek to show that there are no records of the ancient British Druidic religion from 'classical' sources, and that the only sources which are detailed and reliable, and which can to a great extent be checked, are the native British records. The Celtae of southern Gaul may have practised a brutal religion, and they may have had a multiplicity of gods, but this has no connection, and nothing whatsoever to do, with Britain and our British ancestors. The same applies to the various gods, which were imported into Britain by the various tribal and auxiliary military units imported into Britain from all over Europe and the East by the Roman army. The god images of these foreigners were not British, and have no affinity with Britain.

The laughable idea that all across Europe there were totally dissimilar tribes, who were red, or black, or brown, or blonde-haired, and who were short, tall, or medium height, and heavy, medium, or lightly built in their body frames, who spoke different languages, had widely different customs, and were generally foreign to each other, and yet were all 'Celts', needs to be exploded. This academic premise is a total nonsense, and it speaks volumes for the poverty of thinking, and the incapacity to research, of those who spawned and supported it.

What the Khumric records have to say about Bardism, or the practise of Druidism is quite explicit:

> 'Three nations corrupted what was taught them of the British Bardism, blending with it heterogeneous principles, by which means they lost it, the Irish, the Letavian Cymry (Bretons), and the Germans.
>
> 'For three reasons are the Bards titled Bards according to the rights and institutes of the Bards of the Isle of Britain; first, because Bardism originated in Britain; second, because pure Bardism was never well understood in any other country; thirdly, because pure Bardism can never be preserved or continued but by means of the institutes and voice conventional of the Bards of the Isle of Britain.'

Institutional Triads E.W Poems ii. 230.

Letavia was ancient Brittany and Normandy, colonised by the British in the AD 383 invasion of Gaul by Maximus Clemens Maximus. Letavia is still remembered in the town of Lesieux, and in the *Brut Gruffydd ap Arthur* as Londoniesia, and it became Normandy (Northman's Ty = home or house) in AD 911-933.

The Rev J. Williams ab Ithel, M.A. published a full account of the Druidic system in 1852 in the volume titled *Barddas* and subtitled *The Bardo-Druidic System*, in which he shows that the Coelbren Alphabet, its derivations, and symbolic meanings, are inextricably entwined with the Druidic System.

Basically, there were three circles of existence which were -

1- The Circle of Abred, in which all are corporal and dead existences;

2- The Circle of Gwynfyd, in which are all animated and immortal beings;

3- The Circle of Ceugant, where there is only God.

All beings emerged from Annwn, the Other World or the Great Deep of outer space, which was a form of limbo where the least possible life existences survived in a form of coma. From Annwn all life existences entered the circle of Abred, and progressed steadily upwards from the lowest forms of life to the highest form, which is Man. Each being, or soul, had to endure all the known forms of life successively. So, starting off as an amoeba, the entity moved steadily upwards to become say a worm or a sea-slug, and progressed through all the various insect, fish, bird, and animal forms, frogs, sparrows, mice, cats, dogs, wolves, bears, boars, sheep, cattle, and so on. In each life or existence, the soul is gaining all experience, and without gaining all life experience it is not possible to progress upwards to finally become a human being.

This doctrine of the Transmigration of the Soul through successively higher life forms in this Circle of Abred was firmly held, and it was also believed that all life first crawled out of the sea in the simplest life forms. Much of this was published by a theologian in 1846, and must have been known to Charles Darwin, who studied Theology.

At the stage of being a human the soul now has responsibility and has to live a moral life. The penalty for evil-doing and wrongdoing is severe, for the wrongdoer would be demoted on the ladder of ascending life forms. This demotion would mean starting off all over again through the ascending pattern. The extent of the demotion would depend upon the seriousness of the crime. So, an Adolf Hitler would certainly find himself as an amoeba and after a while a water bug being chased by minnows, whilst lesser offenders would find themselves as farm-yard pigs being fattened for slaughter, or whatever.

There was however a way out of this system of re-starts at lower life forms. If a man who had committed a capital crime stopped running, came forward, and surrendered himself, then he was rewarded. The Druids as the administrators of the law would duly execute the confessed criminal, but he was guaranteed to return to his next life as a human being. This avoidance of the centuries of toil moving up the ladder of life was apparently a valued form of pardon.

This voluntary submission for punishment for a crime was known as 'eneidfaddau'. The Laws of Dyfnwal Moelmud (Donald the Bald) specify that the penalty was beheading, or hanging, or being burned alive, the choice being made by the king or the lord of the territory. The idea appears to have been that 'eneidfaddau' propitiated God, and so the reincarnated soul was not placed in so lowly a position as might otherwise have been the case. A murderer who escaped punishment and died a natural death would return in a transmigratory life at a very low level in the order of life. His soul would descend into an animal corresponding to his disposition at the end of his life. Since the Divine Being wishes every human to be saved, then whatever is done to promote that objective and to bring it about speedily must be pleasing to the God.

Some human souls would need to experience several human lives before they finally graduated to their ultimate goal as an angelic soul in the Circle of Gwynfyd. The belief was therefore one involving reincarnation, and the transmigration of the soul. Every soul finally gets to the desired level of the Circle of Gwynfyd. The good soul finally entered the heavenly bliss of the Circle of Gwynfyd whilst the soul of the evil man was recycled back through existences in the Abred. Humanity is a state of liberty where the human can attach itself to either good or evil by choice.

The Circle of Ceugant was the dwelling-place of God, and no soul could aspire to enter this hallowed Circle of Ceugant, where only God himself lived. In British Druidism and Bardism there was only one God. The notion that there were multiple gods in the British religious scheme may have originated from the untenable supposition that the British and Celtic Druid faiths were the same. It may also have arisen from the Roman habit of explaining the nature of other religions in the same pattern as their own pantheon of Jupiter, Juno, Venus, Mars, Mercury, Poseidon, Pluto, Saturn, etc.

The dwelling-place of God was in the sun and this might have caused the confusion in some minds in believing that the British Druids were sun-worshippers. The sun was not seen as God but simply the home of God.

The adoption of basic Christianity into the British Druidic faith would appear to stem from the massive impression that might have been made on at least some Druid minds by the idea that Jesus the Nazarene voluntarily submitted himself to the fate of a sacrificial 'eneidfaddau' whilst being an innocent man who had committed no crime. It is fairly clear from the Secret Messages that the sacrifice was necessary to save the city of Jerusalem in case Pontius Pilate declared a state of insurrection, as was to happen almost thirty years later in AD 70 and finally in AD 132 to 135.

There was no hell as a place of horrific suffering and torment for millions of years in the British Druidic religion. There was simply a place of near non-existence where the soul lingered as if in a coma, unable to advance and develop towards the angelic state of the Circle of Gwynfyd. So, there was no blackmail threat future of endless torture from an avaricious and greedy clergy.

All this brings the investigation back full circle to the subterranean mosaic on the wall of the mausoleum of the Julii beneath the high altar of St Peter's in Rome. Here Jesus is shown riding in the Chariot of the Sun. Modern interpretations have been that Jesus is here represented as Sol Invictus, whereas he may have been shown to have simply entered the abode of the sun to join with God his father.

The Rabbis of Judea also believed in reincarnation and transmigration of the soul, but this ancient belief was quietly silenced around AD 1000 to avoid arousing even harsher Christian persecutions.

Alan Wilson was amazed when he attended a lecture in Columbus, Georgia, in 1992, given by Dr John Ross of the Lakota Souix, to listen to Dr Ross describing the Souix beliefs, which included circles which closely matched the Circles of Inchoation of the ancient British Druid faith.

The Holy Families of Britain

The researches of Wilson and Blackett show in their earlier publications that there were widespread claims of descent from the Holy Family from Jerusalem amongst the ancient British nobility. These hereditary claims can be shown to have originated in the marriages of Arviragus-Gweirydd and Anna, who is said to have been the cousin of the virgin Mary, and the later marriage of King Bran the father of Caradoc II with Penardim a descendant of Arviragus-Gweirydd and Anna.

If the British records and histories can now be re-admitted into the open forum of the nations of Planet Earth, and the hostile Anglo-Saxonism version is condemned as racism, a great number of supposed historical mysteries and puzzles can be dispersed. In line with this just re-admission of British-Khumric records Wilson and Blackett rightly hold that we can take note of entries in the *Long Book of Thomas Trueman of Pantlliwydd*, copied by Iolo Morganwg in 1793.

> 'The three Chief Holy Families of the Island of Britain are as follows -
>
> 'First, the family of Bran, the son of Llyr Lediaith (Llyr of speech impediment); and from this stock comes the family of Caw of North Britain, called Caw Cawlwyd, and Caw of Trecelyn in Anglesey.
>
> 'The second is the stock of Coel Godebog (Coel Hairy Breeches); and from that comes the family of Cuneda Wledig.
>
> 'Third is the stock of Brychan Brycheiniog (of Brecon), who came to this island to teach the Christian faith in the time of Tewdrig the son of Teithfall(t), king of Morganwg, (Glamorgan), and Gwent, and Garth Mathrin (Brecon), and

Erging and Ewyas (Hereford), and the Red Gwent (Gloucestershire between the Wye and the Severn).'

Brychan was, of course, the son of Marchell the daughter of King Tewdrig, and so a first cousin of King Arthur II ap Meurig ap Tewdrig. His father was Enllech Coronogson of Hydwn Dwn, son of Ceredig, son of Cuneda Wledig. As in St Patrick's Life, Ceredig had seized lands in Ireland and made himself a King there. So Brychan was wholly British although born in Ireland.

The first Holy Family of Britain was therefore the Holy Family of Bran and his son Caradoc II. This results directly from the marriage of Bran and Penardim a descendant of Anna. A number of breakaway Holy Families then later emerged as the Holy Blood spread into other noble British lines through intermarriage and female descents. In all there were three major Holy Families of Britain, and the pecking order was related to the seniority derived from descent from the line of Brutus kings. One record lists nine Holy Families in Britain, but these are in effect simply branches of the same family tree, where the bloodline passed through the female line by marriage into another linked noble clan.

So, the Holy Blood of the Jerusalem family permeated down through the noble British bloodlines over the centuries, and was recorded. This is fully described in *Where Jesus is Buried*, and the basis upon which these descents are founded is detailed in *Artorivs Rex Discovered* (both by Wilson and Blackett.)

In brief, the British ancient genealogies record a marriage between the British king of the Midlands area named Gweirydd (George), *alias* Arviragus, and a Judaean lady named Anna who was the adopted daughter, or ward, of the Emperor Claudius I. This marriage would have taken place around AD 44. The lady Anna is stated to have been a close relative of Mary the mother of Jesus the Nazarene, a cousin in one record. The mid to late sixth-century St Cadoc son of Gwynlliw, whose mother was Gwladys a daughter of Brychan of Brecon, records his descent from the Judean lady Anna. Later, the King Hywel Dda (Howell the Good) who died in AD 948, also recorded his family descent from Anna, and these records are emphatic.

The entry in King List No. 1 of the Harleian Manuscript 3859, one of Britain's most illustrious and authentic records, recording the ancestry of King Hywel Dda states:

'Amalech, qui fuit Beli magnus fili et Anna mater ejus, quae dictur esse consobrina Maria Virginis, matris Domini nostri Iseu Christi.'

Chapter 10 - The Myth of Celtic and Roman Britain

Translated, this is: 'Amalech who was the son of Beli the great and Anna his mother, of whom they say the Virgin Mary, mother of our Lord Jesus Christ, to be a blood relative.'

King List No. 10 in this assembly of genealogies compiled for the wedding of Owain son of Hywel Dda, probably around AD 920, has similar information. It stems from a different line of Hywel and Owain's ancestry. This gives 'Eudos son of Eudelen son of Aballac, son of Beli and Anna.'

It is almost certain that Amalech and Aballac are the same person.

Matters get even more interesting in the genealogy of the sixth-century St Cadoc. In Cadoc's father's descent the line similarly traces back to Anna:

'Baallad son of Aballach son of Beli, (and) son of Anna.'

The line of St Cadoc's mother is even more remarkable it traces directly back to the Virgin Mary herself:

'Battlad son of Aballach, son of Beli, brother of Jesus of Nazareth, son of the Virgin Mary.'

The Bible records no less than four brothers and two sisters, (or half-brothers and sisters), of Jesus the Nazarene. The named brothers are James the Righteous, Joses (Joset), Simeon (Simon), and Judas (Jude), and the references are in Mark 6:3, Matthew 13:55, Galatians 1:19, Mark 15:40, and Jude 1. Two sons of a brother were also recorded in the writings of Hegesippus as preserved by Eusebius in his *History of the Church*. These two were arrested in the reign of Domitian AD 86-91, and released as being harmless. The situation is one where it would be extraordinary if there were not a family and descendants.

Another valuable source in another authentic British manuscript is the Jesus College MSS. 20. This again lists the genealogies of Hywel Dda of Dyfed and his son Owain, and again traces them back to Anna. This time there is an additional notation written in Welsh:

'Yr Anna hon oedverch y amherabdyr rufein. Yr Anna honno a dywedi wyr yr cifft y bot yn gyfynnithderb y veir vorbyn.'

This translates into English:

'This Anna was daughter to the Emperor of Rome. That Anna used to be

319

said by the men of Egypt to be the cousin of the Virgin Mary.'

The problem lies in the word here written as 'gyfynnithderb', and there is no certainty that it meant 'cousin' as translated today. It might have had a more indeterminate and less specific meaning when written and may have meant 'kinswoman' or even 'lineal descendant'. The British historical *Bruts of St Tysilio* and *Gruffydd ap Arthur, etc.*, record only one British marriage between Gweirydd-Arviragus and a daughter of the Emperor Claudius I, and the lady is named as Genuissa, or Gewissa. There is nothing unusual in this situation as it was a simple matter of common political policy and expediency for Roman emperors to frequently 'adopt' young foreign princesses, in order to control them and use them as political marriage pawns. The marriage between the belligerent Arviragus-Gweirydd of the British Midlands, who would have been of Ten Tribe Israel descent, with a Judaean Princess would make good political sense.

There are two Annas available to fit with these ancient marriages. One would be Anna the widow of John the Baptist, who would fit as a cousin of Mary. The other, a daughter of the Emperor Claudius, would be Antonia or Anna the daughter of Claudius and Aelia Petina, one of Claudius' four wives. Claudius disowned Antonia and wanted her out of Rome. The effect these records would have had on the fanatical Edwin Guest and Bishop Stubbs and their obsessed followers can only be imagined. In the matter of the cult of Mary, the mother of Jesus the Nazarene, the developments over the centuries not only fly in the face of the evidence, but also border on the quite fantastic. In the fourth century AD at the great conference of Nicea in 325, Mary was a virtual non-entity. Not long afterwards Helvidius and Jovinian were exhibiting the Gospel evidence of the list of the brothers and sisters, and other mentions, of Jesus the Nazarene. Despite the evidence, Didymus the Blind of Alexandria and Hilary of Poitiers were busily constructing the cult of Mary and bestowing upon her the title of 'ever Virgin'. With Jesus having been elected as Very God, there arose the problem of his mother's position. Inevitably in AD 431 at the Council of Ephesus it was proposed that Mary be styled as 'Theotokos', or God-bearing, and this led to 'Mother-of-god'.

Ian Wilson sets out this process of inflationary aggrandisement in his volume *Jesus the Evidence*. There was politicking at the Ephesus Council in 431, on the part of the anti-Mary faction led by Nestorius of Constantinople, who argued that Mary could only be the mother of Jesus in his human condition. These clerics were outmanoeuvred simply by Cyril the Patriarch of Alexandria, who packed the meeting with his own supporters and got an early vote to elect Mary to the pantheon before Nestorius and his supporters arrived. The culmination of centuries of elevations, came in 1854 when Pope Pius IX made it an article of Catholic faith that all believers should regard Mary herself as 'immaculately conceived', and so from the moment of her conception to be incapable of sin. In the twentieth century, Pope Pius XII finally pronounced Mary to be the Queen of Heaven.

The Wilson and Blackett view is that British history is different, as it only records the facts. That British ancient historical records are incompatible with these man-made religious ideologies and voted theories of the Western Church is obvious. The result has been the centuries long onslaught against British history, heritage, and culture as preserved by the Khumry. The arrival of Christianity in Britain in AD 35-37 was obscured, as were the marriage and very existence of Anna and her descendants. Massive evidence of Britain as an advanced organised and highly-civilised state was utterly distorted into a false scenario of alleged barbarism and primitivism. The Roman influence in Britain was hugely exaggerated. Both Arthur I son of Magnus and Arthur II son of Meurig were cast into historical limbo and grotesquely exhibited as fairy stories. Magnus Clemens Maximus son of Crispus the eldest son of Constantine the Great, and legitimate heir, was twisted in to the role of a 'usurper'. The AD 562 comet catastrophe, and the almost immediate discovery of America by Madoc Morfran, were obliterated.

The process of concealments left no stone unturned. King Carawn of Menevia the Emperor of Britain and Northern Gaul became a Belgian Menapii tribesman. The illustrious Helen of the Cross, daughter of Coel, was forged into the daughter of an Illyrian innkeeper. Poor Magnus Clemens Maximus became a Spaniard, and even King Caradoc I son of Arch was transferred to a nebulous descent in eastern Britain. Massive onslaughts were launched against the native Khumric language. Finally, an undefended scapegoat was found in a most honourable, honest, and genuine man, Edward Williams, who was posthumously declared the greatest forger in history and the entire authentic and provable history of Britain was successfully thrown away. With the history went the ancient Coelbren Alphabet and the keys to the past.

The lunatics had at last gained complete control over the asylum.

Chapter Eleven

Back to Britain

The epic migration of the Khumry from somewhere near Armenia and northern Assyria at the time of the assassination of Emperor Sennacherib around 687 BC gives the clue to why Joseph of Arimathea and numbers of the Holy Family from Judea would have made their migration journey to Britain, recorded by Nennius as being 'in the last year of Tiberius' in AD 37, whilst two other ancient sources cite AD 35.

Judean people and the Israel remnant left behind in their homelands would have known of the great march from Armenia and around the south of the Caucasus. They would have known of the Assyrian designation of the Ten Tribes as the Khumry, which some modern American scholars speculatively believe derives from 'the people of Omri'. So, they would have known of the long trek clear across Asia Minor to the great city of Sardis and finally to the Trojan area of Byzantium on the Dardanelles. It was probably common knowledge in the lands around the eastern Mediterranean, and considered to be of little or no importance, that these people had sailed to the great Tin Island set in the great Western Ocean beyond the Pillars of Hercules.

The obvious place for a fleeing Judean community to head for would be the areas of Britain occupied by the Ten Tribes of Israel. There would be some bonds of ancient kinship, even though the religious ideas of Britain would probably be those of the pre-deportation era before c. 720 BC and not those developed in Judea in later eras, and particularly after the exile in Babylonia. Britain would have had the huge attraction and advantage of being outside the Roman Empire and free from the oppression of the Roman blight. Here lay a very powerful island kingdom where they might have protection and religious tolerance.

Down through the centuries it became accepted and commonplace that Joseph of Arimathea came to Britain, and brought with him members of the Holy Family from Judea. The journey would have followed the ancient trade routes to Britain across the Mediterranean and north from the Greek-founded port of Marseilles, and up north along the river valleys of the Rhône and to those of the Saône and the Seine, and also along the Loire. From the estuaries of the Saône and the Seine the much shorter sea crossings could be made to Britain with far less risk. These routes to the Tin Islands, the famed Cassiterides, were specified by the ancient geographers, but were for long largely ignored by historians and archaeologists. Tin was also mined extensively in ancient Brittany (see Herodotus *c.* 450 BC; Pytheas and Timaeus, pre-300 BC; Polybius and Posidonius *c.* 100 BC; Diodorus Siculus; and Strabo, in his *Geographica IV*, 1.14.) The long and dangerous ocean route through the Straits of Gibraltar, north along the Iberian peninsula, and across the Bay of Biscay, was generally avoided.

The traditions, therefore, of Mary the mother of Jesus the Nazarene, along with others of her family, arriving at Marseilles make perfect sense if they were *en route* to Britain.

The Carthaginians had early established a monopoly on the trade with the Iberian tin sources, and the alternatives were the British and Brittany markets which, when reached through the long-established routes of the Rhône, Saône, Seine, and even the Loire. The Carthaginians might control the Straits of Gibraltar, but this route was easily by-passed by Pytheas and other merchant adventurers, using the already established trade routes along the waterways and river systems of Gaul.

The traditions of Joseph of Arimathea in Britain were huge, and formed a centrepiece of the Arthurian romance stories. In these tales it was through Joseph of Arimathea that the legendary Holy Grail was brought to Britain. There was also the enduring traditional record that Jesus the Nazarene came to Britain with Joseph of Arimathea, and this was no problem to the British Church founded in AD 37, but it was a major threat and worry to the Church of Rome, formally established by the British Emperor Constantine the Great in AD 324. Jesus the Nazarene was said to have built an altar to God with his own hands in Britain, and no one in modern times, other than Blackett and Wilson, has gone to look for it and find it.

In the *Life of St David* there is an account of how David visited the altar built by Jesus the Nazarene, and he decided to repair it and to re-consecrate it. Then he had a dream in which he was warned that he should not presume to re-consecrate an altar that had already been consecrated by the Son of God. So, David encased the altar in lead to preserve it and built a chapel around it. It is a simple story, but where is this chapel built by St David to enclose this remarkable altar? Or is this a question that needs to be avoided? The problem lies in the fact that Jesus the

Nazarene came to Britain.

To explain this visit, a whole library of speculation has evolved, all of which completely misses the point that Joseph was leading his family and associates to the safe haven of Britain where their ancient kinsmen of the Ten Tribes of Israel dwelt outside the lands of the Roman Empire. In the swelling pyramid of speculation, Joseph of Arimathea becomes a metal merchant, he is an ocean-going tin-trader, he regularly visits Britain, and in some wilder speculations he owned at least some of the British tin mines (as if the British kings would allow that). In these imaginary trading voyages to Britain for the alleged tin-trading Joseph brought his twelve-year-old 'nephew', Jesus the Nazarene, on one of the voyages. The idea is that a twelve-year-old boy built an altar in Britain.

The alternative is that Jesus the Nazarene was brought to Britain in AD 37 and this is what the British believed and recorded. The result is that either British authentic and correct and provable history is accepted, or alternatively the ideology and dogmas of the Church of Rome are accepted. One has to be correct and the other wrong, for both cannot be correct. The altar preserved by St David in the mid-sixth century may have been built by Jesus the Nazarene in or after AD 37. Predictably the *Lives of the British Saints* have been routinely smeared as being untrustworthy, mystical, or just plain forgeries, yet they usually bear out when tested. One result was that a universal sycophantic stance was adopted by Welsh historical writers in the nineteenth century, all desperately attempting to demonstrate that the ancient Khumric church was orthodox, meaning in line with Rome, when the plain facts are that the ancient British Church was not similar to, or parallel with, or anything like, the Church of Rome.

What is to be done with accurate provable British history that does not conform to the invented dogmas of a Church in Italy? The fact is that there is an ancient ruined chapel which is in the right place, and which by all local tradition contains lead coffers. The place exists. Alan Wilson and Baram Blackett located the Chapel, which St David built to enclose the altar, in the mid-1980s.

This British historical tradition just does not go away because other non-British interests do not like it. Almost every British person is familiar with the words of the hymn 'and did those feet in ancient times, Walk upon England's mountains green, And was the Holy Lamb of God, On England's pleasant pastures seen,' and this hymn raises this very point in plain words.

British culture, heritage, and most of all the history met with exactly the same fate as the cultural heritage of the Aztecs, the Incas, and the other high civilisations

Chapter 11 - Back to Britain

of America. Anything that stands in the way of the religion of Rome is attacked and savagely destroyed with ruthless barbarity. This is why there are barely concealed messages scattered through ancient Khumric manuscripts. Here is the truth of the huge 'Dark Age' antagonisms and hostility between Britain and Rome. Here is the cause of the campaign deliberately to distort and obliterate all ancient British history. The fact that ancient Coelbren texts on written stone contained unwelcome messages would be a sufficient cause for the enemies of truth to allege the alphabet to be false along with the entire history. The fact that the alphabet could be used to demonstrate the truth of the origins and migrations of the British would render it even more dangerous.

The destruction of much of Britain in AD 562 by the comet opened the door to large-scale immigration from western Europe, and it also gave an opportunity to the Bishop of Rome to extend his tax-gathering empire into the Saxon and Angle tribes moving into Britain. No previous Bishop of Rome ever attempted to interfere in the powerful British state. No Bishop of Rome ever claimed the title of Papa or Pope before AD 627 and before Britain was devastated. As for Wales, it can fairly be said that the Church of Rome rode in on the coat-tails of the Normans in the incessant warfare from c. 1090-1300, and which continued sporadically until Owain Glyndwr set up the fully independent Welsh state briefly from c. 1400-1408. Khumric priests routinely went on marrying, and their children were usually hereditary priests after them, but all this is yet another story. Perhaps one illustration is justified, however. When the over-zealous cleric, Gerald de Windsor, a three-quarter Norman, one-quarter Welsh person, was sent into Wales on his famous spying mission for Henry II accompanying the Norman Archbishop of Canterbury, the intent was to spy out the geography, to evaluate the strengths and weaknesses of the people, and to estimate how a conquest might be attempted.

The major problem facing the researchers was the widespread prejudices against all ancient British history which are a direct result of a centuries-long propaganda campaign against our British heritage. In his reports to Henry II, Gerald de Windsor actually advocated the total extermination of the entire Welsh nation, and recommended that the whole country should become one vast hunting and game reserve:

> 'Indeed, it may well be thought preferable to eject the entire population which lives there now, so that Wales can be colonised anew. The present inhabitants are virtually ungovernable, and there are some who think that it would be far safer and more sensible to turn this rough and impenetrable country into an unpopulated forest area and game reserve.'

The stupidity of the advised genocide by this priest can be readily seen from all the many reverses and military defeats suffered by English kings in the centuries-long, grinding process of attempting to enslave the Welsh nation. Amongst many other incidents, Gerald relates how the Normans were totally unable to comprehend the determination of the local Welsh prince to retain possession of Nanhyfer Castle at Nevern, even though a Welsh-Norman marriage alliance was being forged in the area. It never occurred to Gerald that the castle was named after 'the river of the sanctuary' running below it. Gerald was also oblivious to the strange walled-up cave in the cliff below the castle with the cross carved into the cliff and the shaft extending behind the concealed wall. A mass of evidence strongly indicates that this is the most likely depository of the Cross, brought back from Jerusalem by the Empress Helen, the first wife of the Emperor Constantius Chlorus and the mother of Constantine the Great.

The first announcement of this by Wilson and Blackett brought tirades of outrage from an Irish Roman Catholic Priest at Haverfordwest some twenty-four miles away. Father Cunnane (Irish, and therefore a foreigner in Wales), employed by a Church in Rome, made furious attacks on the Welsh Alan Wilson as being a stranger coming into the area and causing disturbances and threatening local ancient relics, of which no one was aware before Blackett and Wilson announced the existence of the concealed wall. It was necessary to point out to Father Cunnane that Alan Wilson's maternal family hailed from the area, and the graveyard at Dinas Cross some five miles away holds many of them, and that Alan lived at Cwm Dewi, five and a half miles away, as a boy, and attended the tiny village school there. A cousin owns a house three miles away, and one of his brothers lives ten miles from Nevern and so on. The Irishman is the alien in Wales; not the Welshman.

The threat which Cunnane clearly perceived is that if there is an ancient wooden cross behind the sealed cave wall at Nevern, then that cross may have blood-stains. These blood-stains might be tested to establish their DNA profile, and so there would be a DNA for the Deity. Under the creeds and dogmas of Western Churches this is an impossibility, and it would affect their beliefs at a stroke.

Next, a local person produced a pamphlet denying that the twelve-foot-high stone-carved Nevern Cross was the great cross of King Howell Dda (the Good), who died in AD 948, and insisted that because of alleged design similarities with other stones it was the cross of a minor prince of around AD 1140. This is also ludicrous as the inscription proclaims 'Higuel Rex' for Howell the King, and there is no way on earth that the minor Howell, who died around 1140, would have dared to call himself 'king' when he was not one. It is the written inscription that dates the stone and not archaeological gobbledygook about guessed design dates based on the cloud cuckoo land notions of the surveyor Collingwood. The essential point is that any attempt to re-establish correct Welsh history meets with open and clandestine assaults from sources with foreign interests and motivations.

Gerald de Windsor actually gives a graphic description of himself and Baldwin, the Norman archbishop of Canterbury, attending a Welsh church service. The congregation assembled, whereupon the local Welsh nobleman walked in accompanied by his military entourage. This lord then placed his spear in a corner and proceeded to conduct the service. When it was finished, he picked up his weapons and walked out.

The Normans were not aware of the significance of Nevern nor of other ancient sacred sites, and the Khumry did not tell them. Nor did they tell the servants of Rome. It occurs to no one that a major Jewish Rabbinical tradition, which was central to their faith, was and is the Jewish belief in reincarnation. This old Hebrew belief precisely matches the ancient British 'Druidic' belief in reincarnation, and is undeniably a major indication that the British Khumry are, as every record collectively demonstrates, the allegedly lost Ten Tribes of Israel.

When kings are not kings

The full extent of the man-made muddles camouflaging ancient British history was a constant source of amazement. Wilson and Blackett finally refused even to contemplate the possibility that the mistranslations resulted from monumental incompetence, and they ceased to worry about the deliberate nature of the multitudes of misdirection. When a series of words forming a sentence, which gives vital information, is exhibited as a list of names of ancient princes, then there is clear evidence of continual conspiracy.

It is inconceivable that the phalanx of clergymen who dominated the mistranslation business in nineteenth-century Wales were unaware that these 'words' forming a sentence in the Khumric language were simply words and not the weird names of otherwise unrecorded kings and princes. The non Welsh-speaking English reader would not have an inkling of the fact that he was being deceived wholesale. Books were relatively expensive and often printed in pre ordered numbers matching the list of subscribers. The subscribers were generally the nobility and gentry who frequently saw the building up of a library as a necessary social asset, and so books were accepted, placed on the shelves, and left there unread. Alan Wilson always carried a small penknife with him when studying in the libraries of Cardiff and elsewhere, so that he could slit open the many, still-joined pages of volumes a hundred and fifty years old yet never before read.

It passes comprehension that these grotesque deceptions of mistranslation have been printed and reprinted for at least a hundred and fifty years. That these versions have allegedly been read by countless thousands beggars belief. The obvious way out of the dilemma was to mistranslate the texts and then to leave the originals in the Khumric language available to those with wit and intelligence enough to read them.

The statements in the ancient texts preserved British Christian ideas stemming from AD 37. Messages which tell of the hyssop in the sponge offered to a man on a cross being drugged are clearly unwelcome.

Remarkable as it may seem the largest part of King-list No. 1 of the impeccably authentic and ancient Harleian MSS No 3859 is in fact not a king-list at all, but simply a message. It begins with 'Cuneda', which is not a name at all, but at best a title; from 'cun', or 'lord', and 'edau', meaning 'restoration'. It then proceeds with a carefully written message thinly disguised as names. King-list No. 2 of this same illustrious British manuscript is also a message. This goes on in many sources. It would pass by those who would study and learn ancient Greek, Latin, Aramaic, and even Chaldean or Chinese, but would never stoop to learn the despised five-thousand-year-old language of the Khumry.

It has to be appreciated that in Khumric lists of descent the most recent name is at the top of the list, and the most ancient ancestor is at the bottom, and therefore whether to read from the top or the bottom is an evident problem. Either way at least one major reason for the deliberate obliteration of virtually all ancient British history is evident. As it can be shown that Western Christianity was founded in Britain and then spread outwards from Britain across Gaul and Italy and elsewhere, the British version of the religion would have great weight as authentic. As British beliefs differ fundamentally from the later-developed Roman version, the reason for the centuries of bitter religious warfare in Britain, and the final suppression of the four thousand years of authentic British history, heritage, and culture, to preserve the Roman Church, is abundantly clear. The animosity between the ancient British clergy and those of Rome is well enough recorded.

The notion that Jesus the Nazarene had come to Britain was very firmly held up until Hanoverian times. William Blake penned his well-known poem *Jerusalem*

Chapter 11 - Back to Britain

in 1804, and it was set to music in 1916 by Sir Hubert Parry.

The uncovering of these messages and the locating of the undeniable physical evidence brought additional problems for Alan Wilson and Baram Blackett. Additional reasons for the unlawful attacks upon them and their project were confirmed, and both were thankful that the insane sadists of the Roman Inquisition were no longer allowed freely to terrorise mankind in the twentieth century. Looming large in their minds, however, was the awesome question of what exactly they should do with the records and with these ancient sites.

The murder of pro-abortion doctors in the U.S.A. by religious opponents leaves no room for any naivety or complacency for anyone getting too close to the truth. Equally Wilson and Blackett were faced with the fact that it was inconceivable that the large number of clerics who had distorted and mangled authentic British history over the centuries had all failed to read and realise what they were mangling and concealing, and why. So, the authorities of both state and church were generally aware of what Alan Wilson and Baram Blackett might discover if they were allowed to exercise their human and democratic rights to investigate freely.

Then there was the basic human problem of what the truth might or might not do to the lives of the dwindling number of people who choose to believe the stories of the Western church. In Britain where churches and chapels are deconsecrated and sold off at an ever-increasing rate to be used as mosques, bingo-halls or markets, converted to dwellings, or simply knocked down for alternative housing development, it might be possible that the truth would actually do more good than harm. So, for some years Wilson and Blackett pondered and moralised over just what to do with this small part of their project.

Publishers, T.V. producers, and the press in Britain were uniformly automatically anti-Welsh, having been educated into the mindset created by the racist Bishop Stubbs of Oxford in the 1850s. Carrying out the research was not nearly as difficult as attempting to overcome the barriers of anti-Welsh prejudice raised by the onslaughts upon genuine ancient British historical records.

There is an important Gwrtheyrn-Victorinus listed in the Welsh *Lives of Saints* who is said to have been a prince of Rome who came to South Wales, and cleared out Irish invaders. In Gwrtheyrn-Victorinus we have a name and chronological match with the Western Emperor Caesar Marcus Piavonius Victorinus Pius Felix Augustus, who was a western Emperor of Britain, Gaul, and Spain, and who died in AD 271. The grandson of this Victorinus was King Euddaf-Octavius, who waged war in Britain with the lieutenants of Constantine the Great from AD 310 to 322 when he finally defeated them. King Euddaf-Octavius then ruled Britain independently until AD 367. The emperor Victorinus left a gravestone near a large grave mound in Glamorgan.

The Western emperors

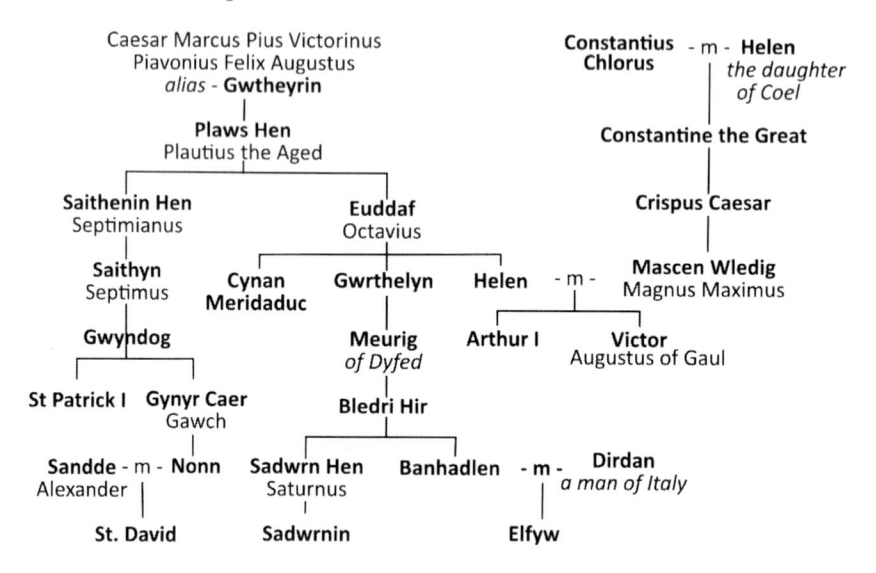

```
Caesar Marcus Pius Victorinus                    Constantius - m - Helen
  Piavonius Felix Augustus                         Chlorus        the daughter
      alias - Gwtheyrin                                            of Coel
             |                                          |
         Plaws Hen                              Constantine the Great
        Plautius the Aged                               |
    ┌────────┴────────┐                          Crispus Caesar
 Saithenin Hen     Euddaf                               |
  Septimianus      Octavius                      Mascen Wledig
      |         ┌────┴────┐                      Magnus Maximus
   Saithyn    Cynan   Gwrthelyn   Helen - m -         |
   Septimus   Meridaduc     |                      Victor
      |                   Meurig    Arthur I    Augustus of Gaul
   Gwyndog              of Dyfed
  ┌───┴───┐                 |
St Patrick I  Gynyr Caer  Bledri Hir
              Gawch       ┌───┴───┐
  Sandde - m - Nonn    Sadwrn Hen   Banhadlen - m -  Dirdan
   Alexander |          Saturnus                    a man of Italy
             |             |                           |
         St. David      Sadwrnin                     Elfyw
```

Cynan Meriadauc, the son of Euddaf, was made King of Brittany by Magnus Maximus when they invaded Gaul in AD 383. Large numbers of other chronologically correct genealogies also attach to this basic line of descents. Meurig of Dyfed was related to Arthur I, and King Meurig was the father of Arthur II some six generations later. Bledri Hir (the Tall) the son of Meurig of Dyfed is the obvious candidate to be the Sir Bleoberis of the mediaeval romance tales.

The list which is not a list

Wilson and Blackett were not prepared for the whole range of defensive devices employed in antiquity to preserve concealed knowledge. These devices included the construction of hidden messages. These were not the complex convoluted stratagems of codes and mathematics so beloved of some researchers and generally attributed to the Knights Templar. Instead, they were barely concealed simple ploys. No foreign person would spot them, as their lack of knowledge of the despised yet most ancient language would simply act to conceal this information anyway.

Chapter 11 - Back to Britain

What was difficult to comprehend was how any of the dilettante pseudo-scholars who, as Khumric speakers, have dabbled in these histories, could ever have missed the messages. As the majority of these scribblers were clergymen and priests, it may be that they saw the messages and decided that the information was just too unwelcome. Unwilling to destroy their own native heritage and yet unable to publish its truths, they probably just fudged the issue by either simply ignoring the texts or instead by mistranslating them. The classic mistranslations are those concerning the Holy Family, those of Arthurs I and II, and the details of the comet disaster. So it seems that to paraphrase Admiral Nelson at the Battle of Copenhagen, they held their telescope to their blind eye and said, "I see no messages".

As the various texts have been the subject of local Khumric interest and discussion by these learned – well, maybe learned - men, for centuries, it took a long while for Wilson and Blackett to realise that there were these barely concealed 'secret' messages in these much-quoted texts. But again, no academic in modern times goes back to original texts, and they usually regurgitate the stale and worn politically correct quotations and theories of legions of others.

It was not until Alan and Baram were looking at old tithe maps in a county archive that they noted something strange. A short verse had been written on the map in one field. The same verse was repeated in the tithe book which accompanied the map. The verse was written in Khumric and a translation into English was offered. Strangely, several of the words in the original text had been mis-spelled if the English version was correct. Given the anti-Khumric attitude commonly adopted, the politically correct act would be to regard the original spellings as illiterate and wrong, and the offered English translation as accurate. Examination of the text showed something very different, and instead of 'if ewes are put into this field they give sour milk', the text read 'this is the field of the queen of heaven'. Alan and Baram were confronted with yet another obviously deliberate mistranslation.

The way in which tithe maps are constructed is this. Large and detailed maps of each parish or sub-division of a parish were drawn showing the exact outline and measured acreage of every field, and every field was numbered. Then a book was compiled listing every field against its sequence number. Against the field number was written the acreage, the name of the owner, the name of any tenant renting or leasing the field, and the tithe due from the field. So, locating a field from a tithe map is a simple matter. Almost all fields in Wales also have specific field names, and the history is written on the land.

A visit to this field under scrutiny in the tithe map was made, and there plain to see was a very large mound of earth. Naturally this very large mound was not listed as any form of ancient or protected monument. The problems with university employees and their ilk were apparent again.

This episode, which led to an investigation of the remarkable history of this strange field with its large earth mound, acted as the trigger to start the conscious search for other hidden messages. To what was a massive and ever-growing project was now added a further project of immense proportions as the whole history and the place names and monuments of the entire surrounding area began to give up their secrets. As the messages were identified, so the sites were found identified and visited. It did not take long before a pattern emerged which showed that it was the very early religious sites that were being coded and concealed.

The messages, which were very simply encoded, showed fundamental differences between original Apostolic British Christianity, and the later Church of Rome. Whilst the Roman Church had no influence whatsoever in early Britain before the powerful British state was devastated by débris from the comet of AD 562, and limited influence with the native population at all times, most certainly in the 'Dark Ages' it was not present in Britain. Not until the majority of the British population was destroyed by the comet, and foreign German tribes began infiltrating the devastated eastern areas of the great island, did the Bishop of Rome dare to send a 'mission' into Britain to these non-British migrants, led by the monk Austin. This is how the archbishoprics of Canterbury and York are 'fringe', almost coastal, edifices.

Original Christianity persisted in the Khumric west and it was not until the Normans and later Angevin and Plantagenet Kings were finally able to dominate the Khumry that the Roman Church rode in on the coat-tails of these military expeditions. It was obvious that there would have been a clear necessity to avoid the inevitable collisions by simply restricting what the Roman Church and its later splinter, the Church of England, were allowed to know.

The sadistic excesses of the Inquisition had little effect in Britain as a whole with its several millennia-long traditions of civilised behaviour, and clearly the hidden messages with their simple codes avoided the threat of this murderous business corporation for centuries. More valuable, however, was the preservation of the sites. These would undoubtedly have been targets for destruction to preserve dogma instead of truth.

Wilson and Blackett soon found however that the problem had not gone away.

As they came upon message after message, and located site after site, they felt a growing unease. It seemed impossible that no one else before them had noted the contents of these statements. Yet no one had made any of them public. More and more it became obvious to them that this was the reason why the host of nineteenth- and early twentieth-century clergymen-authors, who had eagerly dabbled in the manuscripts, had come up with a maze of clear mistranslations. It was more than doubtful that any committed priest would want to read and publish very clear uncomfortable ancient truths of this kind, and find himself defrocked and out of work. Few people today realize that until around 1860 no one could occupy a Professorial Chair in any major English university unless he could first demonstrate his blind religious orthodoxy. Nothing was left to chance by the fearful Establishment.

As regards to mistranslations, the propaganda that there was only a cryptic one-line entry concerning Arthur II son of Meurig in the *Songs of the Graves* is a prime example. The Songs are arranged in three-line verses. A major king, or event, gets one three-line verse. Where there are super-important topics or monarchs there can be two, or as in rare cases, three three-line verses allocated. If King Arthur II ap Meurig had only one line in reference to him, then the question is, what on earth happened to the other two lines? In fact, Arthur II is accorded two three-line verses that clearly identify his grave. Yet for over a hundred and twenty years the Rev Robert Williams, assisted by Skene, was able to deceive and mislead whole armies of would-be Arthurian researchers into the trap of there being one meaningless line of verse. No one thought to check the 'translation'.

The main problem was not in locating messages or in finding hidden sites; it lay in what to do with the information. Wilson and Blackett carefully watched the unfolding controversies that surrounded the alleged Radio Carbon 14 testing of the tiny pieces from the Turin Shroud. Evidence of difficulties was public as the plan to allow seven universities to do the testing under three supervisory bodies was then changed at the last minute to three testing universities and only one supervisory university. Then it is alleged that those in charge cut the small piece of cloth for testing and retired behind closed doors to a private room, from which they later re-emerged with three small sealed metal capsules which they claimed now contained the sample of cloth cut into three.

This was a certain recipe for trouble. Later independent researchers claimed that the piece cut was measured and weighed, yet the three sample pieces in the small metal cylinders, were also photographed, measured, and weighed, at the three universities designated to test them. The combined size and weight of the three individual samples are alleged to be greater than that of the original sample cut from the Shroud. The strange procedure of retiring out of sight into a closed room allegedly to place the three samples in the three small sealed metal cylinders opened the door to more problems than the scientific testing was meant to solve.

The important thing for Wilson and Blackett, however, was that these controversies made them think of how the religious organisations think. If the Cross brought from Jerusalem in *c.* AD 324 by the Empress Helen, daughter of Coel, is actually still behind the wall of the sealed cave at Nevern, in Dyfed, then that piece of timber would perhaps have bloodstains. These could be DNA-tested, and logically it could be held that this would be the DNA of Jesus the Nazarene. The same dangerous DNA situation applies to the Turin Shroud, which is bloodstained.

As a test it was decided to reveal a small part of the evidence leading to the Nevern Cave and to make known the possibility that the Cross, brought home by the Empress Helen in AD 324, was still there. Everything proceeded to take place exactly as Alan and Baram predicted it would. Right on schedule the enemy in the form of BBC Wales Radio telephoned to ask them to come along to a show and tell people what it was all about. They were assured that they would be the main part of the half-hour show. Naturally they didn't believe this, but they went along anyway to see just how the ambush would be set this time. Predictably time passed as the turgid, boring, trivial catalogue of inanities of the programme churned along. It was abundantly clear that they were to be the stupid joke hit at the end, like television news programmes which always try to end with some comic piece of amusement such as 'cat bites dog', and that sort of thing. They considered walking out, but thought it worth staying to see if tactics varied at all. Finally with about three minutes of this entirely forgettable radio trash left, the presenter got around to the matter of a strange, sealed cave at Nevern, in Dyfed.

There was clearly a group which did not want the Cross to be found in Wales, and Baram Blackett and Alan Wilson made forceful representations to the Royal Commission for Ancient Monuments in Wales to guarantee the registration of the sealed cave. This would afford legal protection to the site and deter most of the religious and racist fanatics who might take it into their heads to destroy the site and whatever was there. Everything was back to the old: if there is a two-thousand-year-old bloodstained bit of timber there, it could be DNA- and Radio Carbon 14 tested. If it shows DNA, that DNA could be of one Jesus the Nazarene. If this is done in the interests of British heritage, culture, and authentic history, then non-British and Khumric interests will have to live with it. It is deplorable to sacrifice all British history for a relatively minor vested interest.

Chapter 11 - Back to Britain

All this began with the careful scrutiny of an old tithe map, and the expanding project developing from this one single clue was to prove to be of astonishing importance. The subject is one for another volume, and it is a matter of regret that any mention of this was made in *The Holy Kingdom* against Baram's and Alan's advice.

This, however, is the background against which accurate, provable British history has to struggle. The choice is between accurate, detailed and provable British history, or the mess created by Stubbs at Oxford and Guest at Cambridge, for one cannot have both. For centuries, culminating in the monstrous falsehoods of Bishop Stubbs of Oxford and Edwin Guest at Cambridge, genuine British history and language were attacked and finally suppressed. British publishing is essentially London publishing, and so the suppression of the ancient British truths preserved in Wales has been a relatively simple matter.

In the late 1970s and on through the next two decades Baram Blackett and Alan Wilson were at first bewildered by the outpouring of a veritable library of books packed with semi-romantic speculations, alleging ill-defined mysteries based upon strange imaginings, which inexplicably focused attention onto the South of France. These books purported to allege and investigate unproven discoveries of early Christian origins in these areas. It took some time before they saw that these claims based on finally admitted forgeries were a brilliant smokescreen inexplicably to centre attention onto the wrong ancient dynasty, in the wrong country, and mainly in the wrong era. Laughable claims are made which will cause no sleepless nights in London or in Rome. One volume was entitled *The Grave of God*; which would be a great blasphemy in any religion. Imagine it, GOD is dead. The summation was, however, that without one shred or proof or evidence, a large mountain mass was pointed to, and it was claimed that up there somewhere - site unknown, no records, traditions, or clues - there was a sealed grave (unlocated of course), and in this grave was a gentleman who wandered around Palestine two thousand years ago, and he was God. Publish idiocies and absurdities and make the entire subject appear nonsense.

The problem with a grave with human remains, and records and a history leading to it, is that it sends the theologians and priests soaring into orbit, and into Fantasy Land where they have been for two thousand years anyway. Italian history must not be attacked, nor must Irish history be attacked, nor also must Greek, Egyptian, Jewish, Chinese, or any other history on planet earth be attacked, with one exception. It is perfectly in order to attack and abuse native Khumric-British history, heritage, and culture as viciously as possible in any and every way in a frantic defence of the totally indefensible.

All of which leaves us with the messages. Anyone is free to conjecture just how the location of an anciently sealed cave, recorded in impeccably authentic histories of over a thousand years old, marked with an ancient, crumbling carved cross on a cliff, and where traditionally Christian pilgrims came in multitudes to pray for the vision of the Cross brought to Britain by the Empress Helen in AD 324, would be received in any other country, say France, Spain, Italy, Germany, wherever. There is something rotten in the state of Britain.

Message in the king-list No.2 of Harleian MSS No. 3859

This message deals with the Imperial succession from Constantine the Great. It is necessary to remember that Constantine was British and that he firmly regarded himself as the Head of the Christian Church. With evidence of intermarriage between the British Royal clans and the Holy Family still extant, this assertion by Constantine the Great, the son of the British Empress Helen, may have been well founded.

No.	Name?	
25	Maxim Guletic (Magnus the Wledig = Legate)	Magnus Maximus
26	ap	protect
27	ap Protector	the protected
28	ap Ebiud = Ebythu	to overturn
29	ap Eliud = Eliad ('doing with salve')	the anointed
30	ap Slater = 'stad' (estate) 'er' or 'ter'	of pure estate
31	ap Pincr Misser 'pinc-mi-serr'	I a sprig with the sword
32	ap (successor of) Constans	
33	ap (son of) Constanti Magni (Constantine the Great)	

Constantine the Great died in AD 337, and his son Constans died in 350. Instead of listing the names of those six who acquired the Empire after Constans and up to the accession of Magnus Maximus to the Western Empire in AD 383, this list contains six words. These six words imply a dismissal of these six Emperors from AD 350-383 as illegitimate. As Magnus Maximus was the only son of Crispus the eldest son of Constantine the Great, he was the only legitimate heir.

Those here regarded as the six imposters were:

No. 26   Valentinian II 375-392,
No. 27   Gratian 375-383,

Chapter 11 - Back to Britain

No. 28   Valens 364-378,
No. 29   Valentinian I, 364-375,
No. 30   Jovian, 363-364,
No. 31   Julian the Apostate, 361-363.

As Magnus Maximus can be shown to be the only son of Crispus, who was Constantine the Great's eldest son, it is abundantly clear that Magnus Maximus is here declared the rightful heir after his uncle Constans who succeeded when Magnus was yet a child of some ten or eleven years old.

The text of the message is: -

'Magnus Maximus the protected protector (who was) overturned, the anointed of pure estate, the sprig (descendant) I with the sword.'

As Magnus was removed from Gaul to Spain at the age of one, by the faithful Spanish knight, following the murder of his father Crispus and his mother Flavia in 325, he is the 'protected protector. All this is detailed elsewhere.

Julian the Apostate', who is concealed under 'Pincr Misser', may have been given a double meaning, with 'pincio' meaning 'to cover with sprigs' or 'covering of the sprig'. Julian's return to the old gods may be in 'mis' + 'ser' or literally 'month' + 'stars', an illusion to the planets and constellations being seen as gods.

Message in the king-list No. 16 of Harleian MSS No. 3958

This 'list' is yet another carefully constructed message built up with many misspellings. It is worth remembering that these lists were constructed for the wedding of Owen's son of Howell Dda around AD 920 and Howell claimed direct descent from the Jerusalem Holy Family. The list comprises all the Emperors of Rome from Augustus-Octavian right through to Constans the son of Constantine the Great. It misplaces Nero to succeed Trajan, and why this is not yet clear. There are statements added which refer to the persecutions of Christians by Nero and Diocletian.

1.	Rhun		lavish one.
2.	Neithion	ncith + ion	evening feast + the lord
3.	Caten	cat+ en	a bit/piece + essential spirit.
4.	Caurtom	caur + tom	a giant + heap/dung/manure.
5.	Sergawn	ser + gawn	star + of winter.
6.	Lctan	le + tan	sad + fire (or under).
7.	Catlan	cat + lan (llan = holy estate)	a bit/piece + up

8.	Catel	(catan? = chair, throne,)	chattels.
9.	Decion	dec + ion	beginning + the lord.
10.	Cinis Scaplaut	cinio + scapwrth	the dinner + uncouth.
11.	Lon Hen		the road + old.
12.	Guidgen	gwidw + cen	the widow's + cub.
13.	Caratauc	carados	by concubinage.
14.	Cinbelin	ciniog + Bellach	tattered + further.
15.	Tenhault	tenaut + hawlic	diluted claims.
16.	Constans		
17.	Constantini Magni		

The message appears to be:

'lavish one, the evening feast of the lord, a bit (or piece) of essential spirit, a giant heap (of dung or manure), the star of winter, sad below it (under), a piece of holy estate, the chattels,(belongings), the beginning of the lord, the dinner uncouth (unruly) the old way (road), the widow's cub of concubinage, tattered further the diluted claims.'

It may be that 'Caten' reads as 'catan', for 'bickering or contention', or even 'cader', for 'chair or throne'. Quite what is intended is uncertain, as the message seems to have a number of points. There is a statement that the transfer in AD 324 of the alleged birth date of Jesus the Nazarene from 1st March to 25th December to coincide with the birthdate of Sol-Invictus the Sun god is a nonsense, a heap, or dung, etc.

The 'list' also clearly denies any rights of Imperial succession to those who followed Constans the fourth son of Constantine the Great. It is clear that Magnus Clemens Maximus the son of Crispus the eldest son of Constantine the Great was known to be the rightful heir and successor, and therefore so also were his descendants. These would include Arthur I and Arthur II and all subsequent Morganwg kings. Small wonder that the London régime and the Church of Rome have sought to obliterate this remarkably well-known and recorded dynasty.

Everyone has two parents, four grandparents, eight great-grandparents, and so on with sixteen, thirty-two, sixty-four, a hundred and twenty-eight, etc., in succeeding generations, arriving at a total of 262,144 ancestors in five hundred years and so on.

Wilson and Blackett regard several other very clear messages that appear in *Where Jesus is Buried*, pub. 2021 by Cymroglyphics Ltd.

Age of Arthur, The, Morris 302
Algic Researches, Schoolcraft, H 5
Ancient Bards of Britain, *The*
    Evans, Delta D. 109, 113
Anglo-Saxon Chronicles 159
Barddas, Williams ab Ithel 95
Bardism, William O. 113
Bodleian "KKK" 120, 139-40
Bodleian MSS 572 33, 48, 145, 147, 148, 150, 153
Bodleian MSS Douce 323 69, 70
Bodleian MSS Laud 610 310
Bodleian MSS Rawlinson B.502 310
Britannia, Camden 151
Brut Gruffydd ap Arthur 30, 142, 240, 275, 303, 314, 320
Bruts of England 309
Cambria Triumphans, Enderbie 45
Cambrian Journal 1855 139
Cambrian Journal, The 147
Celtic Art, Bain G. 129
Celtic Grammar, Zeuss 147
De Excideo Brittaniae, Gildas 233
Geneology of Iestyn 105, 107
Gilgamesh and the Land of the Living 95
Gilgamesh, Epic of 95
Gilgamesh, The death of 95
Gulliver's Travels, Swift 15
Henry V, Shakespear 26
History of the Kings of Britain, The 281
Holy Blood and Holy Grail, The, 134
Holy Kingdom, The, Gilbert, Wilson and Blackett 335
Llandaff Charters 159, 268
Mabinogi 95
Morte d'Arthur, Mallory 140

Musical and Poetical Relicks of the Welsh Bards, Jones E. 44
Origanae Celticae, Guest 29, 36
Ruin of Britain, The 306
Seint Gral, Y 95
Seven Tablets of Creation, The 95
St Teilaw/ Lichfield, Book of
St. Finnian, Life of 132
Travels in Syria and the Holy Land, Borchardt, J 80
Triads (institutional) 314
Uruk, King of 95
Y Dyrch (1948) 21

Index

A

Albyne 27, 28, 39-40, Ch. 3, 115, 139, 140, 233, 236

Anson, George and Admiral 136

Ark of the covenant 69, 205-7, 221-9

Arthmael – Arthur 27, 126

Arthur I Iarthun) 27, 30-1, 43, 47, 51, 268, Ch.9, 300, 309, 311, 330, 338

Arthur II (ap Meurig) 27, 30-1, 41, 47, 51, 99, 119, 132, 133, 140, 142, 144, 159, 176, 268, 271-4, 275-6, Ch.9, 303-10, 333, 338

Arthur the Black - see Arthur I

Arviragus - see Gweirydd

Ashurbanipal 95

Ashurnasipal II 192

Assyria 3, 47-8, 87, 95, 100, 103, 106, 192, 205-7, 222-4, 227, 252-3, 261-3

Awen (symbol) 114, 118, 119, 134, 170, 199

B

Babylon/Babylonia 74, 82, 84, 95, 97, 133, 255, 322

Babylonian - Welsh words 252 - 258

Baedan, Battle of 303-7

Bain, George 87, 129-31, 133, 247

Bards - see druids

BBC 64, 65, 118, 141, 269, 334,

Beaumont, H.G. 139-40, 145-7

Bemis lecture 258

Bible (old) 8, 9, 17-8, 35, 37, 49, 79, 172, 229, 253, 262, 319

Bing, Levi 16

Blake, William 328

Borchardt, Johann 80

Brendan, St 12, 14, 15

Bridekirk stone 151-4,

Brutus 14, 27-9, 31, 40, 44, 50, 55, 83, 86, 88, 92, 107, 113, 162, 207, 222, Ch.8, 266-7, 269, 272, 275, 318,

Brychan(s) 126, 276, 279, 280, 282, 283, 284, 306, 308, 317

C

Cadoc St 110, 122, 126, 306, 319

Caer Caradoc 62, 158, 269, 271, 282

Camden, William 151,

Camlann, Battle of 31, 303-307

Canaan 79, 197, 205, 223, 224, 253

Caradoc I (ap Caid) 40, 279, 284

Caradoc II 276,

Caradoc of Llancarfan 20,

Caxton, William 24, 42, 117

Celtic 7, 8, 29, 36, 37, 57-8, 129, 133 -4, 147, 150, 236, 241, 247, Ch 10 (293-296), 312, 316

Chaldean language links 252-8

Cherokee 17

Cockermouth 151

Coelbren alphabet 7-14, 17, 20, 22, 24, 29-30, 31-33, 47-9, 58, 61-4, 67, 86, 101-2, 104, 106-7, 110, 115, Ch. 6, Ch. 7, 231, 236, 240-3, 246, 250, 260-4, 271, 308, 314, 321, 325

Collingwood, W.G. 125-7, 158, 161, 327

341

Index

Columbus Georgia 9, 317

Columbus only theory 16

Columbus, Christopher 15, 33

Cumorah 4

Cynfelyn "Cunobelinus" 53, 89-92, 120

Cyrus (Persian) 202

D

Dafydd ap Gwilym 116

Dafydd ap Gwilym 116, 118, 279

Dafydd Gam 55-56,

Defrobani 28

Delaware Tribal confederation 19

Dimancescu, Dan 258

Druids (and bards) 19, 33, 43-5, 62, 65, 92-5, 109, 113-117, 119, 120, 123, 130, 133-4, 153, 172, 196, 199, 312-7, 327

Dungi / Diocletian 76-83, 89-95, 120

Dykes 308

E

Ealde Cyrcenas - Surrey/Syrians 28, 40-7, 83-8

Elucidator (Coelbren) 10

Ely (Cardiff) 1, 2, 21,

Eski-Sher 243-252

Etruscan 14, 22, 29, 32, 47-50, 102, 106, 112-3, Ch 6, Ch 7, 231, 246, 248, 257

Evans, D. Delta 109, 113

Evans, John (1790s) 66

Evans, John (Blaenavon) 289

F

Fleming (family) 1, 2, 20, 21,

Flynn MP, Paul 24

G

Galletin, Albert 5

Genovesius 308

Geoffrey of Monmouth - see Gryffydd ap Arthur

George I 26, 42

George St - see Gweirydd

Ghomri - people of 260

Gildas St (Aneurin y Coed Aur) 233, 303, 305, 306, 307

Gloucestershire - Red Gwent 118

Glyndwr, Owain 117, 329

Gordium stone 248-52

Grave Creek 1-38 (Chapter 1), 39, 153

Grave Creek tablet 1-38 (Ch. 1), 39, 153

Grave mound(s) 2, 3, 5, 16, 18, 31, 35, 44, 127, 175, 231, 241, 299, 304, 305, 309, 330,

Gruffydd ap Llewellyn 26, 44

Gruffydd Gam 25

Gryffydd ap Arthur (Geoffrey) 30,142, 231, 233, 275, 281, 303, 314, 320

Guest, Edwin 27-31, 34-8, 65, 86, 93, 113, 126, 139, 231, 260, 284, 298-9,303, 307, 320, 335

Guto 'r Glyn 45

Gweirydd (Arviragus/"George") 318, 320

Gwenhwyfar 100

Gwenogfran Evans, J. 62-5, 68, 231, 260, 284, 288, 299

Gwent (county) 3, 24, 42, 101, 104, 138, 141, 162, 241, 266, 283, 308, 309

Index

Gwierydd, Lord 1

Gwilym Tew 117

Gwrgan Mawr 269, 271-2

Gwydion ap Don 116

Gwynedd 21, 26, 27, 32, 44, 60-2, 102, 273-4, 278-9,

Gwynlliw 101, 110, 122, 306, 318

H

Hakluyt, Richard 21

Henry II 47, 123, 325

Henry IV 24, 117

Henry V 25, 55-6,

Henry VI 137

Henry VII (Tudor) 25, 26, 27, 41, 120

Henry VIII 26, 41

Hereford - Erging and Ewyas 118

Herodotus 50, 58, 106, 202, 203, 206 7, 323

Holy Cross 49

Holy Family 44, 137, 272, 317-21, 322-4, 331, 336, 337

Holy Greal 229, 323

Hueil 306

I

Iestyn ap Gwrgan, King "Justin" 20, 54, 56, 105, 107

Ieuan Du'r Bilwg 117

Ifor Bach ap Meurig 123

Illtyd St 127, 159, 306, 308,

Inca bones 19-20

Indiana 1, 19, 21,

Iolo Goch 117

Ithael II, King 274

Ithael, King 99, 121, 127, 159, 176

J

Jefferson, President Thomas 8, 9, 17

Jomard, Prof 11, 12

Jones, Clayton Councillor 289, 290, 295

Jones, Dr. Owen 66,

Jones, Edward (bard) 44, 120

Jones, John Dudley 285

K

Kemp, George S. 64, 128

Kentucky (state) 2, 19, 20, 22, 23, 33, 114, 258,

Kimmerians 50, 206, 262, 263-4

Kimmeroi 50, 206, 222, 257

L

Larthia Scianti 191-2

Layard, Austin 50, 81, 139, 205, 261

Lenni Lenape 19

Lewis & Clarke 9

Lewis of Coety 125

Lexden Mound 89-92, 120

Lief Ericsson 12, 15

Lincoln, Henry 85

Llandaff Charters 121, 159, 268, 271, 273, 275, 283, 309

Llandaff, Bishop of 121, 154

Llan-illtyd Fawr (Llantwit Major) 99, 122, 127, 279

Llan-iltern 100

Llewellyn Moel y Pantri 117

Llongborth 31, 304-5

Lluyd, Edward 51, 156-7, 282

Lydia / Lydian 11, 263 4

M

Index

Mabinogi 95, 167, 169, 283, 307, 308

Madoc (Gwynedd) 1170 1, 2, 8, 12, 20, 21, 32, 123,

Madoc Ap Meurig - "The Cormorant" 1, 2, 15, 21, 47, 49, 66, 269, 273, 310, 321,

Magnus Clemens Maximus 49, 280-1, 308, 338

Magnus Maximus - see Mascen Wledig

Mandan 9

Map, Walter 1, 2, 20, 21,

Marie Llwyd 93

Marwnad Gruffydd Llwyd 117

Mascen Wledig / Magnus Maximus 27, 30, 43, 47, 267, 270, 281, 301, 311, 336-7,

Menevia - St David's 269, 307, 321

Meurig ap Tewdrig, King 27, 31, 100, 133, 142, 159, 163, 269, 271-2, 276, 283

Meurig of Dyfed 330

Mewdrad ap Llew, Modred 31, 52, 304-5

Michael, James B. (Jim) 1, 2, 9, 11, 15, 18, 19, 20, 21, 23, 33, 258,

Modred - see Mewdrad

Moelmud 96, 116, 315

Morgan, Henry 279

Mormon(s) Latter Date Saints 4, 5, 34

Morris, Prof. John 302-10

Morton, Dr Samuel 16

N

Napoleon 12, 34, 42, 90, 296,

Nefydd (of Gweirydd) 1, 20

O

Ogham 8, 131

Ojibwa 5

Olsen, Dana 1, 2, 21

Omri 260, 261, 322

Orwell, George 27, 41

Owain ap Hywel 319

Owain Vinddu 267, 281, 309, 310

Owen Gwynedd 12

Oxford, University of 9, 11, 27, 28, 29, 30, 33, 35, 36, 37, 40, 49, 51, 63, 65, 66, 113, 120, 141, 156, 175, 261, 285, 329

P

Page, Prof. 11

Patrick, St 19, 278-282

Pebiau Glafoerog, King 269, 272

Pelasgian 14, 29, 49, 113, 165, 242

Penmachno 269

Pennington, Dr. Joy 114

Pennington, Prof. Lee 114

Pontypridd 19, 92, 93, 257, 295

Powell, John Wesley 16

Printing ban 24, 30, 42, 117, 138

Pughe, William O 66, 112

R

Radio Carbon 14 (RCD) 16, 96, 333

Rawlinson, Henry 261

Rhitta Gawr 30, 309

Rhys Goch Eyri 117

Runic (alphabets) 7-11, 139, 153

S

Sargon II 205 252, 261-3

Index

Sayce, Henry 81

Schoolcraft, Henry 4-18, 33-38, 39, 47-50, 58, 153

Shakespeare, William 26, 56, 279

Sinclair, Earl Henry 12, 15

Skene, W.H. 81, 231, 333,

Smith, George (researcher) 81

Smith, Joseph 3, 4,

Snake(s) mounds 19

Soissons = Sassy 30, 281, 309, 311

Songs of the Graves 31, 231, 309, 333,

Squier, E.G. 16

Stubbs, Bishop 27-37, 50, 65, 86, 93, 113, 126, 139, 231, 260, 284, 298-303, 307, 320, 329, 335

T

Talhairarn (bard) 116

Taliesin (520-590) 116, 119

Teilaw / Teilo St Book of 154-8

Toithfallt Tudfwlch 122, 126, 156-9, 160-163

Teithrin 110, 122, 270

Tewdrig ap Teithfallt, King 31, 126, 158-63, 271, 275-6, 283,305

Thomas, Cyrus 16

Thomas MP, George 287-8

Tintagel 161-3, 272, 276

Tomlinson, Abelard 3

W

Wallum Ollam, the 19

Wheeler, Sir Mortimer 191, 286

William of Malmesbury 86

William of Orange 41

Williams ab Ithel 95

Williams, Edward (Iolo) 48-9, 63-8, 104, 110-4, 120, 134, 164, 321

Williams, Edward (Taliesin) 134, 136-7

Williams, Griffith John 62-8, 104, 110, 114, 118, 231, 260

Williams, John 9, 29, 49, 112-3, 164

Williams, Mary 64

Williams, Oliver (Cromwell) 44

Williams, Revd. Robert 30, 51, 231, 314, 333

Williams, Richard 42

Williams, Sir Ifor 63

Wright, William 81

345